隧道工程英语
English for Tunnel Engineering

郭敬谊　韦良文　主编

人民交通出版社股份有限公司
China Communications Press Co.,Ltd.

内 容 提 要

本书是我国首部实用性、专业性较强的隧道工程专业英语教材。全书共14单元，每单元包括3篇课文（精读1篇，扩展阅读2篇），主要内容包括：隧道工程；隧道设施；隧道主体及附属结构；地质勘察；钻爆法；钻挖隧道；沉管隧道；明挖法；隧道开挖与衬砌；隧道通风；隧道照明；隧道给排水；隧道安全规定；隧道合同管理。

本教材可作为大专院校隧道工程相关专业和英文科技翻译专业学生的英语阅读教材，也可作为隧道工程行业的科技人员、商务人员、管理人员的培训教材以及参考用书。

图书在版编目(CIP)数据

隧道工程英语／郭敬谊,韦良文主编．—北京：人民交通出版社股份有限公司,2015.3
ISBN 978-7-114-12158-6

Ⅰ.①隧… Ⅱ.①郭… ②韦… Ⅲ.①隧道工程－英语 Ⅳ.①H31

中国版本图书馆 CIP 数据核字(2015)第 066954 号

English for Tunnel Engineering

书　　名：	隧道工程英语
著 作 者：	郭敬谊　韦良文
责任编辑：	刘永芬　李　娜
出版发行：	人民交通出版社股份有限公司
地　　址：	(100011)北京市朝阳区安定门外外馆斜街3号
网　　址：	http://www.ccpress.com.cn
销售电话：	(010)59757973
总 经 销：	人民交通出版社股份有限公司发行部
经　　销：	各地新华书店
印　　刷：	北京市密东印刷有限公司
开　　本：	787×1092　1/16
印　　张：	20.75
字　　数：	460千
版　　次：	2015年3月　第1版
印　　次：	2015年3月　第1次印刷
书　　号：	ISBN 978-7-114-12158-6
定　　价：	38.00元

(有印刷、装订质量问题的图书由本公司负责调换)

序

在当今经济全球化和区域经济一体化深入发展的背景下，"走出去"、"国际化"发展战略已成为中国工程承包商的一种必然选择。越来越多的中国工程设计、施工企业跨出国门、迈向世界，参与国际工程竞标并承建工程项目。尤其是近十年来，我国的涉外工程经历了跨越式发展，呈现出爆发式增长趋势。这就要求我们不仅要有精湛的设计、施工技术和先进的管理水平，还要拥有一批既有深厚的外语功底，又了解、熟悉、掌握涉外工程技术、商务运作和项目管理等知识的复合型人才。而当前的实际情况是该类型人才还十分匮乏，非常有必要加强这方面的教育培训及人才培养。

隧道是人类改造自然、利用自然最早的地下工程领域之一。如今，随着世界经济的发展和各发展中国家基础设施建设进程的加快，公路、城市道路等交通基础设施及地下空间、输送管道等建设需求越来越大，作为必须穿越山岭和埋置地下的工程，隧道是唯一方案；而在跨越江、河、湖、海的通道工程方案论证中，出于其自身优势及建造技术的进步，隧道在"桥、隧"之争中胜出的场合也日益增多。中国企业走向世界承建工程，隧道是一个主要的也是重要的对象和领域之一。因此，隧道工程方面的复合型技术人才的培养是一项当务之急的工作。

重庆交通大学外国语学院郭敬谊副教授和土木建筑学院韦良文副教授，长期从事隧道及相关工程的教学研究及工程翻译工作，具有良好的专业素养，且积累了大量理论及工程实践经验，积沙成塔、集腋成裘，主编了这本国内首部《隧道工程英语》教材。教材取材新颖经典、内容丰富、结构合理、实用性强，几乎涵盖了目前隧道工程的总体方案、工法、结构工程、附属设施、机电工程、项目管理等所有内容，具有一定的系统性、条理性和科学性，难度适中。本书不仅引用了国外著名隧道案例，同时还介绍了近年来国内的一些特色隧道工程的案例，是国内外隧道技术沟通的桥梁。

我很高兴地看到了《隧道工程英语》教材的书稿，在书稿即将付梓之前，我很乐于将本教材介绍给隧道工程技术、商务、管理工作者和工程翻译者等广大同仁，相信大家能从本教材的学习中获得裨益。也希望将来能有更多类似的著作出现，丰富和充实隧道工程外语体系，培养和造就更多优秀的隧道工程外语专业人才，促进我国涉外隧道工程的不断发展。

中交公路规划设计院有限公司隧道与轨道交通事业部
2014.11.06

前　言

《隧道工程英语》是为适应应用型本科人才培养目标需求,专门针对隧道工程专业英语课程和工程外语类翻译专业的教学大纲要求而编写的;同时兼顾了隧道工程专业科研、设计、施工等技术人员在阅读翻译技术文献、撰写科技论文、技术沟通、商务谈判和专业英语培训时的需要。本教材主要目的是培养和提高本科生和研究生的隧道工程英文文献的阅读理解能力和书面翻译能力。通过本教材的系统学习,学习者将会达到熟悉隧道英语文献的文体风格、提高英文阅读能力及翻译能力、掌握大量专业词汇和标准的表达方式的目标,同时还可以将英语学习与获取专业知识有机结合。

全书共 14 单元,每个单元由 5 大部分组成。第 Ⅰ 部分包含相关主题的 3 篇阅读材料,使学生系统掌握每单元的隧道专业知识及术语;第 Ⅱ 部分为隧道专业术语表,供学生记忆和选用;第 Ⅲ 部分为讨论问题和难句分析及中文译文,旨在活跃课堂和检查学生阅读理解的正确性,帮助学生正确理解原文和提高其英译汉的能力;第 Ⅳ 部分为汉译英翻译案例,通过分析案例,培养学生汉译英的技巧和能力,供学生在翻译练习中参考和模仿学习;第 Ⅴ 部分是汉译英课后练习,供学生课后借助字典、网络和翻译工具提高汉译英的能力和技巧。本教材建议学时为 100 学时,主讲宜由隧道工程专业教师或具备隧道工程基本知识或工程经验的英语教师担任。在使用本教材时,主讲教师可根据教学计划灵活掌握,选择全部或部分内容进行教学。

本教材系统讲解了隧道工程相关知识,并介绍了中国隧道的发展现状,内容选自最近出版的国内外专著、教材、杂志、技术标书、相关设计规范、国内外典型隧道工程的设计和施工文件等。

全书由重庆交通大学外国语学院郭敬谊副教授和土木建筑学院韦良文副教授主编。

在教材的大纲拟定和各章节编写过程中,我们有幸获得了许多国内外隧道工程设计单位和施工单位一线技术骨干、项目经理和总工程师的大力支持和帮助。他们一直参与了我们的整个编写过程,提出了很多有价值的建议,提供了丰富的工程案例资料,甚至亲自修改编写内容,在此一并致以衷心感谢! 他们分别是:中交公路规划设计院有限公司副总工程师/教授级高级工程师刘晓东、副总工程师/隧道与轨道交通事业部总经理/教授级高级工程师刘明虎、张志刚博士、吕勇刚高工、黄清飞博士、林巍工程师;中铁隧道集团股份公司高级工程师朱文会和陈静;中国葛洲坝集团高级工程师吴趋书;重庆市轨道交通设计研究院高级工程师翁承显;上海市隧道工程轨道交通设计研究院工程师曾毅;香港迈进基建环保工程顾问有限公司(Meinhardt Infrastructure and Environment Limited)资深高级咨询专家张忠民(香港);丹麦 COWI 公司(COWI A/S)高级工程师张金屏博士(丹麦);林同棪国际工程咨询(中国)有限公司[T. Y. Lin International Consulting (China) Co., Ltd.]高级工程师吴祥祖;参加过中国二滩水电站和南水北调工程建设的新奥法隧道专家 Hans Herbert Oberpichler(奥地利)和工程师 Günter Müller(德国)。

  本教材是我国出版的首部隧道工程专业英语教材,由于编者水平有限,时间仓促,书中难免有不妥和疏漏之处,敬请读者批评指正。

  联系方式:aliceguoyi@163.com;weiliangwen@163.com

编 者

2014 年 11 月

中国　重庆

目 录

Unit 1　Tunnel Engineering 隧道工程 ································· 1
　Ⅰ. Text ··· 1
　　Text A　Tunnel Classification and General Development Situation
　　　　　　隧道的分类及发展概况 ··· 1
　　Text B　Familiarization with Tunnels 熟悉隧道 ························ 14
　　Text C　Rijswijk Railway Tunnel 赖斯韦克铁路隧道 ················· 21
　Ⅱ. Terms and terminology 术语 ··· 23
　Ⅲ. Questions and difficult sentence analysis 提问与难句分析 ······· 23
　Ⅳ. Translation case study 翻译案例 ····································· 25
　Ⅴ. Assignment 作业 ·· 27

Unit 2　Tunnel Installations 隧道设施 ································· 28
　Ⅰ. Text ··· 28
　　Text A　Main Installations in Tunnel 隧道内主要设施 ············· 28
　　Text B　Some Engineering Cases about Installations in Modern Road Tunnels
　　　　　　几个现代公路隧道设计的工程案例 ··························· 33
　　Text C　Installations of Xiang'an Tunnel 翔安隧道设施 ············ 37
　Ⅱ. Terms and terminology 术语 ··· 43
　Ⅲ. Questions and difficult sentence analysis 提问与难句分析 ······· 43
　Ⅳ. Translation case study 翻译案例 ····································· 45
　Ⅴ. Assignment 作业 ·· 46

Unit 3　Main and Ancillary Structures 隧道主体及附属结构 ······· 47
　Ⅰ. Text ··· 47
　　Text A　Tunnel Main Structures 隧道主体结构 ····················· 47
　　Text B　Ancillary Structures in Track Tunnel 铁路隧道辅助结构 ····· 54
　　Text C　Ancillary Structures in Road Tunnel 公路隧道辅助结构 ····· 55
　Ⅱ. Terms and terminology 术语 ··· 56
　Ⅲ. Questions and difficult sentence analysis 提问与难句分析 ······· 57
　Ⅳ. Translation case study 翻译案例 ····································· 58
　Ⅴ. Assignment 作业 ·· 59

Unit 4　Geotechnical Investigation 地质勘察 ························· 60
　Ⅰ. Text ··· 60

  Text A Summary of Geotechnical Investigation 岩土勘察概述 ………… 60

  Text B Geotechnical Investigations Reports 岩土勘察报告 …………… 65

  Text C Geotechnical Investigation Report of Left Line of Muzhailing Tunnel

     木寨岭隧道左线工程地质勘察报告 ……………………………… 67

 Ⅱ. Terms and terminology 术语 …………………………………………… 74

 Ⅲ. Questions and difficult sentence analysis 提问与难句分析 ………… 75

 Ⅳ. Translation case study 翻译案例 ……………………………………… 75

 Ⅴ. Assignment 作业 ………………………………………………………… 77

Unit 5 Drill and Blast Method 钻爆法 …………………………………… 79

 Ⅰ. Text ………………………………………………………………………… 79

  Text A Working Procedure of Drill and Blast Method 钻爆法工序 …… 79

  Text B Explosives 炸药 …………………………………………………… 86

  Text C A Tunnel Drill and Blast Technical Scheme 一个隧道钻爆技术方案 …… 87

 Ⅱ. Terms and terminology 术语 …………………………………………… 91

 Ⅲ. Questions and difficult sentence analysis 提问与难句分析 ………… 92

 Ⅳ. Translation case study 翻译案例 ……………………………………… 93

 Ⅴ. Assignment 作业 ………………………………………………………… 94

Unit 6 Bored Tunnels 钻挖隧道 …………………………………………… 95

 Ⅰ. Text ………………………………………………………………………… 95

  Text A Tunnel Boring Machines (TBM) 隧道掘进机(TBM) …………… 95

  Text B TBM Tunneling System TBM 系统组成 ……………………… 106

  Text C Nanjing Weisan Road Yangtze River Crossing Tunnel

     南京纬三路越江隧道 …………………………………………… 109

 Ⅱ. Terms and terminology 术语 ………………………………………… 114

 Ⅲ. Questions and difficult sentence analysis 提问与难句分析 ……… 115

 Ⅳ. Translation case study 翻译案例 …………………………………… 116

 Ⅴ. Assignment 作业 ……………………………………………………… 116

Unit 7 Immersed Tube Tunnel 沉管隧道 ………………………………… 118

 Ⅰ. Text ……………………………………………………………………… 118

  Text A Immersed Tube Tunnel Introduction 沉管隧道概述 ………… 118

  Text B Design of Tubes 管节设计 …………………………………… 132

  Text C Some Immersed Tube Tunnel Cases 几个沉管隧道案例 …… 138

 Ⅱ. Terms and terminology 术语 ………………………………………… 144

 Ⅲ. Questions and difficult sentence analysis 提问与难句分析 ……… 145

 Ⅳ. Translation case study 翻译案例 …………………………………… 146

 Ⅴ. Assignment 作业 ……………………………………………………… 148

Unit 8　Cut and Cover Method 明挖法 …………………………………………… 149
　Ⅰ. Text ……………………………………………………………………………… 149
　　Text A　Underground Works Construction by Cut and Cover Method 地下工程明挖法 …… 149
　　Text B　Shoring System 支挡系统 ……………………………………………… 162
　　Text C　Open Cut Section of Xiamen Urban Rail Transportation Line 1
　　　　　　厦门地铁一号线明挖段 ……………………………………………… 170
　Ⅱ. Terms and terminology 术语 …………………………………………………… 174
　Ⅲ. Questions and difficult sentence analysis 提问与难句分析 ………………………… 175
　Ⅳ. Translation case study 翻译案例 ……………………………………………… 176
　Ⅴ. Assignment 作业 ………………………………………………………………… 177

Unit 9　Tunnel Excavation and Lining 隧道开挖与衬砌 ………………………… 179
　Ⅰ. Text ……………………………………………………………………………… 179
　　Text A　Types and Selection of Excavation Methods
　　　　　　隧道开挖方法类型及选择原则 ………………………………………… 179
　　Text B　Heading Mode and Category 掘进方式及类型 ………………………… 187
　　Text C　Tunnel Lining 隧道衬砌 ………………………………………………… 189
　Ⅱ. Terms and terminology 术语 …………………………………………………… 197
　Ⅲ. Questions and difficult sentence analysis 提问与难句分析 ………………………… 198
　Ⅳ. Translation case study 翻译案例 ……………………………………………… 199
　Ⅴ. Assignment 作业 ………………………………………………………………… 200

Unit 10　Tunnel Ventilation 隧道通风 …………………………………………… 201
　Ⅰ. Text ……………………………………………………………………………… 201
　　Text A　Tunnel Ventilation Mode 隧道通风模式 ………………………………… 201
　　Text B　Environment within Subway System 地铁运营环境 …………………… 208
　　Text C　Longquanshan Tunnel Ventilation Scheme 龙泉山隧道通风方案 ……… 213
　Ⅱ. Terms and terminology 术语 …………………………………………………… 216
　Ⅲ. Questions and difficult sentence analysis 提问与难句分析 ………………………… 216
　Ⅳ. Translation case study 翻译案例 ……………………………………………… 217
　Ⅴ. Assignment 作业 ………………………………………………………………… 218

Unit 11　Tunnel Lighting 隧道照明 ……………………………………………… 220
　Ⅰ. Text ……………………………………………………………………………… 220
　　Text A　Lighting of Highway Tunnels 公路隧道照明 …………………………… 220
　　Text B　Lighting of Railway Tunnels 铁路隧道照明 …………………………… 230
　　Text C　Illuminator Installation Construction Lighting of Highway Tunnels
　　　　　　公路隧道照明设备施工 ……………………………………………… 233
　Ⅱ. Terms and terminology 术语 …………………………………………………… 236

· 3 ·

  Ⅲ. Questions and difficult sentence analysis 提问与难句分析 ……………… 237
  Ⅳ. Translation case study 翻译案例 …………………………………………… 238
  Ⅴ. Assignment 作业 ……………………………………………………………… 239

Unit 12 Water Supply and Drain 隧道给排水 ………………………………… 241
  Ⅰ. Text ……………………………………………………………………………… 241
   Text A Tunnel Water Supply and Drain System 隧道给排水系统 ……… 241
   Text B To Drain or to Seal 排或堵 ………………………………………… 252
   Text C Tunnel Waterproofing 隧道防水 …………………………………… 255
  Ⅱ. Terms and terminology 术语 ………………………………………………… 257
  Ⅲ. Questions and difficult sentence analysis 提问与难句分析 ……………… 257
  Ⅳ. Translation case study 翻译案例 …………………………………………… 258
  Ⅴ. Assignment 作业 ……………………………………………………………… 259

Unit 13 Tunnel Safety Provisions 隧道安全规定 ………………………………… 260
  Ⅰ. Text ……………………………………………………………………………… 260
   Text A Tunnel Safety Introduction 隧道安全概述 ……………………… 260
   Text B Fire Safety in Tunnel 隧道消防安全 ……………………………… 271
   Text C Tunnel Fire Disaster Cases 两个隧道火灾案例 …………………… 280
  Ⅱ. Terms and terminology 术语 ………………………………………………… 286
  Ⅲ. Questions and difficult sentence analysis 提问与难句分析 ……………… 287
  Ⅳ. Translation case study 翻译案例 …………………………………………… 288
  Ⅴ. Assignment 作业 ……………………………………………………………… 289

Unit 14 Tunnel Contract Management 隧道合同管理 ………………………… 290
  Ⅰ. Text ……………………………………………………………………………… 290
   Text A Tunnel Construction Contracting 隧道施工合同 ………………… 290
   Text B Part of FIDIC Clause 部分 FIDIC 合同条款 ……………………… 295
   Text C A Contract Agreement 合同协议书 ………………………………… 302
  Ⅱ. Terms and terminology 术语 ………………………………………………… 304
  Ⅲ. Questions and difficult sentence analysis 提问与难句分析 ……………… 304
  Ⅳ. Translation case study 翻译案例 …………………………………………… 305
  Ⅴ. Assignment 作业 ……………………………………………………………… 308

Glossary 专业词汇表 ……………………………………………………………………… 309
References 参考文献 ……………………………………………………………………… 319

Unit 1　Tunnel Engineering
隧　道　工　程

Ⅰ. Text

Text A　Tunnel Classification and General Development Situation
隧道的分类及发展概况

Tunnel is an underground engineering building with portals at both ends and an important part of civil engineering, same as bridge and side slope supporting and retaining structures. It serves any of various functions-highway, railway, pedestrian passageway, water conveyance and gallery of pipelines. However, the standard tunnel definition posed from technological point of view at the tunnel conference of OECD in 1970 and the definition states that any strip-shaped building built by any means and ultimately used below surface of ground with clear span more than $2m^2$ is tunnel. By this definition, the range of tunnel is great and different tunnels can be classified by different criteria and different methods from different points of view. By ground, tunnel can be classified into rock tunnel (soft rock, hard rock) and soil tunnel. By geographical locations, tunnel can be classified into mountain tunnel, urban tunnel and subaqueous tunnel. By construction methodology, tunnels can be constructed by mining method, by cut and cover method, by shield method, by immersed tube tunneling method and by TBM method. By burial depth of tunnels, tunnels can be classified into shallow burial and deep burial tunnels. In cross section, tunnel can take one of the several shapes-circular, horseshoe and rectangular. By sectional area sizing standard defined by ITA (International Tunnel Association), tunnels can be classified into super-large section tunnel (over $100m^2$), large section tunnel ($50\text{-}100m^2$), medium section tunnel ($10\text{-}50m^2$), small section tunnel ($3\text{-}10m^2$) and extremely small section tunnel (less than $3m^2$). By number of traffic lanes, tunnels can be classified into single lane tunnel, double lanes tunnel and multi-lane tunnel. By length, tunnels can be classified into short tunnel (by regulation of rail tunnel: $L \leqslant 500m$; by regulation of highway tunnel: $L \leqslant 500m$), medium-long tunnel (by regulation of rail tunnel: $500m < L \leqslant 3000m$; by regulation of highway tunnel: $500m < L < 1000m$), long tunnel (by regulation of rail tunnel: $3000m < L \leqslant 10000m$; by regulation on highway tunnel: $1000m \leqslant L \leqslant 3000m$) and super-long tunnel (by regulation of rail tunnel: $L > 10000m$; by regulation of highway tunnel: $L > 3000m$). But it is commonly considered that tunnel classification by its purposes is relatively more explicit which is introduced in the following section.

1. Transit tunnel

Transit tunnel is mostly widely used and its function is providing a channel for traffic and movement of people and a free and smooth communication route. The following types are generally included.

1) Highway tunnel

Highway tunnel is the channel specially provided for vehicles. In the old age, the highway built in mountain regions usually winds around mountain to save works cost and the longer road line is preferred to avoid use of tunnel due to its high cost. With the development of social economy, production and the development of great number of expressways, a higher technical standard for road construction is raised requiring a flat and freeway wide road with gentle slope. Hence, when road has to cross or pass through mountain regions, many tunnel solutions are proposed. Building of tunnel plays an important role in aspects of improving the technology of road, shortening the traveling distance, improving the transporting capacity, and reducing road incidents. The domestic tunnel known as Qinling Zhongnanshan Tunnel(秦岭终南山隧道) is in length of 18.1km and its completion has saved approximately 60km by distance and 2 hours by time to cross the mountain Qinling.

2) Rail tunnel

Rail tunnel is the channel specially for train transportation. When a railway crosses the hilly regions, it must overcome the obstacle caused by the big difference of the altitude of the terrain. The slop for railways needs to be flat and gentle with the maximum slope gradient less than 24‰ (two engines pull). However, the hilly regions are usually limited by the terrain and impossible to stretch the rail-line across the regions, since the required elevation cannot be reached by the extension of the rail-line. In this case, the tunnel is a reasonable choice to cross through the hills, and its use can shorten the length of route, reduce slope gradient, improve operation conditions and improve train tonnage rating. For example, 48 tunnels are designed on the route from Baoji to Qinling on Baocheng Line accounting for 37.75% of total extension of the route, which demonstrated roles of rail tunnel in hilly regions.

3) Subaqueous tunnel

Subaqueous tunnel is the channel which is built under stream, river, lake, sea and ocean to provide the channel and passageway for vehicles and trains. When a communication route crosses over the stream, the river, the lake, the sea or the ocean, options of bridges, ferry boats and tunnels can be selected. But bridge is limited by its headroom and ferry boat has limited capacity. If these problems cannot be effectively solved, subaqueous tunnel is a very good solution. And its advantages include being from the impacts of weather, no influence on navigation, less space occupation of its rump and hidden communication facility during war time and thus it has won people's favor more and more. Many national subaqueous tunnels have been built across Huangpu

River in Shanghai and across Pearl River in Guangzhou. The disadvantage of the subaqueous tunnels is their high construction cost.

4) Subway

Subways are constructed underground in urban areas and are the channel for train transportation for the purpose of mitigating urban transportation burden. Subway is one of the effective solutions to the traffic congestions and the traffic jams in the large cities. Train transportation due to its large capacity, high speed, safe and timely transportation of passengers has become a powerful solution to transportation difficulties in the cities with large population. In China the completed underground rail transportation systems established in cities as Beijing, Shanghai and Guangzhou and other cities have played an important role in improving urban transportation and reducing traffic incidents. In other cities such as Shenzhen, Nanjing, Qingdao, Dalian, Wuhan, Shenyang, Chongqing, Haerbin and Chengdu, subways have been under planning and construction.

5) Navigation tunnel

Navigation tunnel is the channel specially intended for ship transportation and sailing. When canals have to cross watersheds, the powerful means of overcoming the difficulty caused by the big difference of the altitude of the terrain is to build canal whose advantages include shortening sailing distance, reducing operation cost, smoothening and straightening river channel, thus the navigation conditions are greatly improved.

6) Pedestrian underpass

Pedestrian underpass is a special underground pass way for passage of pedestrians. Pedestrian underpasses are generally constructed in highly populated downtown areas, which are crowded with passing pedestrians, dense traffic and thus prone to traffic accidents from time to time due to less care, for the pedestrian to cross street, railway and auto route. The function of the pedestrian underpass is to mitigate the traffic load on ground surface, reduce road accidents and facilitate the movement of pedestrians.

2. Aqueduct

Aqueduct is an important constituent of hydraulic engineering and hydroelectrical power plant. Aqueduct consists of the following types.

1) Water supply tunnel

Water supply conduit is built to supply water to hydroelectrical power generator set or mobilize water resources. The water diverted in water supply conduit is the driving power to drive generator sets of the power station. For that purpose, water supply conduit as a structure for water supply is required to have a inner wall with bearing capacity. But sometimes only part of water passes through the conduit and its inner wall is exposed to atmospheric pressure and low water pressure and even without water pressure. Hence water conduits with pressure and without pressure are classified.

2) Tailrace tunnel

Tailrace tunnel is built to discharge the waste water released from generators of a hydroelectric power plant.

3) Diversion tunnel or spillway tunnel

Diversion tunnels or spillway tunnels are built to divert water and discharge the flood in excess of flow limit of spillway and are important structures of hydraulic engineering works. The principal function of diversion or spillway tunnels is flood discharge.

4) Sediment discharge tunnel

Sediment discharge tunnel is built to wash away the sedimentation in reservoir and is a constituent of reservoir structure and its function is discharging mud and sand out of the reservoir by use of the sediment discharge tunnel which is also used to empty the reservoir for inspection or repair.

3. Municipal tunnel

In urban construction and planning, underground space is fully used. Various types of public facilities are placed underground, for which underground galleries are known as urban tunnels. Municipal tunnels are closely related to citizens' lives, work and production and they play an important role in assuring the normal life in the cities and the principal tunnel types are as follows.

1) Water supply tunnel

Water supply tunnel is built for the placement of the urban pipe networks for water supply. In cities, the important task of urban administrative infrastructure construction is the reasonable planning and arrangement of main water pipelines which is closely linked to human life and production activity. The water supply pipeline works shall not affect the urban landscape, shall not occupy ground surface to avoid man-made damage. Hence construction of underground gallery to contain these pipelines is a practical solution.

2) Sewage tunnel

The sewage tunnel is built for urban sewage discharge and conveyance system. The most part of urban sewage needs to be discharged into the rivers outside the cities except for the part which imposes severe impact on environment and is purified and recycled or discharged. That is why the underground sewage tunnel is needed. This type of tunnel generally diverts and discharge sewage by itself and thus takes form of egg mostly. It is feasible that sewage pipe is placed in a duct and the sewage is to be discharged through the sewage pipe. Garbage-blocking grate is placed at the inlet of the sewage tunnel to block the drifting miscellaneous wastes outside and to prevent the wastes blocking the passage of pipe.

3) Tunnel for pipelines

The tunnel is built for facilities of urban power energy supply (gas, heating, hot water). For the tunnel for pipelines in cities, the pipelines for energy supply are placed in the underground duct built for that purposes and the ducts go through treatments for anti-leakage and thermal reservation and the energy can be delivered safely to destinations for production and domestic use.

4) Duct for cables

In cities, to ensure that the electrical power cables and communication power cables are protected from harms or damages of human activities and to avoid the influence on urban aesthetics due to overhanging cables, the appropriate underground ducts are constructed to hold the cables underground.

In modernized cities, the above four types of urban tunnels with common properties are built into one common tunnel known as "common duct" in accordance with urban arrangement and plan. The common duct is the symbol of the reasonable managing and planning of the in frastructures in modern cities, as well as the proper means to use urban underground space and is the orientation of urban administrative planning and construction development.

5) Civil air defense tunnel

The tunnel is built for the purpose of civil air defense and works as a refuge in wartime. The urban civil air defense engineering is constructed to meet the demand of protection from air attack during wars. The civil air defense works is built for providing for people a refuge in case of emergency. Hence, during the civil works construction general requirement for living conditions must be considered. In addition to the arrangement of such facilities as drainage, ventilation, illumination and communication equipment, inventory of drinking water and food and necessary first aid facilities should be considered. The devices for prevention of blasting and impact waves need to be mounted at tunnel portals.

4. Mine tunnel

In mine exploitation, in order to enable the access to mine bed from outside of the mountain and transport the exploited mine stones to outside, the tunnel is built. There are following types of tunnels.

1) Haulage roadway

To make a tunnel through mountain to make access to mine bed and open a roadway step by step to reach all excavation surfaces. The former is known as the principal roadway and serves as the principal access for humans and the transport trunk road to underground mine zone. While the latter is distributed like tree branches to all excavation surfaces, and this type of roadway serves as temporary support to meet the needs of excavation of operators.

2) Water supply tunnel

It intends to supply clean water for use of excavating and extracting machines and pump waste water and catchments out of the tunnel.

3) Ventilation tunnel

Generally underground harmful gases swelling out from the stratum where the roadway passes through by mine tunneling method, the waste gas exhausted from excavators and the air exhaled by workmen are the prime pollutants in the roadway. If the stratum contains any mash gas, it will endanger the workmen's lives in the tunnel. Hence, to purify the air in the tunnel and create the pleasant working conditions, the ventilation tunnel is indispensable to extract the dirty air and bring in the fresh air.

In recent years, the national highway construction has developed rapidly, and 7918 expressway network in length of 85000 kilometers will be accomplished in near future. With large national population, the relevant authority is planning and completing national expressway network to meet people's needs of traveling out and the needs of economic development. Due to the high technical specification for formation of highway alignment when a highway enters into mountain area or heavy hilly area, tunnel is inevitably needed to pass through mountains and hills. Hence to build highway in the hilly and mountainous areas in middle and west China, the length of bridges and tunnels account for large proportion, which varies from 40% to 80%, and their construction is extremely hard. Yet being able to shorten distance in large margin is the outstanding advantage, thus greatly improving the operation efficiency. For example, the Zhongnanshan tunnel（终南山隧道）in Chengyu highway（成渝高速公路）is in length of 3km which is 42km shorter than the original old road. The application of tunnel economized on land and protected ecological environment.

Compared with the developed countries, the national highway tunnel of China started relatively late. But since China's reform and opening up in 1978, the construction of civil works have developed rapidly and the quantity and scale of tunnel construction have been expanded continually. In 1980s, the tunnel in length of over 1000m was initially built in the southeast coastal areas where the economy was relatively well developed. For example the Wutongshan tunnel（梧桐山隧道）in Shenzhen is in length of over 2000m in which full transverse ventilation was applied for the first time domestically. In 1990s, higher and higher requirement was raised for highway tunnel with rapid development of highways, and the significance of tunnel construction has been recognized and valued more and more by people, and highway tunnel projects spread over the entire mainland. Meanwhile tunnel construction and management became more and more complicated and highly demanded. In the construction of Zhongnanshan tunnel（终南山隧道）in Chengyu expressway（成渝高速公路）which was 3160m long and accomplished in previous time, harmful geological problems like rush-ins and mash gas were encountered in the tunnel excavation. The Erlangshan tunnel（二郎山隧道）as part of the Sichuan-Tibet highway（川藏公路）in length of 4000m is located in high altitude and cold areas, and during the excavation such challenges as highland stress and rock burst occurred. The built Qinling Zhongnanshan tunnel（秦

岭终南山隧道) is the longest tunnel in China with tunnel total length over 18km and in the course of its construction almost all types of harmful geological problems were encountered. What's more, the tunnel ventilation and operation environment were complicated and hard. By the end of year 2007, 4673 highway tunnels in total had been built in China, with the total length up to 2556km and the annual rate of increment of tunnel construction has been renewed from time to time in the past 20 years. Other accomplished domestic super-long tunnels are shown in following table 1.1.

Some Super-long Highway Tunnels Constructed and Accomplished in China   Table 1.1

SN	Tunnel name	Length(m)	Location	Number of lanes	Mode of ventilation
1	Qinling Zhongnanshan Highway Tunnel 秦岭终南山隧道	18020	Shaanxi 陕西	2×2	Longitudinal ventilation by sections with 3 vertical shafts 3竖井分段纵向式
2	Dapingli Tunnel 大坪里隧道	12290	Gansu 甘肃	2×2	Longitudinal ventilation by sections with 2 vertical shafts 2竖井分段纵向式
3	Baojiashan Tunnel 包家山隧道	11500	Shaanxi 陕西	2×2	Longitudinal ventilation in sections with 3 inclined shafts 3斜井分段纵向式
4	Baotashan Tunnel 宝塔山隧道	10391	Shanxi 山西	2×2	Longitudinal ventilation with inclined shafts by way of air supply and extraction 竖斜井送排式纵向通风
5	Nibashan Tunnel 泥巴山隧道	9985	Sichuan 四川	2×2	Inclined shaft + vertical shaft longitudinal ventilation in sections 斜井+竖井分段纵向式
6	Mayazi Tunnel 麻崖子隧道	9000	Gansu 甘肃	2×2	Inclined and vertical shaft for air supply and extraction + jet fan longitudinal ventilation 斜竖井送排+射流风机纵向
7	Longtan Tunnel 龙潭隧道	8700	Hubei 湖北	2×2	Vertical pit for air supply and extraction + longitudinal jet fan 立坑送排+射流风机纵向式
8	Mixiliang Tunnel 米溪梁隧道	7923	Shaanxi 陕西	2×2	Air supply and extraction ventilation with single shaft in left(right) bore 左(右)洞单井送排式通风
9	Kuocangshan Tunnel 括苍山隧道	7930	Zhejiang 浙江	2×2	Longitudinal mode + semi transverse flow way (smoke extraction) 纵向式+半横流式(排烟)
10	Fangdoushan Tunnel 方斗山隧道	7581	Chongqing 重庆	2×2	Longitudinal ventilation with 2 inclined shafts for air supply and extraction 2座斜井送排式纵向通风

With rapid urbanization progress in China, particularly the rapid spread of urban construction in mountainous areas, the tunnel which matches the wide boulevards in cities must take large span. With the increase of tunnel span, the construction of the tunnels becomes even more difficult and more expensive. Some highway tunnels with long span built in China are listed in table 1.2.

Some Long Span Highway Tunnels in China   Table 1.2

SN	Name of tunnel	Length(m)	Location	Number of lanes × number of tunnel gallery
1	Baihezui Tunnel 白鹤嘴隧道	1240	Chongqing 重庆	4×2
2	Longtoushan Tunnel 龙头山隧道	1020	Guangdong 广东	4×2
3	Wanshishan Tunnel 万石山隧道	1170	Fujian 福建	underground interchange with largest width of 25.89m 最宽处25.89m 的地下立交
4	Dageshan Tunnel 大阁山隧道	496	Guizhou 贵州	4×1
5	Jinzhou Tunnel 金州隧道	521	Liaoning 辽宁	4×1
6	Yabao Tunnel 雅宝隧道	260	Guangdong 广东	4×2
7	Jinjishan Tunnel 金鸡山隧道	200	Fujian 福建	4×2 Multi-arch 4×2(连拱)
8	Luohanshan Tunnel 罗汉山隧道	300	Fujian 福建	4×2 Multi-arch 4×2(连拱)
9	Kuiqi Tunnel 魁岐隧道	1596	Fujian 福建	27.42m underground interchange at maximum width 最宽处27.42 m 的地下立交

Since the 1990s, with the improvement of the technology of tunnel engineering construction, the link across river in form of subaqueous tunnels is common such as Shanghai Yan'andonglu Tunnel(上海延安东路隧道), Guangzhou Zhujiang Tunnel (广州珠江隧道), Nanjing Xuanwuhu Tunnel(南京玄武湖隧道), Ningbo Changhong Tunnel(宁波常虹隧道) and Xiamen Submarine Tunnel(厦门海底隧道). Some underwater tunnels built in our country are listed in table 1.3. The application of river crossing tunnel is of several advantages and the underwater tunnel influences neither the ground surface nor the ships traffic, and it can be a convenient link connecting to the road network on shore. In 1993, the first immersed tunnel was constructed in China under the Pearl River, Guangzhou. In 1995, the second domestic immersed tunnel was completed on river bed under the river of Yongjiang, Ningbo. The very successful completion of these two immersed tunnels has accumulated rich experiences for further construction of longer immersed tunnels under the rivers of Changjiang and Yellow River and at marine bays in subsequent years. All the 5 links between Kowloon Pennisula and Hong Kong across Victoria Bay in Hong Kong take the solutions of submerged tunnels instead of bridges. Table 1.4 listed some the submarine immersed tube tunnels at home and abroad. It is worthy to point out that the Shanghai Changjiang Tunnel(上海长江隧道) of a total length of approximately 4km with dual 6 lanes, with total investment of 6.3 billion RMB started on December 28,2004 and was inaugurated in 2010. The Nanjing Changjiang Tunnel (南京长江隧道) in length of approximately 4km, with dual 6 lanes, with total investment of 3.0 billion RMB started on September 30,2005 and opened to traffic in 2009. It is concluded that the cost of underwater tunnel is approximately 800 million RMB per kilometer in average.

Some Underwater Highway Tunnels in China   Table 1.3

SN	Name of tunnel	Length(m)	Location	Number of traffic lanes	Mode of ventilation
1	Xiamen Undersea Tunnel (drill and blasting) 厦门海底隧道(钻爆)	5960	Fujian 福建	3×2	Air supply and extraction by vertical shaft + longitudinal ventilation with jet fan 竖井送排+射流风机纵向式
2	Shanghai Changjiang Tunnel (bored tunnel) 上海长江隧道(盾构)	8955	Shanghai 上海	3×2	Transverse ventilation 横向式
3	Nanjing Changjiang Tunnel 南京长江隧道	3825	Nanjing 南京	3×2	Longitudinal ventilation 纵向式
4	Wuhan Changjiang Tunnel (bored tunnel) 武汉长江隧道(盾构)	3630	Hubei 湖北	2×2	Transverse ventilation 横向式
5	Shangzhonglu Tunnel(bored tunnel) 上中路隧道(盾构)	2800	Shanghai 上海	2×2	Transverse ventilation (two level in two directions) 横向式(双层双向)
6	Fuxingdonglu Tunnel(bored tunnel) 复兴东路隧道(盾构)	2785	Shanghai 上海	3×2	Transverse ventilation (two layer in two directions) 横向式(双层双向)
7	Nanjing Xuanwuhu Tunnel (bored tunnel) 南京玄武湖隧道(盾构)	2660	Nanjing 南京	3×2	Longitudinal ventilation 纵向式
8	Dalianlu Tunnel(bored tunnel) 大连路隧道(盾构)	2566	Shanghai 上海	2×2	Transverse ventilation 横向式
9	Waihuan River Crossing Tunnel (immersed tunnel) 外环越江隧道(沉管)	2882	Shanghai 上海	4×2	Longitudinal ventilation 纵向式
10	Pearl River Tunnel(immersed tunnel) 珠江隧道(沉管)	1238	Guangdong 广东	3+3	Longitudinal ventilation (combined use in highway and railway) 纵向式(道路、铁道并用)
11	Ningbo Changhong Tunnel (immersed tunnel) 宁波常洪隧道(沉管)	1053	Zhejiang 浙江	2×1	Longitudinal ventilation 纵向式

Particulars of the Submarine Immersed Tube Tunnels (date processed by Lin Wei)　　Table 1.4

SN	Name of tunnel	Length (m)	Section layout	Number of lanes	Opening	note
1	Chesapeake Bay Bridge-Tunnel (USA) 美国切萨匹克海湾桥隧	1748.94	Two-bore 两孔	Bidirectional Four-lane highway tunnel 双向四车道公路隧道	April, 1964 1964年4月	Two immersed tunnels, all steel shell concrete structure 有两座沉管隧道，均为钢壳混凝土结构
2	BART Tunnel (USA) 美国BART隧道	5825	Two-bore 两孔	Subway tunnel 地铁隧道	1970 1970年	The longest immersed tube tunnel in the world; steel shell concrete structure 为目前世界上最长沉管隧道；钢壳混凝土结构
3	Hong Kong Eastern Harbor 香港西区跨港海底隧道	2200 (immersed tunnel length 1363m) 2200 (沉管段长1363m)	Two-bore two-gallery 两孔两管廊	Bidirectional six-lane highway tunnel 双向六车道公路隧道	April, 1997, total 45 months 1997年4月，工期45个月	12 tunnel elements, monolithic, reinforced concrete structure 12个管节，整体式钢筋混凝土结构
4	Oresund Immersed Tunnel 厄勒海底隧道	3510	Four-bore one gallery 四孔一管廊	Bidirectional four-lane combined highway and railway 双向四车道公铁共用	Inaugurated on July 1, 2000 2000年7月1日正式通车	26 tunnel elements, segmental type, element length 135m; reinforced concrete structure 26个管节，节段式管节长135m；钢筋混凝土结构
5	Shanghai Outer Ring Immersed Tunnel 上海外环隧道	2880 immersed tunnel length 736m (沉管段736m)	Three-bore two-gallery 三孔两管廊	Bidirectional eight-lane highway tunnel 双向八车道公路隧道	June, 2003 2003年6月	7 tunnel elements, monolithic, reinforced concrete structure 7个管节，整体式钢筋混凝土结构
6	Busan-Geoje Immersed Tunnel (South Korea) 釜山海底隧道（韩国）	3240	Two-bore one-gallery 两孔一管廊	Bidirectional four-lane highway tunnel 双向四车道公路隧道	Scheduled in 2010 计划2010年	18 tunnel elements, element length 180m; reinforced concrete structure 18个管节，节段式管节长180m；钢筋混凝土结构
7	Hong Kong-Zhuhai-Macao Bridge-Immersed Tunnel 港珠澳大桥海底隧道	5990 (immersed tunnel length 5664m) 5990 (沉管段5664m)	Two-bore two-gallery 两孔两管廊	Bidirectional six-lane highway tunnel 双向六车道公路隧道	Scheduled in 2016 计划2016年	32 tunnel elements, segmental type, element length 180m, reinforced concrete 32个管节，节段式管节长180m。钢筋混凝土结构

So far, among the completed highway tunnels in the world, the longest highway tunnel is the Aurland-Laerdal Tunnel in Norway with total length up to 24.5km. Generally, the highway tunnels in the world are listed in table 1.5. Among the listed tunnels, Mt. Blance Tunnel linking France and Italy under the peak of Alps is in total length of 11.6km, with the street width of 7.0m, the height of 6m from top slab to pavement, the horseshoe shaped profile, and the lining thickness of 80cm. The level of elevation is 1274m at the entrance portal in France and is 1381m at the exit in Italy, and the maximum burial depth is approximately 2500m, with 2 lanes of converse direction and limit speed of 80km/h designed. The tunnel was commenced in 1959 and opened to traffic in 1965.

Highway Tunnels in Length of over 10km in the Countries Worldwide   Table 1.5

Name of tunnel	Country	Length(m)
Mt. Blance Tunnel	France-Italy	11600
Frejus Tunnel	France-Italy	12901
St. Gothard Tunnel	Switzerland	16918
Qinling Zhongnanshan Tunnel	China	18020
Dapingli Tunnel	China	12290
Baojiashan Tunnel	China	11500
Baotashan Tunnel	China	10391
Arlberg Tunnel	Austria	13927
Gran Sasso Tunnel	Italy	10173
Kan-Etsu Tunnel I	Japan	10920
Kan-Etsu Tunnel II	Japan	11010
Gudvanga Tunnel	Norway	11400
Folgefonn Tunnel	Norway	11100
Aurland Laerdal Tunnel	Norway	24500
Pinglin Tunnel	Taiwan, China	12900
Hida Tunnel	Japan	10750

The development in tunnel technology indicated that the aspects of tunnel technological research are: non-blasting mechanized construction, suitable planning and environment protection, reliable and reasonable design and safe operation. China is a developing country with large population and since the entry into 21st century with the rapid progress and constant improvement of civil facility construction, rapid economic development and constant enhancement of economic power; the number of tunnels and bridges in China has ranked the first in the world. However, the construction equipment and their automation are still to be improved. In terms of the tunnel construction techniques, foreign advanced technology shall be introduced, meanwhile better equipments of tunnel construction should be adopted based on the domestic technological level so that the disturbance to the surrounding rock during tunneling can be minimized and the safety of the tunnel during the works execution can be improved.

Some urgent problems of tunnel construction and maintenance need to be solved and the corresponding technologies are to be developed and made available.

(1) Technologies on tunnel geological survey, advanced geological forecasting, judgment and assessment of the level of surrounding rock.

(2) Tunnel construction methodology, technologies on automated inspection, measurement and early warning of the deformation of surrounding rock at the tunnel, automated concrete injection by mechanized means, lining assembly on site, drainage, construction of long vertical shaft, the construction in deep water and the manual freezing construction method for the tunnel to be built in highly moist stratum and in soft rock.

(3) The technologies of tunnel operation surveillance, highly energy-efficient illumination, optimum automated fan adjustment and controlling, and electrostatic dust removal technology.

(4) Tunnel safety standard, the technologies of tunnel traffic-signal arrangement, tunnel hazard detecting, permeation prevention, tunnel noise reducing and light pollution prevention, tunnel fire prevention, rescue, hazard relieving and life escaping and tunnel peril treatment.

(5) Technology of tunnel fume and gas treatment, technology of waste water recycle and treatment, technology of protection the environment and eco-system in the tunneling area.

The characteristics of modern tunnel construction development are associated with following elements: ①Human scientific and technological progress, particularly the rapid development of computer technology and information technology which enables detailed calculation and analysis of the forces to which tunnels are subjected in course of tunnel excavation and the calculation results and construction control method completely agree with tunnel execution reality; ②The continual improvement and intellectualization of machines and equipments for tunnel advancing which protects the integrity of surrounding rock to maximum extent; ③Higher human demanding on ecological environmental protection; ④The more awareness of human-orientation.

The characteristics of modern tunnel construction development are as follows.

(1) Longer tunnels constructed

With the gradual improvement of road standard, tunnel design theory and construction technology are continually improved and upgraded. The length of highway tunnel increased from 2-3km built in 20th century to kilometers today. The famous tunnels include Japanese Kan-Etsu Tunnel in length of 11.06km, Mt. Blance Tunnel in Italy in length of 11.6, Arlberg Tunnel, Austria in length of 14km, St. Gothard Tunnel in Switzerland with length of 16.8km and Aurland Laerdal Tunnel in Norway in length of 24.5km. Although the history of the national tunnel construction is only over 20 years, but its development is very fast. The national representative tunnels are Qidaoliang tunnel in length of 1.56km, Wutongshan tunnel in length of 2.33km, Shanghai Dapulu tunnel in length of 2.76km, Daxiling tunnel in length of 4.1km, Erlangshan tunnel in length of 4.16km and Qinling Zhongnanshan tunnel in length of 18.02km. The successful completion of these long highway tunnels have owned to many success decisive factors—the implementation of higher standard and class of highway, the application of new construction method and advanced ventilation monitoring technology.

(2) More and more curved tunnels

Driven by new theory for tunnel design and construction method, particularly based on the conclusion and summarization of practical experiences on highway operation and management, the principle of "straight line rather than curved one" in tunnel line selection is broken. In the route selection of modern tunnels, more and more curve tunnels are selected gradually, which is a more common practice in oversea projects. For example, to fit for the terrain and environment conditions a section of curved tunnel in length of 1.2km was designed to constitute a part of Baraschi twin line tunnel in Austria. The principal reasons for the increment of curve d tunnels are: ①to avoid harmful geological areas and improve the safety of tunnel structure; ②to limit travel speed and fully ensure travel safety; ③ to effectively control the dazzling phenomenon brought about by the acceleration when getting out of the tunnel. Curved tunnels are helpful in preventing traffic incidents. For example, the Chongqing Cuntan Tunnel(重庆寸滩隧道), which was opened to traffic on December 28, 2008, was mainly intended for heavy-duty container trucks traveling through Cuntan areas and the tunnel is in total length of 400m, with horizontal plane curve radius of 300m and longitudinal slope gradient of 3%. The curved tunnel with small radius was designed for the purpose of limiting or preventing heavy-duty vehicle from traveling into harbor zone in accelerated speed, which may give rise to traffic incidents and this kind of design embodied human-orientated design concept.

(3) The dominance of longitudinal ventilation mode

In 20th century, over 400 oversea highway tunnels with the length more than 3km adopted full transverse ventilation or semi-transverse ventilation which is mainly represented by tunnels in Switzerland, Austrian and Italy. In recent years, with the practical application of longitudinal ventilation modes in long and large highway tunnels, the ventilation modes of highway tunnels are basically classified into two categories—the transverse ventilation or semi-transverse ventilation represented by Europe and the longitudinal ventilation mode represented by Japan in Asia. With the enhancement of criteria on vehicle exhaust limitation, the control factors are changed from control of tunnel ventilation air flow to control of CO concentration in smoke. Besides, two-bore tunnel design is replacing one-bore tunnel design gradually. Hence, the longitudinal ventilation section by section has dominated. Japan is of the opinions that the segmented longitudinal ventilation with electrostatic dust collector applies to all transportation forms and all highway tunnels of any length. European countries are changing their traditional ideas: in many new buildings or increased twin-line long highway tunnels, the segmented longitudinal ventilation is replacing the old transverse ventilation modes. Many domestic long and large highway tunnels adopted mainly the longitudinal ventilation mode or the segmented longitudinal ventilation.

(4) Twin-bore tunnel replacingone-bore tunnel

The air flow between cars heading in converse directions cannot fully be used in the one-bore bidirectional tunnel so the ventilation equipment capacity is required to be increased. Especially, the incident rate in one-bore bidirectional tunnel is much higher than that in twin-bore unidirectional transit tunnel. Hence in recent years, two-bore unidirectional transit tunnel is replacing one-bore dual traffic tunnel gradually. According to the incomplete statistics reported, over 100 old one-bore bidirectional transit tunnels are being transformed into twin-bored one-way traffic tunnel abroad, which have greatly facilitated to reduce the ventilation difficulty, save energy and reduce traffic incidents. In addition, twin-bored tunnels can greatly improve the traffic volume and satisfy the requirements of fire prevention and disaster relieving and civil defense. The Baraschi tunnel in Austria and Tauern Motorway tunnel are the typical examples of this kind.

All the national expressway tunnels are twin-bore unidirectional transit tunnels. But the highway tunnels of class II and the highways with class lower than II are mainly one-bore dual traffic tunnels. Some one-bore dual traffic tunnels on the highway of class II are also transformed to twin-bored unidirectional traffic tunnel to satisfy the increasing traffic flow. The Xiangyang tunnel (向阳隧道) in urban center of Chongqing is a good example as well as the Bayi Tunnel (八一隧道) built in later time.

5. Diversity of tunnel functions

The principal function of highway tunnels is to provide a passage for vehicles, namely the traffic function. However, the long highway tunnels, particularly super-long highway tunnels which were very difficult and costly to build, would attract the attention and curiosity of the public. Hence sightseeing of tourists has become another apparent characteristics of long and large highway tunnels and the noticeable examples are English channel tunnel, Tokyo Bay tunnel, Hong Kong Bay Tunnel and Shanghai Yanandonglu Tunnel which are of special features and do not only serve as scenery spots but also as extremely important traffic passageway. Before the construction of national Qinling Zhongnanshan Tunnel, Shaanxi Provincial Government once proposed an idea of integrating the traffic function of the tunnel with the natural surroundings and around sightseeing for tourism, so many scenery zones were set up in the completed Qingling Zhongnanshan Tunnel which are systematically combined with the ventilation facilities and the transport system and worth visiting.

In addition to the traffic functions, tunnels are often taken as gallery to accommodate all types of pipes such as water conveyance and electrical cable and gas supply pipelines, communication cable pipelines and other special purpose pipelines. Naturally, these pipelines shall be specially designed and arranged before tunnel works commencement.

Text B Familiarization with Tunnels
熟 悉 隧 道

1. Outline of tunnels

A tunnel is a kind of underground engineering structure with entrance and exit at both ends for purpose of traffic movement, pedestrian's passage, water flow collecting and transport and placement of pipelines. Broadly, tunnel and underground engineering are different in meanings. One refers to the applied science on study and construction of all kinds of tunnels and underground works in respect of works planning, survey, design, construction and maintenance and tunneling is one branch of civil engineering; the other refers to the subsurface buildings built in rocks or soil strata.

Generally in tunnel building, a "pit" in any one of the several certain geometric forms such as circular shape, rectangular, horseshoe shape is dug in strata. Since the opened strata are prone to deformation, collapse, or inrush of water for safety in tunnel excavation, normally support structures or the "lining" are built surrounding the pit with the exception of at the points of stable strata and absence of groundwater. The shape and dimension of the lining shall make loading distribution on the tunnel structure most reasonable which makes the structure both economical and robust.

A tunnel is much more than just a tunnel. It serves any of the myriad functions—highway, railroad or rapid transit artery, pedestrian passageway, fresh water conveyance, cooling water supply, wastewater collector or transport, hydropower and cover methods; in long, prefabricated sections sunk in place as in immersed tubes; by mechanized means such as tunnel boring machines or continuous miners (roadheaders), with the aid of a protective shield in free or compressed air, they eventually be constructed in ways now existing only in our imagination.

In cross section, a tunnel takes one of the several shapes-circular, multicurve, horseshoes, cathedral arch, arched, or flat-roofed and with clear spans of form a few feet to more than 50feet and, in cavern form, much wider. Its length can vary from less than 100feet to more than 30 miles. A tunnel can be located in any of a variety of places—under mountains, cities, rivers, lakes, sea estuaries, straits or bays. Finally, a tunnel is constructed in one of the innumerable media—soft ground, mixed face, rock, and uniform jumbled, layered, dry, wet, stable, flowing and squeezing.

Most of all, a tunnel exists because there is a demonstrated need for tunnel such as: to move people or material where no other means is practical or adequate, or to accomplish the required movement more directly, more quickly, or less obtrusively. The need may be for storage, either short term as for storage of storm water flows to reduce the otherwise high peak capacities required of wastewater treatment plants, or longer term as for storage of vital raw material or products.

A tunnel also is more than a hole in the ground to provide for a desired movement of people or material. To accomplish the movement satisfactorily, one or more of a variety of facilities in simple or complex form must be provided in addition to the continuous space. The most obvious need for highway tunnel is ventilation. Fresh air must be supplied in proportion to tunnel usage. The air also must be of reasonable purity; this requires constant monitoring for pollutants and consequent adjustment of the air supply and exhaust.

Another essential for highway tunnels is some form and degree of lighting (in a low-use rural tunnel, the vehicle's headlights may suffice). In high-use (generally urban) tunnels, a sophisticated system of high-level, adjustable lighting is necessary both for safety and for ensuring maximum appropriate speeds.

While ventilation and lighting are the most obvious day-to-day tunnel operational needs, there is a greater need. That this need may arise only once every 10, 25 or 50 years is unimportant because of the possible consequences when it does. All tunnels used for transport or people musthave adequate fire life safety protections. The need has always been obvious in rapid transit tunnels, but it has only recently been recognized for more spacious highway tunnels.

Fire life safety, ventilation, and lighting are also important to railroad and transit tunnels, although in quite different degrees. Lighting requirements are much reduced, needed more for orientation and maintenance than for passage. However, fire life safety requirements are more rigorous due to the greater number of people transported. BAET (the San Francisco Bay Area Rapid Transit System) gained recognition for the design of close and parallel twin tunnels with appropriately spaced and equipped connecting passageways, now accepted as the best possible layout for providing refuge from a raging fire or deadly smoke. Ventilation takes a somewhat different form, because a train's piston effect can handle a large part of the normal ventilation requirement, especially for transit tunnels and short rail tunnels. For transit tunnels, then, emergency ventilation becomes more important. On long railroad tunnels with diesel locomotives and a high volume of freight traffic, the tunnel ventilation capacity may constrain the tunnel's hourly traffic capacity. The ventilation air flow rate governs the speed the locomotive can attain without overheating and the time required to purge diesel exhaust fumes before the next train can enter the tunnel. In some long tunnels, in order to increase the air flow past the train, unorthodox construction may be required, such as the trackway doors installed at portals at the Cascade, Flathead, and Moffet Tunnels, and at portals and at an intermediate shaft at the Mt. Macdonald Tunnel.

Modern highway tunnels include an elaborate traffic surveillance and control system, a coordinated with emergency ventilation and lighting system, and provisions for protected egress of motorists in the event of a fire and access of fire-fighting personnel. The types of surveillance and control for a highway tunnel depend to a considerable extent on the approach roads. Because a tunnel is confined space and presents psychological hazards, there is a need for more detailed knowledge of traffic conditions, better communication with drivers, and faster and more stylized response to emergencies than on the open road or on bridges.

A tunnel project must start with a comprehensive investigation of ground conditions by collecting samples from drillholes and by other geophysical techniques. An information choice can then be made of machinery and methods for excavation and ground support, which will reduce the risk of encountering unforeseen ground conditions. In planning the route the horizontal and vertical alignments will make use of the best ground and water conditions.

In some cases, conventional desk and site studies yield insufficient information to assess such factors as the blocky nature of rocks, the exact location of fault zone, or the stand-up times of softer ground. This may be a particular concern in large diameter tunnels. To get more information, a pilot tunnel or drift may be driven ahead of the main drive. This smaller diameter tunnel will be easier to support, should unexpected conditions be met, and will be incorporated in the final tunnel. Alternatively, horizontal boreholes may sometimes be drilled ahead of the advancing tunnel face.

Tunnels are dug in types of materials varying from soft clay to hard rock. The method of tunnel construction depends on such factors as the ground conditions, the ground water conditions, the length and diameter of the tunnel drive, the depth of the tunnel, the logistics of supporting the tunnel excavation, the final use and shape of the tunnel and appropriate risk management.

2. Classification of tunnel types

There are many types of tunnels and different methods of tunnel type classification from different points of views. From the viewpoint of geological conditions at tunnel site there are soil tunnel and rock tunnel. By depths of embedment, there are low embedded tunnel and deep embedded tunnel. By locations of tunnel, there are mountain tunnel, underwater tunnel and urban tunnel. By different construction techniques, there are cut and covered tunnel, bored tunnel and immersed tunnel.

Tunnel classification by purposes

Most tunnels are for transport purposes and they are transit tunnels including railway tunnel for trains, highway tunnel for motorcars, subway tunnel for urban transportation, underwater tunnel and underground cross for pedestrians.

Most railway tunnels are built in mountainous regions ata high level. Since a railway requires flat and gentle slope, it is most reasonable for a railway to penetrate through a mountain by digging a tunnel which can make route alignment straight and avoid many unnecessary line extensions. The line can be shortened and its slope gradient can be reduced and operation condition can be thus improved. Thus tunnel solutions are the major selections and therefore more and more railway tunnels are built.

Highway tunnels are not so rigorous in slope degree and minimum curvature radius limitations. In mountainous regions highways choose a longer line in order to avoid a tunnel which is more expensive. But with the development of economy in China the number of highways is increasing and the highway requires a straight and flat route, road surface shall be gentle and wide. A tunnel is also used in highway construction.

A subway is a good solution in a municipality where traffic is crowded and congested. Traffic volume for passenger carriage is large. As a rail transport facility, a subway can carry a large number of passengers by underground passage and provide a better condition for surface traffic. In China many cities have subways which are playing a major and effective role in improving urban traffic conditions and reducing traffic accidents.

An underwater tunnel is built on the river floor or sea floor when traffic route needs to cross a river or sea and can also let shipping traffic sail across a channel or bridge cross over water. In stormy weather or strong wind when ferry transport becomes impossible, a subwater tunnel as a carriage way can be used without being subjected to the influence of adverse weathers.

Pedestrian basement: In urban areas, there are crowded pedestrians and the traffic volume is high. Traffic accidents easily occur. For the reduction of traffic accidents and for the safety of pedestrians, the pedestrian underpass is built for pedestrians to cross the traffic lane.

A hydraulic tunnel is one important component of hydraulic-electric power station. Water passes a tunnel and flows to the other side of the dam. Hydraulic tunnels include water carriage tunnel, tailrace tunnel, diversion tunnel, or spillway tunnel and sand drain tunnel.

Urban public utility tunnel: In cities, all types of public utility facilities as underground duct are arranged. Owing to a continuous development of tunnels, the public utilities are highly demanded and many cities have to utilize underground space to accommodate thus utilities. Urban tunnels include water supply tunnel, tunnel for sewage pipeline, pipeline tunnel, cable power, drainage tunnel and civil defense tunnel.

3. Development of tunnel construction techniques

Tunnel as a type of underground engineering building constructed in strata has been extensively used in fields of transport, mines, water conservation, municipal administration and civil defense.

1) The first advent of man-made tunnels

The first transit tunnel in China is the "crossing-heading" tunnel located in Hanzhong county, Shaanxi province. It was built in 66 BC years for passage of horse wagon and pedestrians. The first tunnel in the world appeared in 2200 BC years. It was an underground channel linking the palace and built by King of Babylon.

2) Scientific technology and inventions and the development of tunnel technology

The advent of survey technique has pushed forward the progress of tunnel engineering technology. People used shed support to support rock layers and lift rock by windlass. Tunnel was excavated from entrances. Tunnel quantity for various purposes increased.

Gunpowder was invented in 14th century and greatly developed tunnel technology. Blasting technique was applied to excavation of Malpas tunnel on canal du Midi in France and turned out to be a great success. Tunnel excavation technology developed rapidly.

In time of Industrial Revolution in 19th century, modern tunnel excavation techniques were developed and many new tunneling methods and approaches emerged. In 1818, Brunel invented shield machine and Italian physicist Erardon proposed a tunneling method of balancing the pressure of bursting water in weak soil stratum by use of compressed air to prevent stratum collapse. Later Co-Chrane, a British invented the method of submarine tunnel excavation by utilization of compressed air.

In 1979, the New Austrian Tunneling Method (NATM) was officially promoted. The concept of this New Austrian Tunneling Method was proposed by Austrian scholar L. V. Rabcewicz in 1950s. It is a construction method by which rockbolt and shotcrete are combined to serve as a principal support means based on tunneling experiences and rock mechanics theory. This new tunneling method was patented and officially named in 1960s through lots of practices and theoretic studies in many countries. This method was developed rapidly in many underground works in Western Europe, Northern Europe, America and Japan. In 1960s, NATM was first introduced in China and was extensively applied in late 1970s and early 1980s. Up to today, all the key and difficult underground works are using NATM which has become one of the basic tunnel construction method adopted in building tunnel in weak and fragmentary rock sections in China.

Most of the tunnels, before the great age of railroad construction, were built in connection with mines, water supply system or canals. The maximum grade at which a steam locomotive could operate efficiently was 2 percent. This fact encouraged the construction of a great many tunnels. As more tunnels were built, many significant technical advances were made in boring both through underwater clay and through rock.

One of the most remarkable tunnel-building feats was the construction of the first tunnel under the Thames River in London. It is still used by the London Underground Railway System. It was dug out of clay beneath the riverbed between 1825 and 1843 under the direction of Sir Mark Brunel, who had designed a tunneling shield that made the work possible. The shield offered the workers protection while they dug out clay and mud in the face of the shield. It was then moved forward by jacks so that the process could be repeated.

One of the first major tunnels built through rock was the Mont Cenis Tunnel in the Alps between France and Italy. It is 14 kilometers long and was built between 1857 and 1871. When construction began on it, progress was drill, which uses compressed air to bore holes in rock, was invented a few years after construction began. Thereafter, the tunneling speed was increased to two meters a day. Like most tunnels, the Mont Cenis was bored from two different headings, one in France and one in Italy, which met in the middle.

Another tunnel under the Alps, the Simplon, remains a major engineering accomplishment. It runs for a distance of 19 kilometers, and at one point, it is more than 2100 meters under the crest of a mountain. It was built between 1898 and 1906, and extraordinary difficulties had to be overcome: extremely high temperatures, rock that burst off the walls because of the pressure springs of both cold and hot water, and layers of soft stone that required special supports. It remains the deepest tunnel ever constructed.

The usual technique for tunneling through hard rock is to drill holes in the face of heading. The holes are filled with an explosive that is detonated after the workers and equipment are withdrawn to a safe distance. After fumes and rock dust have settled the rock brought down by the explosion is removed, often on conveyor belts. In many projects, like the Simplon, a small pilot tunnel is driven before the full diameter of the tunnel is excavated. This technique helps engineers to determine the geological features of the rock through which the tunnel is passing so that many difficulties can be anticipated. In some cases, workers on the main tunnel progress a few meters behind the pilot tunnel so that the latter provides ventilations, always a major problem in tunneling operations.

Shields that are modifications of the one that Brunel developed for boring the Thames Tunnel are used in excavating through clay or soft rock. A shield has a sharp edge that is driven into the tunnel face by hydraulic jacks. The top edge of the shield projects for a short distance in order to protect the works. Behind the cutting edge is the tail, which has a smaller diameter. The permanent lining of the tunnels assembled in this area. The space between the lining and the larger diameter that has been excavated by the forward part of the shield is filled with a grout that is pumped in under pressure. Modern shields are highly mechanized so that many phases of the tunneling process can be performed almost completely by machinery.

Silt, the soft mud that is typical of river beds and other underwater tunneling sites, presents difficult problems. In Brunel's Thames Tunnel, water broke through on several occasions, and the tunnel had to be pumped dry. In addition, Brunel had loads of clay dumped into the riverbed to make it more imperious to water.

Modern engineers, of course, have developed and now use more sophisticated soil stabilization technique when they tunnel through silt, sand or loose material such as gravel. Most of underwater tunnel construction through these materials utilizes shields with compressed air, similar to caissons. The same precaution must be taken to protect works from being exposed to the dangers of extreme pressure.

Another technique that has come into wide use in recent years is the immersed tube system. In this technique a channel is dredged along the line of the tunnel, in other words, silt is pumped out of the waterbed. Piles are then driven along the channel, and prefabricated sections of the tunnel are lowered into place on to the piles. The tunnel sections are closed by temporary faces that are removed after all the sections have been assembled. The joints between the sections are also made watertight at this stage of construction. Finally, the channel is filled in to give the tunnel greater stability. The Maas River tunnel at Rotterdam is an immersed tube. Another is the recently opened tube between San Francisco and Oakland, California, for the Bay Area Rapid Transit System.

A technique that is often used for subway construction is the cut-and-cover method. Workers excavate a trench, inside of which the lining for the tunnel is built. It is then covered over with the earth or other fill that was originally removed. The cut-and-cover method obviously can only be used when the tunnel is immediately beneath the surface. One difficulty is that normal street traffic must often be allowed to continue during construction. In such a case, wooden beams or steel plates are laid down to cover the excavation.

Ventilation is a major problem in all tunnels, but particularly in those to be used by automobile traffic. The exhaust fumes of automobiles contain carbon monoxide, a deadly gas. Most automobile tunnels therefore have two systems of ducts. Huge fan pump in fresh air through one of them, while polluted air is sucked out through the other.

A good example of the complexity of engineering a modern highway system can be illustrated by the Chesapeake Bay Bridge tunnel. This crossing between Maryland and Virginia over one of the principal waterways in the United States is 28 kilometers long. Most of the highway is supported on concrete piles with short spans between them. It was also necessary, however, to leave four ship channels. Two of these are spanned by bridges, but the other two are provided by tunnels. The entrances to the two tunnel sections are from man-made islands in the bay. The tunnels themselves are steel tubes, which were placed in a channel that had been dredged in the bay bottom.

Another great engineering project that is still under construction is the Seikan Railroad Tunnel in Japan. This tunnel, 36 kilometers long, will connect the islands of Honshu and Hokkaido, passing 100 meters under the surface of the strait between them, the strait itself is 140 meters at its deepest point. The routes are now being explored by a pilot tunnel in order to determine the geological formations and types of rock through which the tunnel must be bored. The Japanese are also experimenting with new types of machines called moles, which can bore through hard rock by mechanical means.

Text C Rijswijk Railway Tunnel
赖斯韦克铁路隧道

In the framework of the future plan Rail 21, the Dutch Railway Company has doubled the railway track between the Hague and Delft from two to four tracks. In this track-doubling at the city center of the municipality of Rijswijk, the choice was made for a tunnel which would also house Rijswijk Station. With this, the Railway Company has broken down the barrier that was formed by the old railway line in Rijswijk. This contributions to the improvement of the relationship between the old city center of Rijswijk and the new city district situated on the other side of the railway track. In the planning, the designer drew up a comparative study of the costs, the quality and the construction time of differing variations. Construction by means of a dry construction pit method technically proved to be possible and cheaper than the other variations. With this the positioning underground became financially feasible.

1. Route and station building

Approaching from the Hague, the railway track declines from the Van Vredenburchweg intersection to approximately 5.60 meters. The sunken tunnel section is approximately 1500 meters in length of which approximately 550 meters runs across a closed section under the central urban section of the municipality of Rijswijk. The station is situated in this underground section. Here the tunnel reaches its greatest width at 40 meters. Approximately 150 meters before the intersection with the sunken section of the A4 motorway the railway track reaches surface level again.

The top part of the closed tunnel section in Rijswijk is situated at the same or a bit above the old surface level. The area that became available at the place of the underground track provides space for urban redevelopment. In the construction of the tunnel, consideration has also been taken into account with future building over at certain places. At the closed tunnel section, a public transport intersection has already been realized with an important function in the region of Hague.

The station building which is in the shape of a glass pyramid, is situated above the underground platforms and the closed middle section. Eight small glass pyramids have been incorporated in the roof above the platform to enable ingression of daylight for an increased atmosphere and social security. The pyramids also play a role in case of a disaster. In case of fire in the tunnel, they are automatically opened for the discharge of smoke fumes.

2. Design

The sunken tract positioning is realized in a cutting between tow diaphragm walls. The diaphragm walls reach to within the Pleistocene sand deposits (21 meters) and have an earth-retaining and a water-sealing function. They form the vertical walls of the artificial polder. By means of a permanent drainage, the ground water level in the polder is kept at 7.50 meters. A tunnel floor is not necessary, because there is a natural, poorly permeable, clay and peat layer present which impedes the flow of the ground water from the Pleistocene sand deposits underneath. A drained sand bed suffices as a base for the track construction.

The access ramps are situated outside the artificial polder, for this, watertight open trough constructions of reinforced concrete were built, with the foundations on prefabricated poles made of prestressed concrete.

The foundations and the concrete construction of the tunnel have been calculated for building at a number of places. The roof consists of a layer of reinforced concrete which is supported by the diaphragm walls and three rows of columns made of reinforced concrete. There rubber templates between the bearing columns and the roof. The square columns with 55 centimeters faces have a bored pile foundation which stands on the sand deposit 20 to 28 meters deep. The maximum bearing capacity of the bored piles is 600kN and that for the diaphragm walls is 1500kN per running meter of wall. This bearing capacity ensured that traffic across the layer of the tunnel was possible.

3. Construction

During construction, the rail and road traffic and the lives of those living in the neighborhood continues as normal. That is why the work was carried out phased. In the first phase, the trains remained on the existing track. The contractor commenced on both sides of the track with the construction of the tunnel, including the new outer tracks. In phase two, the existing inner tracks were placed out of the operation. As the trains traveled across the sunken outer tracks, the contractor removed the old inner track and constructed the middle section of the tunnel. In order to commence with the tunnel construction and to have trains traveling across existing track, cables and piping are diverted first, and sheet pile walls are erected along the existing railway track. These sheet pile walls are coupled together by means of anchors so that the railway track remains stable when excavation takes place for the outermost tunnel sections. Then the contractor erects the diaphragm walls and bored piles and casts the prefabricated columns into the bored piles.

The diggers start with the partial excavation after the diaphragm walls have been provided with temporary grout-anchors. Only then does the contractor apply the roof formwork and casts the roofs. Once the roofs are placed, the excavation continues further to a depth required for the construction of a permanent drainage and dewatering system. Thereafter, soil improvement occurs in the "polder" location, after which the contractor can construct the ballast bed, the outer tracks and the platforms. In the same phase, the open trough construction for the access ramps of the outer tracks is made inside a temporary construction pit surrounded by sheet pile walls. After the constructional completion of the tunnel and the access ramps, and the putting into operation of the sunken outer tracks, it is followed by the demolition and removal of the old inner track and the implementation of the middle section of the tunnel.

II. Terms and terminology

highway tunnel	公路隧道
rail tunnel	铁路隧道
subaqueous tunnel	水下隧道,水底隧道
rapid transit artery	高速交通干道
pedestrian passageway/walkway	人行通道
immersed tube tunnel	沉管隧道
prefabricated section	预制管段
jacking pit	顶管井
tunnel boring machine	隧道掘进机
roadheader	巷道掘进机
New Austrian Tunneling Method (NATM)	新奥法
protective shield	保护盾
wastewater treatment plant	废水处理厂
ventilation	通风
air supply and exhaust	供气和排气
degree of lighting	照明度
train's piston effect	列车的活塞效应
raging fire	烈火
deadly smoke	致命烟雾
emergency ventilation	应急通风
portal	隧道洞口
traffic surveillance	交通监控
lighting system	照明系统
ground condition	地基条件
collecting sample(或 sample-collecting)	采样
excavation	开挖
ground support	地基支护
planning the route (或 route-planning)	线路规划
horizontal and vertical alignments	水平和竖向线形
cut and cover tunnel	明挖隧道
bored tunnel	钻掘隧道

III. Questions and difficult sentence analysis

1. Questions for brainstorming discussion

(1) Discuss the types and salient features of transit tunnels.

(2) Please give the names, functions and construction features of the tunnels which you know in your city.

(3) Discuss the characteristics of modern tunnels.

2. Difficult sentences analysis

(1) Tunnel is an underground engineering building with portals at both ends and an important part of civil engineering, same as bridge and side slopesupporting and retaining structures. It serves any of various functions-highway, railway, pedestrian passageway, water conveyance and gallery of pipelines. However, the standard tunnel definition posed in technological point of view at the tunnel conference of OECD in 1970 and the definition states that any strip-shaped building built by any means and ultimately used below surface of ground with clear span more than $2m^2$ is tunnel.

译文:隧道是一种地下工程建筑,两端有洞口,为车辆、行人、输水管道提供通道,与桥梁、边坡支护及支挡结构一样,是土木工程和道路工程的重要组成部分。但是,经济合作与发展组织于1970年的隧道年会上,从技术角度提出了关于隧道的定义:以任何方式修建的位于地面以下的条形结构,其洞室内部净空面积超过$2m^2$为隧道。

(2) Driven by new theory for tunnel design and construction method, particularly based on the conclusion and summarization of practical experiences on highway operation and management, the principle of "straight line rather than curved one" in tunnel line selection is broken.

译文:在新的隧道设计理论和施工技术的推动下,特别是在总结公路隧道运营管理的实践经验后,现代公路隧道的选线已经完全打破了过去的"宁直勿弯"的规则。

(3) In 20th century, over 400 oversea highway tunnels with the length more than 3km adopted full transverse ventilation or semi-transverse ventilation which is mainly represented by tunnels in Switzerland, Austrian and Italy. In recent years, with the practical application of longitudinal ventilation modes in long and large highway tunnels, the ventilation modes of highway tunnels are basically classified into two categories-the transverse ventilation or semi-transverse ventilation represented by Europe and the longitudinal ventilation mode represented by Japan in Asia.

译文:20世纪,国外建成的近400座长度超过3km的公路隧道中,多数为全横向式通风或半横向式通风,以瑞士、奥地利和意大利为代表。近年来,随着纵向通风方式在长大公路隧道的实践后,公路隧道的通风方式基本上分为两个派别,以欧洲为代表的横向式通风或半横向式通风和以亚洲日本为代表的纵向式通风。

(4) The principal function of highway tunnels is to provide a passage for vehicles, namely the traffic function. However, the long highway tunnels, particularly super-long highway tunnels which were very difficult and costly to build, would attract the attention and curiosity of the public. Hence sightseeing of tourists has become another apparent characteristics of long and large highway tunnels and the noticeable examples are English channel tunnel, Tokyo Bay tunnel, Hong Kong Bay Tunnel and Shanghai Yan'andonglu Tunnel which are of special features and do not only serve as scenery spots but also as extremely important traffic passageway.

译文:公路隧道的主要功能是用于汽车通行,即交通功能。但是,对于人类修建的长大公路隧道,特别是特长公路隧道、建设难度很大的隧道以及造价很高的隧道等,会引起公众的关注和好奇心,因此,旅游观光成为长大公路隧道的另一明显特点,突出例子有英吉利海峡隧道、东京湾隧道、香港湾隧道和上海延安东路隧道等,人们不仅将这些有特点的隧道作为观光场所,同时也作为极其重要的交通通道。

Ⅳ. Translation case study

Case 1

Chinese	English translation
隧道设计以"安全、经济、适用、美观"作为基本原则。隧道选址综合考虑洞身地质条件、洞口地形及地质条件、洞外接线工程等因素进行确定,尽量避开不良地质区域;洞身结构基于新奥法原理进行设计,充分发挥、利用围岩自身的承载能力;隧道洞口设计严格控制边仰坡高度,避免大挖大刷,尽量实现无仰坡进洞;隧道防排水设计采用"以排为主、防排结合"的原则,达到排水通畅、防水可靠、经济合理、不留后患的目的。	A tunnel is designed by compliance with the fundamental principle of "safety, economy, applicability and aesthetical effect". The geological conditions at the tunnel body, and the geological conditions and terrain at portals and link line outside the tunnel shall be overall considered to avoid harmful ground to maximum extent. The tunnel body structure is to be designed based on the theory of the New Austrian Tunneling Method so as to fully mobilize the bearing capacity of the surrounding rock itself. In tunnel portal design, the level of inverted slope shall be strictly controlled and deep excavation and cutting shall be avoided for purpose of eliminating inverted slope at tunnel entrance section. In tunnel drainage design, the principle of "dominant drainage and combination of waterproofing and drain" shall be implemented so as to achieve objectives of free drain, reliable waterproofness, economic reasonableness and no potential hazard left.

Case 2

Chinese	English translation
港珠澳大桥是我国继三峡工程、青藏铁路、南水北调、西气东输、京沪高铁之后又一重大基础设施项目,东连香港、西接珠海、澳门,是集桥、岛、隧为一体的超大型跨海通道。	The Hong Kong-Zhuhai-Macao Bridge (HZMB) is a significant infrastructure project as momentous as the preceding national key projects of the Three Gorges Dam, Qingzang Railway, south-north water transfer, west-east gas transport and Jinghu Express Railway. It links Hong Kong in the east and Zhuhai, Macao in the west and is the mega marine crossing project consisted of the bridges, the tunnel and the artificial islands.
项目投资约1050亿元人民币,由三个部分组成:离岸大桥和隧道(主体工程),分别位于香港、珠海和澳门境内的三个口岸设施,以及三地境内的连线。其中,岛隧工程为主体工程的控制性工程,由沉管隧道和东、西人工岛三大部分组成,全长7440.546m,其中,沉管隧道在当今世界上同类工程中最具挑战性。合同工期63个月,为2010年12月至2016年3月。	With an investment of approximately 105 billion in RMB, this crossing link consists of three parts: the Offshore Bridge-and-Tunnel (the Main Construction); the three Boundary-Crossing Facilities (BCFs) in Hong Kong, Zhuhai and Macao respectively; and the Link Roads in the three regions. The Island-and-Tunnel Section, a key part of the Main Construction, includes two artificial islands and an immersed tunnel. This section is 7440.546m in length, of which the immersed tunnel is one of the most challenging constructions of its kind undertaken in the world today. The construction period of the Island-and-Tunnel Section is scheduled from December 2010 to March 2016, altogether 63 months.
岛隧工程结合、长距离通风及安全设计、超大管节的预制、复杂海洋条件下管节的浮运和沉放、高水压条件下管节的对接以及接头的水密性及耐久性、隧道软土地基不均匀沉降控制等技术均要达到世界最高水准。沉管隧道东西人工岛的深厚软土的加固处理、人工岛各部分差异沉降的控制、与沉管隧道的连接、岛、隧运营阶段的可靠性及耐久性等技术,也都具有世界挑战性。	The ventilation and safety design for such a long immersed tunnel (6.7km) is admittedly a tough problem in the international engineering community. Additionally, the precasting of the gigantic concrete tunnel elements, their towing and immersion under complicated sea conditions, the connection of tunnel elements under high water pressure, and the watertightness and durability of the element joints all call for the highest world standards. The control of differential settlement from the soft soil tunnel foundation, the control of differential settlement at each part of the Eastern and Western Artificial Islands, the connection of the immersed tunnel and the artificial islands, and the reliability and durability of the tunnel and islands during the operation phase all present daunting challenges.

continue

Chinese	English translation
项目特点除了超大型工程所普遍具有的规模大、工期紧、难度高、风险大等共性外,还具有社会关注度高、三地政府共建共管、采用设计施工总承包模式等特点,以及白海豚保护区的环境因素、路线穿过伶仃洋航道区、复杂的通航环境,工期及接口限制等限制条件。	In addition to such common features of super large-scaled construction, tight works schedule, high difficult level and high risks, this project bears such features of close attention of the public, adaptation of design-and-build contract mode and the coordination and cooperation of the three regional governments in the project construction and management. Moreover, the environmental constraints are the protective zone of the Chinese white dolphins and the busy shipping channel area of the Lingdingyang Sea where the alignment runs across in additional to the tight construction time and multiple working interfaces.

Case 3

Chinese	English translation
秦岭终南山公路隧道创造了高速公路隧道建设史上的六项之最。一、是世界上第一座最长的双洞高速公路隧道。二、是第一座由我国自行设计、自行施工、自行监理、自行管理,综合技术水平最高的高速公路特长隧道。三、是目前世界口径最大、深度最高的竖井通风工程。隧道共设置三座通风竖井,最大井深661m,最大竖井直径达11.5m,竖井下方均设大型地下风机厂房,工程规模和通风控制理论属国内首创,世界罕见,隧道通风竖井被形象地形容为地球上最大的"烟囱"。四、拥有全世界高速公路隧道最完备的监控技术。隧道每125m设置一台视频监控摄像机,两洞共有摄像机288台,是世界上高速公路摄像机安装最密集的隧道。每250m设置一台视频事件检测器和火灾报警系统,对突发事件采用双系统全方位自动跟踪监控,并根据事件类型提供最有效的救援方案;设计水平世界领先,许多关键技术属国内首创。五、拥有目前世界上高速公路隧道最先进的特殊灯光带,缓解驾驶员视觉疲劳,保证行车安全。通过不同的灯光和图案变化,可以将特长隧道演化成几个短隧道,从而消除驾驶员的焦虑情绪和压抑心理,为亚洲首创。六、首次创造性地提出策略管理理论,并运用了首套策略自动生成软件,在高速公路隧道管理理念中处于国际领先水平。对火灾、交通事故、养护等方面发生事件进行自动监测和管理,只要发生一个事件,策略自动生成软件就会自动生成相应的策略程序进行全方位联动指导,保证秦岭终南山高速公路隧道运营管理的准确性和可靠性。	The Zhongnanshan Highway Tunnel in Qinling set up six records in highway tunnel construction history. First, it is the first longest two-tube highway tunnel in the world. Second, it is the first high-speed super-long highway tunnel which is designed, constructed, supervised, managed by Chinese independently and reaches top technical level on comprehensive basis. Third, the ventilation shaft has largest portal diameter and greatest depth in the world up to date. Three ventilation shafts in total are set in the tunnel and the maximum shaft depth reaches up to 661m and maximum shaft diameter up to 11.5m. Large underground fan rooms are set below the shafts. The project scale and the ventilation control theory are originated domestically and rarely seen worldwide. The tunnel ventilation shaft is vividly described as the "largest chimney" on the earth. Fourth: the highway tunnel is equipped with most complete monitoring and surveillance techniques in the world. One video camera for surveillance is set at spacing of 125m in the tunnel and there are 288 video cameras installed in the two tubes thus being the highway tunnel most densely mounted with video cameras in the world. One video incident detector and fire alarm system are set at spacing of 250m in the tunnel interior. The dual systems are set to track and monitor automatically the emergencies in tunnel in all directions and provide most effective rescue and relieving solutions fitting for the incident type. The design level is advanced world wide and many key techniques are domestic creations. Fifth, the highway tunnel mounted with the most advanced special lighting section in the world up to date mitigating the visual fatigue of drivers and ensuring driving safety. The different lightings and pattern variation, which is the creation in Asia, can divide the super-long tunnel into several short sections thus eliminating the driver's anxiety and depressions. Sixth, the strategical management theory is proposed initially and creatively and the first set of the strategy generates software automatically which reaches top level internationally. Such emergencies as fire hazard, traffic incidents and curing are monitored and controlled automatically. If any accident occurs, the strategy automatically generated software will automatically generate corresponding strategical procedures to give overall union direction thus ensuring the accuracy and reliability of the Zhongnanshan Highway Tunnel operation management.

V. Assignment

（1）在隧道施工机械化方面，早已抛弃了原始的人工开凿方法，机械钻孔已由人力持钻发展到支腿架钻。20世纪80年代在大瑶山隧道中开始采用大型全液压的钻孔台车。

（2）施工方面要进一步提高开挖技术和支护方法，配备完善的施工机械，从目前的半机械化程度，提高到全机械化程度，再进一步达到洞内无人、洞外遥控的高度安全化；要提倡采用科学的管理方法，用调查的信息，制订施工计划，再用实测信息反馈，不断调整计划达到最优方案，使之达到质量高、速度快、浪费少、造价低的目的。

（3）过去，在山区修建公路为节省工程造价，常常选择盘山绕行，宁愿延长距离而避开修建隧道昂贵的费用。随着社会经济和生产的发展，高速公路的大量出现，对道路的修建技术提出了较高的标准，要求线路顺直、坡度平缓、路面宽敞等。因此在道路穿越山区时，出现了大量的隧道方案。

（4）当交通线路跨越江、河、湖、海、洋时，可以选择的方案有架桥、轮渡和隧道，但架桥受净空的限制，轮渡限制通行量，如果这些矛盾得不到有效的解决，水底隧道是一种很好的方案，其优点是不受气候影响，不影响通航，引道占地少，战时不暴露交通设施目标等。

（5）在现代化的城市中，将给水、污水、管路、线路等四种具有共性的市政隧道，按城市的布局和规划，建成一个共用隧道，称为"共同管沟"。共同管沟是现代城市基础设施科学管理和规划的标志，是合理利用城市地下空间的科学手段，同时也是城市市政隧道规划与修建发展的方向。

Unit 2 Tunnel Installations
隧道设施

I. Text

Text A Main Installations in Tunnel
隧道内主要设施

For safe operation and construction of tunnels various installations are designed and arranged in tunnel. The mechanical and electrical appliances are installed in intention of tunnel hazard prevention and risk control. They are traffic control signs to control safe driving, ventilation system to provide fresh air for users and extract waste air, fire protection system for fire hazard detection and fire fighting, lighting system in different tunnel sections and portals to enable driver to overcome "black-hole" effect and "white hole effect" and drainage system to control flooding in tunnel and keep tunnel dry sand safe.

1. Installations for traffic control

Installations for traffic control comprise:

(1) Road signs(up and down, emergency exit, distance to nearest refuge, speed limit, U turn, lay-by).

(2) Traffic lights at tunnels with emergency call provisions [to be placed at the portals, U-turn (turnaround) niches and at trafficable cross-avers].

(3) Traffic guide equipment (floor labeling, side reflectors).

(4) Traffic census. Peak of maximum allowable traffic (with respect to ventilation capacity) is indicated in the tunnel control room.

(5) Height control to catch over-sized vehicles before they enter tunnel (measured e. g. with photo-sensors).

(6) Video-monitoring of those tunnels long than 1500m or with a high traffic density. The entire tunnel length as well as the areas in front of the portals should be monitored.

(7) Modern sensors provide warning of traffic slow down (e. g. due to fire).

The frequency of accident in road tunnels is reduced by 50% compared with open roads. The reasons are:

①Speed limits in tunnels are, in general, accepted by tunnel users.

②Snow, ice, wind, rain and fog can be avoided in tunnels.

③One should, however, take into account of the consequences of accidents in tunnels which are much more severe than that happening on open roads.

2. Installations for telecommunication

(1) Equipment for emergency calls: These have to be provided in tunnels of more than 500m in length with a spacing of 150m. Portals and U-turn niches should be equipped with emergency telephones. Telephone boxes should be provided with glass doors that can be opened toward the tunnel.

(2) Service telephones: These telephones must be provided in tunnels of length over 1000m at every service station and also in every control room. They are dispensable if radio communication facilities are provided.

(3) Radio communication facilities: In those tunnels longer than 1000m or with a high traffic density radio communication should be provided for fire brigade, police and road administration as well as for traffic announcement via radio. Radio re-broadcasting equipment and loudspeakers serve the information of the public.

3. Ventilation system

With reference to tunnel ventilation, two different systems of ventilation should be distinguished: ventilation during tunnel construction (i. e. during the heading of tunnel) and service ventilation (i. e. during the operation of the tunnel), expenditures on the latter amount up to 30% of the total construction costs of tunnel.

Ventilation in road tunnel is intended to guard against pollution, guarantee visibility and in case of fire secure the escape routes, ensure the access of rescue teams and reduce damages and relieve risks. The required fresh air supply should be calculated in accordance with the anticipation of traffic flow to guarantee that the following concentrations (Table 2.1) are not exceeded.

Concentration Limits Table 2.1

CO concentration	100ppm
NO_x concentration	<25ppm
Opacity: extinction coefficient	$<7 \times 10^{-3} m^{-1}$
Air velocity (average over the cross section)	<10m/s

In rail tunnels (in particular metros), cooling, i. e. the removal of warm air (e. g. due to locomotive) is another task of ventilations. Road traffic produces maximum pollution in speeds of 10 to 15km/h. The increase in the number of vehicles equipped with catalyzes resulted in a considerable reduction of fresh air requirements of road tunnels which, depending on the radio of trucks and on the slope, amounts to between 30% and 50%. Four types of ventilation techniques are normally applied to tunnel.

(1) Natural longitudinal ventilations: This ventilation is accomplished by the pressure difference between the portals and also by the piston action of the vehicle.

①Jet fan style ventilation: Jet fan is installed in longitudinal direction of tunnel and one to two jet fans are installed in same plane. When profiling is circular form or horseshoe form, jet fan is hang on arch ceiling while in case of rectangular shaped profiling fan is arranged at corner between ceiling slab and side wall. The spacing of fan arranged in longitudinal direction shall be confirmed subjected to designed traffic volume, designed traffic velocity and power rate of fan. Spacing of decades meters in short and hundreds meters in long tunnel.

②Longitudinal ventilation with shaft: In case of using shaft for air extraction it functions as chimney and is effective. But in order to achieve stable ventilation fans installation is still required. For two-way traffic and one-way traffic in highway tunnel the location of shaft arrangement is different. In two-way traffic tunnel shaft shall be arranged in middle of tunnel while in one-way traffic tunnel shaft position is preferred to be near portal. This way it can be ensured that location of shaft is right at point where pollution concentration is heaviest so that it can be most effective in ventilation. Of course the location of ventilation is also to be considered in combination with needs of construction.

(2) Fans: Fans are placed at spacing of 10 times tunnel diameters and produce longitudinal ventilation. The blowing direction is reversible and large ventilators achieve a higher thrust related to installation costs.

(3) Longitudinal ventilation: In case of longitudinal ventilation it can be considered that the air flow in longitudinal direction in tunnel is uniform from entrance to outlet. This type of ventilation enables the concentration of polluted air increases in form of straight line from entrance to outlet of tunnel. If natural wind is blown into tunnel from outlet (one way traffic) the concentration in tunnel will be increased, in case of two-way traffic the traffic wind (piston wind) will be reduced.

(4) *Semi-transverse ventilation*: *Fresh air is supplied from special pathways perpendicular to the tunnel's longitudinal axis, where the polluted air escapes from the portals (supply system). This is appropriate for tunnels with 2-4km in length and medium traffic load. Alternatively, the used air is extracted through special ducts (extraction system), while fresh air enters through the portals. Thus, the worst air quality is found in the middle of the tunnel. The velocity reaches its maximum near the portals.*

(5) *Transverse ventilation*: *Fresh air is introduced and polluted air (which moves upwards) is extracted perpendicular to the tunnel axis. Air ducts with cross sections up to 30m are used. Not only aerodynamic considerations are taken into account but also the necessity of access for maintenance. Long tunnels may require ventilation shaft or ventilation adits that are driven parallel to the tunnel.* According to the German standards for the equipment and service of road tunnels (RABT), the ventilation system should be used with regard to construction type and tunnel length. If the outlet of polluted air has an adverse environment impact, cleaning (by means of electrostatic filters) should be considered.

(6) Control of ventilation: The following quantities are monitored.

①Air velocity: The average air velocity in the tunnel is measured with ultrasonic transducers.

②Temperature: Air temperature in the tunnel can be derived from the measured propagation velocity of sound.

③*Air opacity*: *Usually this quantity is measured via the intensity loss of a light beam in the tunnel air, opaqued by dust, diesel grime and aerosols from combustion motors. The measuring distance amounts at minimum 15m. As measuring devices are very sensitive to installation and maintenance it is advisable to measure opacity by determining the intensity of scattered light. The required photometer is placed at some appropriate position, which can be up to 500m off the extraction position.*

④CO-concentration: The specific absorption of an infrared beam is measured in order to determine the CO-concentration. If this is kept within prescribed limits. NO_x levels are also admissible.

4. Fire protection in road tunnel

Due to confined space, fires in tunnel can be disastrous. In 1995 a fire in the metro of Baku caused 289 casualties. Other disastrous fires in metro occurred in 1903 in Paris resulted in casualties around 84 and in 1987 in London and took away 31 lives. Between 1978 and 1999, total 97 casualties resulted from accidents in tunnels.

The following reasons to deaths have been reported:

①Obsolete ventilation.

②Inefficient warning system.

③Insufficient communication between the tunnel users and fire authority.

④When the fire broke out only one fireman was on duty and fire fighting was delayed.

(1) Fire-resistant concrete: Fire causes damage of the concrete lining due to spalling. The depth of this spalling increases with the duration of the fire and can reach more than 30cm submerged tunnels in weak rock are particularly vulnerable. The spalling is due to the fast rise to temperature combined with the humidity of the concrete and the structure of its pores. *From 100°C onwards the water entrapped in the pores of the concrete transforms to vapor, whose increased pressure spalls the concrete of high strength (C55/67) are particularly vulnerable. At high temperatures also chemical transformations of the aggregates will occur. Beyond 300°C the strength of the reinforcement was reduced and steel fiber reinforcement increases the thermal conductivity and thus accelerates the heating process. It should therefore be accompanied with ordinary rebars.*

Polypropylene fibers disintegrated beyond 380°C. The resulting pores provide escape route for the vapor, relieve the pressure and thus reduce the spalling. Short fibers are preferable to longer ones. Besides the creation of vapor pressure and deterioration of reinforcement heating affects concrete in following ways:

①Cement stone and aggregate exhibit a different thermal expansion, which leads to thermal stresses. Cement stone shrinks at elevated temperatures.

②In case of temperature above 573°C, the volume of the aggregates increases due to re-mineralization in quartz components (e.g. Granite and gneiss).

③In case of temperature above approx imately 800°C limestone ($CaCO_3$) transforms to calcium oxid (CaO), which disintegrates after cooling and carbon dioxide (CO_2).

To increase the fire resistivity of concrete, it is recommended to avoid mineral that disintegrate at elevated temperatures. Coarse aggregates (>16mm) are particularly vulnerable in this respect and should be avoided.

Fire resistant concretes such as "system Hochtief", or "Lightcem"—concrete have appropriately sized aggregates. The fire protection concrete "System Hochtief" contains 3kg polypropylene fibers per m concrete. This concrete has resisted a standard fire and suffered spalling of up to 1cm depth at only 20% of the exposed surface. A concrete cover of 6cm protected the reinforcement from temperature higher than 300℃.

As an alternative to fire-resistant concrete, protective panels or spray-ons can be used. However, they do not offer protection during construction, hinder the visual inspection of the lining and require a slightly larger excavation cross section since their thickness ranges up to 10cm. For instance, in the Westerschelde tunnel in Holland a heat-resistant cladding with a thickness of 45mm was sprayed onto the lining with robots. Covers are intended to protect the lining against fire for 2 hours.

The following versions of protective panels exist:

①Boards made of glass fiber reinforced concrete whose aggregate is glass foam granulate.

②Perforated metallic plates, with a total thickness of approx imately 35mm they represent the thinnest panels.

③Silicate fire protection boards consisting of special concretes made of high temperature resistant materials.

(2)Fire detectors and extinguishers: Fire detectors are provided to enable fast fire fighting rescue and to prevent further vehicles from entering the tunnel. Fire alarms should also be engaged manually by pressing a button in the emergency call niches and at the portals. In tunnels of length over 1500m, automatic fire detectors should be installed. The following detecting systems can be considered:

①Heat sensor: These sensors should be activated along the entire tunnel length and not only at isolated points. Otherwise, fire detection can be delayed. Resistivity measurements are vulnerable to the harsh conditions within tunnels. The pneumatic principle is more effective: Higher temperatures increase the pressure of air entrapped in copper pipes. This pressure increase is registered by pressure transducers. Fire detectors, based on glass fiber and laser beams (which are increasingly scattered at higher temperatures) can localize accurately the source of heat and (with appropriate software) can even detect heat propagation.

②Gas sensor: These register the reduction of the oxygen content and the presence of combustible gases and toxic combustion products.

③Smoke sensors: In road tunnels these can easily cause false alarms and consequently release full power ventilation, which is very expensive because of its high power consumption.

④Flame sensors: These only register open flames.

⑤Video control: The automatic detection of traffic jams, smoke and fire by means of video control and pattern recognition is a promising innovation and can respond much earlier than heat sensors.

Fire detectors should be highly resistant to break-down. They must be provided with an emergency power supply and the maximum length that may drop out should be limited to 50 ~ 500m (depending on traffic density). The equipment must be robust and capable of withstanding (e. g. Cleaning brushes or loose goods falling from vehicles).

⑥Fire fighting: For tunnels with a length between 600 and 1000m a pressure pipe of at least 100mm diameter is sufficient. This pipe does not need to be permanently filled with water but should be fed at the portals. At each portal water tanks, containing at least 80m water must be provided.

In tunnels with more than 1000m in length, a pressure pipe must be installed beneath the lateral strips of the carriageway and protected against freezing. The pressure at the taps should be between 6 and 12 bars. A supply of 1200L/min for at least one hour must be guaranteed. Water for firefighting is to be available at the emergency call niches with a hydrant and a 120m long water hose. In addition, the tunnel users should have access to two fire extinguishers kept in each emergency call niche. When utilizing sprinklers, it should be kept in mind that droplets fall through the fumes, if they are too large, and therefore do not bind smoke particles. A mist of fine water droplets (0.01mm diameter) can be produced with high pressure (100 bar) and appropriate nozzles. Thus the temperature can be lowered by 700℃ within seconds. The evaporation of water increases its volume by a factor of 1640 and thus chokes the supply of oxygen. The objective of the water mist application is to control the fire rather than to extinguish it. Tests have shown that water mist is efficient even at air velocities of 5m/s. The installation of nozzles can be undertaken in metro stations, in on-board systems in the trains and in road tunnels. E. g. Spraying of water has proved to be beneficial during the shield heading of the Socatop tunnel in Paris. In 2002 a fire was initiated by a rubber tire of a hauling locomotive. Water spraying impeded the spread of smoke and cooled the temperature in the back-up section down to 80℃. This enabled the workers to escape into the excavation chamber, which happened to be accessible at that time.

Text B　Some Engineering Cases about Installations in Modern Road Tunnels
几个现代公路隧道设计的工程案例

1. Engineering case: Refurbishment of The Montblanc Tunnel

The refurbishment of the 11.6m long Mont-Blanc road tunnel after the fire in March 1999 demonstrated various aspects of modern fire protection. The following arrangements have been made:

①Lay-by's signs in both directions at interval of 600m allow heavy loaded truck to stop. Signs at every 600m at turn-around points are also provided.

②Refuges (shelters) are situated on one side of the tunnel at interval of every 300m. They are ventilated via fresh air ducts and put under light overpressure. They are connected to the tunnel by means of airlocks. In case of a fire in front of the refuge, the temperature inside should not exceed 35℃ for 4 hours. After the rescuers can get to the refuges and evacuate the victims from outside the tunnel via escape galleries situated in underground fresh air galleries. In this case the fresh air ventilation is reduced to a minimum.

③Emergency recesses have been placed alternately at intervals of around 100m. They are equipped with emergency telephones, fire extinguishers and glass doors. Fire fighting recesses are located at every 150m with a hydrant at interval of 300m.

④Fans provide up 82.5m/s fresh air for ventilation.

⑤The fire ventilation has an extraction capacity of 150m/s.

⑥Closed circuit TV monitors allows all refuges and bays to be monitored and 150 cameras (one camera every 150m on side wall) allow complete surveillance of the tunnel.

Illumination in road tunnel: Road tunnels must be sufficiently illuminated. The luminance is gradually reduced from the portal towards the interior of the tunnel. Three sections of tunnel are distinguished with respect to illumination. The first two sections are the entrance and transition sections. In the transition section illumination gradually reduces and its length depends on the following values:

①Luminance at the end of the entrance section.

②Luminance in the inner section (fundamental lighting density).

③Adoption of vision to changing illumination conditions and thus, from the allowable maximum speed. The length of the transition section is determined by the time needed by the human eye to adapt from the luminance at the end of entrance section to the one within inner section of tunnel (fundamental lighting). The fundamental luminance applies to the remaining tunnel section. The luminance should be uniform within tunnel. Flickering in the frequency range from 2.5 to 15Hz should be avoided. To facilitate the adoption of human eyes, the portals should be as dark as possible. Therefore, galleries and illumination reduction constructions should be used, if affordable. To achieve maximum illumination and to enable easy cleaning, the tunnel inner walls should be covered with a bright and reflecting, but not dazzling coating, which should be cleaned at regular intervals. A good solution is to mount enamel panels on the tunnel wall. The objectives of interior finishing are:

①Identification of alignment by means of the difference in luminance between walls and road surface.

②Enabling drivers to assess the distance from the walls.

③To hide wires and pipes that diverts attention of the drivers.

To improve the driver's concentration, zones of 20m in length and 10cd/m luminance should be provided at every second lay-by. During black outs of the electric power the emergency call niches and some intermediate points as well as the cross-overs should be illuminated?

Regulations on illumination of road tunnels are continuously improving and take into account recent advances in physiology and illumination techniques.

Drainage of tunnel: The interaction of a tunnel with the groundwater via its drainage is a very important issue. The following waters should be collected and diverted.

①Groundwater (for ecological reasons the withdrawal of groundwater should be as low as possible).

②Day water (precipitation or melting ice entering from the portals).

③Service water (e. g. from washing).

Contrary to the mixed system, where all types of waters are put together, groundwater on the one hand, precipitation water (entering from the portals) and service water (used for maintenance or fire fighting) on the other hand are withdrawn in separate pipes in the so-called separate system ("dual drainage system"), Provisions for non-propagation of fire should be taken for the case of effusion of inflammable fluids.

Longitudinal drains are installed in the sides of the tunnel. Their diameter depends on the slope (at least 0.5%) and on the pipe material and should be at least 15cm. Cleaning and flushing shafts should be provided with a spacing of 50-65m. Water is removed from the carriageway by means of longitudinal drains with diameter >20cm, slope ≥0.5% and cleaning shafts with spacing of 110m. A possible aggressively of the water as well as the danger of freezing should be taken into account.

2. Examples for the installations of modern road tunnels

Kaisermühlen tunnel: The Kaisermühlen tunnel in Vienna is considered to be one of the safest among the 200 Austrian road tunnels. It belongs to the motorway A22 and has a length of 2150m. With a daily traffic load of 100000 vehicles it is one of the most densely used tunnels in Austria. More than 2000 lamps provide illumination; 104 fans are used for ventilation; 7.5km sensor cable are installed for automatic fire monitoring; 2 ventilation buildings with ventilators assure a complete exchange of the tunnel air within 10 minutes. 22 emergency call niches with spacing of 200m and 9 emergency call columns in front of the portals enable contact with the tunnel guard. Fifty robot video monitors control the tunnel. Radio amplifiers and antenna cables at the tunnel roof enable communication for the service teams. A special pipeline fed from the river Donau is provided for extinguishing water. Numerous escape doors in the separating wall and several escape stairhouses make it possible to escape from the tunnel as far as possible. The tunnel control room operates day and night and the tunnel guard is assisted by 13 automatic fire programmes and more than 150 traffic programmes. A concise system of traffic guidance and information helps the users to react to unexpected situations. Three spare power stations and accumulators as well as a mobile and a stationary generator guard against total black outs.

Engelberg base tunnel: Two tubes with 3 drive and one park lane each (maximum excavated cross section 265m, maximum thickness of concrete inner lining 3.50m) accommodate a daily traffic load of 120000 vehicles.

The tunnel has the following equipment:

Power supply by two loops of 20kV;

6.4MW installed transformator power;

2 UPS-plants with 12kVA each;

More than 800km cable of various cross sections;

1200 sodium high pressure lamps 50 to 400W, partially as dual shiners;

6 videos measuring luminance;

2 illumination computers;

4 axial fans with 659kW each for fresh air supply;

3 axial fans with 370kW each for air extraction east tube;

4 axial fans with 240kW each for air extraction west tube;

29 CO-sensors;

4 NO-sensors;

16 monitoring stations for haziness of air;

4 monitoring stations for air flow;

8 fire-detector cable with 625m length;

39 buttons for manual fire alarm release in the emergency call niches;

30 buttons for manual fire alarm release in the control rooms;

2 fire control rooms;

22 color video monitors (11 in each tube);

4 dirigeable color video monitors with zoom at the portals;

2 video cross rails;

6 color monitors;

39 emergency call niches with emergency call devices;

4 transponders for radio;

2 antennas per tube, to emit and receive, separated in 5 sectors;

2 external antennas for radio, BOS and mobile phone;

4 amplifier stations in the cross cross-overs with 8 radio amplifiers each mobile phone;

Transposer and antennas for 5 mobile phone providers.

3. Example of ventilation system in Oresund tunnel

The forced ventilation system in Oresund tunnel: The forced ventilation system ensures that, during normal tunnel operations, the acceptable level of pollution such as carbon monoxide (CO) and nitrogen dioxide (NO_2) are not exceeded and that acceptable level of visibility is maintained. The system dilutes the pollutants automatically as their levels rise above set points.

Whilst the flow or traffic through the tunnel provides a form of natural ventilation itself, when this flow fails to provide adequate renewal of the air, the forced ventilation automatically supplies additional assistance from longitudinal thrust provided by fans.

The system thus ensures a smoke free environment in the event of fire or other emergencies that may occur within the tunnel, e. g. Traffic accidents or toxic spillages. If such an accident occurs, the traffic will stop and natural ventilation from traffic flow will cease also. The longitudinal ventilation fans will then begin to extract smoke and fumes. At the same time air will be blown into the escape gallery to allow emergency teams to reach the scene of the accident.

Acceptable air quality values were established taking into consideration the three levels of traffic flow through the tunnel.

(1) Congested traffic;

(2) Free flowing traffic and;

(3) Maintenance periods.

Data such as outside air pollution, wind effects, traffic emission and re-circulation between tunnel tubes were also taken into account when arriving at the design values.

If traffic accidents occur in the tunnel, minimum values of air velocities have to be maintained to remove the smoke and reduce heat. Such velocity values are either specified in the contract documents or in relevant safety standards such as the PIARC (Permanent institution Association of road council). In the case of the Oresund tunnel, the design criteria were based upon a 100 MW fire.

The ventilation system was dimensioned according to the diagram shown in table 2.2.

Minimum air velocity   Table 2.2

Tunnel tube	Minimum air velocity
Motorway	5m/s
Railway	4m/s

The first step in dimensioning a system is to determine the basic emission of carbon monoxide (CO) and nitrogen dioxide (NO_2) as well as dust levels from rail and road. The potential variation caused by the type and speed of traffic and including correction factors for tunnel gradients also had to be established. The second step is to calculate the fresh air requirement. The third step is to deduct the velocity from the airflow-achieved by dividing the airflow by the area of the tunnel's cross section. The fourth step consists of calculating the net thrust required. The net thrust is the overall performance to be achieved by the fans in fulfilling the required airflow and takes into account the various applicable losses. The last step is to calculate the jet fan net thrust.

Text C   Installations of Xiang'an Tunnel
翔安隧道设施

Xiamen East Passageway (Xiang'an Tunnel) engineering project is the first subsea tunnel of large section constructed by drill and blasting tunneling method. This tunnel is located at the narrowest point at the southwest entrance of the Xunjiang harbor, between the Tutong port in Huli district, northeast of Xiamen Island and the Xiadiancun, Xibing in Xiang'an district. To the northeast of the tunnel site is the enclosed sea bay and to the southeast is the outlet of the bay. The tunnel is of magnificent scale, crossing the marine area in total length of 4200m. The tunnel is of total length of 5.9km of which the length of the section by cut and cover method is approximately 2.9km at sea, approximately 1.5km in intestinal intermediate zones and 1.5km on shore. In the light of the design criterion for high class highways, the calculated travel speed is 80km/h, The maximal dimension of the cross section of the cut and cover tunnel is 17.04m × 12.56m (width × height), the width in construction gauge is 13.5m and the headroom is 5.0m. The said tunnel links Xiamen Island and the land area in Xiang'an district and serves as both the highway and the municipal motorway, and it is an optional export channel for the Xiamen City.

The East Passageway Project is the key engineering project of Xiamen city, as well as the most important constituent of the east wing out of in "the two wings of Xiamen". The project construction has been planned for over 20 years. The greatest burial depth of the tunnel is approximately 70m below the sea level and is the first subsea tunnel in China as well as the first subsea tunnel that is self-designed and constructed by domestic experts independently. This given tunnel is located in the east of Xiamen and links the land area by crossing the sea. After its completion, this tunnel will be one of the five major links which are as the Xiamen Bridge, in north Xiamen, the recently built Xinlin Bridge, the Jimei Bridge and the Haicang Bridge in the west thus forming a road network and forming an economic circle of Xiamen island. After the completion of East Passageway, great proportion of vehicle flow to or from the island can be diverted particularly assuring the effective traffic moving in severe climate and meanwhile forming the golden tourist route line Jinmen-Dadeng-the East Passage-Xiamen Island-Haichang. Subject to the plan, the motorway of passageway is designed to be bidirectional with six-lanes, with the travel speed of 80km/hour is designed and connected into the shores are connected by the interchanges and class freeways on land respectively. This project will fulfill become the fifth passageway into and out of the island under the Xiamen municipal plan, which will be connected to the national motorways, the provincial-level roads in north and the urban road network in south and it will be connected with all major nodes in the road of the city.

1. Constitution of the ventilation system

The ventilation system is comprised of the large axial flow fan mounted in the two ventilation shafts and the jet fans mounted in the tunnel. Two air supply axial flow fans of 280kW and two air extraction axial flow fans of 185kW are installed in the ventilation shafts on the shore of Xiamen and two air supply axial flow fans of 450kW and two air extraction axial flow fans of 185kW are mounted in the ventilation shafts on the shore of Xiang'an. 13 groups (each group has 3 sets) in total of 39 jet fans of 30kW, are installed in the traffic tunnel: 6 groups in total of 18 jet fans in the left bore and 7 groups in total of 21 jet fans in the right bore and 20 jet fans of 15kW are arranged in the service gallery.

2. Functions of the ventilation system

In the normal operation, the tunnel ventilation system should be able to control the concentration of the toxic gas inside the tunnel).

(1) CO concentration: 200ppm;

(2) VI concentration: $0.007m^{-1}$.

In the normal operation, the tunnel ventilation system should be able to dilute the unpleasant smell in the tunnel.

(1) Air exchanges: 3 times in the daytime and 2 times at night;

(2) Velocity of the exchanging air: 3.0m/s.

In traffic jam, the ventilation system shall be able to control the concentration of toxic gas in the tunnel.

(1) CO concentration : 300ppm, in less than 20mins' time;

(2) VI concentration: $0.007m^{-1}$.

In occurrence of fire in the tunnel, the ventilation system shall be able to effectively control the wind direction and speed, and meet the requirement for fire fighting and the discharge of toxic smoke.

Control flexibly the air flow direction in the tunnel in respect of the requirement of the fire fighting and the smoke extraction.

Velocity of the air of smoke extraction: 3.0m/s.

With the aid of tunnel surveillance system, the tunnel ventilation system can effectively control the air speed and pressure in all ventilated sections of the tunnel by adjusting the quantity of running fans, the rotation speed, the angle of impeller, and the opening extent of air valve of the running fans, and keep the sectionalized ventilation system in balance and avoid generating short circuit flow among all ventilated sections.

In the normal operation, the ventilation system can keep the electrical substation, the ventilator room and the ground embedded transformer in good ventilation.

3. Illumination system

The illumination system in Xiamen East Passageway (Xiang'an tunnel) and associated compatible works is comprised of the installation of the illuminative equipments in the subsea twin-bored bidirectional six-lane highway tunnel, the illumination in the service gallery arranged between the two parallel traffic bores, the illumination system on the link roads and the plazas and interchanges in Xibing on the shores at ends of the tunnel, and the installations and commissioning of the ducts for TV. The principal works amount is comprised of the illumination installations in total of 13684 sets in the main tunnel and the service gallery; 205 sets for the street lights and high posted lamps; 108 km's installation of all types of cable trays; 483km's placement of various control cables and low-tension cables; and 107 different types of distribution boxes for lightening.

4. Three major systems

1) Surveillance and communication systems

The surveillance system is the traffic engineering and facility surveillance and communication systems along the Xiamen Xiang'an tunnel and the link lines on shores(ZK5+908.893 ~ K14+675, in total length of 8.766km).

2) Toll collection system

One toll collection station is arranged on the side of Wutong (namely the Xiang'an tunnel toll collection station). The open toll collection mode is adopted (toll collection at the exit of the island and no chargement at the entrance of the island), and it is a combination of the semi-automatic manual mode and the electronic toll collection mode.

Totally 12 lanes of toll collection are set in the toll plaza, of which 5 are lanes of ETC (Electronic Toll Collection) and 7 are lanes of MTC(Manual Toll Collection).

3) Complex pipeline works

The pipeline works is the affiliated works of the project, which includes the works and related operations of the reserved communication pipelines and the manholes in the tunnel.

5. Firefighting system (1)

The execution contents include: the fire water tank, the water supply facility for the foam-water sprinkler firefighting system, the installation of the facilities and pipes in the pump room, the pump room ventilation equipments' installation, the maintenance, the water pressure testing, the flushing and inspection for acceptance during the execution.

Two pump rooms are arranged in the firefighting system in Xiang'an tunnel and the pump rooms are placed at the tunnel portals at both ends respectively. Fire hydrant and pump sets are arranged in the fire pump rooms respectively on the bank of Xiamen and Xiang'an, which include two fire hydrant pumps (one is on duty and the other stands-by) spare to each other and two pressure stabilizing pumps spare to each other.

Water spray pump sets: two spray pumps with one on duty and the other standing-by spare to each other and two pressure stabilizing pumps with one on duty and the other standing-by. spare to each other.

Foam pumps sets (entirely made by stainless steel) including two foam pumps with one on duty and the other standing-by (spare to each other).

The firefighting pump room also includes other power distribution equipments, control equipments and pipes.

The installation of the power distribution facility (mainly including the low pressure control cabinet, two power sources conversion boxes, the power cables, and the cable tray in connection with) associated with the fire system in Xiang'an tunnel involved has the following main works quantity listed in following table 2.3.

The Principal Works Quantity of the Given System   Table 2.3

Partial works	Location	Quantity
Installation of fire pipes and equipments	Fire pump room in Xiamen and Xiang'an	Equipment footing works execution
		Water pump installation
		Air pressure tank and foam tank installation
	The fire water tank on ceiling at tunnel portal	Fire water tank and associated parts on the banks
	The pump rooms inside the main tunnel pipe trench and the ones on the banks	Pipes and fittings installation
	Left side of traffic lane of main tunnel	Alarming valves and their fittings installation
		Water formed foam nozzle installation
	The pipe works outside the tunnel	Out-door pipe trench and valve-well room
		Water pump coupler and out-door fire hydrant installation

continue

Partial works	Location	Quantity
Ventilation system in the pump room	The firefighting pump room on the banks	Air pipe and the fittings fabrication and installation
		Air extraction fan installation
Low voltage power supply and distribution	The power distribution for the fire pump rooms on both banks, the fire pump and the ventilation system	Power distribution cabinet (control cabinet) installation
		The installation of the cable trays and the cables
		Fabrication of the cable end and the isolation testing
		Secondary extension

The arrangement of the firefighting system are as follows.

Foam-water spray firefighting system is arranged on the left side in the travel direction on left and right line of the main tunnel. Two fire tubes of DN250 are led out from the water outlet pipe from the water spray pump in the fire pump rooms in Xiamen and Xiang'an respectively and are placed in the fire pipe trench on the left side of the travel direction of the left and the right line and the tubes are put all through the tunnel to supply water to the foam-water spray firefighting system. The signal butterfly valve and the current indicator are arranged on the water spray tube in the pump room.

Two foam liquid tubes of DN65 is led out from the outlet liquid pipe of the foam pump in the fire pump rooms in tunnel ends on sides of Xiamen and Xiang'an ends respectively and is placed in the fire pipe trench on the left side in the travel direction on the left and the right lines and the whole pipe line is put all through the tunnel to supply foam liquid to the foam-spray firefighting system of each tunnel. The Stainless steel signaling butterfly valve and the current indicator are placed on the foam liquid tube in the pump room and the effective capacity of the foam storage tank allows the system's pumps in three sections to jet for at least 30 minutes at the same time. Usually, the whole system is filled with original foam liquid contained in the pipes of foam in front of the proportion able mixer. The water formed foam liquid to be applied in the system must be the environmentally-friendly foam liquid which can be directly charged into rain pipe after spray-released.

Totally 482 sets of foam-spray firefighting system are arranged on the left and the right lines of the main tunnel with each set in length of 25m and 7 nozzles of large distance coverage range are arranged, and that is totally 3374 nozzles. In total of 482 sets specialized foam spray control valve boxes are arranged on the left and the right lines of the main tunnel and one electrical deluge valve is set in each box, which turns on the foam spray system. In addition, two signal butterfly valves (constantly open), the foam liquid proportion mixer, the balance valve, the foam liquid check valve, the pressure switch, the foam liquid ball valve, the foam liquid control electromagnetic valve, and the testing drainage pipe are installed. Each foam-water spray firefighting system corresponds to its fire alarm system by sections. The system operation sequences are: the occurrence of fire hazard, the action of fire detector, the confirmation of central control room and activation of the deluge valve, the foam liquid control electromagnetic valve, the starting of the water spray pump system, and the action of foam pump. The actions of signaling valve, the opening state of deluge valve, the electromagnetic valve and the current indicators shall be all displayed in the central control room.

The portable fire extinguisher is placed in the B-type fire box which is set every 50 meters and start at the second type B fire box (B-type fire hydrant) from the entrance.

The interior and exterior pipe trenches are arranged respectively at the portal in Xiamen, the portal in Xiang'an and in the middle of the tunnel to form a fire prevention network.

6. Fire fighting system (2)

This given project is the fire prevention and its associated works in Xiamen east channel passageway (Xiang'an tunnel), which involves mainly about the fire hydrant system and fire alarming system in the fire prevention works. The fire hydrant system is comprised of the twin pump rooms and the twin ring network.

The main tunnel and the service gallery are equipped with the fire hydrant system and two firefighting ducts of DN150 are led out from the water outlet pipes of the fire hydrant mounted in the fire pump rooms in Wutong and Xiang'an, and the two ducts are placed in the fire trench on the right side of the travel direction of the left and right lines, and on the firefighting support on the right wall of the service gallery. The whole pipeline goes all through the tunnel and supplies water to the fire hydrants of each tunnel. The fire hydrants are placed every 50 meters and one butterfly valve is mounted every fire sets of hydrants on the firefighting duct at interval of every fire hydrants. The air valve is placed at the highest position of the main pipe and the water discharge valve is mounted at the lowest position. When the water pressure at the outlet of fire hydrant exceeds 0.5MPa, the stabilivolt hydrant shall be adopted.

The automatic fire alarm system is comprised of the optical fiber signal processor, the optical fiber optical grating fire detector, the transmitting optical cable and the necessary accessories. The fiber brag grating fire detector is connected to the fiber brag grating signal processor.

The manual operation fire alarm system is comprised of the fire alarm controller, some manual operation fire alarm buttons, the transformer and the smoke-sensitive detector of equipment and the connection cables. The manual operation alarm buttons and the point-typed mode smoke-sensitive detector are connected to the fire alarm controller on by means of trunk line.

The main engine of the fiber brag grating detecting system must be connected to the fire automatic alarm controller via the RS232 and RS485 communication interfaces to conduct the effective communication with the fire alarm; to upload the error information of the fiber brag grating detection system to the upper fire alarm controller; and to reset the fiber brag grating detection system.

Temperature-sensitive optical fiber of the automatic fire alarm system is suspended

180mm below the tunnel ceiling and is suspended by with steel wires. The fire alarm main machine is installed between the central control room, the No. 1 transformer cave, the No. 2 transformer cave and the fire alarm controller, and the signal is transmitted with the connection optical fibers.

The manual alarm buttons are placed every 50 meters next to the fire box and the point-typed detectors of the central room and the transformer stations transmit the signals via the signal trunk line to the central computer of the fire alarm system.

II. Terms and terminology

road signs	道路标识
traffic lights	交通灯
speed limit sign	限速标识
traffic census	交通控制
height control	机动车高度控制
oversized vehicles	超高车辆
video-monitoring	摄像机监控
u-turn (turn-around) niches	掉头区
emergency telephone	应急电话
service telephones	公共电话
radio communication	无线电通信
firefighting equipment	消防设备
fire hydrant	消防栓
fire hose	消防软管
fire extinguisher	灭火器
fire ax	消防斧头、太平斧
foam extinguisher	泡沫灭火器
ventilation facilities	通风设施
axial fan	轴流风机
ventilator	通风机
semi-transverse ventilation	半横向通风
tunnel portals	隧道洞口
unbound	上行
downbound	下行

III. Questions and difficult sentence analysis

1. Questions for brainstorming discussion

(1) What are the main facilities and their respective performances in a transit tunnel?

(2) What are the principal modes of ventilation in a highway tunnel and what facilities are involved?

(3) Discuss the importance of fire equipment and facilities in a tunnel.

2. Difficult sentences analysis

(1) Semi-transverse ventilation: In order to facilitate air exchange in tunnel of section forms other than circular shaped section in 1934 when British was building Mosi tunnel (length of 3226m) solution of reducing duct section as much as possible was investigated. Semi-transverse ventilation system was applied for the first time with successful result.

译文:半横向式通风:为了对于除圆形断面之外的其他断面形式的隧道换风便利,1934年,英国人在修建莫尔西隧道(长3226m)时,对尽量减少管道断面的方式做了研究,首次采用半横向通风系统,取得了很好的效果。

(2) Transverse ventilation: The Holland tunnel in New York City, USA is constructed by shield heading and tunnel section is circular in shape. The air supply duct is arranged beneath carriage way and upper part as air extracting duct and air flows from downside toward upside flowing in transverse direction. This is the first application of full transverse ventilation in the world.

译文:横向式通风:美国纽约市的荷兰隧道,采用盾构法施工,圆形断面,所以车道下面作为送风道,上部作为排风道,气流从下往上横向流动。这是世界上首次采用全横向通风方式。

(3) Air opacity: Usually this quantity is measured via the intensity loss of a light beam in the tunnel air, opaqued by dust, diesel grime and aerosols from combustion motors. The measuring distance amounts at minimum 15m. As measuring devices are very sensitive to installation and maintenance it is advisable to measure opacity by determining the intensity of scattered light. The required photometer is placed at some appropriate position, which can be up to 500m off the extraction position.

译文:空气不透明度:其数量通常为穿过隧道内空气的光束能量损耗的测量值,这是因为空气因内燃气产生的灰尘、柴油垃圾及气溶胶而使得隧道内空气变得不透明所致。测量距离至少为15m,由于测量设施对于安装和维修很敏感,因此建议通过确定分散射光的强度来测量不透明度。按要求将光度计布置在合适位置,该处距离排气位置500m。

(4) From 100℃ onwards the water entrapped in the pores of the concrete transforms to vapor, whose increased pressure spalls the concrete of high strength (C55/67) are particularly vulnerable. At high temperatures also chemical transformations of the aggregates will occur. Beyond 300℃ the strength of the reinforcement was reduced and steel fiber reinforcement increases the thermal conductivity and thus accelerates the heating process. It should therefore be accompanied with ordinary rebars.

译文:从温度100℃起,夹在混凝土孔隙中的水开始变为蒸汽,随着气体压力增大,使得高强混凝土(C55/67)特别容易剥落。在高温下,也将发生集料化学转变。当温度超过300℃,钢筋强度下降,钢纤维钢筋增加传热性,从而使加热过程加快。所以应该加配普通钢筋。

Ⅳ. Translation case study

Case 1

Chinese	English translation
在韦依克隧道中,首次将3台通风机为一组安装在每条隧道管廊中,增加隧道顶部局部空间,供安装这些通风机。通过将通风机按组划分,布置在整个隧道管廊宽度内,使得隧道通风效果大大增强。因此,通风机的数量也大大减少。	The Wijker tunnel is the first tunnel in which the ventilators are grouped in three clusters per tunnel tube. A local increase in the tunnel roof provides space for the storage of these ventilators. The effectiveness of the ventilation is strongly increased by dividing the ventilators per cluster across the width of the tunnel tube. Due to this, the number of ventilators is substantially limited.

Case 2

Chinese	English translation
韦依克隧道的另一项创新是所谓的反光照明灯,经过在韦尔赛隧道中试用后决定采用该照明灯。采用该照明后,该隧道中第一段的强亮度,直射照明形成了从白天光线到暗光段的过渡段。因此,没有必要进行其他设计来逐渐增加隧道入口处的白天光线。	Another new item in the Wijker tunnel is the so-called counter-beam lighting which was decided on after a test in the Velser tunnel. In this, a high and directed lighting level in the first section of the tunnel forms the transition from daylight to the darker tunnel sections. Other designs for the gradual decrease of the daylight at the tunnel entrances are therefore not necessary.

Case 3

Chinese	English translation
隧道路段交通设施的人性化设计指:在某一时期内,对某一地点,地区的交通设施进行人性化改造,既包括对道路交通标志,标线的设计与设置,也包括对道路本身的设计与设置。它是以满足隧道交通参与者的需求为依据,以服务和方便交通参与者为终目标,并随着交通法规的调整,交通环境的发展而变化。韦依克隧道被列为一级隧道,允许运输有毒和有害物质的车辆通过。设置了专门设施尽可能防止灾难发生。为此,隧道管廊的混凝土墙安装了抗高温面层,各段混凝土结构之间的接头处安装了保护层,以防止有害物质的可能侵入。	The humanized design of traffic facilities in road tunnel sections means: the humanized improvement of the regional traffic facilities at some locations within some time period including the design and setting of road traffic signs, mark line and also including the design and setting of road itself. The humanized design is performed based on meeting the needs of tunnel participants, aims at the ultimate goal of serving and facilitating the participants and changes along with the adjustment of traffic laws and development of traffic environment. The Wijker tunnel is a tunnel classified into category 1, which also provides for the passage of transports of toxic and hazardous substances. Special facilities prevent the occurrence of disasters as much as possible. To this end, the concrete in the tunnel tubes is clad with a heat resisting layer and the joints between the various sections of the concrete constructions have been protected against possible penetration by hazardous substances.

V. Assignment

（1）射流风机要占用隧道断面空间，但省去了洞口风道式通风的风道与风机房。射流风机的基本布置方式有两种，一种是沿隧道纵向等距离布置，其间距宜在 100~150m，可以保证风流均匀扩散，每个设置断面上设一至两台风机，一般悬于拱顶。在确定隧道建筑限界时，必须保证风机的位置。在电气化隧道中风机不要与拱顶的电力线路太靠近。另一种是集中布置在洞口。

（2）在隧道内设置人行道和自行车道时，从安全和舒适的角度考虑，全横向式通风最为理想，其送风口通常设在两侧距车道面约 1m 高的位置上，这就能保证行人最先呼吸到新鲜空气。全横向式通风沿隧道纵向几乎没有风流动，使行人感觉不到风速产生的不舒适，也可以保证自行车的稳定和安全。

（3）车辆在隧道中行驶的过程中，会排放出大量的有害气体（如 CO、CO_2、NO_2、SO_2 及烟雾等），这一方面致使洞内空气恶化，不仅会影响驾乘人员的舒适感，还会对其身体健康造成损害；另一方面洞内大量烟雾使能见度降低，给行车安全带来直接威胁。因此，通风的目的就是：对有害气体（主要是 CO）进行稀释，保证隧洞内卫生条件；对烟雾进行稀释，保证隧洞内行车安全；对异味进行稀释，提高隧道内行车的舒适性。

（4）为了解决以上各种问题，即使在白天也必须在隧道设置合适的照明设施，把必要的视觉信息传递给司机，防止因视觉信息不足而出现交通事故，从而提高驾驶上的安全性和增加舒适感。我国《公路隧道照明设计细则》(JTG/T D70/2-01—2014)规定 300m 以下的行人稀少且交通量不大的隧道可不设照明，但二级以上公路隧道长度超过 100m 时，必须有可靠的照明设施。

（5）我国目前公路隧道总里程已建成 2000km，隧道照明电费是高速公路运营成本的重要组成部分。一些运营商由于不堪高额照明运营费用的重负，不得不关灯节电，以牺牲安全的办法来降低运营成本。因此，如何在满足规范的前提下降低隧道照明能耗，已成为高速公路隧道运营中迫切需要解决的课题之一。这对于保持国民经济的可持续发展、保护环境以及保证行车安全都具有重要意义。

Unit 3　Main and Ancillary Structures
隧道主体及附属结构

I. Text

Text A　Tunnel Main Structures
隧道主体结构

Traffic tunnel structure consists of two parts: main building and ancillary building. *The main building of a tunnel is intended to maintain stability of a tunnel, ensure traffic safety and operation and is composed of tunnel body lining and tunnel portals. When collapse or stone fall easily occur at portal sections cut and cover tunnel shall be built additionally.*

1. Tunnel limit and clearance

Tunnel clearance refers to the space surrounded by inner profile line of tunnel lining. The tunnel clearance is determined in accordance with "tunnel construction limit". Tunnel construction limit refers to the space range in which no any obstruction is allowed within regulated certain width and height to ensure normal operation and safety of all types of traffic in tunnel. Generally tunnel construction limit refers to the profile line of inner edge of lining which cannot be invaded.

1) Railway tunnel construction limit

In China locomotive and trains of various types and specifications are running on railways. Through overall investigation and statistics the cross section required are specified as "locomotive limit" which can satisfy maximum required cross sectional dimensions of various types of locomotives and trains. In addition, different situations of loading cargo on train are also considered and all the train loaded cargo including extended cargo allowed by code is not allowed to go beyond range of train limit.

For purpose of all types of buildings on railway, "railway approaching construction limit" is specified which refers the clearance space range which all buildings on railway are not allowed to invade in to ensure smooth passing of running trains without any scratch and touch.

Tunnel is permanent building on railway line which cannot be dismantled and altered once its construction completion. Based on consideration of "building approaching limit" a few spaces are reserved and enlarged properly for installation of illumination, communication and signal equipments.

2) Highway tunnel construction limit

Highway tunnel construction limit comprises carriage width (W), lateral width (L), and walkway (R) or inspection passageway (J). When planning walkway width allowance (C) is included.

In design of highway tunnel limit the space relations between all types' carriage ways and highway equipments should be fully studied. Any part (including the space allowances necessary for tunnel ventilation, illumination, safety, surveillance and internal decoration and other ancillary facilities) shall not invade into tunnel construction limit.

The design of road tunnel should take into account of the expected traffic capacity, safety measures (emergency exits, evacuation tunnels, lay-bys, vehicle turn around points), provisions for breakdowns, horizontal and vertical alignment, widths of the several elements and vertical clearances in accordance with the regulation prevailing for a considered tunnel.

Capacity: The traffic capacity depends on several factors, among them the width of the lanes, the percentage of heavy vehicles, the longitudinal inclination etc. The traffic capacity in tunnels appears to be slightly higher than in open sections of a highway. This is possibly due to increased concentration of drivers in tunnels. According to the French regulations, the traffic capacity of bi-directional urban tunnels is 2200pcp/h (passenger cars per hour), for bi-directional mountain tunnels it is 2350pcp/h. The speed in bi-directional tunnels should be limited to 80-90km/h.

Width: For traffic lanes, the recommended width is 3.50m (in North America: 3.65m). The width of traffic lane markings should be no less than 15cm. For safety reasons, the width of the roadway should be no less then 8.50m, so as to enable a heavy goods vehicle to overtake another vehicle that is stopped without completely interrupting traffic in the opposite direction. The hard clearance is intended to:

(1) Increase lane capacity;
(2) Provide a redress space for drivers crossing the edge line;
(3) Provide an emergency lane to give access to rescue services;
(4) Facilitate maintenance activities.

And it should have a width of 2.50-3.00m. The width of the hard clearance can be reduced to a minimum of 0.50m if their functions as emergency and breakdown lane are taken over by a central median strip having a width between 1.0 and 2.5m.

Walkways: Walkways are used by staff, and in case of incidents, by pedestrians. They also serve to enable door opening (from stopped cars and also emergency escape doors etc.). The recommended width is 0.75m. Regular pedestrian and bicycle traffic should not be allowed in tunnels. The walkway should be raised 7 to 15cm above the carriageway with a vertical kerb. Alternatively, walkways can be demarcated by roll-over kerbs. In this case, they can also be used by breaking down cars.

Vertical clearance: it should be distinguished between the following two headroom.

(1) Maximum headroom: design height of heavy goods vehicles, plus necessary allowance for dynamic vehicle movements. Recommended value is 4.20m.

(2) Mechanical headroom: additional allowances for signs, luminaries, fans etc. Vary between 0.20m and 0.40m. The headroom over walkways should be 2.30m (if the walkways are accessible also to cars via roll-over kerbs, then the forementioned headrooms should be kept).

Climbing lane: If the speed of heavy vehicles drops below 50km/h, a climbing lane of 3.00 m width should be planned.

Lay-by's: Lay-by's are planned to accommodate breakdowns. Their spacing should decrease with increasing traffic density. It should be noted that it is improbable that a breakdown occurs exactly where a lay-by is to be found. A variant of lay-bys are turn-around points.

For a daily traffic volume exceeding 10000 vehicles per lane, a twin tube tunnel with uni-directional traffic should be considered. Two tubes are much safer and also preferable for maintenance reasons. In case of fire, a twin tube with cross walks and cross drives offers better chances for escape and also better access for rescue services. Note that the supplementary construction of the second tube faces a reduced geological risk, as information from the first heading can be used.

3) Cross sections

The shape of a tunnel cross section is also called profile. Various profiles are conceivable, e. g. rectangular ones. The most widespread one, however, are circular and (mostly oblate) mouth profiles. The choice of the profile aims at accommodating the performance requirements of the tunnel. Moreover it tries to minimize bending moments in the lining (which is often academic, since the loads cannot be exactly assessed) as well as costs for excavation and lining. Further aspects for the choice of the profiles are: ventilation, maintenance, risk management and avoidance of claustrophobia of users.

A mouth profile is composed of circular sections. The ratio of adjacent curvature radiuses should not exceed 5 ($r_1/r_2 < 5$). The minimum radius should not be smaller than 1.5m. Note that in the case of weak rock the lower part of the lining also receives load from the adjacent ground. Therefore, a curved profile is advisable from a statical point of view also in the invert.

After accomplishment of tunnel main structure in order to ensure safe passing of motorcars or vehicles and enable normal operation of tunnel some ancillary installations shall be furnished including safety installations for hiding from traffic, electric communication signal, water control and drainage facilities. Due to difference of traffic the installations in rail tunnel and road tunnel are different.

Rail tunnels: Often a choice between the economically preferable one tube with two tracks and the safer twin tubes is necessary. Required cross sections have been specified by the rail companies. The German Rail (DB) prescribes a radius of 4.9m for circular sections of one-track high speed train tunnels. For two-track tunnels cross section of 92 to 101 m are required. With improved electric wire suspension this area can be reduced to 85 m.

The aerodynamic air pressure rise due to the entrance of a high speed train into a tunnel may cause discomfort of the passengers (unless the cars are pressure-tight) and constitutes load acting upon the lining. The prevailing aerodynamic effect can be understood if we consider a piston entering with a high speed into a tube. Neglecting the gap between piston and tube we observe that the piston moving with the velocity V imposes the same velocity upon the air in front of it. This gives rise to a compaction shock that moves ahead with the velocity.

In reality, air can escape backwards through the gap between train and tunnel wall. Thus, the pressure in the air cushion pushed ahead of the train rises gradually, as the length of the gap increases. When the bow shock front reaches the portal, then a refraction shock travels backwards to the piston/train and causes there a sudden pressure drop. Realistic figures can only be obtained numerically. With respect to double tracks in one tube, one should take into account that a high speed train should not encounter a freight train inside a tunnel, because it could be endangered by falling items.

Alignment: For the choice of the proper alignment, several aspects must be taken into account: geotechnical, traffic, hydrological and risk management issues. The main geotechnical aspect is to avoid bad rock and adverse groundwater. The choice of alignment depends also on the excavation method (drill and blast or TBM), noise and ventilation ①the disposal of polluted air should not impair abutters; ②ventilation shafts should not be too long should be considered. In road tunnels, straight alignments longer than 1500m should be avoided, as they could distract the driver. Furthermore, to avoid excessive concentration on one point, the last few meters of a tunnel should have a gentle curve in plan view.

A dilemma is the choice between a high level tunnel and a base tunnel. On the one hand a high level tunnel is much shorter and has reduced geological risk (because of the reduced cover). On the other hand the operation is more expensive because of increased power consumption and increased wear of the wagons. Velocity is reduced and traffic interruption or delays during winter must be factored in. A base tunnel is much longer, therefore, much more expensive and difficult to construct. But it offers many operational advantages. Consider e. g. Engelberg tunnel on the Stuttgart-Heilbronn motorway, the old high level tunnel had a length of 300m and access ramps with a 6% slope. As a result, heavy trucks had to slow down, which lead to traffic jams. The new base tunnel (completed in 1999) has a length of 2×2.5km and a maximum slope of 0.9%. Each tube has three drive lanes and one emergency lane. Thus, the traffic capacity has increased dramatically.

Further aspects for the choice of alignment are as follows.

Depth: For tunneled under crossing, a sufficient cover is needed to avoid surface settlements and daylight collapses. It requires longer ramps.

Longitudinal slope (s): There are following limitations.

$s = 0.2\% - 0.5\%$, for water drainage;

$s < 2\%$, for rail tunnels;

$s < 15\%$, for road tunnels (due to exhaust gases). Inclinations of more than 3.5% make ventilation more difficult, as it has to overcome the chimney effect. The latter becomes particularly important in case of fire. Therefore, considerably lower limits for longitudinal inclination are recommended: $s < 4\%$ in bi-directional road tunnels. If the tunnel length exceeds 400m, then the inclination s should not exceed 2%.

With an increasing slope the production of exhaust gases also increases, therefore, ventilation costs rise.

2. Tunnel lining types

The main structure of highway tunnels mainly comprise tunnel body lining structure and tunnel portal structures which are determined mainly subject to the geological conditions at tunnel site, consideration of rationality of its structural forces, construction methodology and construction technical levels. With the people's accumulated experiences of tunnel engineering practice and more and more knowledge of surrounding rock compression and performance of lining structures, various structural shapes suitable for different geological conditions have been developed and approximately following categories are classified. There are number of ways in which to classify linings. The linings can be classified according to:

(1) Shapes (vertical wall lining, curved wall lining, circular profile lining, rectangular profile lining, flared tunnel ling);

(2) Forms (monolithic lining, shotcrete and anchor bolt lining, composite lining, assembled lining);

(3) Materials (brick or stone lining, concrete lining, reinforced concrete lining and steel sheet lining).

Portals: *Length cuts in slope debris should be avoided as well as large jumps in illumination (to avoid high illumination costs in the tunnel). Thus tunnel entrances in east-west direction should be avoided and the distance between two consecutive tunnels should not be too small.*

3. Functions of tunnel portals

Portals shall be provided at both ends of tunnel and portals have following functions.

(1) Reducing earth and stone excavation works amount at portals. The road cut within range of portal sections are excavated by landform and geological conditions by some prescribed side slope. When the tunnel embedment depth is large the excavation works amount is large. Provision of tunnel portals can serve as earth retaining wall and can reduce earth and stone excavation amount.

(2) Stabilizing side slope: due to that the rock on side slope is subjected to weathering from time to time the loose stones on slope surface easily fall down. Since the side slope is too high, the stone mass on upward slope whose stability is hardly maintained can also roll down slope surface and stones fallen down can sometimes block the tunnel portal or even damage track of railway line thus causing threat to passing trains. Provision of tunnel portal can reduce the elevation of side slope of road cut of approach section, shorten slope surface length of from upward slope so as to stabilize side slope and upward slope.

(3) Diverting surface water flow: Surface water flow mostly gathers at tunnel portal and if the water catchments are not discharged, it will immersed railway and impair safety of traffic. Tunnel portal built can divert the flow into side ditch and keep tunnel portal in normal and dry condition.

(4) Decorating tunnel portal: Tunnel orifice is the only exposed part of tunnel and is the

appearance of front face of tunnel. Portal building is also a kind of decoration of tunnel. Especially the tunnels near cities shall be aesthetically treated to make city more beautiful.

4. Types of tunnel portals

Circular frame of portal: When the stone at portal is hard and stable rock of rating I and topography is steep and lack of drainage requirement, a type of unbearing simple portal circular frame portal should be provided and it can reinforce tunnel portal and reduce water droplet effect on portal after rainfall. Tunnel portal is simply decorated.

The circular door frame is slightly backward and its inclination is consistent with that of upward slope on top. The width of circular frame matches with external appearance of portal and is generally no less than 70cm and the surface of extruding upward slope shall be at least 30cm to enable the water flowing down upward slope to drop front face of portal.

End wall typed portal (Figure 3.1): End wall typed portal applies to wide and extensive landform region where the rock is basically stable and rated I to III. The function of end wall is to support upward slope of tunnel portal and maintains its stability and gather and discharge the water flow on upward slope. For this type of tunnel door one end wall which can resist longitudinal thrust of mountain body is only set on right front face of tunnel opening, and it can not only work as retaining wall but also can support the upward slope on front face of portal and collect the surface water flow from upward slope into drainage ditch.

The configuration of end wall generally uses uni-thickness straight wall and volume of masonry straight wall is smaller than that of other types and works execution is easy. The wall body tilts backward slightly with inclination degree approximately 1:10. Thus it can undertake smaller pressure of earth and stone than vertical wall and is favorable to resistance against overturn of end wall.

Wing wall typed portal (Figure 3.2): When the geological conditions at tunnel portal are poor and longitudinal thrust of maintain body is large in additional to end wall typed tunnel portal one-sided or two sided wing wall can be added called wing wall typed tunnel portal. The wing wall and end wall work jointly to resist against the longitudinal thrust of mountain body and increase capacity of portal against skidding and overturn. Thus wing wall typed portal applies to rock of rating IV-VI. The front faced end wall of wing wall is generally uni-thickness straight wall and tilts slightly backward with inclination degree of 1:10. The front face of wing wall is perpendicular to end wall and top inclination in consistence with gradient of upward slope. Water flow trench is provided on wall top diverting the water from trench on tunnel top to side drain by road cut. The footing of wing wall is placed on stable foundation and its embedment is identical to foundation of end wall.

On top of tunnel portal the drainage ditch between end wall and foot of upward slope generally takes shape of trench form 60cm wide and 40cm deep and trench bottom shall have drainage slope with gradient of 3‰. The form of drainage trench is subjected to topography of portal and door configuration. One way down slope drainage is mostly applied and can divert water to low hill on one side of portal or to side ditch by road cut. When landform does not allow one-sided drainage two ways drainage can be applied and divert water to both sides of end wall. Water flows out of wall from the reserved water outlet at back of end wall called "dragon's mouth" or "suspension ditch" and the water can be also diverted to top of wing wall and can flow into side trench by road cut along inclined trench.

Figure 3.1 End Wall Type Portal

Figure 3.2 Wing Wall Type Portal

Column typed portal (Figure 3.3): *When landform is steep and geological conditions are poor, there is possibility of down slide of upward slope. In addition to constraints of landform or geological conditions wing wall is not provided. Large column pier with large sections can be set in middle of end wall to increase stability of end wall. This type of portal wall face has outstanding profile and is pleasant looking and suits application near city or within scene areas. For long and large tunnel column typed portal looks spectacular.*

Step typed portal (Figure 3.4): When portal is situated sloppy area by mountain and the side slope by one side of portal is high, in order to reduce elevation of upward slope and exposed slope length, the top of one side of the end wall can be changed to gradually incremental step typed form to suit landform features and to reduce earth-stone excavation volume of upward slope.

Figure 3.3 Column Type Portal

Figure 3.4 Step Type Portal

Skew portal: When route direction skews with contour line of landform portal can be made to be consistent with contour of landform to enable horizontal sides of portal to be approximately symmetrical.

Cutting face tunnel portal (Figure 3.5): When tunnel portal section has one section of cut and cover tunnel lining because within some range behind portal backfilled earth dominates and thrust and slide force of mountain is small cutting face portal can be applied. It is named thus due to its structure similar to bamboo cylinder which is cut. This type of portal is extensively applied in construction of road tunnels. The special features of bamboo cutting face tunnel are reduced damage to vegetation cover and favorable to environmental protection, suitable for all types of rock types. Its application conditions are relatively symmetrical landform and not too steep landforms. Since the topographical conditions at portals are various and geological conditions are also variant, the types of portals shall be set as appropriate based on above mentioned basic portal types.

Figure 3.5 Cutting Face Tunnel Portal

Text B Ancillary Structures in Track Tunnel
铁路隧道辅助结构

1. Refuge recess

Whena train is passing through tunnel in order to ensure safety of pedestrian, maintenance staff and repair equipment in tunnel cave chambers are built on bilateral side walls of tunnel uniformly and alternatively for hiding from passing train and are thus called train avoiding cave which are classified into large cave and small cave according to its sizes.

2. Arrangement of the refuge recess

One large train hiding cave is arranged at interval of 300m in tunnel with gravel bed for rack. In tunnel with integral track bed for easiness of pedestrian hiding from train and smaller maintenance and repair works amount a larger hiding cave is built at spacing of 420m on each side of track. When tunnel length ranges between 300-400m one large refuge recesses can be arranged in middle of tunnel. When tunnel length is less than 300m larger refuge access can be omitted. If the connection bridge or road cutting exist at both ends of tunnel while there is no refuge platform or no platform outside the trench by both sides of road cutting a larger refuge recess shall be considered by taking tunnel into consideration.

Small refuge recess: No matter it is gravel rack bed or integral rack bed one small refuge recess shall be considered at spacing of 60m on each side wall in single track tunnel and at spacing of 30m on each side wall of twin track tunnel. In arrangement of smaller refuge recess shall be considered in combination with larger refuge recess. No smaller refuge recess shall be considered at location of larger refuge recess. Care shall be taken that no refuge recess shall be arranged at varied section of lining, connection of different lining types or at point of deformation joint. If there is rural towns and villages in vicinity of tunnel and crowds of people are expected to pass through tunnel or smaller curve radius and shorter visual distance larger refuge recess shall be considered in conjunction with tunnel.

3. Ancillary building for electrical power and communication facilities

Cable trench: All types of power cables through tunnel such as power cables for lighting, communication and signals must be protected by cable trench to prevent damages to cables due to moisture, rotting and vandalism.

Cable trench is cast with concrete and is arranged in parallel to and close to drainage trench and is placed on side of track or on opposite side to drainage trench (in case of one-sided drainage trench). Fine grained sand bed is placed in trench. Top of the trench cover plate shall be in level with top face of refuge recess or top level of rack bed. When power cable trench is parallel to drainage trench and on same side it shall be in level with cover plate of power cable trench. The power cables for communication and signals can be arranged in same trench and can be placed in separate trench also but must be separate from electrical power cable trench.

Power relay box for signal and unmanned voice increase station recess: Relay for signals shall be arranged in tunnel and signal relay box recess shall be arranged on same side of power cable trench and recess width and depth shall be 2m uniformly and center width is 2.2m.

Ventilation shaft: When tunnel length is large ventilation shaft shall be built to provide ventilation to sections of tunnel. For example the Gotthard tunnel in Switzerland has three ventilation shafts. In addition, when the longitudinal slope of long and large tunnel is gable slope contaminated air often accumulates at slope crest. In tunnel construction in order to increase excavation working face vertical shaft or inclined shaft are built additionally as ancillary tunnel which can be used as ventilation duct in operation. Ventilator is arranged on ceiling of shaft or inclined shaft and fine ventilation can be produced by fan and shaft ventilation.

Text C Ancillary Structures in Road Tunnel
公路隧道辅助结构

Emergency lane and lay-by: Lay-bys are planned to accommodate breakdowns of motorcar. The spacing of lay-bys should decrease with increasing traffic density. It should be noted, however, that it is improbable that a breakdown occurs exactly where a lay-by is to be found. A variant of lay-bys are U turn points (turn-around points). When motorcar breaks down in tunnel, it should drive off main traffic lane immediately for handling and emergency lane or lay-by is the place for stoppage of emergency, and especially in long tunnel faulty motorcar should leave traffic lane as soon as possible, otherwise traffic jam even traffic incident will occur. Thus in super long and long expressway tunnel and highway tunnel emergency lane for breakdowns should be arranged. In order to provide refuge and hiding for motorcar in fire hazard, U-turn (turnaround facility) point should be provided in tunnel of length over 10km.

The spacing between lay-bys and emergency lane should be subjected to possible sliding distance of breakdowns and manpower pushing distance. Generally speaking, it is hard to ascertain its distance for example the sliding distance of car is larger than truck's and manpower pushing is easier; sliding distance on downslope is larger than that on upslope and pushing is power-saving. Based on experience the spacing of emergency lanes or lay-bys may be set to be 500 ~ 800m. In China, the associated parameters of emergency lanes or lay-bys are taken in accordance with the recommended values set by PIARC (parliament of international association of road committee). For the tunnel of length over 2km emergency lane (lay-by) of width 2.5m and length of 25 ~ 40m shall be arranged at spacing of 750m.

Walkways: Walkways are used by staff, and in case of accidents, by pedestrians. They also serve to enable door opening (from stopped cars and also emergency escape doors etc.). The recommended width is 0.75m. Regular pedestrian and bicycle traffic should, in general, not be allowed in tunnels. The walkway should be raised 7 to 17 cm above the carriageway with a vertical kerb. Alternatively, walkways can be demarcated by roll-over kerbs. In this case, they can also be used by break down cars.

Climbing lane: Climbing lane of 3.00m in width should be arranged if the speed of heavy vehicles drops below 50km/h.

II. Terms and terminology

ancillary buildings	附属建筑
refugee access	行人,行车横洞和预留洞室
emergency lane and lay-by	紧急停车带
ventilation shaft for operation	运营通风竖井
lighting for operation	营运照明设施
sunlight shed, sunlight grid, dimmer section	遮阳棚,遮光格栅,减光段
drainage	排水设施
drainage ditch, interception	排(截)水沟
drainage pipe	排水管
cable trench and other trenches for pipelines	电缆槽与其他设施预留槽
escape corridor	逃生管廊
escape route	逃生线路
climbing lane	爬坡车道
end wall typed portal	端墙式洞门
cross section	横断面
tunnel clearance	隧道净空

Ⅲ. Questions and difficult sentence analysis

1. Questions for brainstorming discussion

(1) What are the principal buildings and their respective functions in rail tunnels?

(2) What are the principal shapes of portals for highway tunnels?

What is the shape of the portals of tunnels you know? Please describe the tunnel name, location and its surroundings.

(3) Please explain why the longitudinal slope gradient cannot be 0 in highway tunnel.

2. Difficult sentences analysis

(1) The main building of a tunnel is intended to maintain stability of a tunnel, ensure traffic safety and operation and is composed of tunnel body lining and tunnel portals. When collapse or stone fall easily occur at portal sections cut and cover tunnel shall be built additionally.

译文：隧道主体结构旨在维持隧道稳定性，确保交通营运安全，由隧道洞身衬砌和洞口组成。如果洞口段易发生坍塌或坠石，应加修明洞。

(2) The shape of a tunnel cross section is also called profile. Various profiles are conceivable, e. g. rectangular ones. The most widespread one, however, are circular (mostly oblate) and mouth profiles. The choice of the profile aims at accommodating the performance requirements of the tunnel. Moreover it tries to minimize bending moments in the lining (which is often academic, since the loads cannot be exactly assessed.) as well as costs for excavation and lining. Further aspects for the choice of the profiles are: ventilation, maintenance, risk management and avoidance of claustrophobia of users.

译文：隧道横截面的形状又称作截面。截面可以是各种各样的，例如：长方形。但是，最普遍采用的截面形状是圆形（多数是椭圆形）和口形。截面形状的选择主要基于满足该隧道的功能要求。此外，还应尽量减小衬砌的弯矩（该弯矩不能精确估算，因为是理论弯矩），同时减少开挖和衬砌成本。选择截面形状的其他考虑因素为：通风、维护保养、风险管理以及防止隧道用户发生幽闭恐惧症。

(3) Length cuts in slope debris should be avoided as well as large jumps in illumination (to avoid high illumination costs in the tunnel). Thus tunnel entrances in east-west direction should be avoided and the distance between two consecutive tunnels should not be too small.

译文：应避免泥石坡的长距离开挖以及照明亮度的大起大落（以避免高昂的隧道照明成本）。因此，应避免隧道两端进口呈东西向布置，并且两个相邻隧道的距离不应太短。

(4) When landform is steep and geological conditions are poor there is possibility of down slide of upward slope. In addition to constraints of landform or geological conditions wing wall is not provided. Large column pier with large sections can be set in middle of end wall to increase stability of end wall. This type of portal wall face has outstanding profile and is pleasant looking and suits application near city or within scene areas. For long and large tunnel column typed portal looks spectacular.

译文：在地形陡峭并且地质条件差的地段，仰坡可能发生滑坡。除了地形或地质条件的限制以外,也没有翼墙。可以在端墙的中部打入大直径的大墩柱,以增强端墙的稳定性。该类洞口墙面有突出的截面,美观,适合周边城市或风景区。在长大隧道中,该类洞口显得壮观。

IV. Translation case study

Case 1

Chinese	English translation
该隧道太长,不能从两个服务建筑供电。这就是为什么在隧道的中央管廊内布置变电器。除了该基础设施以外,该隧道还有一个应急供电设施。该电源利用热和能组合,产生的热能加热附近郊区的住户。 该隧道采用条形照明带,在入口斜坡道处,增加进口照明,代替传统的遮阳百叶窗。	The tunnel is too long for a provision of power from the two service buildings. That is why two transformers are placed in the middle of the central tunnel canal. Besides this basic facility, the tunnel has an emergency power supply. The power supply makes use of combined heat and energy, whereby the generated heat energy heats up the residences in the adjacent suburb. The tunnel is provided with strip-shaped lighting, at the access ramps this is supplemented with entrance lighting, which replaces the traditional sun louvers.

Case 2

Chinese	English translation
两种不同的交通工具使用皮埃特·海茵隧道(Piet Hein Tunnel),即道路交通和有轨电车。因此,综合考虑了两种不同的安全标准。道路交通的安全理念认为采用一些用户自救的措施,而轨道隧道安全理念认为机车不停车,直接穿过隧道以后,乘客才可以下车。 道路交通隧道内每50m布置急救站,该急救站配有灭火和通信设备。为了防止相对小的事件发展为一场灾难,道路车辆应尽早停车。如果必须离开车辆,驾乘人员可以步行经过连接隧道两管廊之间的逃生隧道撤离该隧道。 如果轨道电车管廊发生事故,那么,该电车不得不停车,交通控制员关闭该道路隧道的南侧管廊的交通通行,使轨道电车的乘客可以使用公路管廊作为逃生通道而撤离事故现场。	Two different types of transport make use of Piet Hein tunnel: road traffic and trams. Thus, a combination of two different safety standards was assumed. The safety philosophy for the road traffic tunnel assumes some measure of self-rescue by users, while that of the tram tunnel assumes that carriages do not stop but drive through the tunnel before the passengers may disembark. The road traffic tunnel is provided with aid stations every 50 meters which contain fire extinguishing and communication equipment. In order to prevent relatively small incidents from turning into a disaster, the road traffic is halted at an early stage. If it is necessary to leave the vehicle, motorists can leave the tunnel on foot via the escape corridor between the two traffic tubes. If an accident occurs in the tram tube whereby the tram is forced to a halt, the traffic controllers halt the road traffic in the southern tube of the road traffic tunnel, so that the escape tram passengers can use the roadway as an escape route.

Case 3

Chinese	English translation
交通控制和探测系统每天24h监控隧道内交通并及早发现问题。为此,该隧道安装了彩色照相机、交通停滞探测器以及喇叭、高频天线和对讲机。该隧道的监控由控制室操作,该控制室设在1J隧道顶部。皮埃特·海茵隧道(Piet Hein Tunnel)的监控在另外增加的一层楼操作,1J隧道将进行大修以保持与皮埃特海茵隧道(Piet Hein Tunnel)同等的安全水平。	Traffic controlling and detection systems monitor the traffic 24 hours per day and detect problems at an early stage. For this purpose, the tunnel is equipped with color cameras, stagnation detectors, loud speakers, HF aerials and intercom. The surveillance of the tunnel takes place from a control room, which is situated at the top of the lJ tunnel. The Piet Tunnel is operated from an extra floor. The lJ tunnel will undergo a major maintenance to attain the same level of the safety as the Piet Hein tunnel.

V. Assignment

(1)洞门墙基础必须置于稳固地基上,这是因为通常洞口位置的地形地质条件比较复杂,有的全为松散堆积覆盖层,有的半软半硬,有的地面倾斜陡峻,为了保证建筑物稳固,应视地形及地质条件,将洞门墙基础埋置足够的深度。基底埋入土质地基的深度不应小于1m,嵌入岩石地基的深度不应小于0.5m。

(2)一般隧道开挖是从两洞口相向掘进开挖,或从其中一个洞口单向掘进。但在特长隧道因工期、经济、施工、地形、环境等条件限制,有必要分成多个工作区段进行施工,多数情况下要设辅助工作坑道。此外,为了保证隧道营运期间的安全,也需要设置安全避难通道。辅助坑道按坡度不同,分为横洞、平行导坑、斜井和竖井。选择哪种形式,取决于地形、地质、工期、通风需要、运输能力及安全等级等。

(3)竖井的位置选择必须考虑地形、地质、与主坑道的衔接、完工后的处理等条件。特别是设在山谷部分的竖井多数延长短,要研究防止井口附近地表水和泥沙的流入措施。当存在平面位置稍偏离一点,即有可能产生大的地质变化的情况时,必须重视地质调查。

(4)当隧道埋深较浅,上覆岩(土)体较薄,采用暗挖法较困难时,则应采用明挖法来开挖隧道。用这种明挖法修筑的隧道结构称为明洞。明洞具有地面、地下建筑物的双重特点,既作为地面建筑物,用以抵御边坡、仰坡的坍方、落石、滑坡、泥石流等病害,又作为地下建筑物,用于在深路堑、浅埋地段不适宜暗挖隧道时,取代隧道的作用。另外它还可以利用与公路、灌溉渠立交处,以减少建筑物之间的干扰。

(5)隧道内的路基结构应具有足够的承载力,尤其要求在有丰富地下水的条件下也能满足要求,这就要求有良好的排水设施。衬砌背后应设置盲沟和导水管,在车道板下面铺设透水性好的路基材料,必要时设置仰拱。在确定隧道纵坡时保证排水沟排水顺畅,保证路面有1%~1.5%的横坡等。

Unit 4　Geotechnical Investigation
地 质 勘 察

Ⅰ. Text

Text A　Summary of Geotechnical Investigation
岩土勘察概述

Geotechnical engineering is the branch of civil engineering that deals with soil, rock and ground water and their relation to the design, construction and operation of engineering projects. Nearly all civil engineering projects must be supported by the ground, and thus requires at least some geotechnical engineering information.

Geotechnical engineering is closely related to engineering geology, which is a branch of geology. Individuals from both professions often work together, each making contributions from his or her own experience to solve practical problems. The combined efforts of these two professions are sometimes called geotechnics.

Geotechnical engineers usually begin by assessing the underground conditions and the engineering properties of the various strata and this process is called site exploration and characterization. It usually involves drilling vertical holes called exploratory borings into the ground, obtaining soil and rock samples and testing these samples in a laboratory and tests in-situ (in-place) may also be involved.

The next step is to perform engineering analysis based on the information gained from the site exploration and characterization program. The analytical tools used to perform these analyses are collectively known as soil mechanics and rock mechanics.

Thus, soil mechanics and rock mechanics are to geotechnical engineering what structural mechanics is to structural engineering. In both fields, "mechanics" refers to the analytical tools, while "engineering" is a broader term that also includes the rest of the design and construction process.

The analysis results are used to develop geotechnical input for design processes. The design process also includes engineering judgment, experience from previous projects, and a sense of economics. However, regardless of the results from these analyses, geotechnical engineers are reluctant to deviate too far from design criteria that have proven worthy in the past. This is why understanding a customary standard of practice is so important.

Geotechnical engineers work as part of a team, which also includes other professionals, such as structural engineers, architects and others. Many design issues can be resolved only through a team effort and contribution, so the final design drawings and specifications reflect the combined expertise of many individuals.

Geotechnical engineer does not stop his work at the end of the design phase, for it is very important to be involved in the construction phase as well. Geotechnical services during construction typically include:

(1) Examining the soil and rock conditions actually encountered and comparing them with those anticipated in the design. This is especially useful when the project includes large excavations, because they expose much more of the subsurface conditions than were seen in the exploratory borings. Sometimes the conditions encountered during construction are different, and this may dictate appropriate changes in the design.

(2) Comparing the actual performance with that anticipated in the design. We may do this by installing special instruments that measure movements, groundwater levels, and other important characteristics. This process, which is called observational method, can also produce changes in the design.

(3) Providing quality control testing especially in compacted fills and the structural foundations.

A rational approach for selecting soil and rock properties for engineering design can be summarized as a logical procedure that encompasses the general activities of site investigation and field testing, laboratory testing and interpretation and engineering design. This step-by-step process is presented in brief as below.

1. Site investigation and field testing

(1) Review available information: The best place to start the process of material property selection is to review any and all information that may be available. There are several sources for this information, many of the sources being in the public domain and readily available at modest expense.

(2) Identify required material properties: No investigation should be initiated without specific goals being established that are related to design and construction issues that must be considered for example performance requirements, engineering properties that are needed and the type of structure that is to be constructed.

(3) Plan site investigation: Historical information, which will provide anticipated subsurface conditions, coupled with knowledge of the specific design will allow an efficient site-specific investigation strategy to be developed. Contingency plans should be considered based on anticipated variabilities in subsurface conditions. Sampling intervals should be identified and an in situ testing program should be developed.

(4) Conduct site investigation and filed testing: Once the investigation strategy is developed, it is ready to implement. Findings should be communicated to the geotechnical design engineer during the field work and modifications to the number and types of samples and testing should be

determined, as required.

(5) Describe samples: Results from the field investigation program and subsequent laboratory identification of samples should be compared to the anticipated conditions based on historical information. Selected laboratory samples can be reviewed by the design engineer to obtain first-hand observations. These samples should be used for performing simple laboratory index tests.

(6) Develop subsurface profile: Using results from the field investigation and the laboratory index tests, a detailed subsurface profile should be developed by the geotechnical design engineer. It is helpful at this step to review the initial site investigation objectives and expectations to be assured that the materials are consistent with expectations.

(7) Review design objectives: An on-going evaluation of field and available laboratory data relative to the design objectives should be performed during the implementation of the site investigation. If adjustments are needed or if additional data needs are identified, procedures should be initiated to obtain the necessary information.

2. Laboratory testing and test interpretation

(1) Select samples for performance testing: Prior to initiating the project-specific laboratory-testing program, the design engineer should review the recovered samples and confirm the testing that needs to be conducted (i. e. , type, number and required test parameters). If possible, selected samples should be extruded in the laboratory and reviewed by the design engineer.

(2) Conduct laboratory testing: Once the samples have been reviewed and the testing program is confirmed, it is time to continue the index tests and initiate the performance-testing program (with index test correlation for quality assurance). Preliminary results should be provided to the design engineer for review.

(3) Review quality of laboratory data: If the data and interpreted laboratory test results are not consistent with expectations or if results indicate that the sample was disturbed, it is necessary to review progress and make adjustments. On some projects, results at this stage can be used to plan and initiate a more detailed and focused phase of investigation. A phased investigation approach is particularly helpful on large projects and in cases where there are many unknowns regarding the subsurface conditions or specific project requirements prior to conducting the proposed site investigation program.

(4) Select material properties: The laboratory and field test results should be interpreted and compared to project expectations and requirements. The role of the design engineer at this stage is critical as the full integration of field and laboratory test results must be coupled with the site-specific design. If test results are not completely consistent, the reason(s) should be evaluated, poor data should be eliminated, and similarities and trends in data should be identified. It may be necessary to return to the laboratory and conduct an additional review of sample extrusion, selection and testing.

3. Engineering design

Perform design: At this final stage, the design engineer has the necessary information related to the soil and rock properties to complete the design. Additionally, the design engineer also has the first-hand knowledge related to the variability of the deposit and of the material properties. Design activities can proceed with knowledge of these properties and variabilities.

The above process is logical and is generally followed on many projects. *In many cases, old "rules-of-thumb" and "status quo" approaches can result in an unconscious "by-passing" of critical steps.* In particular, selection of the correct engineering property tests, their interpretation, and summarization are often poorly performed. Rigorous attention to this procedure is required to assure efficient and thorough investigation and testing programs, especially since many projects are fragmented in which drilling, testing, and design are performed by different parties.

Occasionally geotechnical services continue beyond the end of the construction. For example, sites prone to long-term settlements may require monitoring for months or years after construction. Post-construction activities also can include investigations of facilities that have not performed satisfactorily, and development of remedial measures.

4. Use of correlations to assist property selection

If time and budget were not an issue, the design engineer could obtain as many samples as necessary and conduct as many laboratory or in situ tests as desired to obtain a complete assessment of subsurface soil and rock conditions. Engineering properties could be quantified and any inconsistent data could be set aside; additional testing could then be initiated. Unfortunately, time and budgets are major issues and the design engineer must make critical decisions at several steps throughout the design to obtain the most reliable and realistic soil and rock property information. A critical step in obtaining these properties lies in the selection of a specific test and the interpretation of the test results. For any number of reasons (e. g. Cost, sampling difficulties, etc.), it may be difficult to obtain the specific parameter(s) of interest. Fortunately, the design engineer can often use well-developed and/or site-specific correlations to obtain the designed parameter. Also correlations serve as a quality assurance check on determined test results.

Correlations to engineering properties come in many forms, but all have a common theme: specifically, the desired correlation utilizes a large database of results based on past experience. In the best case, the correlation and experience have been developed or "calibrated" using the specific local soil; in other cases, the correlation may be based on reportedly similar soils. The reliance or use of correlations to obtain soil and rock properties is justified and recommended in the following cases: specific data are simply not available and are only possible by indirectly comparing to other properties; a limited amount of data for the specific property of interest are available and the correlation can provide a complement to these limited data; or the validity of certain data is in question and a comparison to previous test results allows the accuracy of the selected test to be assessed. *Correlation in general should never be used as a substitute for an adequate subsurface investigation program, but rather to complement and verify specific project-related information.*

(1) Specific data are unavailable: Several examples of this type exist. Most notable is the strength of the uncemented clean sand. Undisturbed sampling is prohibitively expensive and

correlation to standard penetration testing (SPT). Cone penetration testing (CPT) and other in situ tests results have been shown to be quite reliable. As another example, suppose that the strength of a soil in triaxial extension is desired and only triaxial compression data are available. By reviewing previous published comparison of compression and extension test results for similar soils, it is possible to approximate the triaxial test extension tests results.

(2) Limited data are available: For a given application, suppose that only a few, high-quality consolidation tests were performed. Compression properties were found to correlate well with Atterberg limits testing results. It is therefore concluded that additional consolidation test results are not required and that numerous Atterberg limits tests can be used to confidently assess compression properties.

(3) Assessing data validity: Consider that results from tests on two similar soils are inconsistent. By comparing the results to those for similar soils it may be possible to identify whether the data are simply inconsistent of is some of the data are incorrect.

Regardless of the specific correlation, the following critical components need to be explicitly recognized:

(1) The selected correlation is only as good as the data used to develop the correlation. Many correlations for sands were developed for clean, uncemented, uniform sands primarily for assessing liquefaction potential. Be careful in using this correlation to assess properties in a well-graded silty sand deposit. Select the appropriate correlation carefully.

(2) A correlation provides an "approximate" answer and will undoubtedly exhibit scatter among the data points. Assess the data and the scatter by using upper and lower bound (i. e. Best case/worse case) scenarios in the design calculations.

(3) The selected correlation will be most accurate if "calibrated" to local soil conditions.

5. Use of observational method

Once an appropriate value for the design has been selected, it is possible to complete the design and proceed to construction. There is one final step that can be performed to validate the data and possibly improve the accuracy of the selected value. This three step process involves: using the design value and the actual estimated loading to predict a field response; systematically monitor the field performance; and "back calculate" the actual property of interest. This process of prediction, monitoring, and reassessment is known as the observational method (Terzaghi and Peck, 1967).

Two examples of this technique follow:

(1) In soil, this use of piezometers to monitor the rate of pore pressure dissipation and measured settlements of a large area fill can result in a more accurate estimate of the compressibility and time rate of consolidation characteristics of soft soil as well as provide information to maximize the rate of fill placement.

(2) In rock, the use of instrumented rock bolts and displacement monitoring instrumentation can provide valuable information regarding the kinematics of block stability and the strength of the jointed rock mass.

The observation method is an invaluable aid and ideally should be a part of every geotechnical project. Sadly, this approach is often overlooked due to budget concerns and in many cases is not even considered by the design engineer. Where appropriately used, the observation method can have significant benefits not only to the project at hand, but also for other projects in the area because a full-scale assessment of the engineering properties can be made. It is strongly recommended that the observational methods be included as a basic tenet of all projects.

Text B Geotechnical Investigations Reports
岩土勘察报告

It should be clearly distinguished between the raw data from laboratory and field test results and their interpretation. Referring to so-called design-build contracts, the owner should not present interpretation of construction behavior that might define or limit construction means and methods. However, he should present sufficient data from investigations to avoid that the bids are too diverse and difficult to compare.

According to SIA 199, the following documents have to be worked out:

1. Description of the ground

(1) Geology: Geological layout, formation of the relevant soils and rocks. In this respect, the most important parameters for soils are: structure and density, for rocks: structure, joints, weathering.

(2) Hydrological conditions: Groundwater flow and its relation to surface water, circulation within pores, joints, karst, permeability. Influence of groundwater on tunnel (e.g. aggressivity against concrete) and influence of the tunnel on groundwater and sources on the ground surface.

(3) Geotechnical conditions: This item contains all geotechnical properties relevant to excavation and support.

(4) Possible additional statements: They refer to possible gases such as CH_4, CO_2, H_2S, radioactivity (radon), rock temperature, earthquakes, active joints, rockslide, and dangerous substances such as quartz, contaminations.

2. Rating the ground

This item contains prediction on excavation and usage of a tunnel, based on the above stated ground properties. One of the main aims is to recognize hazards (e.g. Cave-ins, daylight collapses, rock bursts, gas explosions, surface settlements) and to plan countermeasures. The hazards and countermeasures have to be compiled in the so-called safety plan. Hazards have to be classified into the following degrees in table 4.1.

Degree of hazard　　　　　　　　　　　　　　　　　Table 4.1

Degree of hazard	1	2	3
Occurrence	improbable	possible	probable

Judgment of the ground comprises statements on excavation and support. i. e.

(1) Method of excavation, length of advance step, over excavation, drilling, support of tunnel wall and face.

(2) Draining and stabilizing measures such as grouting, freezing support with compressed air.

(3) Reusage or disposability of the muck.

Geological, hydrological and geotechnical reports should contain above mentioned contents and shall be composed in following structure.

(1) Contract and relevant questions.

(2) Provenience of data, used documents.

(3) Executed experiments with documentation of method.

(4) Description of the ground.

(5) Conclusions, recommendations, open questions, missing data, supplementary investigations.

(6) Annex with plans (drawings).

(7) Annexes with data, profiles of sounding and drilling, results of laboratory and field measurements.

The conditions encountered during excavation have be assembled in the final report.

3. Presentation of data

The provenience of all data should be clearly documented. Hence, it should be distinguished between measured data and data taken from bibliography, experience, estimation and assumptions (so-called soft data). When referring to measured data, one should add the measuring method, the number of measurements, scatter and uncertainty of the values.

It should also be distinguished between the measured data (factual information) and the extracted conclusions (interpretation). Thus, it has to be distinguished between the Geotechnical data record that contains the exploration data, and the geotechnical baseline records that summaries and interprets the data. This distinction has often contractual implications. However, factual information and some degree of interpretation are, virtually, inseparable.

The behavior of rock is described with reference to some distinct properties. Therese can be assessed verbally by judgment (e. g. "weak rock"), but in the sense of rational approach, properties should be quantifiable. Attention should be paid to the definitions of properties. To be more specific, some properties are rigorously defined by means of constitutive equations. E. g. Young's modulus is defined by means of Hooke's law $\sigma = E\varepsilon$. It should be asked whether the underlying constitutive equation is realistic for a particular material (e. g. Reference to E makes no sense for sand or water). Some other properties, such as "abrasivity" cannot be described in the frame of equations. In such cases one has to resort to some whatsoever arbitrarily prescribed procedures. Apart from rock abrasivity, there are also other properties which cannot be specified properly. This is the case, e. g. with rock toughness, which is understood as the resistance to cutting. All attempts to further specify the toughness failed so far.

The specification of measurable quantities occurs on the basis of:

(1) Direct laboratory or field measurements.

(2) Empirical correlations with other quantities.

(3) Consideration of scale effects.
(4) Judgment from similar situations.
(5) Back analysis.

Text C Geotechnical Investigation Report of Left Line of Muzhailing Tunnel
木寨岭隧道左线工程地质勘察报告

The left line of Muzhailing Tunnel is located in medium-high mountain areas in Qinling. The tunnel is set to penetrate through ground of the Muzhailing, the watershed between Zhanghe River and Yaohe River crossing the two counties as Zhangxian and Mingxian with the tunnel portals proposed at position around 900m south of Dacaotan station in alluvial deposit fan area on west bank of Zhanghe. The tunnel route runs through gullies as Xiaogou, Shizuigou, Nanshuigou, Dazhangou and Wayaogou and the exit portal is at position near Houjiata on right side of Suzigou. The tunnel is in total length of 18460m from entrance at chainage number CK171 + 800 to exit chainage number CK190 + 260. The entrance portal is at level of 2549.88 m while the exit at 2390.94m. The maximum embedded depth of tunnel body is approximately 715m with minimum embedded depth around 30m.

This tunnel penetrates through Muzhailing, the watershed between Zhanghe and Yaohe and crosses transversally the two counties as Zhangxian and Mingxian. The most terrains which the tunnel runs through are steep hilly areas where few people tread and the communication is difficult except that. Only a few villages as Sanli, Yazhawan and Luzha and one communication tower are accessible by road. Since this tunnel is located in terrains of medium-high mountainous areas in Qinling, and ground surface level is generally between 2390 and 3214m and the natural slope gradient is greater than 50°. Gully is in deep cut in shape of letter "V" and at the foot of the slope there are mostly slope colluvial-deposits of and collapse deposits. The villages along the line mostly are located at gentle slope in mountains and gulley bottoms. This area is located at the transition zone from semi-humid weather of temperate zone and humid weather of high and cold zone, which is featured with low temperature, short frost-free seaon and rich precipitation. and the temperature, is low; frost-free season is short and precipitation is rich.

In accordance with the weather data from weather bureau show that, for years the annual mean temperature is 5.8℃ with the lowest temperature of −24.3℃ (February 9, 1972) and highest temperature of 33.3℃ (July 25, 2000), frost-free period of 90-120 days; relative humidity is 69%; for years the annual mean precipitation is 560.8mm with annual maximum precipitation of 709.3mm, daily maximum precipitation of 61.5mm, maximum precipitation in 1 hour is 54.0mm, and the maximum precipitation in 10 minutes is 30.4mm. The areas Chapu, Meichuan, Zhongzhai and Baozhi are of less rain with annual precipitation less than 550mm. The precipitation in the surveyed areas mainly concentrates in the duration from May to September during which period the precipitation amount accounts for more than 78% of whole year's precipitation. Heavy rain (greater than 25mm/d) breaks out 2.1times/year at average for years. The mean evaporation capacity for years is 1199.6mm equivalent to twice the precipitation amounts. The maximum depth of frozen earth is 0.90m.

In accordance with the "Code for Seismic Design of Building" and "The Ground Motion Parameter Zoning Map of China" (GB 18306—2001), in the project site area, the peak ground acceleration (PGA) is 0.15g and, the period of response spectrum characteristics is 0.45s equivalent to basic earthquake intensity of 7 in magnitude degrees.

According to shear wave test report and by the analysis in compliance with the table 4.0.1-2 in "Specification for Seismic Design of Railway Engineering" (GB 50111—2006), the construction site at the tunnel location in tunnel site range falls into category II.

The principal folds and faults in fracture structures in relation to this route section is grassland anticlinoria which form a large angle with the tunnel. where the route crosses in large angle. s. In the characteristics, The characteristics of folded zone is in length of over 200km and width of 20-40km with core of upper Devonian series and bilateral wings of carboniferous system and Permian strata with wing angles of 50°-70° and distributed along the : axle distributes in shape of "S" in NWW-EW direction. , in length of over 200km and width of 20-40km with core being upper Devonian series and bilateral wings being carboniferous system and Permian strata with wing angles of 50°-70°.

The major faults in connection with in relation to this tunnel section is Meihu-Xinsi fault zone F_2, developed in south wing of above mentioned grassland anticlinoria trending in direction of N65-80W. Surface of the fault zone is most inclined northward in inclination angle of 30°-70° bearing apparent compression-shearing features. The developed secondary faults in this section include f_9, f_{10}, f_{11}, f_{12}, f_{13}, f_{14}, f_{15} and f_{16} and most of these faults are covered with Quaternary system with apparent topographical features. In conjunction coupling with the results of observation stations and sound Magneto telluric method of geophysical explorations of controllable sources, the morphology and characteristics of all the faults are described respectively as below.

F_2: is tis the main regional fault in this region and the, it is compression-shear type fault, in attitude N58°W/60°N, developed in the demarcation between Devonian system and Carboniferous system. The fault zone with the hanging wall sandstone ($D_3^{S_s}$) and footwall sandstone ($C_1^{S_s}$) is made of fault breccias, fault mud and cataclasite. The route fractured at CK172+800 ~ CK172+980 with crushed zone in width around 180m showing in topographical form of big gully.

f_9: is of unclear property, predicted to be reverse fault in altitude N54°W/89°S. Both hanging wall and foot wall are slate ($C_1^{S_l}$), consisting of fault breccias, fault mud and cataclasite. The route crossed through this fault at location of CK174+770 ~ CK174+870 and crushed belt is in width around 100m.

f_{10}: is the reverse fault in altitude of N61°W/86°S. The both hanging wall and foot wall are slate($C_1^{S_l}$), consisting of fault breccias, fault mud and cataclasite. The route crossed this fault at location of CK175+170 ~ CK175+345 and the crushed belt is in width around 175m.

f_{11}: is the reverse fault in altitude of N60°W/60°N. The hanging wall is slate($C_1^{S_l}$) and the foot wall is limestone mixed with sandstone and slate ($C_1^{L_s+S_s+S_l}$). The fault consisted of fault breccias, fault mud and cataclasite. The route crosses through this fault zone at location of CK175+620 ~ CK175+700 and the crushed belt is in width around 80m.

f_{12}: is the reverse fault in altitude of N60°W/80 ~ 89°N, developed at the demarcation between Carboniferous system and Permian system. The hanging wall is limestone mixed with sandstone and slate ($C_1^{L_s+S_s+S_l}$) and the foot wall is conglomerate mixed with sandstone and slate ($P_1^{C_g+S_s+S_l}$). The fault consists of fault breccias, fault mud and cataclasite. The route crosses through this fault zone at location of CK175 +970 ~ CK176 +310 and the crushed belt is in width around 340m.

f_{13}: is the reverse fault in altitude of N60°W/56°N. The hanging wall is conglomerate mixed with sandstone and slate ($P_1^{C_g+S_s+S_l}$) and the foot wall is conglomerate ($P_1^{C_g}$). The fault consists of fault breccias, fault mud and crushed rock. The route crossed through this fault at the location of CK177 +125 ~ CK177 +300 and the crushed belt is in width around 175m.

f_{14}: is of unclear property, predicted to be reverse fault in altitude of N84°W/89°S. The hanging wall is sandstone mixed with carbon like slate ($P_1^{S_s+cS_l}$) and the foot wall is sandstone mixed with slate ($P_1^{S_s+S_l}$). The fault consists of fault breccias, fault mud and crushed rock. The route crosses through this fault at location of CK178 +125 ~ CK178 +275 and the crushed belt is in width around 150m.

f_{15}: is the reverse fault in altitude of EW/56°S. The hanging wall is sandstone mixed with carbonous slate ($P_1^{S_s+cS_l}$) and the foot wall is sandstone mixed with slate and the foot wall is sandstone mixed with slate ($P_1^{S_s+S_l}$). The fault consists of fault breccias, fault mud and crushed rock. The route crossed through this fault at location of CK181 + 925 ~ CK182 + 150 and the crushed belt is in width around 225m.

f_{16}: is the reverse fault in altitude of N52°W/72°S. Both the hanging wall and foot wall are sandstone mixed with carboneous slate ($P_1^{S_s+cS_l}$). The fault consists of fault breccias, fault mud and crushed rock. This route crossed this fault at the location of CK187 +467 ~ CK187 +597 and the crushed belt is in width around 130m.

In this preliminary survey, all gullies through which the Muzhailing Tunnel route runs crossed through was investigated with emphasis and flow amount was measured. Water sample was taken from the gullies near the tunnel site and the gullies where fold and fault crossed through were taken to water regular chemical test and isotope tritium analysis. The drainage division range through which Muzhailing Tunnel crossed was basically consistent with the location of original Muzhailing Highway Tunnel. Hence, in this survey process, this highway tunnel site was investigated with emphasis and the water inflow in Muzhailing Highway Tunnel was accurately measured. During the tunnel inflow forecasting and predicting, in addition to full analysis and utilization of the measured hydrological geological data on Muzhailing Highway Tunnel, such approaches as building model of underground runoff modular building, analogue method, underground hydrodynamic method, atmosphere precipitation permeation method were used.

1) Medium water yield area in fissures in bedrock (Ⅰ)

Mainly distributed in belt of Dapingcun-Shizuigou on north side of the tunnel and in Nanshui gully on south side of the tunnel. The water abundance demarcation line and limestone lithology demarcation line and boundary of fault are almost in alignment. In this medium water abundance zone, unit normal inflow amount is in range of 964.7-1025.4 $m^3/(d \cdot km)$. The fault zone under tunnel body, fissures in soft hard rock, karst of limestone and lithological decomposition sections are principal zones of groundwater water yield where rock joint fissures were developed and connection was fine and were the main passageway of possible inflow generation. Hence, during the construction time, the advanced forecast shall be performed during works execution and drainage facility shall be enhanced.

2) Water-shortage area in fissure in bedrock(II)

Area II_1: Mainly distributed in belt of entrance of super-long tunnel, small gully and large gully. In this region the spring flow amount is in range of 7-12 m^3/d. Being subject to tectonic influences, the joint fissures of bedrock is developed and the rock body was relatively fragmentary. The calculated underground runoff modules was in range of 293.6-372.4 $m^3/(d \cdot km^2)$ and unit normal inflow in range of 769.0-835.3 $m^3/(d \cdot km)$.

Area II_2: Distributed in middle section of the tunnel. The sandstone, slate, breccias joint, fissures were undeveloped, developed and groundwater was undeveloped. But in the section of the tunnel crossed at bottom of river valley or in tunnel section of small burial depth groundwater was developed. The calculated underground runoff modules in this section is in range of 79.4-95.97 $m^3/(d \cdot km^2)$ and the unit normal inflow amount is in range of 547.4-744.8 $m^3/(d \cdot km)$. The groundwater in the tunnel area fell into the category of the typical penetration—runoff cyclic system and the supply source to groundwater mainly came from atmospheric precipitation, snow melted water and surface trench water. In the tunnel area, gully was developed and those gullies generally constituted one small and relatively independent groundwater cycle system. The division ridge of mountain ridge and gullies were groundwater supply areas in various drainage basins and there was lack of or only weak hydraulic connections among systems. Slope terrain enables atmospheric precipitation, snow-melted water to be discharged in forms of sheet flood, spring water. In dry period, although runoff on surface water supplies water to groundwater, runoff surface water amount is rather limited hence its supply to groundwater would not be in large amount. Based on the inflow amount classification through geo-hydrological calculation and the medium water abundance sections, weak water abundance section classified by tunnel geo-hydrological characteristics, the tunnel engineering geo-hydrological conditions were assessed and evaluated as below:

(1) Entrance section CK171 +800 ~ CK173 +600 was weak water yield zone (II_1). Rocks there were severely subject to influences of the reverse fault F_2 and the joint fissures were relatively developed and the groundwater was mainly stored in crushed zone in the fault and the fissures in weathered bedrock. When the tunnel crossed through this section, the possible occurrence of big inrush and inflow was small but the possibility of inrush generated on the hanging wall of fault still existed when tunnel was crossing the reverse fault F_2. The main supplies to the groundwater were atmospheric precipitation, snow-melt, surface trench water and hydrochemical water of type HCO_3—Ca.

(2) The section of CK173 +600 ~ CK177 +400 was medium water yield zone (I). The lithology of this section ground was limestone and sandstone, and f_9, f_{10}, f_{11} and f_{12} normal fault

crossing zones. The rocks were severely influenced by the water subject to severe influences and thus the joint fissures were developed. Karst fissure water was developed but distributed unevenly. It was calculated and predicted that the unit maximum inflow amount was 964.7m^3/(d·km) at the location of tunnel crossing in this section and when the tunnel penetrated through crossing this section, the unit maximum inflow was 7332.0m^3/d. When the tunnel crossed the fault zone, lime rock section and lithology demarcation point zone, sudden inrush might occur. The groundwater mainly received the supply of atmospheric precipitation and the groundwater was of no corrosion.

(3) Section CK177+400 ~ CK181+600 was a water yield zone (II_2) where and was the section where the tunnel was of shallow burial depth. The rocks were subject to severe tectonic impacts. The joint fissures were developed and the groundwater was mainly stored in the intraformational joint fissures and lithology of rocks. Basically no big inflow would occur in the section of the tunnel. According to the calculation, the predicted unit normal inflow was 632.8m^3/(d·km) at the location where the tunnel crosses this section. The main water supplies to the groundwater was the atmospheric precipitation and the groundwater was of no corrosion.

(4) The section of CK181+600 ~ CK182+200 was medium groundwater yield zone (I) and was the section where tunnel burial depth was small. The rock was subject to severe tectonic impacts and the groundwater was mainly stored in fault f_{15}, sandstone and slate contacting zones. The tunnel-crossing section was rich in groundwater yield. According to the calculation, the predicted unit normal inflow in this section reached 1025.4m^3/(d·km) and maximum inflow of 1230.4m^3/d at the location of the tunnel's intersection with this area. crossing. The main water supplies to the groundwater were atmospheric precipitation, snow-melt and fissure water in bedrock. The groundwater was of no corrosion.

(5) Section CK182+200 ~ CK186+500 was water shortage lacking zone (II_2) where the tunnel was of great burial depth. The rocks were subject to severe tectonic impacts and joint fissures were developed but weakened with their increased depth. increment of depth. According to the calculation, the predicted normal inflow in the section was 547.4m^3/(d·km) with the maximum inflow of 4707.6m^3/d at the intersection of the tunnel with this area. location of tunnel crossing and the maximum inflow of 4707.6m^3/d at the location of tunnel crossing. Possible big inrush might occur in the section at lithology demarcation point. The main water supplies to the groundwater were atmospheric precipitation, snow-melt and fissure water in long and wide joint. The groundwater was of no corrosion.

(6) Section CK186+500 ~ CK187+800 was water short zone (II_1). The rocks were subject to severe tectonic impacts. Joint fissures were developed. The groundwater was mostly stored in the fissures of introformational joints of rock. Basically, no big inflow will occur in the section of tunnel site but at the locations where the tunnel intersects with the belt influenced by fault f_{16} and shallow burial section of gully, large scaled groundwater inflow would occur. According to the calculation, the predicted normal inflow amount in this section was 769.0m^3/(d·km) at the location of the tunnel. The main water supplies to the groundwater were atmospheric precipitation and surface water. The groundwater was free of corrosion.

(7) Section CK187 +800 ~ CK190 +260 was water shortage zone (II_2). The rocks were subject to severe tectonic impacts. Joint fissures were relatively developed. The groundwater was mostly stored in the fissures in weathered bedrock and in the fissures of intraformational joints in rock. According to the calculation, unit normal inflow of 744.8m^3/(d · km) was predicted in the section at the location where the tunnel crossed. The maximum inflow at the location of the tunnel's crossing was estimated to be 1832.2m^3/d. No sign of large amount of big water inrush sign would occur in this section at the location of the tunnel's crossing but swell of groundwater may be found in the section of shallow embedment across the gully. Some amount of weathered fissure water was contained in the tunnel exit. The main water supplies to the groundwater were atmospheric precipitation, snow-melt and surface water. The groundwater was free of corrosion.

This tunnel crossed the region with following adverse geological conditionsgeological development mainly including landslide, debris flow and rock deposits etc. as described as below:

1. Landslide

Dapping landslide: located on the left bank of gully on east of section CK176 +030 is a rocky ancient landslide zone with its plane of typical "dustpan shape" with its front edge into reaching gully bed. The landslids zone is in length of 700m and average width of 360m. The landslide body consisted of slate in carboniferous system. The landslide zone was around 30m thick with its upper part consisting of crushed stone around 5-15m and relatively integrated lower part. This landslide formation cause was the tectonic. The tectonic landslide was resulted from fault f_{12} and the landslide body was located on north side of this fault while the edge on south side was the crushed belt of this fault. This landslide was formed in early time and now there is no sign of deformation and is stable, its current state was free of deformation signs and was in stable state. The route, in form of tunnel, crossed the landslide zone at around 100m west side of its rear edge and thus was escaped free from the impacts of this landslide.

The upper stream landslide of Zhangou: a rocky landslide located on the right bank of Dazhangou gully on east side of the section CK186 +070. The bed of the slide consisted of Permian slate mixed with sandstone. The slide body consisted of slate and sandstone breccias and was in estimated thickness around 20m with plane state in "dustpan shape". The middle and rear part of the slide body formed platform terrain with steep front edge. The slide body was 210m long and of average width of 250m. The landslide in current state presented stable state without any sign of deformation. The route in form of tunnel with shallow burial depth of approximately 320m crossed west edge of the landslide and thus free from the effect of the landslide. in form of tunnel with burial depth around 320m and was free from the effect of this landslide.

Wayaogou No. 1 landslide: is a loess landslide located in the right bank in middle stream of Wayaogou on east of section CK189 +240 with its (the branch gulley on right side of the downstream of Suzigo. The rear edge of this landslide was in form of "circular-backedround-backed armchair". The slide body was Quaternary weathered loess of thickness around approximately 10-15m. The slide bed consisted of tertiary system sandstone and breccias. The upper loess slide along surface of bedrock and its front edge penetrated down into reached the bed of gulley. The landslide body was in average slope gradient of 30° and in length of 280m, width around 320m. The front edge of this slide body was avoided and the slope face was subject to severe scour of rain. Fine gulley was developed and of with poor stability. The route in form of tunnel penetrated down into the lower bedrock at the front edge of the landslide and the tunnel burial depth was around 70m and thus free from the impact of surface earth landslide.

Wayaogou No. 2 landslide: a loess landslide located on the left bank of the downstream of Wayaogou (right branch gulley on the downstream of Sizigou) east side of the section CK189 + 670. The rear edge of this landslide was in form of "circuarcircularround-backed armchair" and the slide body was Quaternary weathered loess. The upper loess slided along the surface of bedrock and its front edge penetrated down into reached the gulley bed and were subjected to the scour of flood. The landslide body was of average slope gradient of 25°. The slipping mass was in length of 400m and approximate width around 450m. The slipping mass of this landslide was free stood and the gully on slope surface developed, crushed and of poor stability developed on the slope surface. The route in form of tunnel penetrated through the bedrock at the location of around 100m apart away from the west edge of the landslide and the tunnel was thus free from impact of the earth landslide.

2. Debris flow

The debris flow on slope surface debris flow at the tunnel entrance: is the slope surface debris flow on the slope surface on west bank of Zhanghe River at the tunnel entrance in the section CK171 + 590 ~ CK172 + 190 on the west bank of Zhanghe River. The great deposit of diluvial crushed stones were largely deposited was in with thickness less than 5m and its frequent activities were found took place in rainy seasons. The entrance portal of tunnel starts commenced at the location of CK171 + 800 on the route under great effect of the debris flow.

The debris flow of the small gulley in west side of on west side of Jiudianzi: located in the section at location of CK172 + 860 ~ CK172 + 990 and the downstream of one gully on the west of Jiudianzi, namely passage section of this debris flow gulley abundant in which diluvial deposited crushed stone and soil was rich. Within the flow area, solid and loose substances mainly originated from the slope deposited layers on the slope surface and dominant sandstone fragments of carboniferous system dominated. The tunnel route penetrated down below the gulley in form of the tunnel and was thus free from impact of the debris flow.

The debris flow of the northern branch gulley of Laoyoudian: was the branch gulley on the left bank of upper stream of Laoyoudian Gulley and located at location of Nanshuigou at CK181 + 630 ~ CK181 + 910 of Nanshuigou, was a section of debris flow deposit section and deposit diluvial crushed sandstone with deposit thickness greater than 5m. Within the drainage basin, deposited breccias on the slope surface were abundant rich and the debris flow activity is found took place frequently. The tunnel on the route penetrated down under the gulley and was thus free from impacts of the debris flow.

Luzha debris flow: located at CK183 + 950 ~ CK184 + 280, namely the discharging area of discharge areas of debris flow from 4 gullies in as Hualiwan, Woniupingwan and Mazigou and others so forth. The diluvial deposits of debris flow was deposits of debris flow were abundant rich and were mainly crushed stone soil with thickness greater than 5m. The tunnel foundation on the route penetrated down under the gullies and was thus free from the impact of the debris flow at that location.

Dazhangou debris flow: located at the section range of CK186 + 265 ~ CK186 + 350, namely the formed section formed on upper stream of Dazhangou debris flow. There was small quantity of diluvial crushed stone soil in the gulley and the mountains in upper stream gulley area was mountains in upper stream gulley area were well covered with vegetations. The rock weathering was weak and the loose stratum substances on the slope surface was in thin layer mainly of harmful gulley entrance belts. The tunnel on the route penetrated down through under the gulley and was thus free from the impact of the debris flow at that location.

3. Talus

One talus adverse geological ground developed at location CK175 + 880 ~ CK175 + 970 of route. That talus was subjected to impacts of faults f_{11}、f_{12} and was the deposits from collapsed steep terranceterrace of bedrock of the fault and the deposit was in thickness ranging 3-7m and basically was original rock deposits. The tunnel on this route penetrated down into and through under the talus and was thus free from its impact.

II. Terms and terminology

engineering geology	工程地质学
geotechnics	地质学
settlement	沉降,沉降量
depth of burial	埋深
seepage	渗流
site exploration	现场勘探
drill	钻孔
exploratory boring	勘探钻孔
sampling intervals	取样间距
standard penetration testing (SPT)	标准贯入试验
cone penetration testing (CPT)	静力触探试验
Triaxial test	三轴试验
consolidation	固结
Atterburg limits	阿太堡限度,含水限度
jointed rock mass	节理岩体
observational method	观察法
piezometers	压力计,压强计

III. Questions and difficult sentence analysis

1. Questions for brainstorming discussion

(1) Discuss the main works of Site investigation and field testing in tunneling.

(2) Discuss the importance of investigation for tunnel engineering.

(3) Discuss the parts included in a tunneling investigation reports.

2. Difficult sentences analysis

(1) Thus, soil mechanics and rock mechanics are to geotechnical engineering what structural mechanics is to structural engineering.

译文：因此，土力学和岩石力学对于岩土工程就像结构力学对于结构工程一样重要。

(2) The analysis results are used to develop geotechnical input for design processes.

译文：分析结果用于设计过程中的岩土参数输入。

(3) In many cases, old "rules-of-thumb" and "status quo" approaches can result in an unconscious "by-passing" of critical steps.

译文：在很多情况下，旧的"经验法则"及"依照现状"法能在关键步骤中无意识地成为"旁门左道"。

(4) Correlation in general should never be used as a substitute for an adequate subsurface investigation program, but rather to complement and verify specific project-related information.

译文：总之，关联绝不能代替充分的地下土层勘察计划，而是补充并证实特定项目相关的资料。

IV. Translation case study

Case 1

Chinese	English translation
地勘 　地勘按照国际标准执行。地勘技术要求中要求地勘需按照英标执行。 　地质资料的准确性与精细程度，对隧道基础方案选择以及控制不均匀沉降至关重要；应通过多种勘察手段（物理勘察、地质钻孔及室内试验、原位测试如CPTU、十字板、标准贯入试验等）分阶段逐步开展勘察工作，以准确掌握隧道区工程地质情况，提供准确的设计参数。 　勘察阶段可分为初步设计勘察、施工图设计勘察以及补充勘察；现场勘察量应满足各阶段的要求，初步设计阶段钻孔间距应不大于150m，全部钻孔完成后勘探点间距应在50m之内。	Soil-investigations 　The soil-investigations shall be carried out to high international standards. The technical specification of the soil-investigations requires that the soil-investigations shall be carried out in accordance with the British Standards. 　The accuracy and level of the detailed geology data is vital to the selection of tunnel foundation solutions and the control of differential settlement. Therefore different methods should be used (physical investigation, boreholes, and laboratory test and in-situ test, e.g. CPTU, vane shear, SPT and so on) in different phases to get attain a correct understanding of the site conditions so as to provide accurate design parameters. 　Investigation could be divided into the stages of PD, DD and supplementary investigation. The site investigation works amount in each phase should meet the corresponding requirement for each stage. PD borehole shall be made at interval no greater than 150m. The final survey point spacing should be within 50 m after the completion of all the boreholes.

continue

Chinese	English translation
对于沉管隧道基础,勘察工作中应特别关注地基的压缩性指标、渗透系数。 地勘将包括较小间距的 CPTU 探孔,以及成对布置的 CPTU 孔和钻孔用于对比修正岩土参数和室内试验结果(三轴试验和固结试验)。 土层分类将按照英标和中国标准进行。	For the immersed tunnel foundations the soil investigation should focus on the compressibility and permeability of the ground. The soil investigations shall consist of closely spaced CPTUs, CPTU placed in pairs and boreholes for site calibration of soil parameters and laboratory test results (e.g. triaxial tests and consolidation test). Stratum stratification shall be made in accordance with both the British Standards and Chinese Standards.

Case 2

Chinese	English translation
碎屑岩类孔隙裂隙水 碎屑岩类风化裂隙孔隙水主要分布在基岩风化节理裂隙中,含水岩组主要由白垩系沉积岩组成。地下水位不定,该类地下水水量一般较小,仅在局部风化节理裂隙发育地带可形成富水,局部可接受上部松散岩类孔隙水补给外,径流是其主要的补给和排泄方式。 AA002-2 桩+700 ~ AA002-3 桩+580m:长度约 2.85km。海岸平原,地形稍起伏,地表植被较发育,以灌木、杂草为主。地层主要为细砂,灰黄色,干,稍密~中密,揭露厚度 3.0m,未揭穿,用锹可挖掘,土石等级为Ⅱ级。勘察期间未见地下水。	Fissure water of clastic rock type The pore water of weathered fissure of clastic rock type is mainly distributed in the weathered jointed fissure of bedrock and the aquifer is mainly formed by sedimentary rock of Cretaceous period. The level of groundwater is unstable and the amount of this type of groundwater is generally small and abundant water can be developed only in the developed locally weathered jointed fissure. Except that local parts can receive the water supply from upper fissure water of loose rock type and the stream run off is mainly water supply and discharge pattern. The section from stake No. AA002-2 + 700 to No. AA002-3 + 580m is of approximate length of 2.82km and is coastal plain with slight fluctuation of landform. The top vegetation cover is well developed with mostly bushes and wild grass. The stratum mostly consists of fine sand which is greyish yellow in color, dry and slightly dense to medium dense; The penetration depth into the stratum is only 3.0m instead of through penetration and thus can be made with shovels. The exposed soil-stone is in class Ⅱ. No groundwater was seen during survey period.

Case 3

Chinese	English translation
样本跟踪 无论实验室试验在内业开展还是分包给其他单位,样本都很可能获得一个实验室识别编号,该编号为不同现场编制的识别编号。应该列出一个实验室编号和现场编号对照表。该表还能提供追踪信息,确保每个样送达到实验室。当要求开展实验室试验时,申请单上应该包括现场识别编号和实验室编号。电子表或数据库有助于管理样本识别数据。	Sample tracking Whether the laboratory testing is performed in-house or is subcontracted, samples will likely be assigned a laboratory identification number that differ from the identification number assigned in the field. A list should be prepared which matches the laboratory identification number with the field identification number. This list can also be used to provide tracking information to ensure that each sample arrived at the lab. When requesting laboratory testing, both the field identification number and the laboratory identification number should be used on the request form. A spreadsheet or database program is useful to manage sample identification data.

Chinese	English translation
样本储存 　　在储存和运输非扰动土样本的时候,应尽量保持其含水率和自然状态一样。样本应避免阳光直射,哪怕是短暂的照射。非扰动土样本应直立摆放保存,样本顶板向上。	Sample storage 　　Undisturbed soil samples should be transported and stored so that the moisture content is maintained as close as possible to the natural conditions. Samples should not be placed, even temporarily in direct sunlight. Undisturbed soil samples should be stored in an upright position with the top side of the sample up.
样本处理 　　如果对非扰动土(原状土)样本处理不小心,可能导致重大扰动,以至于对设计和施工产生严重的直接影响。应该一直由经验丰富的人员处理样本,以确保样本结构整体性和天然水分。用于加工样本的锯子和刀应该干净、锋利。尽可能缩短加工时间,尤其在某些部位,保持水分是关键。样本存放应该避免阳光直接照射,防冻或遭受雨水。	Sample handling 　　Careless handling of undisturbed soil samples may cause major disturbances that could lead to serious design and construction consequences. Samples should always be handled by experienced personnel in a manner that ensures that the sample maintains structural integrity and natural moisture condition. Saws and knives used to prepare soil specimens should be clean and sharp. Preparation time should be kept to a minimum, especially where the maintenance of moisture content is critical. Specimens should not be exposed to direct sun, freezing, or precipitation.
选择样本 　　选择具有代表性的样本用于实验室采样和试验程序中最重要的方面之一。所选样本必须代表所勘察的地层结构或沉积层。高级实验师,地质学家及/或者岩土工程师应该研究钻孔记录,了解现场地质情况,在挑选试验样本之前,仔细目测样本。应该根据样本的颜色、外形及结构特征挑选样本。不连续、带有杂质的样本可能会在实验室中过早断裂。如果这些特征不突出,位置是任意的样本,就不一定在现场导致那样的断裂。应该注意局部断裂破坏,但不能选作代表该沉积层。	Specimen selection 　　The selection of representative specimens for testing is one of the most important aspects of sampling and testing procedures. Selected specimens must be representative of the formation or deposit being investigated. The senior laboratory technician, the geologist and/or the geotechnical engineer should study the drilling logs, understand the geology of the site, and visually examine the samples before selecting the test specimens. Samples should be selected on the basis of their color, physical appearance, and structural features. Specimens should be selected to represent all types of materials present at site, not just the worst or the best. Samples with discontinuities and intrusions may prematurely fail in the laboratory. If these features are small and randomly located, however, they would not necessarily cause such failures in the field. Such local failures should be noted but not selected as representatives of the deposit.

V. Assignment

(1)调查与测绘是工程地质勘察的主要方法。通过观察和访问,对隧道通过地区的工程地质条件进行综合性的全面研究,将查明的地质现象和获得的资料,填绘于有关的图表与记录本中,这种工作统称为调查测绘(调绘)。

(2)对沿线居民调查访问,可以了解有关问题的历史情况及当地与自然灾害做斗争的经验,这对于直接观察,往往是必不可少的补充。在某些情况下,这种方法显得尤其重要。例如,对历史地震情况的调查,对沿线洪水位的调查,对风沙、雪害、滑坡、崩塌、泥石流等不良地质的发生情况、活动过程和分布规律的调查,都离不开调查访问。

(3)工程地质条件包括岩层性质、地质构造、岩层产状、裂隙发育程度及风化程度、隧道所处深度及其与地形起伏的关系、地层含水程度、地温及有害气体情况、有无不良地质现象及其影响等。

(4)初勘阶段主要以调查和测绘为主,配合物探,并充分利用以往地质资料,只有当不进行钻探,试验工作不足以说明地质情况而影响方案的选定时,才作代表性的钻探试验工作。调查和测绘是隧道地质勘探最基本、最重要的勘探方法。

(5)随着社会发展,人们对环境保护要求提到议事日程,保护环境,改善环境已列入国家法律,因而在隧道设计、施工中必须提高对环境保护的意识。否则,会给周围环境造成不良影响,致使周围环境质量下降,对于环境保护问题,应按照国家颁布的法律规定中有关规定。

Unit 5　Drill and Blast Method
钻　爆　法

Ⅰ. Text

Text A　Working Procedure of Drill and Blast Method
钻爆法工序

In ancient times rock was bored with hammer and chisel. From the 16th to the 19th Century stoking was applied. The tunnel face was heated by fire and subsequently cooled with water. As a consequence, cracks appeared that made the rock easier to excavate. Rock blocks were removed by splitting. Wooden spikes were placed into drilled holes; added water caused swelling of the spikes and split the rock. The drill and split method is also applied nowadays, where the rock is split with the aid of steel chisels. This method is applied where vibrations due to drill and blast have to be avoided. The maximum excavation rate with this technique is 1m per 24h.

For practical reasons the excavated profile does not coincide with the intended one. Under profile (i. e. deficient excavation) can be detected by means of templates or geodetic devices. Subsequently the remaining rock has to be removed (scaling) with excavator or cautious blasting.

Over profile (also called over break), i. e. surplus excavation (over excavation) can be due to bad geological conditions, and is thus inevitable, and /or due to improper excavation. It causes additional costs for the contractor, as it has to be filled with shotcrete. Thus, the distinction between both types of over break is of economic importance. A certain amount of over break, represented by a strip of the width should be allowed for, as required by the technical equipment. It should be specified by the contractor. A strip of the width is to specify the "geological" over break, i. e. the over break imposed by the geological conditions.

1. Tunnel construction operation by method of drilling and blasting

The principal construction procedure of tunneling by drilling and blasting comprises excavation, mucking, supporting and lining. The construction process by this method is to dig out soil and stone from strata to form tunnel profiling in compliance with design and carries out necessary supporting and lining to constraint the deformation of surrounding rock and ensures long term safe use of tunnel. To assuring proceeding of principal procedures necessary power and mechanical equipment shall be furnished and its necessary ventilation, lighting, drainage and control and anti-dust facilities shall be equipped with.

2. Excavation by drilling and blasting

Drilling and blasting excavation operation is the primary one in tunnel construction by drilling and blasting method and blastholes of some whole diameter and depth is drilled and chiseled in rock body in the operation and charge explosive in the bore for blasting so as to reach objective of excavation. Excavation operation accounts for the large works quantity in whole tunnel works quantity and its building cost accounts for 20% to 40% of total tunnel cost. Hence excavation by drilling and blasting is a key and fundamental operation in tunnel construction.

Excavation operation shall meet following requirements:

(1) Excavating profile by design requirement (including requirements on shape, size, surface flatness, under and over excavation amount).

(2) Rock blast mass degree (size of rock blast) shall be moderate and rock blast disposal range shall be concentrated relatively for easiness of muck loading and transportation.

(3) Works quantity of blast holes is small and advancing speed is fast and takes shorter operation cycle time and equipment and material for drilling and blasting shall be saved as much as possible.

(4) Blasting shall reduce damage of vibration to surrounding rock under precondition of capacity of blasting is fully mobilized to ensure stability of surrounding rock.

(5) Reducing damages to construction plant and equipment and supporting structure and reducing damage to surroundings (particularly when blasting tunnel portal section).

3. Rock blasting mechanism to break rock and relevant concept

The blasting reaction of explosives is redox reaction of organic materials and has special features of high temperature, high pressure and high speed. The explosion process of explosives is propagation process of explosive wave namely is the process of explosion generating gas and initiating acting. When explosive charges are exploding in rock (earth) body, the explosive wave bombarding rock surface and is propagating in form of impacting wave in rock body thus forming dynamic stress field. The impacting wave is of short acting time and its energy density is extremely high and causes comminuted damages to the rock surrounding blast holes.

The drill and blast method consists of several subsequent steps (drilling, charging, tamping, ignition, extraction of fumes by ventilation, mucking loading and unloading and disposal, support and lining).

Step one: Drilling of blast holes

Drilling patterns depend on the size and shape of the tunnel and the quality of the rock to be excavated. Rock that is badly fractured will require a lesser number of holes than massive formation with few seams. There must not only be enough volume in drill-holes to permit placing sufficient explosives to break out the rock, but the holes must be placed sufficiently close in blocky rock so that the resulting muck will be in small enough pieces to be handled efficiently by the mucking machine. It is possible to estimate the number of drill holes for a given rock condition based on physical characteristics of the rock and theoretical design of the explosive charge required. The required pattern must be determined by trial and error. It is unusual that a given condition will be as estimated or continuous for any great length of tunnel. It is more usual that the conditions will change from round to round. It is necessary for an experienced tunnelman to be at the heading during each round where changing conditions are being experienced so that the drill pattern can be adjusted as required. Rotary and percussion drilling is applied to drive blast holes within a diameter range from 17 to 127mm (mostly being about 40mm) with drilling rates of up to 3m/min into rock. The prescribed positions, orientations and lengths of blast holes must be kept precisely; therefore, the drilling equipment is mounted on tire carriages, called jumbos, with 2-6 booms. The length of the blast holes corresponds to the advance step (usually 1-3m). To achieve good blast results, the advance step should not exceed the minimum curvature radius of the tunnel cross section (parallel cut).

The commonly used blasting method in tunnel is blasting by drilling blast holes and the main contents consist burn cut hole technique, determination of number of blast holes, arrangement of blast holes and charging and ignition.

The number of blast holes range between several tens to over one hundred. By location of holes, blasting effect, hole arrangement and relevant parameters the hole types are generally classified into following three types:

(1) Burn cut hole.
(2) Relief hole.
(3) Trim hole.

Types of cuts: The quality of cuts will influence blasting quality and directly influence successful blasting of whole tunnel. According to construction method, size of excavation profiles and difference surrounding rock conditions and rock chiseling equipment the cutting ways can be classified into inclined cut hole and straight cut hole.

Angled cut hole including conical cut hole, wedge cut and single inclined cut. Vertical wedge cuts and conical cuts are most commonly applied in tunnel blasting.

Straight cut includes cylindrical cut and spiral cut.

In order to enable the rock to break out of its confined conditions ahead of the tunnel face, it is necessary to eject some of the rock back into the tunnel(临空面) to form exposed face which is also called free face, the excavation face exposed to air to make room for the expansion of the main body of rock. Formerly, this was accomplished by using a number of cut holes(掏槽眼), usually four to six drilled in a wedge or pyramid shape near the center of the face, with the apex in the direction of advance. *These holes should be drilled a little beyond the depth of the other holes and are blast first so that the rock within the cut holes would be thrown into the open tunnel.* Sometimes this throw is for a considerable distance, causing damage to timber or steel sets and more time for mucking the scattered rock. This method has been largely replaced by the "burn cut", which provides one or more large holes near the center of the face, not loaded with explosives, into which the rock inside the first ring of closely spaced loaded holes expands when blasted. These large holes are up to 5 inches in diameter. The advantage of the "burn" cut(直眼掏槽) is that all drill holes are approximately parallel to the tunnel, rather than at an angle, and the rock is not thrown so far from the face as with wedge cuts（锲形掏槽）. The burn cut hole may be enlarged by loading and exploding closely spaced surrounding holes so that all shot rock（爆碎石料）is ejected from the hole, thus making more room for the expansion of rock from following explosions. This is called a cylinder cut（桶形掏槽）. The holes outside the cut holes and inside the perimeter are called relief holes（辅助眼,扩大眼）whose function is to reduce disturbance to surrounding rocks. One set of relief holes may be sufficient in small headings. For large headings, two, three or more sets may be necessary to prevent an undue burden on the trim holes（周边眼）. The outside holes along the perimeter are called trim holes. The bottom holes（底板眼）are called lifters（底部炮眼）.

  The most economical drill is a jackhammer, which should be supplied with a wet head when used in a tunnel. Because horizontal drilling with a hand-held drill is very tiring, jack legs or air legs have been developed to support the drill on extendable pneumatic legs, which, in turn, are supported by the tunnel floor or drill jumbo platform. A refinement is ladder drilling, in which the air leg drill propels itself along a steel ladder frame. Although one man can operate an air leg drill, a helper per one to three drills is available to get the best production. For drilling in high labor cost countries, 1/3 to 4 inches bore drifter drills with automatic feed devices, mounted on hydraulically positioned booms supported on drill jumbos, have been found to be most economical. One miner can supervise several automatic drills（and, on some of the Swiss tunnels, as many as seven）. Union regulations may limit this to fewer and even require helpers on each drill, greatly increasing the cost. Prior to the advent of hydraulic booms, drills were mounted on pipe column bars spanning the width or height of the tunnel. Later the column bars were supported on jumbos.

  Drill jumbos have made it possible to drill any size tunnel full face. With decks at 6 to 8 feet spacing, the hydraulic boom-mounted drills can cover the entire face, drilling holes at any angle. Jumbos are of three general types. Main line track-mounted jumbos ride on the haulage track. They are pulled back to a side near a face when not in service. This type is suitable for small tunnels. Straddle track jumbos are designed to ride on wide gauge track to permit haulage on the main line through them. They straddle the haulage track, so when not in service they need to be hauled back only far enough to avoid damage from the blast at the tunnel face. This type is suitable for large tunnels. Rubber-tired or crawler-mounted jumbos are suitable for use in tunnels using truck haulage. Jumbos are designed so that deck platforms cover the entire width of the tunnel. The sections outside the frame or interfering with haulage can be dropped on hinges to provide clearance for moving the jumbo away from the face and to permit trains to pass through the straddle-track type. A minimum of 25 square feet of face should be allowed for each drill in small tunnels. In larger tunnels, enough drills should be provided to limit the number of holes per drill to a maximum of 8 to 10 per round.

  Tungsten carbide bits are now almost universally used for rock drilling. Bits integral with the 7/8 inch or 1 inch drill rods used with air drills are usually 11/2 to 15/8 inches in diameter, and thrown away after their useful life of 400 to 900 feet of drilling. This bits used with 11/4 inches diameter drifter drill steel are detachable and in sizes from 11/2 to 17/8 inches. They have a life of 300 to 400 feet of drilling in hard rock such as granite. Bits require sharpening on a grinding wheel after 40 to 50 lineal feet of drilling.

Drilling time taken: Rock will penetrate up to 4 feet/minute, depending on the hardness and quality of the rock. The drills are mounted on a drill jumbo (凿岩台车) that must be parked several hundred feet away from the face. Time for moving the jumbo to and from the face and for changing steel and moving drills from hole to hole must be added to the actual drilling time. Actual production will usually be from 1 to 2 feet/minute, allowing for lost time.

Step two: Charging

Lengthy charges are applied in tunneling. Charging depends on the types of explosive. Cartridges (药包) are pushed with the help of rod, powders (such as "ANFO", a mixture of ammonium nitrate and fuel oil) and emulsions are cast or pumped into the boreholes.

The types and quantity of explosives:

There are several types of explosives. Explosive gelatin like ammongelite or gelamon are plastic, have a high strength and develop large gas volume (approximately 800L/kg). They are water resistant and allow safe handling. The detonation speed is 6.5km/s. Explosives are an important cost issue. *The required amount of explosives increases with decreasing tunnel cross section and increasing rock strength. It ranges between 0.3 and 4.3kg/m.*

Step three: tamping

Explosion is the "instantaneous" transformation of the solid (or fluid) explosive into a mixture of gases called fume. To achieve pounding, the fume must be contained, i.e. its expansion must be hindered. This is why blast holes are tamped, i.e. plugged. Since the impact of the fume is supersonic, the strength of the plug is immaterial. Thus, a sufficient tamping is obtained with sand or water cartridges. In long blast holes even the inertia of the air column provides a sufficient tamping. Tamping increases pounding of the rock and reduces the amount of toxic blast fumes by improving the chemical transformation of the charge. Tamping, in particular with water, is also a countermeasure against dust production.

Step four: Ignition

Detonation is oxidation, where oxygen is present in compound form within the explosive. The reaction from propagates within the explosive with a detonation velocity which amounts up to 8km/s and depends on the chemical composition, size, containment and age of the explosives. The detonation front leaves behind the fume, which is a highly compressed gas mixture. 1kg explosives produce gas volume of nearly 1m under atmospheric pressure. The highly compressed fume exerts a large pressure upon its containment. The energy content of an explosive is not overly high, but the rate at which this energy is released corresponds to a tremendous power. Modern explosives are inert against hits, friction and heat. They can only be ignited with a (smaller) initial explosion. Therefore, ignition occurs through electric detonators and detonating cords.

Electric cords consist of a primary charge, which is susceptible against heat, and a less susceptible secondary one. The primary charge is ignited by means of an electric glow wire. A retarding agent can be added in such way that the explosion is released some milliseconds after closing the circuit. The detonators are placed in the bottom of the blasting holes. Electric detonators have a higher retardation accuracy (which is important for smooth blasting) and can be ignited with a coded signal.

Denoting cords (from 5 to 14mm) have a core made of explosive and are ignited with an electric detonator. The detonation propagate along the cord with a velocity of approx imately 6.8km/s. Modern variants ("Nonel", "Shockstar") are synthetic flexible tubes, whose inner walls are coated with 10-100g/m explosive (Nitropenta). Detonating cords allow bunched ignitions with only one electric detonator. The power of detonators reduces with time, but appropriate storage ensures a long life.

Distribution of charges and consequence of ignition:

The explosion aims at breaking the rock into pieces which are manageable for haulage; avoiding over break or insufficient excavation profile (so-called smooth blasting) and not disturbing the surrounding rock. To this end, several schemes (drilling and ignition patterns) have been empirically developed for the distribution of charges and the consecution of ignition. It is distinguished between production and contour drill holes. The most efficient excavation is obtained if the fume pushes the rock against at free surface. This can be achieved, e.g. with a V-cut ("edge" or "fan" out). The blast holes in the central part of the face are conically arranged and ignited first. The surrounding blast holes are ignited consecutively with a delay of some milliseconds. Thus the rock is progressively pared, from the cut to the contour. Parallel blast holes ("parallel cut") are easier to drill precisely and enable longer advance steps but require more explosive than conically arranged ones V-cuts). Several unloaded drill holes are provided in the parallel cut, creating thus a cavity against which the detonation pushes the rock. Thus the efficiency is increased. For smooth blasting, the contour holes have a small spacing (e.g. 40-50mm) and are charged with detonating cords. Smooth blasting helps to minimize the costly after-treatment (post-profiling).

In case of anisotropic, jointed or stratified rock, the distribution of blast holes and the ignition pattern have to be adapted to the structure of the rock. The various work steps for drill and blast are repeated cyclically. Adjusting and optimization of the blasting scheme with regard to the individual rock properties are therefore recommended. This can be accomplished by the aid of computers.

It is important that the holes in the drill pattern be blasted in the proper sequence to obtain the best breakage and muck pile formation. To accomplish this, electric detonators with built-in delays of fixed periods are used. These have largely replaced the caps and different lengths of fuse in earlier days. The cut holes are fired first, followed by the inner set of relief holes and progressively toward the outer relief holes. The corner relief holes perform best if fired after the adjacent holes have fired. Trim holes are usually fired in rotation with the bottom holes heavily loaded and fired last for hand mucking. For machine mucking, top holes are usually fired last.

Step five: mucking

The excavated material in a tunnel is known as muck and the loading of it into vehicles for transportation is known as mucking. Loading the muck on truck and transporting it out of tunnel is an important procedure in improving tunnel heading progress. This operation often accounts for 35% to 50% of total excavation time and is critical to tunnel works progress speed. Thus correctly selected loading machine and transportation vehicles and their preparation, determination of rational muck loading and transportation proposal, maintaining and properly repairing the transportation access, reducing mutual interference, improving muck loading efficiency is critical to speeding up tunnel works progress, particularly to speeding up larger and long tunnel works construction speed. In choosing mucking methods the size of tunnel profiling, geological condition of surrounding rock, excavated volume in one excavation, associated capacity of machines, economics and construction time requirement shall be taken into consideration comprehensively. Muck loading and transportation operation consists of three procedures: loading, transportation and unloading. After a round has been blasted, some of the rock that has been broken loose will hang in a precarious position, endangering the safety of the crew. On returning to the face after a blast, the walls and roof should be washed down to permit careful inspection of the rock surface. The first operation is to scale down any loose rock in the tunnel roof or sides that might cause injury to personnel. This usually takes only a few minutes and is accomplished while equipment and services are being brought forward and prepared for mucking. The largest capacity mucking machine that can operate in the tunnel without restricting motion will usually produce the best results. In tunnels using rail for haulage, mucking machines are usually of two types, rail-mounted with a bucket arranged to scoop up the muck and cast is back over the top of the machine directly into cars such as the Conway, which can not only discharge into the cars but also acts as a minor storage reservoir while cleaning up. In very small tunnels, it is usually more economical to use an air motor for power. If all other equipment, such as pumps, is also operated by air, it is unnecessary to extend a power cable into the tunnel, thereby saving its cost. For larger tunnels, the cost of air for power becomes too great and is usually replaced by electrically driven equipment. In tunnels using rubber-tired hauling equipment, the mucker can be a caterpillar tractor-mounted or rubber-tired loader. In larger tunnels, revolving shovels are sometimes used, either powered electrically or with diesel engines where the tunnel is wide enough to permit the truck to stand beside the shovel.

In larger tunnels, rubber-tired front end loaders are sometimes used either as conventionally built or (preferably) with the bucket arranged so it can discharge into a truck standing alongside ventilation.

4. Tunnel ventilation during construction

Tunnels must be constantly supplied with fresh air to provide works an adequate amount of quality air, to remove smoke, dust and fumes from the heading, to cool hot tunnels, to dilute natural gases and to remove the exhaust of diesel engines. A tunnel may not be safe to enter even when no operations are in progress because of carbon dioxide from decaying timber or methane gas that may exude from the tunnel walls. The ventilation system is designed to bring fresh air to the tunnel face through a pipe called the fan line, or to draw it through the tunnel by exhausting through the fan line. A blower can be made reversible so that air can be either blown into the tunnel through the line or sucked out through the line. The most common system in use at present consists of light gauge (20 to 26) spirally-crimped pipe with axivane type of in-line electric fans. These have better efficiently when blowing in one direction, so they are usually installed to exhaust air from the face through the vent pipe. It is undesirable to blow air into the heading because it forces the smoke and noxious gases from the blast to travel the full length of the tunnel, creating a hazard to the men working away from the heading or passing through the contaminated air. For short lines or blowing air from the end of the main ventilation duct to the face, "Ventube", a flexible collapsible tube, made by impregnating selected fabrics with a high grade rubber, is sometimes used. The end of the ventilation line should be kept generally within 40 feet of the face.

No one should be allowed to return to the face until the smoke, dust and fumes from the explosives have been expelled. Even explosives with the best fume characteristics produce toxic gases that may be dangerous to breathe. Spraying the muck pile will reduce dust; dissolve soluble toxic gases and can displace non-soluble gases in the muck pile to permit their earlier removal by the ventilation system.

The most commonly encountered dangerous natural gas found in the tunnel is methane (CH_4). It is odorless. Air mixtures with 5% to 15% CH_4 by volume are flammable and will explode in confined areas. Methane, being lighter than air, tends to gather in pockets in the roof. The gas is most commonly found in coal seams, shales and in regions where oil and natural gas is found. Detection can be made by several methods. Flame, safety lamps, designed to indicate the percentage of gas, have been commonly used. Regulations now require the use of electrically operated methane detectors. A spark from equipment or from striking a steel tool on rock can cause an explosion. When such conditions are encountered, it is necessary to use "permissible" equipment designed to prevent sparking. Permissible dynamite is also available where required. In order to prevent concentration of methane above a safe level, it is necessary to provide ample ventilation with small blow pipes or exhaust ducts, directed into pockets where the lighter methane gas tends to concentrate. Concentration of methane gas should be kept to not over 1%. If it exceeds 1.5%, the men should be withdrawn from the areas of excess concentration.

Fans must be operated continuously while men are working underground. If they are not operated when the tunnel is idle, they must be turned on sufficiently in advance of men entering the tunnel to clear it of contaminated air. Atmospheres in all active areas of tunnels should contain at least 19.5% oxygen, and not more than 0.005% carbon monoxide, 0.5% carbon dioxide, and 5ppm nitrogen dioxide. There should be no harmful quantities of other toxic gases, fumes, mists or dusts. Instruments should be available for testing the quality of air and quantity of pollutants.

Text B Explosives
炸　药

In explosive emulsions(乳化炸药), oil serves as the combustible agent(可燃剂). Oxygen is delivered from salt (nitrate) (硝酸盐) solutions available within droplets of 10m diameter. These droplets are covered with a 10m thick oil film. They develop a gas volume of 1000L/kg and a detonation speed of 5.7km/s. They are water resistant, safe in handling and can be pumped into the blast holes or placed within cartridges. The non-explosive components are separately delivered to the construction site, where they are mixed together. Compared with explosive gelatines(凝胶炸药)the strength of explosive emulsions is reduced and therefore about 10% more blast holes are needed. On the other hand, their fumes are less toxic (having, though, a pronounced smell of ammonia), so shorter ventilation is needed and the spoil is less contaminated.

Explosive powders are also safe but not water resistant. With gas volume of 1000L/kg and a low detonation speed of approx imately 1.5m they push rather than shatter the rock.

A recent development is the so-called non-explosive explosives line BRISTAR or CALMMITE. These are expansive cements. Mixed with water and cast into boreholes they expand. Thus developing pressures up to 600 bars and tearing up the surrounding rock.

There are two types of explosives (called powder, in tunnel parlance) in general use for tunnel excavation. They are nitroglycerine dynamites and ammonium nitrates. Dynamites are mixture of nitroglycerine and other substances. They are rated in strength according to the percentage of nitroglycerine. They are manufactured in ratings of 15% to 90%. The energy produced per pound is not in proportion to the percent of nitroglycerine. The blast effect is determined not only by strength, but also by density and velocity. Density can be expressed by the number of cartridges of a particular size contained in a 50lb case. There may be only one-third as many of the denser cartridges as the least dense. In hard rock, the dense dynamites are required to break the rock, so these are generally in tunneling. Cartridges are manufactured in various sizes. Gelatine dynamites are dense and most water-resistant, and up to a 60% rating they have better fume characteristics. Thus, they are preferred for tunneling (40% and 60% gelatins are best adapted to tunnel work).

Ammonium nitrate, in the form of fertilizer prills, when mixed with from 1% to 12% carbon black, powdered coal or fuel oil, has become a favorite explosive in tunnel work because of its lower cost (5% to 7% by weight of fuel oil gives the best performance). It requires a dynamite cartridge in each hole primed with an electric blasting cap to cause it to explode. Ammonium nitrate is not water-resistant so it can only be used in relatively dry tunnels or when encased in plastic bags. Powder companies now market ammonium nitrate prills ready mixed with the necessary admixtures, although mixing can easily be done on the job. This powder may be pneumatically placed in the drill holes.

In order to detonate dynamites it is necessary to insert a blasting cap in one cartridge in each hole. Blasting caps are manufactured for instantaneous explosion or with 15 or more delays and with various wire lengths up to 100 feet. Ordinary delays provide for time intervals from 1/2 to 2 seconds or more between delays. Milliseconds delays have time intervals in the order of hundredth of a second.

The amount of powder required to break rock out from a tunnel heading is much greater than in an open cut because of its confined location. Smaller tunnels require more explosives per unit of excavation than do larger tunnels. Rocks with low RQDs requires less powder than those with high RQDs. Harder massive formations require more powder than softer formations.

Text C A Tunnel Drill and Blast Technical Scheme
一个隧道钻爆技术方案

1. The tunnel excavation and drill and blast design scheme

In this part all the tunnels are short and unidirectional heading from inlet or outlet is planned.

During the tunnel excavation, efficient and control blasting must be adopted to ensure construction safety. YT28 type air-led rock drill and the blasting operation approach of wedge cut are used in heading. Excessively long cyclical penetration depth shall be controlled to avoid generating hazardous blasting effect beyond the limit of safety code. In the said project, the respective cyclical advancement length of 3m for the rate Ⅲ surrounding rock, within 2m for rate Ⅳ surrounding rock and within 1m (not exceeding 2m at lower bench) for rate Ⅴ surrounding rock are designed. While poor strata are encountered, the blasting technician shall improve the drilling depth and blasting parameters in time according to the field situation.

2. Tunneling method

Drill and blast method is used in tunnel excavation. The theory of the New Austrian Tunneling Method is used as guidance to the execution and smooth face blasting. The explosive material is emulsion explosive and the perimeter cut is charged with $\phi25$ small cartridge for smooth surface blasting and rest other holes take $\phi32$ cartridges. Rock mucking is transported with ZL-50 loader with aid of 5t dumper directly to the disposal yard designated by employer.

Smooth surface blasting parameters:

(1) Coefficient of not coupling. The rational coefficient of not coupling shall make the cut hole pressure lower than the rock wall dynamic compressive strength and higher than dynamic tensile strength. Usually, 1.5-2.5 as the coefficient of no coupling is used and 1.7 is selected;

(2) E, the spacing between the holes in smooth surface blasting is generally 8-15 times diameter of blast holes. In the rocks with developed joint fissures, smaller value shall be taken. In the rock with sound integrity, greater value can be taken and 45cm can be used;

(3) W, the minimum lines of resistance. The smooth surface thickness or the distance from perimeter cut to the adjacent auxiliary cut takes 60cm which shall be the minimum line of resistance of smooth face cut at blasting initiation and generally shall be greater than or equal to the spacing between the holes in smooth surface.

3. Tunnel excavation parameter design

1) Construction method and procedure

The construction shall strictly observe design requirement and the principle of New Austrian Tunneling method. In soft ground, the tunnel body excavation shall observe the principle of short drill depth, weakened blasting, strengthened support and lining in early stage. Construction temporary monitoring and surveying shall be strengthened to ensure construction safety. While the disagreement of actual surrounding rock type with design data is encountered in works execution, the supervisor and designer shall be contacted in time and the construction scheme shall be adjusted accordingly to ensure safe excavation and smooth progress. The vehicle station and power distribution room in tunnel shall be expanded after the tunnel shape is formed.

2) Blast holes types

(1) cut hole; (2) relief hole; (3) contour hole.

Explosive Charge Structure is shown in table 5.1.

Explosive Charge Structure Figure   Table 5.1

Structure form	Schematic figure	Statement
interval explosive charge of not coupling	毫秒微差导爆管雷管; 导爆索 炮泥 φ25mm小药卷 φ32mm药卷; 导爆索-detonating cord; 炮泥-stemming plug; φ25mm small cartridge-φ25mm小药卷, φ32mm cartridge-φ32mm 药卷; 毫秒微差异爆管雷管-millisecond micro difference ignitor detonator	1. This figure illustrates the smooth blasting hole charging structure; 2. The detonator outside hole time retardation; 3. Detonating cord initiating blasting
coupling continuous reverse primer charge	导爆管 炮泥 φ32mm药卷; 导爆管-detonator; 炮泥-stemming plug; φ32mm cartridge-φ32mm药卷	This figure illustrate the structure of cut hole, auxiliary hole and bottom hole explosive charging

3) The blasthole layout for tunnel excavation

Excavation by upper and lower bench method in rate III surrounding rock:

(1) Upper bench smooth face blasting, using inclined cut hole, considering 3m cyclical drill depth, the smooth face blasting parameters and holes layout are given below (Table 5.2, Figure 5.1).

Upper Bench Rock Blasting Parameters in Level-III Surrounding Rock   Table 5.2

Blasting sequence	Blast holes	Hole quantity	Hole depth (m)	Detonator section	Explosive quantity (kg)	Note
1	cut hole	4	3.2	1	9.2	1. Each cycle drill depth of 3.0m, blasting efficiency 87%, each cycle earth volume 249.75m³; 2. Unit explosive consumption 0.6kg/m³; 3. Smooth blasting hole trace rate 90%
2	cut hole	6	3.2	3	13.8	
3	auxiliary hole	5	3.1	5	10	
4	auxiliary hole	9	3.1	7	18	
5	auxiliary hole	12	3.1	8	24	
6	auxiliary hole	15	3.1	9	30	
7	perimeter hole	44	3.1	10/11	30.8	
8	bottom hole	20	3.1	12	14	
total		126			149.8	

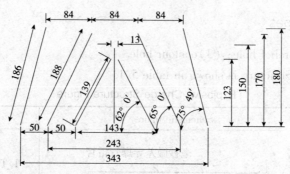

Figure 5.1 Upper Bench Cut Hole Layout(cm)

(2) Lower bench smooth blasting is given in table 5.3.

Lower Bench Rock Blasting Parameter in Level-III Surrounding Rock   Table 5.3

Blasting sequence	Blast holes	Hole quantity	Hole depth (m)	Detonator section	Explosive quantity(kg)	Note
1	auxiliary hole	39	3.0	1-5	78	1. Each cyclical drill depth of 3.0m, blasting efficiency of 87%, each cyclical earth volume of 84.1m^3;
2	perimeter hole	8	3.0	5	5.6	2. Explosive unit consumption is 1.1kg/m^3;
3	bottom hole	11	3.2	7/9	7.7	3. Smooth blasting hole trace rate is 90%
total		48			91.3	

Right and left sided cut jumping excavation is designed as per 3m and the perimeter cut and auxiliary cut charging structure is same as that at upper bench(Figure 5.2).

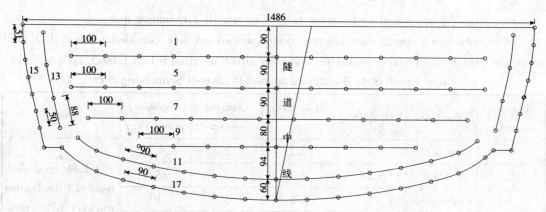

Figure 5.2 Lower Bench Blast holes Layout(right side and left side are separated)(mm)

4) Blasting network

To ensure safe explosion propagation of blasting detonating network, improve blasting quality, reduce blasting harm and facilitate constructional operation, in combination with the matured construction technology and experiences of my company, the blasting network for purpose of the given project proposed to adopt compound momentary difference priming network(复式微差起爆

网络). The detonating network uses plastic detonator and four-way connection and explosion initiating device for priming. To control the hazardous effect of blasting, the maximum explosive quantity in a single blasting shall be 1.5kg with distance of 15-40m from civil residence, and 25kg with more than 40m away. The maximum explosive charge for one blasting operation is 150kg.

To ensure the efficient coordination of blasting network design and field execution to facilitate blasting execution and avoid any wrong distribution of detonators, signs are used and each hole is marked with bamboo sign indicating the hole number, hole depth and locations of all the detonator sections.

II. Terms and terminology

drill and blasting	钻爆法施工
drill hole	钻孔
blast hole	炮眼
surrounding rock conditions	围岩状况(条件)
drill and split	钻裂
presplit	预裂
charging	装炸药
tamping	封堵炮孔,炮孔堵塞
ignition	点炮
extraction by ventilation	通风排气
anti-dust facility	防尘设施
over excavation (overbreak)	超挖(超爆)
mucking	出渣
lining	衬砌
support	支护
burn cut	直眼掏槽
wedge cut	锲形掏槽
cylinder cut	桶形掏槽
relief cut	缓冲辅助眼
perimeter cut	周边眼
bottom cut	底眼
roof cut	顶眼
drill jumbo platform	钻孔车台车
pneumatic leg	气腿
initial spalling	初期剥落
dynamite, explosive	炸药
blasting cap	起爆雷管(火帽)
stemming	炮泥
stand-up time	自稳时间

nitroglycerine	硝化甘油
ammonium nitrates	硝酸铵
gelatin dynamites	胶质炸药
explosive emulsions	乳化炸药
muck	石渣
mucking	出渣
apex	顶点
jackhammer	手提钻
tunnel parlance	隧道用语
detonation	引爆,爆轰
oxidation	氧化反应
detonation velocity	爆轰速度
chemical composition	化学成分
detonating cords	引爆线,导爆索
electric detonator	电雷管
electric glow wire	导电线
primary charge	主装药
secondary charge	副装药
retarding agent	延迟剂,延期药
smooth blasting	光面爆破
nonel	诺雷尔管,由瑞典科学家诺雷尔发明
nitropenta	四硝酸酯
propagate	传递,传爆
contour blasthole	周边钻孔眼
parallel cut	直眼掏槽,平行掏槽
free surface	自由面
detonation speed	炮轰速度

III. Questions and difficult sentence analysis

1. Questions for brainstorming discussion

(1) Discuss the main steps of drill and blasting tunneling.
(2) Discuss the types of cuts and their individual function.
(3) What can we do to reduce overbreaks in drill and blasting?

2. Difficult sentences analysis

(1) In order to enable the rock to break out of its confined conditions ahead of the tunnel face, it is necessary to remove some of the rock outstanding the tunnel face to from an exposed face which is also called free face.

译文:为了使岩石从隧道面前方的狭窄空间中爆炸出来,有必要去掉一些突出于隧道面的岩石,形成暴露在大气中的开挖面,也叫自由面。

(2) These holes should be drilled a little beyond the depth of the other holes and are blasted first so that the rock within the cut holes would be thrown into the open tunnel.

译文:这些孔应该比其他钻孔稍微钻深一些,首先爆炸这些钻孔,使这些掏槽中的岩石被抛掷入隧道中。

(3) The required amount of explosives increases with the incremental decrease of tunnel cross section and increase of rock strength.

译文:随着隧道横截面逐步减小和岩石强度增加,炸药需求量增大。

(4) In case of anisotropic, jointed or stratified rock, the distribution of blast holes and the ignition pattern have to adapt to the corresponding rock structure. All explosion operation procedures are repeated in cycles. Adjusting and optimization of the blasting scheme with regard to the individual rock properties are therefore recommended.

译文:如果是各向异性,节理或层状岩石,炮眼的分布和点燃方式必须适应相应的岩石结构。循环重复各钻爆作业步骤,因此,建议根据不同个体岩石特征,调整和优化钻爆方案。

Ⅳ. Translation case study

Case 1

Chinese	English translation
炸药的性能取决于所含的化学成分。掌握炸药等爆破材料的性能,对正确使用、储存、运输炸药,确保安全和提高爆破效果,具有重要意义。炸药的主要性能为:敏感度,爆速,猛度,殉爆距离,爆炸稳定性和临界直径,最佳密度,管道效应。	The property of explosives is mainly subjected to its chemical components contained. Good knowledge of the property of explosives and explosive materials is of significance to correct use, storage, transportation of explosives and to ensure safety and to improve explosion effect. The primary property of explosives include: sensitivity, sensitivity, explosive velocity, brisance, distance of detonation by influence, explosive stability and critical diameter, optimum density and pipe effect.

Case 2

Chinese	English translation
在乳化炸药中,油起着可燃剂的作用。氧气从直径10m的硝酸盐溶液液滴中获得。这些液滴表面覆盖着10m厚的油膜,这些油膜形成1000L/kg体积的气团,传爆速度为5.7km/s。这些液滴防水,操作安全并能泵入炮眼或装入药卷。非爆炸成分单独运达施工现场,然后当场与滴液混合。	In explosive emulsions(乳化炸药), oil serves as the combustible agent(可燃剂). Oxygen is delivered from salt (nitrate)(硝酸盐) solutions available within droplets of 10m diameter. These droplets are covered with a 10m thick oil film. They develop a gas volume of 1000L/kg and a detonation speed of 5.7km/s. They are water resistant, safe in handling and can be pumped into the blast holes or placed within cartridges. The non-explosive components are separately delivered to the construction site, where they are mixed together.

Case 3

Chinese	English translation
炸药压实：爆炸是固体(或液体)炸药瞬间转化为气体混合物即烟雾的过程。为了实现猛烈冲击，烟雾必须加以限制，即必须阻止烟雾扩散。这就是为什么要压实即用封盖堵住炸药的原因。由于烟雾的冲击力速度达到超声波速度，封盖的强度微不足道，因此，采用砂或水填充才能达到足够的压实强度。在长炮眼中，甚至气柱的惯性也能达到充分压实的效果。通过提高充装炸药的化学变化，压实增加了岩石的冲击力，降低了爆炸毒气量。特别是采用水压实，还是一个抗粉尘的有效措施。	Tamping: Explosion is the "instantaneous" transformation of the solid (or liquid) explosive into a mixture of gases called fume. To achieve pounding, the fume must be contained, i. e. its expansion must be hindered. This is why blast holes are tamped, i. e. plugged. Since the impact of the fume is supersonic, the strength of the plug is immaterial. Thus, a sufficient tamping is obtained with sand or water cartridges. In long blast holes even the inertia of the air column provides a sufficient tamping. Tamping increased pounding of the rock and reduces the amount of toxic blast fumes by improving the chemical transformation of the charge. Tamping, in particular with water, is also a countermeasure against dust production.

V. Assignment

(1)隧道工程中常使用的凿岩机有风动凿岩机和液压凿岩机。另有电动凿岩机和内燃凿岩机，但较少采用。其工作原理都是利用镶嵌在钻头体前端的凿刃反复冲击并转动破碎岩石而成孔。有的可通过调节冲击功大小和转动速度以适应不同硬度的石质，达到最佳成孔效果。

(2)近年来，由于重型凿岩机投入施工，尤其是能钻大于100mm直径大孔的液压钻机投入施工以后，直眼掏槽的布置形式有了新发展。

(3)裂爆破实质上也是光面爆破的一种形式，其爆破原理与光面爆破原理相同。只是在爆破的顺序上，光面爆破是先引爆掏槽眼，接着引爆辅助眼，最后才引爆周边眼；而预裂爆破则是首先引爆周边眼，使沿周边眼的连心线炸出平顺的预裂面。

(4)周边眼原则上沿着设计轮廓均匀布置，间距和最小抵抗限应比辅助眼的小，以便爆出较为平顺的轮廓。

(5)裂缝形成的机理，国内外进行过不少研究，但目前还缺乏一致的认识。

Unit 6　Bored Tunnels
钻　挖　隧　道

I. Text

Text A　Tunnel Boring Machines (TBM)
隧道掘进机(TBM)

Tunnel boring machines (TBM) are used to excavate tunnels in virtually all types of ground and under widely different physical conditions. The hard and soft rock TBM with full-face rotating heads and their development from soft ground shields are elaborated. Roadheaders (boom headers) are also discussed here because of their growing role in the softer rock tunnels and caverns. The innovative ranging mobile miner, which combines some of the advantages of the roadheader and the TBM and can be used in harder rocks, is also covered.

The functions of a TBM are simple enough:
(1) To excavate the ground;
(2) To remove the material excavated;
(3) To maintain line and grade of the excavation;
(4) To support the excavated tunnel temporarily until permanent support can be provided;
(5) To handle adverse ground conditions.

These five simple requirements become less simple when the necessary qualifying conditions are added. The functions must be performed:
(1) Safely;
(2) Reliably;
(3) Continuously for many months;
(4) Through any and all ground conditions;
(5) Quickly;
(6) Economically.

Throughout the development of TBM, a term which implies a rotary action, designers have built on the successes and the failures of their predecessors. In recent years, there has been a great deal of healthy cross-fertilization between designs of machines for hard rock and those for soft ground. _Today's TBM is likely to have been designed specifically for the anticipated ground conditions and is likely to use technology from both hard rock and soft ground machines._

A TBM is subjected to heavy stress and much abuse during its service life. It is worth reflecting that a typical hard rock TBM may be called upon to cut through a wall of rock considerably larger in area than the wall of an average room, the wall being made up of rock of up to 10 times the strength of normal concrete. It must do this steadily, day and night, for many months, perhaps under corrosively saline water inflows, and almost certainly, at some point, through uncooperative ground. Only the state of the art in metallurgy and mechanical design can create a machine that can accomplish this.

1. Historical development

Like many other technical developments, the TBM was designed in concept by men of genius long before the technologies of metallurgy and motive power were advanced sufficiently to meet the challenges the designs imposed. In the period starting in the early 19th Century, numerous tunneling machines were built, largely in United States and Great Britain, many of them with features that can be recognized in the modern TBM. Before that time, soft ground was excavated and supported by hand mining methods, then from the protection of a shield, then from increasingly mechanized shields. The rock tunnels were excavated by explosives set in holes drilled into the face. Subaqueous tunnels in both rock and soft ground were not attempted until the early 19th Century, and the poor success rate led to the development of the shield, and its subsequent mechanization into a TBM.

The history of TBM started with soft ground shields of the type developed by Marc I. Brunel (the senior Brunel) and J. H. Greathead in England. These shields progressed by breaking the excavation into small compartments excavated by hand. The first Brunel shield, patented in 1818, excavated these compartments and advanced the shield in a spiral pattern, with lining segments following in the same spiral. The shield did not rotate, but the spiral arrangement of the head meant that the miner excavated along a spiral path at right angle to the direction of the tunnel. Since the miner was the cutterhead, a case could be made that this was a rotating head "machine", but the verdict is best left to the reader. The first subaqueous tunnel under the Thames at Rotherhithe may have been started in 1827 using one of two Brunel designs patented in 1818, but it was completed nine years later by a newer Brunel-designed compartmented shield, and one with no hint of rotary action in its operation. The completed tunnel lay idle for many years until the dawn of the railway age put it to work, a function it still performs well 160 years later.

The coming of the railway age was a great stimulant to tunnelers. The next two shield tunnels were both successes at least in execution, and were built concurrently in New York and London.

2. Excavation under external water pressure

Until recently, TBM designs were categorized by the hardness of the ground to be encountered or, more precisely, expected to be encountered. While this is clearly an important design consideration, the quantity and pressure of groundwater is as important an influence in the design or selection of the TBM. In a hard rock tunnel, the water inflows are likely to be localized, volcanic lava formations being a notable exception. Water inflows are unlikely to erode or weaken rock in the area of the inflow, whereas water from soft rock or soft ground is likely to carry some of the ground with it. In water-bearing ground, this usually calls for a full watertight lining to be erected within the tail shield of the TBM, the assembled lining ring being extruded from the tail shield through a pressure resisting circumferential seal. Owning to cost or schedule constraints, this is usually the permanent tunnel lining.

The idea of compressing the air inside a tunnel to reduce water inflows, and thereby support the ground, was first tried under the Hudson River in 1879. The technique was successful in a second attempt in 1889 and was used on many subsequent tunnels. Working under compressed air and decompressing after such work was found to be hard on the human body. Limits on time worked under compressed air developed such that other means had to be found to make such tunneling economical. In 1964, the Robbins Etoile TBM used air pressurization of the face ahead of a bulkhead in driving subway tunnels in Paris. But air is compressible, and carries almost explosive potential when compressed to several atmospheres. Preferable are the incompressible semi liquid slurries, which, like water, can transmit, but do not store pressure when under pressure.

Greathead had patented a shield in 1874 that had a face through which slurry could be circulated under pressure to support the face and remove the spoil. The ground was dislodged by being poked by excavating tools through stuffing boxes in the bulkhead. There is no record that it was built. In 1960, E. C. Gardner successfully built a tunnel in Houston, Texas, using a shield with a rotary arm excavator in front of a bulkhead. Water was pumped into the face, and water and spoil slurry pumped out of the invert. The slurry may have played some role in supporting the ground. In 1964, J. V. Barlett patented a Bentonite Slurry TBM, which worked well in London, and in 1974 Ways and Freytag A. G. used their Hydroshield, which used slurry in combination with an air chamber pressure regulation system. These machines, together with a series built by the Tekken Kenetsu Co. , have driven tunnels in very difficult ground and groundwater conditions. The main disadvantage of the slurry TBM is that the spoil removal systems are at the surface, and the inlet and discharge lines must be extended as the tunnel advances. During this extension of the pipes, care must be taken that pressure is not lost at the face. A small leak can produce a large pressure drop and loss of ground support. The circumferential seals between tail shield and the exterior of segment ring are difficult to keep fully watertight under pressure.

In 1963, the Japanese company Sato Kogyo designed an earth pressure balance TBM, which eliminated the need for slurry and, with improved tail seals, made it possible to maintain pressure at the face. Removal of spoil was by screw conveyor inside a pipe, in which the pressure drop to atmospheric level took place. Earth pressure systems are today the preferred system for TBM operating below the groundwater table, and the TBM is designed so that it can operate with or without the system. Spoil removal from high-to-low pressure areas is key to the success of the system.

As soft ground and rock TBM built on each other's experience, they shared more and more features. By the 1980s, of the 11 machines used in the soft chalk of the Channel Tunnel, most were rock machines, but at least 2 were adaptations of soft ground TBM, and 3 had earth pressure balance (EPB) features. The latter were the French undersea TBM, designed to excavate and erect lining under 10 bar external water pressure in fractured and faulted rock.

3. Components of a modern TBM

A modern TBM is a complex system of interdependent parts. A fully equipped TBM can occupy as much as 1000 ft of tunnel, and be made up of mechanisms of cutting, shoving, steering, gripping, exploratory drilling, ground control and support, lining erection, spoil removal, ventilation, and power supply. All of these items must advance with the tunnel heading, and items such as track work, power supply, and ventilation ducting must be extended behind the TBM as it advances.

The key word in the preceding description is interdependent, since all mechanisms must be able to function at a rate consistent with the advance of the cutterhead. Deficiency in performance of any part handicaps the heading advance rate and affects project schedule and cost.

4. Cutting the ground

A TBM excavates rock or soft ground by the rotation of an assembly of teeth or cutting wheels under pressure against the rock face. The teeth, known as drag bits and made of very tough alloy steel tipped with tungsten carbide, excavate softer rocks and soils by a ripping action. As a rough guide, they are suitable for rocks with strength of up to 13000psi (90MPa). The earliest TBM used drag bits. Cutter wheels, again made of tough alloy steel, excavate rock by rolling crushing action under pressure against the rock sufficient to fracture the material. Cutter wheels are suitable for use in rocks up to 40000psi (275MPa) at rates of advance competitive with or exceeding those attainable with drill-and-blast methods of excavation. For even harder rocks the rolling cutters are of different design, embodying carbide buttons in a single-or multiple-disk-shaped wheel. The buttons pulverize the rock. The degree to which the rock is broken is a measure of the energy needed to excavate a unit volume of tunnel. Much work has been done in the past two decades on the mechanisms of rock cutting by drag bits and cutter wheels. The references contain several reports on this continuing work.

The magnitude of the thrust against the face and the torque at the cutterhead are varied to suit the conditions anticipated or encountered. Rotational speeds are slow, typically around 5rpm. The speed at the periphery of the cutterhead is held to 400-500ft per min. The thrust of a modern machine can exceed 2000000Ib, and the load on each cutter 64000Ib. The torque capacity can be as high as 13000000Ib. More than 150 Robbins TBM ago, the machine that began the modern development of the TBM at Oahe Dam, had a thrust of 100000Ib and a torque of 281000Ib.

Soft ground machines can require even higher toque, earth pressure balance machines requiring the highest torque. A rule of thumb for torque on such machines in ton meters is 2 to 2.5 times the diameter in meters cubed.

The cutter wheels move at different speeds across the rock face, depending upon their radial distance from the center of the head. The segment of the wheel in contact with the rock is in a straight line, but it is moving and cutting in a circular path. This subjects the cutter wheel to a sideways twisting action that demands great lateral strength and bearing capacity. The torsion loading on wheels and bearings is reduced by splaying the cutters slightly outward from the line of advance. The outer cutters and the gauge cutters are splayed outward. It is the gage cutters that control the diameter excavated and that give the tunnel its smooth finish. The loading is particularly severe on the cutters nearest the center of the head, where the cutters have a substantial component of rotation about a diametric axis as well as the conventional axial rotation. The effect increases on larger-diameter wheels. Some machines use smaller center wheels for this reason.

The cutter wheels or drag picks are arranged in what at first may appear to be a haphazard pattern over the cutterhead. Closer inspection will show that the wheels are arranged radically to cut grooves separated by a few inches, and circumferentially located to give as balanced a thrust as is practicable to the cutterhead. The pattern of the cutters on the head is an important design feature, since balanced loading on the cutters and the power train is a major factor in component durability.

5. Removing the spoil

As the spoil, or muck, falls from the excavated face, it is picked up by the scoops rotating with the head. In a typical arrangement, the scoops, or buckets, empty into a hopper, which feeds a conveyor belt, which in turn carries it to dump cars at the rear of the train for hauling out of the tunnel. In some tunnels a conveyer belt or trucks are used instead of a train for spoil removal. When the TBM is designed to operate under external water pressure, however, the first part of this handling sequence is not practicable because of the pressure differential between the groundwater and the inside of the tunnel. Means must be found to pass indeterminable mixtures of the rock, soil, mud, and water through the watertight bulkhead of the machine through some form of pressure lock. This is not an easy task.

One spoil removal approach involves the use of two end-to-end encased screw conveyors rotating at slightly different speeds. The conveyors are set at an angle to each other, and the second rotates slower than the first, creating a moving blockage at the angle, in which the pressure drop is achieved. A second technique uses a singe screw conveyor with a breech discharge mechanism to discharge onto a conveyer belt. The arrangement operates like a breech-loading rifle mechanism in reverse, with the spoil taking the place of the bullet.

6. Main bearing, motors and gearboxes

Behind the cutting head is the main bearing, which must absorb the full thrust of the machine. Because of its size and location, failure of the main bearing in operation is a serious occurrence, and as a result the maintenance and treatment of this key item is critical. In this same area the cutterhead main drive motors and gearboxes are located. Machines designed to operate under external water pressure incorporate a watertight bulkhead at this point.

7. Steering shoes, grippers and shove jacks

Arranged around the body of the TBM just behind the cutterhead are the steering shoes, hydraulically operated pads that bear against the ground selectively to keep the TBM on line and grade. These shoes and the grippers also serve to prevent rotation of the body in reaction to the head rotation. If the ground is suitable, the TBM will be designed with gripper pads—large circumferential pads that are thrust hydraulically against the ground to provide a firm base against which the cutting head can be thrust forward. If the ground is soft, the pads will be unable to develop the requisite bearing, and this, together with the need for immediate ground support, leads to the adoption of precast linings. The machine is then designed to develop the thrust necessary for cutting from thrust or shove jacks bearing on the ends of the ring of segments. The erected segment rings are grouted in place, and the liner acts as a long hollow horizontal friction pile against which to shove. In the absence of grippers, this friction pile must also provide torsion reaction resistance for the rotating cutterhead. The grouting also serves the important purpose of providing early support for the heavy loads imposed by the segment erectors and other TBM equipment, which follow behind the cutterhead. Thus the TBM and the lining design must be designed to work together. It is common that the highest loadings the lining will experience will be the combination of grouting loads and the longitudinal forces caused by the TBM shove jacks.

8. Ground support equipment

The ground support equipment is installed behind the main bearings as close to the excavation as is practicable. This can consist of complex precast liner erectors, or relatively simple rock bolting drills, or steel rib erectors, or shotcrete machines, depending on the ground being designed for. In this area will be located any forward ground exploration drills or ground modification grouting rigs. If the machine is designed to use precast linings, it might be built in two parts, front and rear, the one telescoping over the other. This permits the cutting head to move forward a limited amount independently of the lining erector section, which must be stationary during the erection sequence. By this means the excavation, which is a continuous process, can proceed during the lining erection process, which is a cyclical process. This has not yet been achieved in a machine required to operate under external water head because of the need for annular seals where the two outer shells slide over each other, an arrangement that has not be made to work entirely satisfactorily.

9. Backup facilities

At the rear of the train are located the backup facilities, which must be extended behind the TBM as it advances. These include the high-voltage electrical cable reel, ventilation ducting, track-laying equipment and catenaries, if used, and water and drainage lines. At various points along the train, grouting equipment is located to fill the annular space between the segment and the ground, and to redrill the grouted areas to ensure adequate filling of the voids by proof grouting. The support train for a fully equipped TBM can extend as much as 1000ft. If precast linings are used, a large part of the remaining TBM train will be taken up by conveyer belts, segment hoists and gantries, which move the segments from the cars that brought them in and orient them correctly for installation. Through the same area, conveyer belts will carry spoil to the muck cars. Fitted into this restricted space will be the transformers and switchgear, the TBM operator's cabin, and the worker amenities. The difficulty of replacing major items of equipment at the front end of this train during the work will be readily appreciated.

10. Operation of TBM

Steering: If allowed to move forward unattended, a TBM would not advance in a straight line. Variations in ground conditions would deflect it; gravity would tend to move it downward, and buoyancy might tend to move it upward. In addition, the reaction from the rotation of the cutting head and the cutting forces themselves would tend to move the machine from a straight path. Steering a TBM is an art and one not easy to practice off-site.

Steering is achieved by selective use of grippers and shove rams, with some machines being fitted additionally with steering shoes at the front end, these being smaller versions of gripper pads. Guidance on a modern machine is almost invariably by the surveyor such that when the laser beam passes through the center of both targets the TBM is on course.

Why is precise steering so important? In a drill-and-shoot excavation, the tunnel is of necessity oversized, and the forms used for final lining will straighten out short-term irregularities, converting them to lining thickness irregularities. As a result, linings in drill-and-shoot tunnels are usually more than adequate. A TBM bore is also oversize, but only by a few inches to permit steering of the machine, and possibly for tail-shield clearance to segmental liners. If the tunnel is to have a precast lining and the lining is to be expanded against the ground, the finished tunnel will follow the alignment and irregularities of the excavation. Such irregularities, and even some wandering off course, can be tolerated in, say, a water supply tunnel, but in a subway rail tunnel, and even more so in a high-speed rail tunnel, accuracy of alignment and grade is critical. In rail tunnels, the owner is buying a track laid to a precisely specified line and grade, and the tunnel is merely an inconvenience en route. The track geometry rules and the tunnel must be set out to accommodate the track, not vice versa. Thus for every inch of cross section out of alignment allowed in the specification as a construction tolerance, the tunnel must be built two inches larger in diameter to maintain the clearances. Experience teaches that it is the most prudent and economical course to make the construction tolerance a generous one.

Accuracy of grade can be as important as alignment. For high-speed rail tunnels, both rate of change of grade and deviations of track alignment are very gradual indeed, so much as to create virtual straight line alignment and grade. The change of grade can be deceptive because engineers are accustomed to studying geologic sections, which for clarity and convenience of presentation have a greatly expanded vertical scale. An example of this is the published profile of the English Channel Tunnel, a difficult thing to present pictorially. The impression given is of a vertical tunnel alignment that rises and falls to follow the good tunneling ground, with a change in elevation of about one eighth of the undersea length of tunnel. In fact, the change is about 100m in the undersea length of 38km, and to natural scale the entire profile would be contained within a straight pencil line 19cm long and half a millimeter thick. There is little room for deviation from either azimuth or grade in a long high-speed rail tunnel.

11. Advancing the TBM

While a TBM operation is considered a continuous process, which it would be if excavation were the only operation, it is in fact a cyclical operation, particularly if a lining is being installed behind the machine as it advances. The excavation is continuous until the limit of extension of the thrust ram is reached. At that point the excavation stops, the rear of the machine is supported (either by a second set of grippers or jack legs), and the main grippers move forward as the thrust rams are retracted. At this point, temporary support or permanent lining is paced, and the cycle begins again. To advance, the TBM must develop thrust to enable the cutters or bits to penetrate the ground. In its simplest form, found in the hard rock TBM for an unlined tunnel, a TBM consists of the cutting head, motors, main bearing, and front grippers, connected by hydraulic cylinders to a rear frame and a second set of grippers. In some machines the hydraulic rams are skewed to resist rotation force. Double-shielded TBM, which are intended to make the cycle truly continuous, are discussed in the section on ground support equipment earlier in this chapter.

The operator controls the thrust on the cutterhead and also the speed of rotation. Too much thrust and too slow a rotation will tend to stall the machine or burn out the clutches. Too little thrust and too fast a rotation will not move the machine forward and may result in a churning action where the cutterhead turns in place and material falls from the roof, creating an overhead chimney, which can be dangerous, particularly in undersea tunnels.

The operator has no direct view or feels of the ground conditions or the parts of the TBM and thus must deduce the conditions from the array of instruments and video screens in the compartment. Ground is seldom uniform for long, and changes can be sudden or deceptively subtle. A great deal rides on the operator's skill in advancing and steering the TBM.

Where the TBM is designed to work under external water pressure, the designer and the operator face yet another challenge. In all advancing and steering operations, the operator must be constantly award of changing ground conditions. A good operator makes for good advances. A poor operator can destroy the TBM.

12. Ground support erection

If the project schedule and ground conditions permit, a contractor will usually prefer to install the permanent lining in the tunnel after excavation is complete. This makes for a simpler TBM, and he can first concentrate on excavation and temporary support, with greatly simplified logistics. A tunnel can be lined faster, and the equipment used more efficiently, using movable forms when the support lines carrying air, power, communications, and water to and from the working place have been removed. However, project schedules and ground conditions are not always compatible. At the other end of the difficulty scale, the schedule is tight and the ground requires immediate support. The final lining in such a case is then likely to be precast and installed as close as practicable behind the cutterhead. If the ground is highly variable, the project will probably be equipped to handle the poorest ground condition.

In rock tunnels, temporary support erection equipment can be installed well forward on the machine, and this will consist of rock bolting equipment or a steel rib erector, usually the former. When precast segments are used, the temporary support is not needed, since the segments are erected as soon as close behind the cutterhead as are practicable.

In all tunnels where they are used, the precast segments arrive a ring at time into the heading. As there are usually several shapes of segment in a ring, they must be offered up in the correct order. They arrive at the face usually lying parallel to the line of the tunnel. They are picked up, rotated into position, and held in place by building bars cantilevered from the body of the machine, or by thrust jacks bearing on the front of the segment, until the final segment is in place. This last segment may be a wedge to expand the ring hard against the ground, in which the case the rings may not be bolted but rely on ring compression and thorough grouting to hold them in place. Alternatively, the segments may be bolted and perhaps gasket for watertightness. Where the TBM is operating under external water pressure, the completed ring must be built within the tail of the TBM and extruded from the tail of the TBM past a system of seals between the outside of the ring and the inside of the rail shell. The favored tail seal is a triple row of wire brush seals kept generously supplied with thick grease.

If the machine is designed to use precast lining, it might be built in two parts, front and rear, one telescoping over the other. This permits the cutting head to move forward a limited amount independently of the lining erector section, which must be stationary during the erection process, which is a cyclical process. This has not yet been achieved in a machine required to operate under external waterhead, because of the need for annular seals where the two outer shells slide over each other, an arrangement that has not been made to work entirely satisfactorily.

Once erected, the rings must be grouted into place as soon as is practicable, starting at the invert and working up to the crow. Proof grouting is repeated at various points behind the first-stage grouting to ensure complete filling of voids. The grouting serves several purposes. The TBM support equipment following behind the head transmits heavy loads from the erectors and gantries to the invert of the tunnel. A solid footing is necessary to support these loads. The horizontal tube formed by the segments is subjected to heavy axial loads during the shoving and needs to be grouted in place if the segments are not to move around during the shoves. The grout also serves to bind the segments and the surrounding ground into a coherent structural ring, which gives the lining its strength and stability. Lastly, the grout serves to cut off water flows outside the lining, both in radial and longitudinal directions.

13. The TBM temporary support and permanent lining

A minority of rock tunnels require neither temporary support nor a permanent lining. The majority require some degree of structural support and lining for protection from rock falls or groundwater inflow, or for hydraulic smoothness. The tunnel use and the ground condition will determine the need for a final lining. The amount and the extent of support and lining can only be estimated at the time the work is priced. The accuracy of such estimates, or in some cases, the lack of such estimates, is a common aspect of tunnel construction litigation.

TBM excavation is a continuous process, whereas installation of temporary support and permanent lining are cyclical process. An early planning decision, therefore, is whether two or three operations should be tied together. For example, if ground conditions permit, the contractor may elect to support the ground temporarily as he excavates the install the permanent lining later, after holing through. This gives him less logistic congestion, but it may extend the overall schedule. Alternatively, and depending on the requirements for the finished tunnel, he may elect to support and line the tunnel with a segmented precast concrete lining as he excavates, eliminating the need for temporary support. He may elect to go partway between these two approaches, and lay a precast concrete invert behind the TBM, installing temporary support as necessary, and complete the lining of the arch later.

It should be recognized that tying the TBM and the lining operations together means that the work will progress at the speed of the slower operation, with the potential for inefficiencies in crew usage. Some alleviation of this disadvantage can be gained by designing a double-shielded TBM to permit limited relative movement of the excavation and lining system as discussed in the previous section. However, this improvement will be minor if there is a fundamental mismatch between the rates of excavation and support installation.

It is considerations such as the preceding that make the question of what type of lining is best for the job in the conceptual stage a difficult one for the engineer to answer with assurance. Unless some imperative dictates the nature of the lining from the beginning, the best support and lining methods will not become clear until late in the design process. Even then, the decision will lack the important input of the contractor until the successful bidder is determined.

14. The decision to use TBM

The economics of tunnel construction are extremely site-sensitive and resist generalization. Most tunneling contracts are bid competitively. The decision whether or not to use a TBM is usually left to the contractor, although the bid specifications may lean, or appear to lean, toward or away from use of a machine. If the owner feels the case of use of a TBM is clear, he may require its use. In a privately financed project, the interest cost during construction and the urgency of the need for early revenue may take precedence over construction costs.

Listed and discussed here are some of the factors that are likely to influence a contractor in his decision of whether or not to use a TBM in a rock tunnel.

15. Factors favoring use of a TBM in rock

(1) Adequate geologic data.

(2) Timely geologic data, which should be complete before insurance of invitation to bid, not just before bid date.

(3) Geologic data that indicates reasonable uniformity of rock quality and behavior throughout the drive.

(4) Low to moderate water inflow expectations, preferably based on pump tests with quantitative, rather than qualitative, estimates of flows.

(5) Rock not excessively hard or abrasive.

(6) Circular cross section of tunnel or crown. A noncircular section, such as a horseshoe section with a circular crown, can usually be driven circular and enlarged by a pass of an invert excavator or subsequent drill-and-blast benching excavation.

(7) Single portal access. Unless the tunnel length justified the use of two TBM, access from both ends of a tunnel reduces the competitiveness of a TBM in terms of construction schedule. To complete a tunnel from one heading by TBM when both ends are available at least twice as fast as a drill-and-blast heading. Access from shallow intermediate shafts or adits further increase the demands on the TBM advance rate.

(8) Access by portal rather than shaft favors the TBM for large tunnel diameters, where heavy TBM sections must be lowered to tunnel elevation for assembly underground. A portal permits assembly of the TBM outside the tunnel, a distinct cost and schedule advantage.

(9) Long tunnels. The drive must be long enough to warrant the heavy initial expenditure in purchasing the TBM. Equipment costs for drill-and-blast construction are usually lower.

(10) Availability of the right type of and the right diameter TBM. During its working life a TBM must be well maintained, since its performance in the last quarter of the drive is as important as in the first three-quarters. Because many of the working traits of the machine are known, and because modifications improving the performance may have been made, availability of a suitable used TBM is a big advantage to a bidder, who also knows his competition may have to allow many months of lead time for delivery of a new TBM.

(11) Availability of skilled labor. TBM require different skills and crewing from those for other tunneling techniques.

(12) Ready sources of adequate electric power. A TBM require as much as 5MW of installed power.

16. Factors not favoring use of a TBM in rock

(1) Inadequate or unconvincing geologic information.

(2) Mixed-face excavation or the likelihood of it.

(3) Heavily faulted areas and/or wide fault zones. In this case and in item 4 below, a TBM may help support the poor ground, or it may be trapped by ground movement behind the face. Such situations should be considered separately on their merits and demerits.

(4) Short stand-up time. Tunnels in rocks requiring support when excavated will stand unsupported for a period; this is known as stand-up time.

(5) Very hard, abrasive, or swelling rock.

(6) Geologic formations known to be unpredictable. For example, glaciated formations with deep valleys into the bedrock; karstic limestone or volcanic lava formations.

(7) Short tunnels.

(8) Variable geology requiring frequent changes in excavation and support methods.

None of the unfavorable or favorable factors should be taken as absolutes. Every project is different, and a careful weighing of all factors, with a good measure of judgment, will go into the final decision. A little luck has been known to help.

17. Measuring TBM performance

The measurement of performance of a TBM must serve the needs of a variety of people: the contractor, the manufacturer, the owner of the work, and the tunnel engineer. Not all have the same interest. The contractor is interested in the percentage of time the TBM is cutting rock. The manufacturer is interested, in addition, in the percentage of time the TBM was available to operate since, for reasons behind the manufacturer's control, the TBM may not have been used to its fullest capacity. The owner shares this interest.

The designer and the student of tunneling are also interested in the instantaneous rate at which the TBM advances through the ground: the rate at which the TBM can penetrate the ground for short periods. All are interested in forecasting further advance rates, in analyzing problems and correcting them, and in minimizing the often painful shakedown time during the early days. During this "learning curve", TBM have problems, operators have problems and crews have problems.

The objective during these days is to establish the optimum thrust, torque, and cutter wear for the ground, to minimize the cycle time, and to settle the work crew into a steady and safe routine. Performance is measured primarily for internal project reasons, with the objective of improving performance on the project. Because of this, what is included or excluded in measuring a particular activity is likely to be job-specific. However, when the performance of several projects is to be compared, we find there is little standardization of input.

Text B TBM Tunneling System
TBM 系统组成

Because of the number of large tunnels now under consideration where the use of TBM is contemplated and where squeezing conditions may become important, the following discussion is extended, even though not based on a great deal of current experience.

It is only with the advent of the modern tunnel boring machine that construction methods have been freely adapted to tunnels of circular cross sections. Even so, it was not until after 1970 that TBM design had advanced to the point where more tunnels were completed by TBM than by drill-and-blast methods. In the mid-1970s, Japanese slurry shields for deep soft ground tunnels were being manufactured in sizes up10m in diameter. Machine tunneling in truly hard rock did not become generally successful until about this same time. Improvements in mechanical design and development of large diameter single-disk cutters improved the performance of TBM exceeding 6m in diameter before 1980. Even larger machine, 9m diameter and greater were used in limestone with a compressive strength of 175MPa in Chicago. At the present time, 12m machines are being constructed for major tunnels in Taiwan with difficult conditions anticipated near one portal and at several fault crossings.

The Stillwater tunnel second contract was the first was the first project for which a TBM was specifically designed to penetrate squeezing ground. The machine was successful, although a second machine modified from a conventional design was more successful. Both designs recognized the need for adaptation to the squeezing conditions, but the actual amount of radial reduction in tunnel diameter was comparatively small. Had it been much greater, it is unlikely that the conventional machine could have worked.

The majority of examples of tunnels in squeezing ground are related to the crossing of faults. TBM have been troubled in this situation by inrushes of water carrying sand and finely divided rock or by blocks of rock jamming between the cutters. The second of these problems has been dealt with in many tunnels in otherwise normal conditions. The primary solution is the use of a cutterhead design that allows only a limited projection of the cutters forward of the cutterhead using a face shield ahead of the structural support element. The second development is a design that permits worn cutters to be changed from within the tunnel, so that no access is required in front of the cutterhead. There has, as yet, been no easy solution for the problem of the cutterhead and its buckets being choked with sand and rock fragments while unrelenting water flows are in progress. It becomes a difficult and slow process of cleaning out and gaining progress slowly until the affected area has been cleared. Also in such conditions, the presence of a shield is important to protect the machine and to provide temporary support to material with no stand-up time. In some circumstances, if the condition is known to exist or to be likely to exist, probing ahead to identify the precise location can give an opportunity to stabilize the ground with grout injections, keeping a bulkhead thickness ahead of the excavation at all times. It is sometimes possible to allow most of the water to drain out of the ground, but this is not a reliable approach to prediction of construction methods. Shielded TBM have been used successfully in such conditions, but unfortunately the use of a long shield militates against successful use in squeezing ground.

The other major problem, whether or not in a fault or shear zone, is the closure of the ground around the cutterhead shield and any protective shield behind the cutterhead. Many TBM including that used on the first contract at Stillwater, have been immobilized because the load on the shield system was too high to permit the machine to advance. An indication of the way to approach this problem was offered by the use of a short shrinkable shield on the machine used on the second contract from the inlet portal.

It is not anticipated that tunneling in squeezing ground or fault zone will ever become a simple, routine operation because of the erratic variability of conditions. However, current opinion is that virtually all tunnels can be attacked by TBM methods whenever there is an economic advantage in doing so.

As previously noted, the difficulty of predicting rock behavior in squeezing ground has played a major role in the development of observational methods for determination of rock support requirements. However, if tunneling by TBM is selected, some of the flexibility of the observational method is removed, and decisions must be made at the time the TBM is designed as to the amount of ground movement to be anticipated or permitted and the design of the support system to accept the loadings implied at different stages.

Since squeezing of soft rock does usually lead to immediate instability, it should be possible and practical to delay major support installation until a high percentage of the total strain has taken place and ground loading has been reduced. Sixty to seventy percent of the potential ground movement has usually taken place within about three diameters of the working face. If the total amount of squeezing is not great, it may not be necessary, or even desirable, to delay support installation so long.

Ideally, final support is not installed until convergence is less than one millimeter per month. The loading associated with a given amount of convergence depends on the parameters of the project. One must also consider any long-term requirement for the tunnel to carry water. Finally, it must be realized that if groundwater is to be totally excluded from the tunnel, the final lining must be designed to carry the full hydrostatic head unless the aquifer is fully sealed off by consolidation grouting. If groundwater is admitted, whether in a controlled manner or by allowing local cracking of the lining, then only seepage pressures need to be accounted for. In the case of weak squeezing ground or faulted rock with an unknown potential for swelling behavior, the latter alternative appears undesirable.

The principal components of a TBM affected by the difference between tunneling in squeezing and nonsqueezing ground are discussed here.

Cutterhead: Many different cutterhead designs have been used over the years, from the earliest flat heads with multiple disk cutters through domed heads, rounded edge, flat heads, and conical designs. These days the cutterhead geometry is selected on the basis of the ground it is expected to penetrate. It has been found preferable to arrange that at least the gauge cutters be designed to be changed from behind, and it is possible to arrange this system for all cutters. A spoke design allows ready access to the working face and simplifies design in some respects. However, such machines offer little support if weak ground is encountered and it is generally considered prudent to use a closed-face machine. Also, to protect the cutters and cutter mounts, a lighter false face is provided so that the cutter disks protrude only a short distance. In conventional designs, the cutterhead is provided with its own shield as part of the cutterhead bucket system. The conventional design creates a drum about 1.2m long almost in contact with the ground. In squeezing ground this shield is vulnerable to the pressure exerted by rock movement. It is therefore better that the shield be smaller in diameter than the excavation and that it be tapered toward the rear. The gauge cutters should be arranged to protrude beyond the main body of the cutterhead.

If the cutterhead is not in close contact with the ground, provision must be made to provide stable support in its place. This will be the equivalent of a sole plate as used for overcutter compensation in earth pressure balance machines. However, to provide for varying amounts of overcut, the support will need to be hydraulically actuated. Since it will be subjected to substantial shear loading, the design will have to be very stiff.

Propulsion: A TBM requires a reaction against which to propel it forward. This reaction can be obtained by shoving directly against the tunnel support system with jacks spaced around the perimeter of the machine or by developing friction resistance against the tunnel sidewalls.

The thrust needed to keep the cutterhead moving forward would be about 14000kg per cutter. Because the ground is week, it would be desirable to limit the bearing pressure on the tunnel walls because the weak rock would fail under even light loads, especially perpendicular to the direction of foliation. This would accelerate the rate of squeezing and might increase the total strain. At the same time, it would be desirable to limit the length occupied by the grippers so as to minimize the necessary distance between the working face and any support system. This would probably require that there be multiple grippers covering most of the circumference but of limited length to minimize uneven bearing on the squeezing rock surface.

Shield: If any shield is felt to be desirable or necessary, it should be short and shrinkable, following the example of the inlet portal TBM at Stillwater. Many TBM have been stuck because the ground has moved on to the shield and exerted sufficient load to stall the machine.

Erector: It is desirable to have complete flexibility in selecting the point at which ring erection is to take place. Therefore, the erector should be free to move along the tunnel, mounted on the conveyor truss. A ring former should also be used to maintain the shape of the last erected ring until it has been grouted, if concrete segmental lining is used.

Spoil removal: Conventional conveyor to tail car systems or single-conveyor systems designed for the tunnel size selected is appropriate.

Back-up system: To keep the area between the grippers and the ring erection area as clear as possible, any ancillary equipment such as transformers, hydraulic pumps, etc. should be kept clear of this space at track level.

Operational flexibility: It is envisaged that the system outlined above would be capable of handling either steel ribs or precast concrete supports. If shoving off the supports were to be selected for TBM propulsion, the degree of flexibility would be less than the use of a gripper system. It would also be more vulnerable to problems in any circumstance where the convergence rate was markedly higher than expected.

Text C Nanjing Weisan Road Yangtze River Crossing Tunnel
南京纬三路越江隧道

The project of Nanjing Weisan Road Yangtze River Crossing Tunnel is one of the most important components of the river-crossing system for Nanjing urban expressway and the most accessible link which connects the old city center area, Hexi new city area and Jiangbei new city area. The project is located between the Yangtze River Bridge and the Nanjing Yangtze River Tunnel at Weiqi Road, approximately 5km downstream of Nanjing Yangtze River Bridge.

This project connects Puzhu road in Pukou district at the north of river from the north and Dinghuaimen Street (Line S), Yangtze River Avenue (line N) at the south of river from the south. SG-1 bidding section includes Pukou link road (including the toll plaza fill), open excavation section of Jiangbei tunnel, launch shaft of TBM of Jiangbei tunnel, tunnel shield tunneling section, Meizizhou ventilation shaft, TBM receiving shaft on south bank of the river, the open cut section of line N on the south bank of the river, the open cut section of line S on the south bank of the river, the open cut section of the ramp line NA on the south bank of the river, the open cut section of the ramp SB on the south bank of the river, the link line on the south bank of the river and the tunnel interior structures, decoration, and the working shaft wind tower buildings.

This project designadopts solution is a twin-bore double level, type X 8-traffic lane bored tunnel.

The features of this project can be summarized with following seven words.

Large: Super large diameter shield tunneling with excavation diameter up to 14.96m. This tunnel is one of the largest tunnels by TBM method.

High: There are three high value technical parameters for the shield tunnel construction: high water pressure (up to 0.77MPa), high quartz content (up to 65%), high accuracy of segments joining and placement. All the three parameters are of top level at home.

Thin: The thickness of cover soil of this river-crossing tunnel is shallow. The local thickness of cover soil on line N tunnel is only 0.6 times of the diameter.

Long: The advance distance in one operation of shielded boring reaches up to 4135m.

Dangerous: The tunnel penetrates through sandy rubble stratum with high content of quartz and composite stratum and unrecognized obstacle sructs may exist. All the strata at deep foundation pit are saturated with aqueous weak soil, silty fine sand stratum. The engineering technology level and construction risk is high.

Congested: This tunnel adopts the structure of double level 4-lane. In course of heading the cavity space is narrow and small in which pipelines are densely placed and transportation is busy. Interior structure works progress must follow tunnel body excavation closely and multiple works sequences fore and aft and up and down are carried out concurrently, which demands a strict and scientific construction arrangement.

Complicated: This project includes several multiple construction sections and construction technologies involved are highly comprehensive. The complex environment and various uncertainties make high difficulty of the organization and coordination.

This tunnel crossing Yangtze River from river floor has larger diameter by TBM method, long advance length of heading in operation, complex TBM penetration geological conditions for TBM penetration. The main engineering technical difficulties are tunnel boring excavation by TBM and deep foundation pit works and other aspects such as:

(1) Design of geological condition adaptable toted TMB cutter disc and cutting tool.

The geological information shows that the TBM is supposed to penetrate such strata including mucky soil, clay, silty fine sand, and pebble round gravels, muddy rock and silty sandy rock. Among the soils, silty fine sand, pebble circular gravel and silty sandy rock contain highest contents of quartz which greatly wears cutting machines. The selection of cutter types of TBM and cutter arrangement design shall enable the cutting wheel of this TBM to suit both clay cutting and sandy soil cutting so that it works well for boring in both weak soil and composite stratum. And the general purpose and compatibility of cutting and heading in various strata as well as the replaceability and substitutability of cutters should be considered.

(2) Design of watertightness of TBM under high pressurized operation condition.

The maximum water and soil pressure on TBM at the riverbed is up to 0.77MPa which is a challenge to watertightness design of the TBM, including the designs of overall high pressure resistance of shield shell, seal of main bearing, seal of tail, technological design of cutter replacement under constant pressure and high pressure. Both the possibility of operation and operation safety should be ensured.

(3) Shield tunneling in composite stratum.

The geological information showed that there are more than one but up to seven strata (composite strata) on one section of submerged tunnel. The structures of the stratum are also different: The upper stratum is clay and the lower stratum is sandy soil; The upper stratum is weak soil and lower stratum is gravel; The upper stratum is weak soil and lower stratum is sandy rock. It is a challenge to the cutter maintenance, control of TBM pose and alignment, and the balance of the heading face which greatly increases the difficulty of shield tunneling.

(4) Slurry control in long distance shield tunneling.

Heading length by TBM can reach up to 4135m in one operation which greatly raised increases the requirement on slurry control in works execution. The safety of slurry transport over long distance and the changing pressure balance during heading shall be ensured. In addition, as the tunnel penetrates the strata with high content of quartz and slurry transport distance is long, the demanding wear resistance of pipes and pumps are necessary.

(5) Trench formation for diaphragm wall in high water pressurized silty fine sand strata.

The ventilation shaft at Meizishou is immediately adjacent to Yangtze river dam and the top strata are dominantly muck, silty clay, silty fine sand strata. The fence structure uses diaphragm wall whose base penetrated into rubble stratum with penetrated depth up to 63.75m. Due to poor self-stability of weak top stratum, the water and soil pressure on side walls of trench is fully resisted supported by slurry during execution where there is high water pressure, and trench wall is prone to failure due to collapse and the trench formation is extremely difficult.

(6) Stratum improvement with super depth high pressurized jet grouting piles.

Highly pressurized jet grouting piles for reinforcement has depth exceeding 50m (Meizizhou ventilation shaft) while regular highly pressurized jet grouting pile has effective reinforcement depth less than 30m. In reality practice design requirement can only be met by implementation of new workmanship and, new method.

The selection of TBM type requires purposeful design given different geological features of different projects so that the TBM can have better adaptability. By analyzing the geological and hydrological features of given project and referring to the opinions of TBM manufacturers at home and abroad towards TBM type selection under given geological features, slurry pressure balance TBM is proposed for the following main reasons:

(1) Slurry shield can reduce construction risk.

The water and soil pressure is high in stratum which has lots of pebbles and water. Using soil pressure balance boring method is not helpful to improve muck soil and soil plug can hardly form. And it is not good for the control of surface subsidence and large amount of additives are needed which will increase works cost. However, the slurry shield can reduce the risk of this type. Besides, due to existence of long distance sandy pebble, application of slurry shield can more effectively ensure construction safety.

Since the tunnel site contains pore water in loose deposited sandy gravel pebble stratum and groundwater is abundant rich, there is risk of works suspension once great inrush of water occurs. While slurry shield has sound adaptability, it can greatly improve construction efficiency and effectively avoid ground surface settlement and cave-in.

(2) Slurry shield is suitable for geological conditions.

In light of geological factors analysis, long distance pebble stratum and hydrological conditions are suitable for using slurryshield.

In conclusion, in light of engineering conditions, geological features, construction time and requirement based on the experiences on TMB selection for similar works, this given project is suitable for using slurry pressurized balance type TBM.

1. The analysis on the adaptability of proposed slurry shield to the geology

1) The suitability of long distance heading in sand-pebble stratum

Sand-pebble stratum contains high content of quartz which is highly abrasive to cutterhead, cutting machines and mud drain pipelines. The following performances of TBM should be considered with emphasis when procuring shield:

(1) Capability of balancing the water and soil pressure on heading face;

(2) High abrasion resistance of cutter disc, cutting tool and slurry pipelines;

(3) Rational design of cutter disc and cutting tools and proper opening of cutter disc and reasonable position of opening;

(4) Waterproof and sealing of shield body under high water pressure condition;

(5) Performance of in shell with pressure;

(6) Tail void grouting can be performed under high water pressure;

(7) Capable of crushing larger pebble to effectively prevent pipe blockage.

2) Capacity of treating large pebble and boulder

The stratum which the tunnel penetrated crossed through contains pebble in diameter in range of 60-150mm generally with maximum grain size of 200mm. In the sand-pebble stratum, the soil is loose. In order to accommodate heading in the pebble stratum, the fore tearing knife is equipped which can effectively protect the scraper knife and panel of the cutter disc.

In order to fragment the boulders to enable the fragmented to be discharged via drain pipe, one two-jaw plate crushing machine is mounted in front of the mud drain pipe at the bottom of slurry balance hold. The maximum size of pebble is 800mm which the crushing machine can fragment is 800mm and isolating grids are equipped to limit the size of stone fragments from entering into slurry drain pipe.

3) Excavation in mudstone and sandrock stratum

To ensure the excavation in sandrock and mudstone stratum, the rocks is broken by means of double bladed hobbing cutter. In the project, the rock strength is classified as moderate to hard rock ranging between 70-80MPa in average. The double-bladed hobbing cutter is featured with easy activation (small torque of activation) and the application of double-bladed hobbing cutter can both break rock and reduce unbalanced wearing and is suitable for this project.

4) Excavation in compound stratum

In order to suit the advance in different geological conditions, alternative application of the hobbing cutter and the scraper cutter is designed. The scraper cutter is used in weak soil section while the hobbing cutter in hard rock sections.

2. Suitability for high water pressure

The cutting tool check and maintenance of the cutting tool, main bearing sealing, slurry hold door and tail void sealing are designed accordingly for TBM under high water pressure. In the selection and arrangement of the cutting tools, the application of two launch hobbing cutter and rolling cutter which can be replaced in constant pressure can avoid operation under pressure.

The main bearing sealing can resist the designed pressure of 10bar with the designed life exceeding 10000h. The sealing lubrication grease can be automatically controlled and grease injection pressure can be automatically adjusted according to the water and soil pressure of the stratum. The grease injection amount and abrasion of sealing and temperature can be checked automatically.

The door of slurry hold is specially sealed to ensure the complete seal between air pressure tank, which can avoid the check and maintenance of stone crushing machine.

The solution of Tail sealing adopts the design under high water and soil pressure is adopted which is the design at home and abroad, including 4 steel wire brushes and 1 steel plate brush, 1 emergency sealing and the sealing strength against water pressure exceeds 10bar. The first two sealing brushes can be replaced inside tunnel and the freezing pipes are built in tail and all various types of reinforcements are designed at connections which ensure the safety in element replacement operations.

3. Suitability for long distance transport of slurry

Advanced Warman slurry pump imported from Australia is used and the slurry pipes with large power, large flow amount, high flow speed and large diameter are adopted. Slurry treatment system with well known brand is adopted and slurry index is strictly controlled. Site slurry laboratory is set up and slurry engineers are hired for slurry management.

4. Suitability for fast excavation

In the general design of the shield machine, the requirement for tight works schedule of the time limit for the project is fully considered and the maximum excavation velocity is 5cm/min which is an advancing speed in large diameter shield machine at home and abroad. Under high water pressure, the resistance of water and soil pressure under high water pressure against TMB is fully considered in the total thrust of advancing and the maximum thrust is 278400kN which is higher by 30% than that of average TBM.

5. Technological advancement of TBM

The TBM applied in this project adopts the internal state-of-art and the modern advanced design of the latest successful works so that. And the smooth, safe, rapid excavation of the given project can be ensured. Design of two launch rolling cutter is used and operation under pressure can be avoided.

Design of constant pressure replaceable rolling cutter/cutter is used and different cutter arrangements are used for different strata and flowability of muck can be ensured. The advantages and special features of various types of cutters are fully developed.

The design of 19 inches rolling cutter is used and the service life of the cutter is improved. The advanced detecting devices for cutter abrasion and cutter disc face abrasion are used and can perform automatic check and guide cutter replacement. The advanced tail void measurement system is used to provide support to segment type selection and can ensure the segment installation quality. The spare power generation set can start automatically by PLC and can meet the power needs for pressure reservation after power failure, segment installation and emergency power supply. The slurry treatment system adopts the three-graded pressurized filtering and it meets the environmental protection requirement for zero release.

II. Terms and terminology

Tunnel boring machines (TBM)	隧道掘进机
shield	盾构
Earth pressure balance (EPB) shield	土压平衡盾构
slurry shield	泥水平衡盾构
segment	管片
jack	（盾构）千斤顶
blade	切削刀
tail avoid	盾尾间隙
cutter head	切削刀头
back filling	背回注浆
rear void	盾尾空隙
shield work shaft	盾构工作井
shield launching	盾构始发
shield arrival shaft	盾构接收井
shield cradle	盾构基座
temporary segment	负环管片
frame	反力架
sealing gasket	防水密封条
back-fill grouting	壁后注浆
articulation shield	铰接式盾构
U-turn, turn around	调头
curve in small radius	小半径曲线
position and stance	姿态

ovality	椭圆度
mucking	出渣
main bearing	主轴
erector	管片拼装器
scraper cutter	刮刀
hobbing cutter	滚刀

Ⅲ. Questions and difficult sentence analysis

1. Questions for brainstorming discussion

(1) Discuss the most important functions must be met for TBM tunneling.

(2) What principal factors should be considered in selecting TBM?

(3) Why is precise steering so important for TBM tunneling?

2. Difficult sentences analysis

(1) Today's TBM is likely to have been designed specifically for the anticipated ground conditions and is likely to use technology from both hard rock and soft ground machines.

译文:当今,TBM 往往针对可预见的地基条件而专门设计,并通常采用适合于坚硬岩石和软地基的设备技术。

(2) Like many other technical developments, the TBM was designed in concept by men of genius long before the technologies of metallurgy and motive power were advanced sufficiently to meet the challenges the designs imposed.

译文:早在冶金和动力技术进步足以满足设计的挑战之前,就像许多其他的技术发明创造过程一样,天才们进行了 TBM 的概念设计。

(3) As soft ground and rock TBM built on each other's experience, they shared more and more features. By the 1980s, of the 11 machines used in the soft chalk of the Channel Tunnel, most were rock machines, but at least 2 were adaptations of soft ground TBM, and 3 had earth pressure balance (EPB) features. The latter were the French undersea TBM, designed to excavate and erect lining under 10 bar external water pressure in fractured and faulted rock.

译文:由于软弱地基和岩石的 TBM 借鉴相互工程经验,两者具有越来越多的共同特征。到 20 世纪 80 年代,11 台 TBM 用于海峡隧道中的白垩软弱地基,大多数是岩石机,但是至少 2 台机器是软弱地基 TBM 机,3 台机器具有土压平衡特征。后者是法国设计用于在 10 块破碎和断裂构造岩石中下开挖和管片安装的海底 TBM。

(4) Accuracy of grade can be as important as alignment. For high-speed rail tunnels, both rate of change of grade and deviations of track alignment are very gradual indeed, so much as to create virtual straight line alignment and grade.

译文:纵坡的精确性和线形同等重要。在高速铁路隧道中,坡度变化率和轨道线形的偏离的确在很大程度上是渐变的,形成最终的直线线形和坡度。

IV. Translation case study

Case 1

Chinese	English translation
TBM 是一个表示旋转动作含义的术语,在其发展的全过程中,设计师门基于前人成功和失败的经验,建造了 TBM。最近数年来,用于坚硬岩石和软弱地基的 TMB 设计相得益彰。	Throughout the development of TBM, a term which implies a rotary action, designers have built on the successes and the failures of their predecessors. In recent years, there has been a great deal of healthy cross-fertilization between designs of machines for hard rock and those for soft ground.

Case 2

Chinese	English translation
从 19 世纪初开始,建造了大量隧道开挖机,主要是在美国和英国,这些机器的许多特征在现代盾构机上得到体现。之前,软弱地基的开挖和支护采用矿山法,然后采用盾构保护,最后逐渐机械化盾构。岩石隧道的开挖采用在开挖面上钻孔,填充炸药的方法。岩石和软弱地质的水下隧道直到 19 世纪初才开始尝试,其成功率很低,因此产生了盾构以及随后的机械化盾构用于 TBM。	In the period starting in the early 19th Century, numerous tunneling machines were built, largely in United States and Great Britain, many of them with features that can be recognized in the modern TBM. Before that time, soft ground was excavated and supported by hand mining methods, then from the protection of a shield, then from increasingly mechanized shields. The rock tunnels were excavated by explosives set in holes drilled into the face. Subaqueous tunnels in both rock and soft ground were not attempted until the early 19th Century, and the poor success rate led to the development of the shield, and its subsequent mechanization into a TBM.

Case 3

Chinese	English translation
现代 TBM 是一个复杂体系,其中各部分相互独立。装配完整的 TBM 可占据隧道长度 1000 英尺,有切割,铲土、操纵转向,夹紧,钻探,地面控制与支撑,衬砌安装,除渣,通风及供电几大功能组成。所有这些作业必须与隧道掘进一起前进,当 TBM 在掘进时,铺设轨道工作,供电及通风管道的铺设必须同步向前延伸。	A modern TBM is a complex system of interdependent parts. A fully equipped TBM can occupy as much as 1000 ft of tunnel, and be made up of mechanisms of cutting, shoving, steering, gripping, exploratory drilling, ground control and support, lining erection, spoil removal, ventilation, and power supply. All of these items must advance with the tunnel heading, and items such as track work, power supply, and ventilation ducting must be extended behind the TBM as it advances.

V. Assignment

(1)为了提高止水性,有时要安装几段盾尾密封材料。对于安装的段数问题,必须根据盾构的外径,地质条件,施工过程中是否必须更换盾尾密封材料等条件决定。为了做成可更换的结构,有时采用螺栓、螺母进行连接。考虑到管片可能使密封材料遭到破损,需十分注意连接方法。

（2）盾构是由承受外部作用的荷载,保护内部的钢壳部分和其保护下面的工作面部分进行开挖,在后部组装衬砌及具有掘进机能的各种设备组成。

（3）盾构是开挖土砂围岩的主要机械,由切口环,支承环及盾尾三部分组成,也叫作盾构机械。在人力开挖式盾构的切口环中,装备有支挡装置,支撑环作为承受支护千斤顶反力的部分,并且作为盾构千斤顶等设备安装的空间,或者用来作为进行推进操作的场所。

（4）盾尾密封材料一般是安装在盾尾板和管片外表面之间,是以防止注浆材料和地下水漏入盾构为目的。在土压式盾构和泥水加压式盾构中,还有保持其各自压力的。

（5）钢管片的材质均匀,强度易被保证,具有良好的焊接性;由于重量比较轻,易于施工,在现场进行加工和修理也比较容易;但与混凝土类管片相比,钢管片易变形,当千斤顶推力和回填注浆压力过大时,有可能被压坏。

Unit 7　Immersed Tube Tunnel
沉 管 隧 道

I. Text

Text A　Immersed Tube Tunnel Introduction
沉管隧道概述

Definition of immersed tube tunnels: Immersed tube tunnels are composed of prefabricated sections placed in trenches that have been dredged in river or sea bottoms. The sections are usually constructed at some distance from the tunnel location and made watertight with temporary bulkheads. They are then floated into position over the trench, lowered into place and joined together underwater. The temporary bulkheads are removed, and the trench is backfilled with earth to protect the tubes. Immersed tubes have been widely used for highway and rail crossings of soft-bottomed, shallow estuaries and tidal rivers or canals in which trenches may be excavated with floating equipment.

General descriptions: Under favorable conditions, the immersed tube method is the most economical construction for any type of underwater tunnel crossing. Tunnel sections in convenient lengths, usually 300- 450ft (Denmark's Guldborgsund Tunnel has the longest element length, 690ft) are placed into a pre-dredged trench, joined, connected, and protected by back-filling the excavation. The sections may be fabricated in shipyards on shipways, in dry docks, or in casting basins depending on the type of construction and available facilities. A prerequisite for this method is a soil with adequate cohesion, which permits dredging of the trench with reasonable side slopes that will remain stable for a sufficient length of time to place the tubes and backfill.

The top of the tunnel should be preferably at least 5ft below the original bottom to allow for an adequate protective backfill. Where grade limitations and bottom configuration make this impractical, the tunnel may project partly above the bottom and be protected by a backfill extending about 100ft on each side of the structure and confined within dikes. The fill must be protected against erosion by currents with a rock blanket, protective rock dike, or other means. There have been cases where ships in confined channels have used anchors as turning pivots in wharfing operations. This practice, although contrary to navigation rules, may require deeper backfill over a tunnel in such a location or special protection by rock cover, concrete slabs, or other means.

Tides and currents must be evaluated to establish conditions to be met during dredging and tube sinking operations. Nearby shellfish areas must be identified so precautions can be taken during construction to prevent damage from silting due to dredging or backfill spillage.

Dredging and backfilling operations should be executed so as to minimize disturbance to the natural ecological balance at the construction site. <u>Permits for construction and jurisdictional conflicts with other governmental agencies over environmental protection, natural resources, and local conditions must be evaluated and resolved. Approval of these agencies should be obtained during the preliminary dredging stage.</u>

1. Advantages and disadvantages of immersed tube tunnels

For underwater tunnels, the immersed tube concept offers several advantages compared with mined or shield-driven tunnels.

(1) The tunnel has the minimum possible depths. For an approach gradient fixed by operating criteria, this usually means minimum tunnel length.

(2) Almost all construction is accomplished from above the ground or water surface, in normal working conditions. This promotes better quality of construction, particularly for control of water seepage.

(3) Most of the constructions are related to standard materials and operation using readily available labor skills.

(4) there are no major time-dependent construction constraints such as:

①Provisions for control of water inflow to permit the work to proceed under atmospheric pressure, such as in mined tunnels.

②Measures required to stabilize the working face, as shield-driven tunnel.

③Repetition of construction activities offers opportunities for higher efficiency.

Major disadvantages of immersed tunnels compared with mined or shield-driven tunnels are as follows.

(1) Potential for disruption of existing facilities if the trench must be extended pass the shorelines.

(2) The need for special equipment to construct foundations.

(3) The need for special equipment to place and join the tube sections.

(4) Selection of acceptable dredging methods and construction of underwater dikes if needed in environmentally sensitive areas.

(5) Environmental objections to disturbances caused by trench dredging and backfill placement.

(6) Selection of suitable sites for a casting yard for concrete tube tunnels.

(7) Selection of a disposal site for the dredged spoil material excavated from the trench. This can create serious environmental problems if not resolved in early planning. In the Fort McHenry Tunnel Project, as a result of the early planning in preliminary engineering, the 3.5 million yd^3 (2.7 million m^3) of dredged material from the trench excavation was used in construction of a new port facility.

Other limitations on immersed tube construction include:

(1) There must be sufficient duration of slack tidal current to permit lowering the tube-preferably at less than 3ft/s(1m/s) over a duration of 2 hours.

(2) The bottom must not be so soft and unstable that the trench cannot be kept open.

(3) The site must be reasonably free from rapid deposition of fluid silts, which can alter the density of water in the trench and affect the balance of buoyancy at tube placement.

2. Settlement of immersed tube tunnels

Under normal conditions, immersed tube tunnels are relatively insensitive to soil settlement, because their buoyant weight differs only slightly from that of the original submerged soil or the adjacent backfill. However, when the soil types and the loading pattern vary significantly along the tunnel alignment, differential settlements will take place. The distribution of loads may create significant bending moments, which although secondary in nature, can be critical. The assessment of anticipated settlement is particularly important in the design of concrete tunnels. Concrete is brittle and susceptible cracking compared with steel, which is ductile. In recent European practice, dilatation joints have been placed every 60ft to minimize the bending stresses due to settlement.

3. Concrete immersed tunnels

The advancement in immersed concrete tube tunnels in Europe was heavily indebted to the successful improvements of three major design and construction features: crack control, watertightness, and foundation and placement systems.

Crack control: Uneven shrinkage is the major cause of cracking in concrete structures. For concrete immersed tunnels, a number of remedies have been used for crack control.

(1) Increasing impermeability of concrete by selecting suitable cement content and aggregate size and by other means.

(2) Reducing differences in temperature between the core and outer layers of the walls during concrete placement, including the bottom slab, roof slab, and between opposite sides of construction joints.

(3) Introducing dilatation (expansion) joints every 60ft along the element. These joints reduce the high tensile stress due to shrinkage, and the stresses induced from possible settlement of the subsoil or foundation course.

Watertightness: watertightness in concrete tunnels is an important part of the design. Major areas of improvements include:

(1) The increased impermeability of concrete.

(2) Improvements to construction joints between walls and top and bottom slabs.

(3) Improvements in dilatation joints.

(4) Improvements in element joints.

In Holland, following the completion of the Maas Tunnel and up to the construction of the Vlake Tunnel in 1975, extensive waterproofing systems were used. In general, the system used contained a steel membrane for the bottom slab, copper stripping for the joints, and three exterior layers of impregnated fiberglass with asphaltic bitumen on sidewalls and the roof slab, followed by a layer of polyester foil with additional concrete cover for the roof slab. Recent European practice for shallow concrete tubes has favored reliance on crack control, impermeable concrete, and improved joints. For deep concrete tubes, exterior waterproofing is still favored.

Foundation and placement system: After the introduction of the sand jetting method for the Maas Tunnel in 1942, tunnel designers in Holland developed the sand flow method. The new method eliminated the use of a gantry system riding on the roof of the tunnel element and provided better control for the sand flow pattern in locations where high velocity of currents, up to 6.5ft/s, are common.

Improvements in placement techniques include the introduction of three-point temporary support system for the placement of elements during construction of the foundation system. The three-point support system used since 1969 makes use of a single pivotal support at the adjoining (outboard) end of the element, ensuring easier adjustments for alignment and reducing the number of correction required in making the joint.

4. Concrete tubes

Configuration: rectangular reinforced concrete sections are generally used for tunnels with four or more traffic lanes, particularly where concrete is more economical than steel. A design for a highway tube with two three-lane roadways (with central upper compartments for cable ducts and lower compartments for emergency exit) is shown in the figure below. It is the cross section of Zeeburger Tunnel which completes Amsterdam's peripheral ring road system under the heavily used navigation channel of Buiten. The 2900ft long cross contains three 370ft long immersed tube elements, all supported on pile foundations. The six-lane tunnel has two 34.5ft wide roadway sections with a total width of 87.6ft and a height of 23.7ft. The major features of the tunnel include the elimination of external water-proofing and special connection devices for pile connection.

Construction of tubes: The sections are constructed in dry docks or in temporary dewatered basins located near the site, which are flooded for floating the tubes. Unless a dry dock or outfitting basin is available for construction in the dry, these facilities must be constructed for the project, with resultant increased costs and time of construction. The Hong Kong Cross Harbour Road Tunnel was originally designed as a four-lane, rectangular, prestressed section, but an alternative tender was made for the twin steel single-shell section. The steel section was constructed, at a saving of several million dollars and 1-1/2 years of construction time. The base and roof slabs and sidewalls of rectangular concrete tubes are of massive reinforced concrete as determined by structural and functional requirements. In general, concrete has a compressive strength of 4000psi, and reinforcing steel a 60000psi yield point corresponding ASTM designation A-615. Since the tubes are solidly supported in the construction basin, the concreting sequence is not critical. However, concrete placement requires stringent quality control to assure crack control. Usually, alternate longitudinal sections varying from 20 to 60ft are poured, and then the intermediate sections are placed, to minimize shrinkage. The base slab is poured over a waterproofing membrane, and walls and top slab are placed by means of movable steel forms to provide smooth and accurate interior surfaces.

The concrete tube may be heavy enough for sinking, in which case it has to be supported by pontoons for floating into position. If the completed section is buoyant, it has to be ballasted for sinking. Temporary ballast may be placed internally, using water, sand, or ballast blocks, or permanent ballast consisting of gravel or lean concrete may be placed on top of the section.

Prestressing: Since concrete thickness is determined largely by the weight required to prevent uplift, prestressing is economical only for very wide sections. Obtaining watertightness by prestressing alone, without membrane, is controversial.

Waterproofing: The improvement in achieving watertightness was one of the factors for the advancement of concrete immersed tube tunnels in Europe. According to recent Dutch practice, a concrete immersed tunnel can be water-tight if one of two design parameters is used effectively: crack control to achieve impermeability of the concrete, or an independent waterproofing system. The measures necessary for watertightness and crack control were discussed previously. The following waterproofing types are examined.

Steel membranes made of 1/4in. structural steel plate have been applied to several concrete box tunnels as a waterproof enclosure. All joints are welded, and anchors are welded to the skin to bond it to the concrete. With temporary stiffening, the plates may serve as a form for the concrete. For the tender design of the Great Belt project in Denmark, a continuous steel plate was used along the circumference of the cross section. In most cases, a steel plate has been used to waterproof the base slab and at least a portion of the side wall. The recently completed Conwy Tunnel in England used a 1/4in steel membrane for bottom slab and sidewalls. The top slab is protected by two layers of bitumen covered by concrete. Special attention needs to be given to the joint between the steel plate and the bitumen membrane. The steel membrane is protected against corrosion by cathodic protection.

Multi-ply membranes of fabric and coal-tar layers can be applied to the top of box sections, at least four plies being used. To protect the membrane against damage during handling and placing of tubes, it is covered with a thin layer of poured concrete, bricks, or planks of concrete, asphalt or wood. Due to the difficulty of attaching such a membrane, and in protecting it later, it is not practical to use it on the sidewalls or the bottom.

Plastic membranes made of synthetic neoprene or vinyl type rubbers have been developed for waterproofing concrete structures. Sheets of this material about 1/8in thick can be attached to the roof and sidewalls with special adhesives. Due to the difficulty of protecting the membrane on vertical sides against damage, use of this method has been limited.

Epoxy coatings, mostly of coal-tar epoxy to waterproof the sides and tops of tunnel sections, have also had a few applications. Great care is needed in preparing an epoxy mixture in order to retain adequate elasticity and adhesion and in its application to the concrete surface. The coating may be applied by bush or sprayed on a completely dry surface. Protecting such a coating or membrane on vertical sides against mechanical damage is extremely difficult. Primary emphasis has been on using concrete as an impermeable barrier with improvement in crack control and in expansion joints, details, and element joints.

5. Weight control of tubes

Final weight: Final weight of the completed tube, including main structure, inferior finish, and backfill, has to be controlled to counteract buoyancy forces. Thickness of concrete is more often determined by the weight required than by structural strength.

Weight of tubes at various stages: This has to be controlled in accordance with construction procedures. Tubes built in dry docks are solidly supported by keel blocks, and the only criteria are the loading on the supports and on the dock floor. These do not impose any serious restrictions on the construction sequence. When concrete is placed while the tube is floating, as in the steel shell type, the sequence of pouring concrete is governed by several factors: keeping the tube on an even keel; increment of immersion producing hydrostatic pressure on the steel plate; and longitudinal bending moments from unequal loading.

Factors of safety against buoyancy: The fundamental difference between recent European and U.S. practices for the selection of safety factors against buoyancy arises from the difference in construction methods between concrete box and steel shell design. There are two contributing factors for the difference; the use of distinctly different materials for watertightness (structural steel versus structural concrete) and the use of final ballast. In U.S. practice, steel shell plate design generally is not controlled by stress considerations. It is primarily a watertight membrane and the maximum stress occurs during construction. Also, the dimensions of the concrete lining of a steel tube tunnel are not controlled by stress, but by buoyancy. The steel shell's ductility provides a variety of options in placing the final ballast and the structural concrete. The ballast is generally placed during sinking, allowing the steel shell to be used as a vessel for long-distance towing with the minimum freeboard available.

In contrast to the steel shell tunnel, concrete tube tunnel design is controlled by the quality of concrete for crack control, temperature control, shrinkage, and creep control. The concrete tube usually cannot be used as a vessel for transporting elements to the site because the entire ballast concrete (usually at the bottom slab) is placed in the casting yard. This allows better quality control. As a result, a concrete tube generally will have negative buoyancy, requiring pontoon type equipment for transport. European immersed tubes are usually constructed relatively close to their permanent locations, as the large concrete sections are difficult to transport. By contrast, U.S. steel tubes are frequently fabricated at a considerable distance from the tunnel site.

In European practice, the required factor of safety for buoyancy at the element's permanent state is 1.05, *based on minimum weight and maximum water density, excluding the friction forces from backfill and excluding the weight of operational installations, finish work, pavement, safety walks, and backfill.* Generally, no design guidance is given for the factor of safety to be observed during concreting, transporting, or sinking. The required additional temporary ballast during the dewatering of joints between tube elements is left to the contractor. The final factor of safety against buoyancy including total weight of the element and backfill, excluding friction is generally greater than 1.15. It must be noted that Dutch practices is not to specify a factor of safety against uplift, but rather to specify instead a minimum residual bearing stress, to be maintained under maximum uplift, minimum-weight conditions.

For U. S. practice, the following is recommended: After placing the tube in the trench and before backfill is placed or interior finish, including sidewalks, ledges, and roadway pavement are completed, a minimum factor of safety of 1.10 is required. This may be achieved by adding temporary or permanent ballast. The specific gravity of the water in the silt from adjacent dredging operations or sludge from other sources must be checked.

After dewatering of joints and removal of the end bulkhead, and prior to completing the interior concrete lining and backfill at the joint, the structure should have a minimum factor of safety of 1.02. The completed structure should have a minimum factor of safety of about 1.2, not including backfill. With backfill in place, the factor of safety against uplift of the tunnel is usually at least 1.5 or more.

Checking of weight is done by computation of weight of structural and reinforcing steel and accessories and continuous checking of unit weight of concrete samples. In determining the volume of the concrete, the volumes of embedded structural steel, reinforcing steel, conduits and pipes more than 2 inches in diameter, and all boxed-out niches should be deducted. The weights of available aggregates are determined, and the mix is designed for weight as well as for strength. If local aggregates have insufficient weight, it is usually more economical to use more distant sources of supply of heavier material instead of increasing the concrete volume of the tubes.

6. Preparation of trench

Dredging sections: The trench must be deep enough to allow for a foundation course below the tunnel, the height of the tubes, and preferably a minimum of 5ft of protective backfill. Under certain conditions, a shallower trench may be used for short distances, with the tunnel projecting partly above the natural bottom of the tunnel. The side slopes depend upon the soil characteristics and may vary from near vertical in rock to 1:4 in soft material. Generally, a slope of 1:1.5 is feasible. In unusually deep trench sections, an intermediate berm may be required.

Payment for dredging may be based on fixed quantities determined by a side slope selected on the basis of borings and slope stability studies, say 1:1.5 in reasonably firm soil, giving the contractor the option to steepen the slope to, 1:1 at his own risk or flatten it to 1:2 with a unit price payment on overweight if actual soil conditions require this.

Rough dredging: This is usually done, at the contractor's choice, as a continuous operation. Hydraulic dredges are used where suitable for depth and material and where disposal areas are within economical pumping distance. For greater depths or barge transportation of soil, clamshell dredges are used. For harder materials, dipper dredges are used.

Fine dredging: Fine dredging to final dimension is done two or three tube lengths ahead, to keep the time interval between it and the placing of the tube to a minimum.

Removal of silt: Just prior to the placing of the foundation course, the trench is checked for accumulation of silt or sloughing of the dredged slopes. Any such accumulation is removed by clamshell, suction dredge or air lift.

7. Tube foundations

Several methods have been used to prepare the foundation supporting the tubes. Since the weight of the tubes including backfill is not much greater than that of the displaced soil, accuracy of alignment is the most important function, bearing capacity being a second consideration.

Screeded foundation course: The finished dredging is carried to a minimum 2-3ft below the bottom of the tube. A cover of course sand or well-graded gravel is placed in the trench and leveled to accurate grade. The gradation of these materials may vary from 1/4 to 1-1/2 inch in light currents, or may go up to 6in stones where heavy currents occur. The leveling is done by dragging a heavy screed, made of a grid of steel beams, over the surface in successive passes, adding material as needed. The screed is suspended from winches on a carriage rolling on tracks supported on an assembly of two steel barges yoked together. The tracks are adjustable to parallel the grade. The rig is anchored in correct position. Adjustments are made in the screed suspension to compensate for tide level changes. The foundation for a 300ft tube can be screeded in two or three setups. *For the 58 tubes of the BART tunnels in San Francisco, a special screed rig was built consisting of a steel truss of 240ft in length, supported by flotation tanks that could be partly ballasted with water to reduce buoyancy, permitting anchoring the assembly against tide level changes, thus eliminating adjustments during screeding.*

Accuracy of screeding usually allows a tolerance of ±1-1/2in in elevation for a 300ft tube for a highway tunnel. The tubes for the San Francisco Trans-Bay tunnel were set within a tolerance of ±1-1/2in of theoretical grade.

Jetted sand and sand flow foundation: The first jetted sand foundation was used for the Mass Tunnel in Holland in 1946. Since then, a number of tunnels have been built using this method, where a sand-water mixture is jetted under the tunnel element while the element is positioned to line and grade on temporary supports. The jetting is accomplished through a horizontal pipe within the opening between the tunnel and the dredged trench. A sand jetting gantry with a tower is constructed over the top of the tunnel, moving along the tunnel to facilitate the jetting operation. The reach of the jetted sand is adjusted by a nozzle on the jetting pipe to change the exit velocity. On the average, the sand constitutes about 0-15% of the sand/water volume. Packing of the sand is usually loose, with a void ratio of approximately 40%. The minimum thickness of the sand foundation was determined to be 3ft to ease the jetting operation. In early tunnels, including the Maas Tunnel, the establishment of a regular flow pattern was not easy to achieve because of the fixed position of the supply pipe (perpendicular to tunnel axis). In later tunnels, this was changed, where the supply pipe revolved around the vertical pipe located at one side of the tunnel and connected to a gantry that rode along the temporary bridge on top of the tube. The primary disadvantage of the jetting method is that the major part of the operation takes place at the surface, which can be a handicap for a busy channel. Because of this disadvantage, the design of the Western Scheldt Tunnel in Holland in 1969 proposed a sand flow method.

The sand flow method, as it was named later was an improved version of the method proposed for the Western Scheldt tunnel. In the Vlake Tunnel project, a sand barge and pumping units were moored along the shoreline allowing a clear channel for navigation. Two sand flow lines were provided within each tube, connecting to two sets of discharge openings located in the bottom slab with an assumed radius of deposit of 36ft for each. For a 412ft element, a total of 26 discharge points were used, 13 for each half of the bottom slab. Discharge valve openings contained rubber-coated steel balls on the underside of the slab. During the pumping, sand and water mix will push the ball down, allowing inflow to pass. When pumping is stopped, the ball will be forced back to its seat by hydrostatic pressure. The sand flow method not only provided a clear channel for navigation, it also secured better control for a uniform sand flow pattern, which was very desirable for conditions with high currents.

Pile foundations: In unusual circumstances, where the soil under the tunnel is too weak to support the tunnel and backfill, and cannot be economically excavated and replaced with firm material, the tubes may have to be supported directly on pile bents. These are driven and cut off underwater to grade. Various cushioning systems are used between the tops of the piles and the bottom of the slab to mitigate the tolerance in practical pile cut-off elevation.

A weak layer of soil may be strengthened by driving a series of compaction piles. These are driven so that their tops are 1 or 2ft below grade and are covered with a screeded foundation course.

Recently in Holland, several immersed concrete tunnels with interesting features of pile foundations have been constructed. In 1961 the IJ tunnel in Amsterdam was constructed on pile foundations consisting of eight 3.5ft diameter cast-in-place concrete piles with pile cap at 100ft intervals. The boring and concrete placement for the piles was accomplished with the help of fixed pontoons with four legs. Only the top 30ft of the piles were reinforced. The pile caps placed over the piles were constructed by diving bells suspended from floating double pontoons. The connections of tunnel elements to the pile cap were achieved by connecting 1in thick rubber bags to the bottom slab of the tunnel elements set at the preestablished pile cap locations to receive the bags, and then filling the retained volume by pressure grout from inside each tunnel element. The elements were held in theoretical position by temporary support during the connection operation.

In 1990, American's Zeeburger Tunnel was constructed on a pile foundation using 1.65ft diameter steel piles driven to a depth of about 140ft along the outer walls of the tunnel elements, spaced at 9ft centers. The accuracy required for connecting piles to the tunnel elements was achieved by using vertically adjustable serrated locking pieces. Initially, tunnel elements were supported temporarily by two piles while the serrated connection piece was lowered to engage the pile head. Final connection was established by engaging the upper piece of the serrated connection to the lower piece by applying pressure grout to the connection devices.

Mortar injection as foundation course: Over the past decade in Japan, the mortar injection method has been frequently used as a foundation course. The system includes placement of mortar while the tube is supported by temporary support jacks. The base slate is designed to include $4m \times 4m$ spaced injection orifices through which a low-viscosity bentonite mortar is injected at pressures 0.1-$0.2 km/m^2$ higher than the local water pressure to form a continuous foundation.

Injection of the mortar is monitored by ultrasonic gap meter to check the clearance between the bottom slab and the top of the grout. Generally, low-viscosity, low-segregation bentonite mortar is used with balanced mortar pressure to obtain required strength in the foundation course. Generally a 500mm thick grout is used. To retain the mortar within the foundation limits, a stopper bag and crushed stone combination is used along the edges of the foundation. Before placing the tubes on the temporary supports, stopper bags are placed at the inner end of the temporary supports and the crushed stone along the outer edge of the foundation. The bags are inflated with water before injection of the bentonite. Bags used in combination with crushed stone prevent the grout from moving out of the foundation limits. The system was first used on the Tokyo Port tunnel in 1976, and its use has since become common practice in Japan.

Tube placement: The tubes are moved from the construction basin or outfitting site with a freeboard of about 12-18in. Heavy concrete box sections may have less freeboard, and to ensure their buoyancy they may be supported by pontoons or barges, which then form part of the lay barge. The methods of placing vary somewhat according to the type of foundation support and type of joints between tubes. In tidal waters, the actual placing is scheduled during slack tide. In rivers with constant flow or where slack tides are extremely short, the effect of the current on the tube while it is being lowered must be analyzed. This is particularly important for wide rectangular sections, where water pressure may upset the equilibrium of the tube while it is suspended on wire ropes with a relatively small positive weight. The specific gravity of the water in the bottom of the trench is checked to gauge the adequacy of the ballast.

The lay barge consists of two or more steel barges. These are placed parallel, with sufficient space between them to clear the tube, and connected with transverse girder bridges that carry for lowering winches. The assembly is further stabilized with diagonal wire ropes. The lay barge is held in position by wire ropes extended from winches to heavy anchor blocks placed on the bottom at distances of several hundred feet. The anchoring devices must have an adequate factor of safety to resist the maximum current pressure and wind forces on the barge and tube. The capacity of the lowering winches and wire ropes is determined by the net positive weight of the tube during placing. This may vary between 100 and 400 tons, depending on the size of the tube and the contractor's choice of sinking equipment. Load-limiting devices may have to be installed on the lowering winches to prevent overload on the wire ropes, if there is danger of sudden surges in water level to which the tube cannot respond quickly enough. By imposing speed restrictions on passing vehicles during lowering, this danger can be minimized.

In some cases, two whirly cranes mounted on barges have been used to support the tubes during placing. This limits the lowering weight to about 100 tons, but it permits more precise adjustments of the position of the tube without moving the barges.

(1) Placing on screeded foundation.

After ballasting, the tube is slowly lowered until it nearly touches the foundation. Its inboard end is kept clear of the outboard end of the previously placed tube. After a final alignment check, it is then moved against the other tube as required to make the connection at the joint and set down on the foundation. If the weight of the tube is light, as when handled by cranes, additional ballast must be placed as soon as the connection is made—either by filling all tremie pockets with concrete or by temporary heavy concrete blocks—to secure the tube against uplift.

(2) Placing tubes on jetted or sand flow foundation.

In Europe the selection of temporary support for the jetted sand or sand flow foundation is usually left to the contractor. The temporary support may vary from concrete foundation blocks to inflatable bags, depending on the selected immersing system.

In early tunnels, temporary foundations were cast in dry dock and attached to the tunnels, usually four per tunnel unit. In recent construction, temporary blocks are placed on the bottom of the trench separately before the tunnel unit arrives. This reduces the depth requirements for the dry blocks. Generally, temporary foundation blocks are placed on gravel foundation by a screeding gantry with hydraulic legs, or longer strokes. An average concrete block will have 15ft × 15ft × 3ft dimensions to receive the rams from hydraulic jacks located inside the tube, in order to keep the tunnel element on alignment and at proper grade. Recently, the number of temporary foundations has been reduced to two supports located at the outboard end of the element being placed. Two seats on the unit in place provide the support for the inboard end. Unlike the screeded foundation, one important factor that must be recognized by the designer is the settlement characteristics of the jetted sand or sand flow foundations. For both systems, after the removal of temporary supports, the tunnel element can settle as much as 3in. An average settlement of 3/8in. can be expected under normal conditions. For this reason, in Holland, immersed concrete tunnels are designed with dilatation joints every 60-75ft coinciding with the ends of modular units. These joints are designed to transfer shear and therefore will prevent differential settlement between segments and, at the same time, will allow rotation. As a result, the concrete tube will act like a series of linked structures following the combined settlement of the sand foundation and the subsoil strata without inducing longitudinal bending moments. For a successful uniform, approximately 0.02in in average diameter, which is the cause of settlement of a foundation course (not a well-graded material).

One of the everlasting challenges of this type of foundation system is the quality assurance during sand flow or jetting. Over the years, a number of instrumentation system have been developed to correlate the water pressure at discharge, sand packing of the mixture, the amount of sand supplied, jacking pressures at the temporary supports, and echo sounding of the outside walls in order to assess the uniformity of the sand foundation and to minimize the upward pressure against the base slab. During the Vlake Tunnel construction, 2.8in. settlement took place at the last injection point. This was assumed to be related to silting during the sand flow operation. For two 412ft long and 90ft wide units of the Vlake Tunnel, a total of 13000 yd^3 of sand was used within 200 working hours (30 days). In spite of all the instrumentation mentioned above, correlation between the mixture and pressure at the nozzle and the upward pressure at the base slab was not conclusive. Since then, the foundation placement time for sand flow foundations has been improved. The recently completed Liefkenshoek tunnel in Antweep required 60 working hours for the placement of foundations of an element 460ft long and 106ft wide.

8. Alignment control

To check the horizontal and vertical position of the tube during placing operations, temporary survey towers are mounted on the tube near the ends. These project above the water and carry survey targets. To control transverse level (roll) of tubes and to ensure coincidence of the target location with that of the tube below, a vertical plummet was installed in the survey towers of the Trans-Bay tube in San Francisco in relatively deep water.

On the first tube placed at each end, two survey towers are mounted, one near each end to correctly place the tube. The tower at the outboard end is left in place until the next tube is placed. The position of the inboard end of each following tube is governed by the tube already in place, so that a survey tower on these tubes is needed only at the outboard end. After the towers have served their purposes, they are disconnected by divers and reused.

Instruments for checking the alignment are mounted on each shore. On long tunnels or where horizontal curves occur, additional instruments are set on pile-supported platforms in the water. Theodolites are used. Where more elaborate survey towers with vertical plummets are used, instruments can be mounted on them, sighting on targets located on the shores. A final check of the position is made after the tube has been placed and connected to the previously placed section.

Generally, in the United States, tunnel elements are placed by suspending them from catamaran barges, where all load lines and alignment control cables are anchored. In Europe, the horizontal control is made through fairleads from the elements connecting to freestanding anchors. This option permits positive control of the outboard end of the tunnel. However, the operation is more complex and time consuming. In the United States, before construction of the BART tunnel, the tunnel elements were joined by use of a tremie seal joints. Gasketed joints were used for the first time in the United States on the BART tunnel. In this type of joint, horizontal correction for small errors cannot be accomplished by control cables from the barge. Corrections are made usually by the placement of shims, which can be frustrating at times. A method using an adjustable wedge system was first developed for construction of the Fort McHenry tunnel. A set of wedges, about 16ft long, 1.5ft wide, with varying thickness up to 4-1/2in were placed on each side of the rubber gasket seal at the horizontal centerline of the section. Once the joint is dewatered and the wedges bare, a follow-up survey of the in-place tube will indicate how accurate the initial setting is. If further correction is needed, the joint is refilled, permitting the wedges to be reset for final desired positioning. The entire operation can be controlled from the surface by a hydraulic system that takes not more than 1/2 hour to operate on average. The time-saving feature of the wedge system can be an added advantage in constructing tunnels under busy harbors.

9. Joints between tubes

Tremie joints: Tremie joints have been used in a number of steel shell tubes and are still applied when relatively few sections are required. A circular steel collar plate, of the same diameter as the tube shell, is welded to the outside of the end bulkhead and projects 4ft. To the lower half of this collar on the outboard end of the tube, a 3ft wide hood plate is welded with filler, half its width projecting beyond the end of the collars. A similar hood plate is welded to the upper half of the collar at the inboard end of the tube. The fillers provide an annular clearance of 1in. between hood plates and collar. When the following tube is lowered, its inboard collar plate fits into the lower hood of the previous tube. On the horizontal diameters, where upper and lower hood plates meet, each carries a heavy welded bracket with a hole for a 5in diameter steel pin. The hole in the upper bracket is round: the one in the lower is elongated to provide about ±1.5in tolerance. After the tubes are pulled together by four steamboat ratchets, operated by divers, to match the brackets, the divers insert the tapered end steel pins, which are secured to the brackets by wedges driven through slots in the pins.

Curved closure plates are inserted in guides attached to the vertical edges of the rectangular end dam plates. Either sheet pile section or steel angle guides are used to form the guides to connect the curved plates to the dam plates. Sometimes, a series of sheet piles in a curved configuration has been used instead of closure plates. The piles are driven into the bottom of the trench, the foundation course having been omitted at the joints, so that an enclosed space is provided by them and the end dam plates, which is filled with tremie concrete. To prevent concrete from flowing inside the joint, the annular space between hood pates and collars is caulked by divers. Care must be taken to ensure that the tremie concrete flows across the bottom of the joint, and that at the top it is level with the top of dam plates. This provides an adequate seal of the joint with only minor leaks, if any. Any leakage must be sealed off by grouting, before the joint can be completed. To dewater the joint, valves are provided in the end bulkhead of the previous tube. The joint is then entered through the watertight doors mounted in the end bulkheads. Before opening the bulkhead doors, the air in the joint should be tested for explosive gases due to possible decomposition of organic matter in the water trapped in the joint.

Sectional linear plates are welded to T-sections on the interior of the collar plates to form a continuous watertight steel membrane for the tunnel. The space between these liner plates and the collar plates is filled with grout under 10psi pressure. Then the interior portions and the dam plates are removed, and the interior concrete lining is placed, thus completing the joint. The same process is used for completion of regular gasketed joints. Linear plates are welded to the T-section after successful completion of initial sealing and before concreting.

Rubber gasket joint: In this type of joint, the initial seal of the joint is provided by the compression of rubber gaskets attached to the face of one tube and bearing against a smooth face on the adjoining tube. While various shapes of gaskets have been used, the principle is the same. The tube being placed carries a continuous gasket on the periphery of its inboard face. After lowering, the tube is moved close to the outboard smooth-faced end of the tube in place so that hydraulic coupling jacks, extending from one of the tubes, can be engaged into mating parts on the other tube. These jacks pull the tube into contact and give an initial compression to the gasket. This seals the joint sufficiently for it to be drained from the inside, which brings into action the entire hydrostatic pressure on the far end of the tube, compressing the gasket, temporarily sealing the joint. Positive stops are provided to limit the compression of the gasket to its design range. After dewatering, the joint then can be entered through the doors in the end bulkheads, and the permanent connection made.

A single gasket of large dimensions was used on the Deas Isand Tunnel and on similar concrete box tunnels in Europe. The tip of the gasket provides the initial seal. Under final pressure, the body of the gasket is compressed to about half its height and carries the entire load.

A double-ring gasket of smaller cross section was used in the Trans-Bay Tube of BART. The gaskets are attached to a continuous bracket-type extension of the tube structure. The cantilever lip on the outer gasket is deflected by the pull of the jacks and provides the initial seal. Upon dewatering of the joint, the gaskets are compressed to one-half of their height. A steel bar welded to the face provides a definite (limit) stop to the movement that avoids any variation in the final spacing of the joint. Valved drain lines bleed the water between the gaskets to the interior during compression. The gaskets made the joint watertight, permitting the welding of the interior liner plates and completion of the concrete lining.

Coupling jacks: Large single coupling jacks mounted at the center of the bulkhead in each bore have been used in Deas Island and other similar tunnels. They must be controlled from inside the tube, and a diver has to enter the open joint to check that they are properly engaged. Once pulling has started, they are no longer accessible if trouble develops.

Multiple, externally mounted jacks—similar to large automatic railroad couplers—were used in the San Francisco Trans-bay tube. Two of these were mounted on each side of the tube: one near the top, the other near the bottom. They were at all times accessible to divers for checking. Should one have malfunctioned, the other three would have been sufficient to close the joint. After the gasket was compressed, the coupler bars were wedged in position and the hydraulic jacks were removed for reuse. The hydraulic control hose lines were extended to a control panel on the lay barge. The system worked exceptionally well for all 58 tubes. Since completion of the BART tunnel, similar couplers have been used successfully in other projects.

Closure Joints: In long tunnels with many tubes, it is usually most expedient to start placing the tubes from both ends, with the closure joint somewhere out in the waterway. In the 58 tube Trans-Bay Tunnel, tube No. 7 was the last one placed. To provide for fabrication tolerance, which may be cumulative, and for adequate clearance in placing the last section into the space, the closure joint must allow for adjustment. Rubber gaskets cannot be used because no hydrostatic compression is available. A tremie joint with extra long hood plates was used in the Trans-Bay tube, providing a 24 in allowance for clearance. It was sealed in the same way as described for the regular tremie joint. Due to very tight fabrication tolerance required was less.

Special joint for seismic movements: The San Francisco Trans-Bay tube BART is located in a highly seismic area. Although it does not cross any active faults, the tunnel structure, including the joints, is capable of elastically absorbing deflection from seismic waves originating anywhere in the area's major faults. Where the ends of the submerged tube section join the massive ventilation buildings, particularly at the San Francisco side, differential movements in any direction may occur between tube and building, amounting to as much as 4 in. A patented composite telescoping and sliding joint allows for these motions. For transverse sliding or rotation displacement, two neoprene gaskets are attached to the tube end, held under compression against a Teflon-coated steel plate on the building side by a series of short steel wire ropes. A telescoping joint of similar construction permits longitudinal motion. Provisions are made for retightening of the ropes by threaded sockets and nuts if needed. Flexible neoprene-impregnated fabric covers attached to the outside of the joints protect the outer gaskets and Teflon areas from the backfill.

Tolerance in fabrication and placement of tubes generate small misalignments between adjacent tubes, which require adjustments to the installation of interior finish elements such as ceiling panels, lighting fixtures, roadway pavements, curbs, and walkways. For this reason it is usually advisable not to mount attachments for finish elements on the interior of the tubes during fabrication, but rather to drill attachments into the concrete lining after the tubes have been placed and their final alignment and profile have been surveyed. This will ensure the necessary visual continuity within the entire tunnel.

10. Backfill

Locking fill: A special fill is placed in the trench to about half the height of the tube to securely lock the tubes in position after there are connected. This is a well-graded material that compacts easily on placing. It may be sand or coarser material, depending on available source. Material used has been well graded, usually ranging in size from 1-1/2in to No. 100 mesh size, but sizes up to 8in have been used in strong currents.

Sand may be placed through tremie pipes or by clamshell bucket, which is opened only when reaching the bottom. This is also used for coarser material.

Ordinary backfill: Ordinary backfill to fill the trench to a depth of at least 5ft above the tube may be any reasonably firm material available. In long tunnels, soil excavated from the trench may be used as backfill over tubes that have been placed in other parts. Backfill should be free from clay balls, chemically inert, and material passing the No. 200 mesh sieve should not exceed 20% by weight.

Protection against scouring: Where part of the tunnel projects above the original bottom, or where strong currents prevail, the backfill is protected with a rock blanket 2 or 3ft thick. The size of the stone depends upon erosive action of current and usually varies between 1 and 10in. The width of the blanket should be at least 100ft on each side of centerline or confined within dikes.

Text B Design of Tubes
管 节 设 计

1. Design considerations

Although construction methods for steel tube and concrete tube tunnels are different, the design process is similar. For each tunnel type, evaluation of the following design considerations will be most beneficial in establishing the basic design parameters:

(1) Project limits and interfaces.

(2) Design codes and standards.

(3) Selection of materials (structural steel, structural concrete, and others).

(4) Applicable loads and surcharges.

(5) Probability and magnitude of accidental loads such as sunken ships, anchor dropping,

dragging ship anchors and others.

(6) Acceptable design flood levels.

(7) Realistic tunnel fire scenarios and fire safety and other emergency requirements.

(8) Determination of self-weight for applicable loads and variation in specific gravity of construction materials.

(9) Assessment of water (sea) conditions such as wave heights, current velocities, current directions, swell and surf conditions, and density variations.

(10) Yearly statistics of weather conditions and weather windows (pressure, wind, rain, temperature visibility, and others).

(11) Establishing design-basis earthquake if applicable.

(12) Tidal effects.

(13) Internal or external explosions due to terrorist attack or other causes.

(14) Applicable operational system and safety requirements.

(15) Navigational requirements.

(16) Concrete cover, minimum reinforcement, shrinkage, and crack control limits.

(17) Corrosion control system selection.

(18) Selection of method of analysis, use of ultimate limit state, serviceability limits state, or both.

(19) Selection of loading combination and load factors for each design stage or condition.

The fundamental difference between recent European and U. S. practice for the design of immersed tube tunnels stems from the use and limitations of two distinctly different materials, concrete and steel. In general, for the U. S. practice, steel shell plate is not controlled by stress consideration. It is primarily a watertight membrane. The shell plate thickness is chosen to limit distortion under fabrication, or to permit reasonable spacing of stiffeners to avoid excessive buckling and to ease placement of concrete for the liner. Maximum stress occurs during construction, launching, towing, and placement of interior concrete if the placement is performed while tubes are afloat.

Under final service conditions, stresses in steel tube tunnels are relatively uniform, resulting in smooth stress flow in a lightly stressed structure. This is highly desirable since the shell plate serves as the primary waterproofing membrane. Concrete lining of the steel tube tunnel is not controlled by stress, but by buoyancy. Since neither the steel shell nor the concrete lining is controlled by stress, the use of ultimate limit state analysis is not warranted. For this reason, design analysis for steel tube tunnel in the United States generally is controlled by serviceability limit state and the design is verified for accident loads using the ultimate limit state. Cracking of the concrete lining is of little concern, since the waterproofing is provided entirely by the ductile steel shell plate.

In contrast to the steel tube tunnel, concrete tunnel design is controlled by the quality of concrete for crack control, temperature control, shrinkage, and creep control. Therefore, the proper use of material control factors, durability and safety class factors of ultimate limit states plays an important role in the design and analysis of concrete tube tunnels. This is a particularly important issue for the recent Dutch immersed concrete tube practice, where watertightness depends wholly on the concrete being crack-free, and exterior membrane waterproofing is eliminated.

2. Selection of cross section

For a railroad, transit, or vehicular tunnel, selection of cross section is dependent on vertical and horizontal clearances, number of lanes or tracks, type of ventilation system, and required air duct areas. Typical cross section configurations are circular, octagonal, arch, and rectangular. The number of bores depends on the number of tracks or lanes. Transit and railroad tunnels are usually ventilated by the piston action of the train, and except for fire protection they do not require air ducts. Vehicular tunnels more than 500ft in length usually require ventilation. A full transverse ventilation system requires both exhaust and supply air ducts, and a semitransverse system require either a supply or exhaust duct. Ideally, the exhaust duct is located above the roadway and the supply duct beneath it. The configuration for a two-lane single bore is best suited to a circular or octagonal shape tunnel, which structurally is the most efficient. The flat-bottomed arch shape is suited to single-bore tunnels with a semi-transverse ventilation system. Rectangular shapes for multilane single or multiple roadways have center or side duct locations, which reduce the depth of the structure and dredging. For a single bore with a semi-transverse supply ventilation system, location of the supply duct above the roadway has been used, but it requires reversible fans for emergency exhaust during a fire.

3. Setting the interior geometry

An optimized geometry satisfying the operational requirements of an immersed tube tunnel is the principal objective of the design process. Optimization of geometry applies not only to the dimensions of the cross section, but to the length of the tunnel element. For steel shell tubes, considerations include selection of fabrication methods for subassemblies; number of girder welds, number and location of mitered joints to accommodate vertical and horizontal curves, diaphragm spacing, use of stiffeners, constraints imposed by fabrication practices and tube-launching facilities and the availability of material.

Optimization of the interior dimensions of a circular cross section can be accomplished by use of available software programs, where minimum radius for the shell plate can be obtained from coordinates of roadway or trackway, and the vehicle clearance envelope, including space requirements for signs, signals, and other installations.

Element geometry and layout can be a significant factor in cost optimization, particularly for tunnels with alignment curved in horizontal and vertical directions. For long tunnels, it may require a number of iterations before reaching an optimized element geometry that satisfies the alignment requirements and the local steel fabrication and production constraints. Before initiation an interaction of profile optimization and tube module length selection, discussion with local steel fabricators and shipyards or dry docks will be beneficial. In selecting the modular length, two items will control the process: the plate widths, and the lifting capacities. Separation of horizontal and vertical curves in the alignment is desirable. While miter locations need not relate to module length, significant cost savings can be achieved if the miter locations are close to the beginning or end of a module. Miters that actually coincide with the joint location are therefore not used. Precise alignment of the plate edges may involve repositioning of the module or the "strutting" of the plates. Optimization of these operations will result in significant cost savings.

4. Loading conditions

For the design of the tubes, loads from the structure's weight, water pressure, earth pressure, and superimposed live loads must be considered. Other loads can consist of accidental loads such as a sunken ship, anchor dropping, vessel grounding, temporary load such as earthquake, or permanent loads due to special surcharge. The design loads are usually classified into two general categories: construction-phase loads and final in-place loads.

Construction-phase loads include those imposed during the fabrication, launching, towing, outfitting, and placing operations. The significance of these loads varies with the type of construction. For tubes fabricated in a dry dock or a graving basin, the stresses induced during fabrication, launching, and outfitting can be controlled easily. For steel shell immersed tube tunnels fabricated on shipways and outfitted in flotation, these stages can induce large stresses if not controlled by the proper sequence of concrete placement operation.

Final in-place loading conditions include normal and temporary loads. Normal loads include the dead load, water pressure, earth pressure, and superimposed live load that the structure is expected to encounter during normal operating conditions. Temporary loads include additional loads produced by unexpected events such as earthquakes, floods, anchor dropping or vessel grounding, explosion loads, and others. For quick preliminary analysis, basic components of the normal in-place loading conditions can be reduced to the elements for a circular section. The loads can be explained in the following manner:

(1) Uniform distributed load—top. This is usually equal to the weight of the soil above the structure and the normal uniform surcharge load.

(2) Uniform distributed load—side. This load results from the uniform load located above the structure and is equal in magnitude to the appropriate coefficient of lateral pressure times the magnitude of loading components.

(3) Wedge shape horizontal load—side. This load results from lateral pressure of the soil located below the top of the structure.

(4) Quadrant loading: This load results from the vertical soil load located below the top of the structure at the corners, which, for simplicity, is balanced by a uniform reaction along the bottom of the structure. For rectangular cross sections, quadrant loading does not exist unless the top of the tunnel section is sloped at its extremities.

(5) Buoyancy force: This load consists of the buoyant force acting on the structure balanced by the weight of the structure. If the weight of the shell of the tube is uniformly distributed around the circumference and is sufficient to cause fu submergence, there will be no bending in the shell. The assumption that the weight is uniformly distributed is not strictly correct since some of the weight is concentrated near the bottom, in the roadway slab, the sidewalks and ledge etc. Also part of the tremie concrete is not placed until after the tube rests on the bottom of the trench. Analysis

has shown that these ventilations have a relatively slight effect on the stresses in the shell of the tube.

(6) Water surcharge: This load results from the weight of water located above the top of the tube. When the tube is completely submerged, the additional uniform water pressure caused by the depth of water above the top of the tube causes a uniform compression around the ring, but no bending moments.

5. Design loads

Design loads for stress analysis are based on boring information and the specific gravity of water at the site. For stability against uplift, assuming 3000psi concrete with 1/2-1in. maximum size aggregate, the unit weight of concrete is usually 145pcf; structural and reinforcing steel is 490pcf; and water is 64pcf.

For checking buoyancy during flotation, the usual weight of concrete is assumed to be 147 pcf, and steel and water weights are the same as for stability against uplift. Specific gravity of silt-laden water in the trench must be considered. During construction of the Washburn tunnel in Texas, an overnight freshet washed silt into the trench before a recently placed tube had been backfilled and the tube floated to the surface.

Factors of safety against uplift were discussed earlier. Stability calculations should be based on the net volume of concrete. Weight of all conduit, pipe, reinforcing steel, and structural steel should be included. The calculations should be based on the full length of the tube. The critical condition for stability against flotation occurs after the tube is on the bottom and connected to the previously placed tube. After the joint has been dewatered and the end bulkhead has been removed, and prior to completing the interior concrete at the joint, with no backfill in place, the factor of safety should not be less than 1.02. If this factor of safety cannot be maintained, temporary ballast, such as sinking blocks, should be provided.

Water level is usually assumed to be mean sea level. Where the fill over the tube extends above water level, maximum movements occur in the tubes with minimum water level. Where the surface of the fill is below water level, the moments are not affected by the elevation of the waver surface, but the direct thrusts in the shell of the tube will increase with higher water levels.

For a tunnel profile set below the existing sea bottom, the depth of submerged earth is usually calculated as the distance from the top of the structure to the existing sea bottom prior to construction. This accounts for any siltation into the trench that may occur in the future.

Live load surcharge depends on the future use of the area above the tube. Usually, 500psf is assumed unless definite loads are known. In industrial areas, a surcharge of 1000psf is not unusual. On the McHenry Tunnel in Baltimore, Maryland, a 2000psf surcharge was used on the east end of the project to accommodate a future cargo facility.

The seismicity of the project site must be investigated. The alignment should be located clear of any active faults. Particular attention should be directed to any abrupt changes in structure mass or in the stiffness of the subsurface materials. Seismic articulation joints may be provided where unacceptable movements or stress levels are anticipated.

6. Construction phase

The construction phase consists of the fabrication, launching, towing, outfitting and placing operations. Fabrication, launching, towing, and outfitting stresses are a function of the construction method. For construction in a dry dock or casting basin, stresses produced by these operations are usually not significant. For fabrication on shipways and outfitting in flotation, these stresses can be very large. In the following paragraph, shipway construction and outfitting in flotation will be discussed.

Fabrication and launching stresses depend on several items, including the type of structural system (single or double-shell), the method of fabrication, the length of the tube modules, the method of erection on the ways, the blocking between ways of support of the modules, way spacing, slope of the ways, and launching method. During these assembly stages, each module and tube section should be self-supporting or should be locally reinforced for local buckling, lifting, and launching stresses. In addition, transverse deflections of the modules should be checked, and if required, internal spider bracing frames should be installed to maintain the diameter of the shell plate, to permit proper fit-up for the circumferential butt welds between the tube modules.

Depending on the launching system, keel concrete may have to be placed prior to launching. If keel concrete is poured prior to launching, after the pouring the weight of the steel shell and keel concrete should be transferred from the temporary blocking to the launching sleds prior to launching. End launching may require reinforcement of the shell and diaphragms. Temporary longitudinal reinforcing of the top of the shell to preclude longitudinal buckling may be necessary. For side launching, the steel shell and diaphragms may require local strengthening over each sliding way. In evaluating these stresses, the keel concrete should be considered to be longitudinal beam acting with the shell plate and diaphragms. Stresses in the shell and form plates should be investigated for water pressure at launching.

There have been occasions where steel immersed tubes have been towed in excess of 1000mile to an outfitting site. On several projects, the route from the fabrication site to the outfitting site involved towing on the open seas. Wave conditions for the selected route must be investigated and the tube analyzed to span between wave crests. For simplicity, the tube is modeled as a thin-shelled beam stiffened by the longitudinal stiffeners. The critical unit compressive stress for buckling is the same as discussed below for the outfitting operation. Fabrication, launching, and towing stresses generally are the responsibility of the contractor, since they depend on the method of fabrication and transport.

During outfitting while floating and except for the end bulkheads, the weight of the tube is uniformly distributed longitudinally and is supported by the buoyancy forces. The end bulkheads, however, impose concentrated loads, creating hogging moments along the tube element. Depending on the weight of the end bulkhead, the hogging moments will result in tensile stresses at the top and compression stress at the bottom of the tube element. This is highly desirable since the shell plate can sustain higher tensile stresses than the compression stresses at this stage of the construction. Placing the keel concrete prior to launching not only protects the bottom portion of the shell plate during launching, but it will also help to resist the compression stresses and buckling tendencies created by end bulkheads' hogging moments. As the placement of interior concrete proceeds, the added longitudinal moments produced by concrete placement will counteract the hogging moments, neutralizing the shell plate stresses along the tube element.

In addition to the longitudinal moments, the steel shell and stiffening diaphragms are subjected to circumferential bending moments resulting from the exterior water pressure. For double-shell construction the form plates are not made watertight, to minimize the pressure acting on them and to permit the shell plate to resist all the water pressure.

A typical sequence of concrete placement by stages is shown, the length of pour for each stage is a function of convenience in form-placing operations, the quantity of concrete that can be conveniently placed in a single shift, and the longitudinal moments and shears that the shell can withstand. Insofar as possible, pours should be symmetrical about the transverse and longitudinal centerlines of the tubes in order to maintain trim of the tube and reduce the water pressure on the shell plate. Experience has shown the stages and sequence indicated and usually results in the most favorable design and construction conditions.

Moments, shears, and head of water acting on the shell plate and diaphragms due to the unbalanced weight of bulkheads and the fresh concrete are calculated for each stage and length of pour. Usually, the critical condition occurs during the placing of the haunch pour for sequence 5. At this stage, the shell and diaphragms are fixed at the top of the keel concrete, and the head of water against the shell extends from the top of the keel to approximately the horizontal axis. The pressure of the fresh concrete against the inside of the shell is usually neglected. The resulting circumferential moments are resisted by the shell plate and the diaphragms, with longitudinal distribution of loads by the shell plate and longitudinal stiffeners.

Text C Some Immersed Tube Tunnel Cases
几个沉管隧道案例

1. Busan-Geoje Immersed Tunnel, Korea

Busan-Geoje fixed link involves the construction of an 8.2km motorway connecting Busan to the island of Geoje. The connection includes a 3240m immersed tunnel—one of the longest and deepest in the world and two cable-stayed bridges, each 2km in length. The total length of the 3.6km with two 170m long cut and cover sections at both ends.

The design of the immersed tunnel includes the structural design of tunnel elements, joint, foundations and tunnel protection, west approach cut and cover structure, east approach cut and cover structure, ventilation buildings and all related mechanical, electrical and communication system.

The immersed tunnel is designed for two lane traffic with emergency and crawler lane where appropriate. The central gallery in the tunnel, between the motorway lanes, will contain utilities and an escape route.

The immersed tunnel consists of 18 pre-cast tunnel elements placed in a dredged trench at a maximum water depth of 50m the first time a concrete segment immersed tunnel is constructed at such depth. The outer dimension of the elements is 180m long, 26.5m wide and 10.0m high. The maximum gradient is 5%. The design life of the tunnel is 100 years.

(1) Due to soft soils the tunnel foundation includes soil-improvement (sand compaction piles and cement deep mixing). Towards the western landfall the tunnel elements are placed inside a subsea embankment above the existing seabed. Hydraulic model testing was carried out to establish stone sizes on the tunnel roof and to study the overall stability of the tunnel during a typhoon event. The design of the tunnel protection at the eastern portal includes a risk analysis of ship impact.

The tunnel elements were constructed in a casting basin, up to 5 elements in each batch. The elements are cast in segments of 22.5m.

(2) Each element consists of 8 segments and was tied together longitudinally before float-up by a number of post-tensioning cables. The cables are cut when the element is placed in the final position.

After flooding of the casting basin the elements were towed to a mooring area for temporary storage. Transportation of the elements, 36km under sheltered conditions, took place just before immersion. The immersion site is offshore.

The foundation methods and temporary works for immersion were developed in cooperation with the contractor, taking into account the actual soil conditions and the severe wave conditions on site during immersion. Extensive physical testing and numerical models were carried out to determine sea-conditions under which safe immersion would be able to take pace. The tunnel elements were placed directly on a leveled gravel bed and, in some cases, ground underneath. Optimization of methods and temporary works was carried out during construction with input from the designer.

2. Oresund tunnel

In Europe, immersed tunnels are mainly used for motorways to cross rivers. Theses crossings are normally relatively short, at around 500-600m; Netherlands examples range between 77m for the Pr, Margriet tunnel and 1265m for the Piet Hein tunnel in Amsterdam. Immersed concrete tunnels are thus normally moderate in length, and at 3510m immersed length Drodgen Tunnel is by far the longest immersed concrete tunnel in the world. This was dictated not by the width of the navigation channel but by environmental requirements. The required "zero solution" for the Baltic, combined with restriction on the amount of compensation dredging, could only be achieved by a more than 3500m long tunnel.

The use of longitudinal ventilation by booster fans gives a further dimension to the length of the tunnel, as in an immersed tunnel the additional space around the clearance envelope is for economic reasons reduced to an absolute minimum.

Initially, immersed motorway tunnel always had transverse ventilation system, which requires additional longitudinal ventilation ducts and buildings at the portals. The Maas tunnel has such a transverse ventilation system including ventilation towers at the portals. Longitudinal ventilation, by which fresh air enters through the entrance of the tunnel and is propelled through the whole length of the tunnel to the exit, was used for the first time in 1961 in Germany's Rengburg Tunnel.

Followed by the Coen tunnel, this became more or less the standard type of ventilation for motorway tunnels in the Netherlands, but in other countries it took much longer before longitudinal systems were accepted. Before the Drogden Tunnel, the 1265m Piet Hein tunnel in Amsterdam held the record of the longest longitudinal ventilation immersed tunnel. Having a system to actively control traffic flow into the tunnel to avoid excess pollution levels was used to enable a longitudinal ventilation system in the unprecedented length of the Drogden Tunnel.

The length of the Drogden Tunnel and its straight horizontal and gradual vertical alignments opened up the possibility of unconventional production methods of the elements. Industrialized construction had been considered previously for projects in the Netherlands but they proved to be uncompetitive for short crossings. Before the Oresund Link, concrete elements for immersed tunnels had all been produced in a casting basin or dry dock, in the open air, and below ground water level.

In some cases the casting basin location was far from the site and elements had to be towed considerable distance over open sea: 85km, 70km, and 175km for the Sydney Harbour, Wijker and Pier Hein tunnels respectively. Only smaller immersed cable ducts and conduits and service tunnels had been produced using industrialized and repetitive production method. In several instances elements have been produced in line in ramps, as for the Pr. Margrier tunnel in Netherlands.

The construction method for the Drogden Tunnel elements was an industrialized process in a ground level production hall, wherein factory and controlled climatic conditions allowed for high and constant quality. This method adds a new chapter in the history of immersed tunnel construction is expected to be used again in the future, where appropriate.

Permanent watertightness is essential for all submerged structure. For concrete immersed tunnels it can be secured by an external membrane or b the concrete itself. Early concrete tunnels all have membranes of various types, but in 1975 the Vlake tunnel in the Netherlands was constructed without an external membrane, relying wholly on the watertightness of the concrete. This was made possible by avoiding hydration cracking by artificial cooling, and the method has been successfully used for all immersed tunnels built in the Netherlands since 1975. For the service tunnels crossing the Holland, hydration stresses in the young concrete were avoided by casting the whole cross-section in one. After casting, which took place in a vertical position, the sections were turned 90 degrees to the horizontal for assembling.

Among other reasons the construction of the first concrete immersed tunnel, a new technology was developed. This was the installation of a sand layer by jetting sand/water mixture under tunnel elements while they were temporary supported by jacks. Release of the jacks brought the elements to rest on the sandbed.

Before the USA type of tunnels were founded on a gravel bed, which was not considered feasible for concrete tunnels because of their greater width and limited flexibility.

Sand jetting normally takes place from a barge above the element. As this obstructs ship traffic the sandflow method was developed and used for the first time for Vlake tunnel (1975). This method enabled a sand/water mixture to be pumped through pipes from the riverbanks under the tunnel. For many years sandflow has been used to found concrete immersed tunnels, but because of its size, the subsoil, and time constraints, the Drogden Tunnel drove the further development of a new technology, already used to found caisson in Singapore. This made it possible to place a gravel bed on the seabed within strict tolerances.

All the four outstanding features of the Drogden Tunnel and the successful completion of the whole Oresund Link will doubtless boost the use of immersed tunnel, a technology with its own range of application and within this several advantages over other construction methods. The special features will bring longer, deeper and perhaps even floating immersed concrete tunnels closer to reality in the second century of their history.

3. Malmo City tunnel, Sweden

The new city tunnel under the central part of Malmo forms the final part of the Oresund link between Malmo and Copenhagen. It links the existing railway network from the central station to the Oresund link. The project consists of a 17 kilometer double-track railway line and three stations of which 6 kilometers and two stations are underground.

The underground section consists of 4.6 kilometers twin-bored tunnels and 360 meters cut and cover tunnels at the southern end and 1.6km cut and cover tunnel and station at the northern end. The bored tunnels were excavated with two earth pressure balance TBMs with external diameter of 8.9 meters. The tunnels were excavated in Copenhagen and Bryozoan limestone which is fractured and, in places, highly permeable and contains layers or noodles of flint with un-axial compressive strength of up to 200MPa. The TBMs were each equipped with 55 disc cutters which had to be frequently inspected and changed.

The tunnels are lined with precast concrete rings of an internal diameter of 7.9 meters. Each ring consists of 7 segments plus a key. One segment is 1800mm wide and 350mm thick.

Thirteen cross-passages connect the two main tunnels every 300-400 meters, and they serve as emergency routes for passengers and house electrical and mechanical installations. Two of the cross-passages will be combined with access shafts for rescue personnel.

The Triangeln station is a mined station. It has cut and cover boxes at each end where escalators, lifts and equipment are installed. The main part of the station is a 250 meters long cavern, 28 meters wide and 14.5 meters high. The central platform is 14.5 meters wide with central support columns. The station is 25 meters below ground level with a 10 meter cover of limestone. The construction is close to St. Johannes Church and other buildings. Groundwater is controlled by a dewatering and re-charging system in combination with a grout curtain surrounding the station cavern and boxes. The excavation was carried out in stages with a central audit where the central station columns were cast prior to excavating the side audits. Excavation of the larger side audits were carried out with a top heading, bench and invert.

4. Hong Kong-Zhuhai-Macao Bridge, China

The Hong Kong-Zhuhai-Macao link (HZM Link) is a three-lane high-speed connection cross the Pearl River delta between Hong Kong SAR and the city of Zhuhai (mainland China) and Macao SAR on the western side. The link consists of an immersed tunnel, low bridges and two man-made islands.

(1) The top of the tunnel is placed at 28 meters below the water level making the tunnel very deep. The feasibility study included a comparison of an immersed tunnel solution and a bored tunnel solution as well as an environmental impact assessment, construction risk and operational safety etc.

The immersed tunnel is 5.4km long making it the word's longest immersed tunnel. In the conceptual design the cross-section was established based on operation requirement such as space for traffic, ventilation and other electrical and mechanical equipment. The external tunnel width is 40 meters and the height is 10 meters.

(2) The foundations at the shallow part of the immersed tunnel are in very soft soil which makes it necessary to combine soil-improvement, piles and direct foundations. The conceptual design was also used as the technical part of the bidding proposal for winning the design contract of the preliminary design.

5. Limerick immersed tunnel, Ireland

(1) The Limerick southern ring road will provide an east-west bypass of Limerick City for both regional and local traffic. The ring road will pass the River Shannon and allow unrestricted shipping traffic to the Ted Russel Dock in Limerick. A number of cross options (low-level bascule bridge, high-level fixed bridge and immersed tunnel) have been considered with due consideration of environmental and aesthetic constraints and soil conditions.

(2) The preferred option is a tunnel comprising a dual-tube immersed concrete tunnel with a length of approximately 700 meters including adjoining cut and cover tunnels at each end.

The open ramp on the northern bank was temporarily drained and used as a construction dock for the tunnel elements. On the southern bank the ramp will combine with an embankment across Bunlicky Lake.

The works entailed major excavations/dredging and foundation of structure in very soft, organic clays and very hard limestone.

The tunnel and adjoining roads and bridges will be designed, built, financed and operated as a public-private partnership (PPP) scheme.

The tunnel is to be operated by the PPP concessionaire for a period of 30 years. Construction works started after award of the concession contract in 2006. Four years after the tunnel was opened for traffic in June 2010.

6. Copenhagen district heating tunnel, Denmark

As part of a modernization project the district heating Production Company, Energi E2 decided to move production in Copenhagen from two old production plants to a completely new production block located at the Amagervaket plant.

In order to connect the new plant with the existing distribution network KE decided to build a tunnel for the pipe. The project comprised 4km of bored tunnels and three shafts in total.

The heating pipes in the tunnel convey either hot water or steam.

(1) The steam pipes are built as steel in steel pipes with vacuum between the outer and the inner pipe.

(2) Despite of this insulation, the surface temperature of the steam heating pipes reach 100°C and ventilation is required to keep a uniform operation temperature of around 50°C in the tunnel. Prior to maintenance, the ventilation can be increased to further reduce the temperature to around 35°C.

These conditions are quite demanding to the structural design. The solutions must be able to resist the expansions resulting from the temperature rise during operation, and also the chemical reactions associated with detrimental processes tend to run much faster at elevated temperatures.

Consequently, it was decided to design the segmental lining without traditional reinforcement and use steel fiber-reinforced concrete (SFRC) instead. The advantage of the SFRC is that it reinforces the surface zone during construction, and even if it corrodes in the surface zone the associated volume changes will not damage the concrete due to the small size of the steel fibers.

The shafts were designed with retaining walls of secant piles penetrating well into the limestone. From the feet of the piles down, the retaining structure was made by sprayed concrete lining (SCL) technique, which was also used for the TBM launch and receipt chambers at the bottom of the shafts.

To avoid decomposition of the wooden piles forming the foundation for numerous historic buildings groundwater tables were not lowered during the works.

The project was tendered as a "late partnering" project, and shortly after the civil works contract was signed with the joint venture MT Hojgaard-Hochtief JV, a partnering agreement between the client, the contractor and the consultant was signed. The agreement included a definition of joint success criteria, responsibilities, day-to-day organizational set-up, a conflict handling model, milestones and associated bonuses as well as a target maximum total price.

The late partnering was intended to best benefit the combined knowledge of all the parties to find optimal solutions for the project and thereby avoid the budget overruns. This intention was fully met, and the project was finalized on time and approximately 5% below the maximum target price.

7. Shanghai Yangtze River Tunnel and Bridge Project

Shanghai Yangtze River Tunnel and Bridge Project are located at the South Channel waterway and North Channel waterway of Yangtze River mouth in the northeast of Shanghai, which is a significant part of national expressway. It is an extremely major transport infrastructure project at seashore area in China at Yangtze River mouth and also the largest tunnel and bridge combination project worldwide.

Shanghai Yangtze River Tunnel and Bridge (Chongming Crossing) alignment solution is the planned western solution which is implemented firstly based on the Shanghai over urban planning, and comparison between east and west alignment and in combination of various aspects. The western alignment starts from Wuhaogou in Pudong, cross Yangtze River South Channel waterway to Changxing Island and spanning Yangtze River Mouth Channel waterway to east of Chongming Island.

Yangtze River begins to be divided into 3 levels of branches and have 4 mouths flowing into the sea. The South Channel waterway is mixed river trench. The intermediate slow flow area forms Ruifeng shoal which is relatively stable for a long time. The natural water depth makes it as the main navigation channel. However, the North Channel waterway is located in the middle part of river, which is influenced by the south part and branch transition into North Channel waterway. So the trench varies alternatively and the river map is not as stable as South Channel waterway. Therefore, after iterative discussion by several parties, finally the solution of South Tunnel and Northern Bridge is selected.

The total project is 25.5km long, among which 8.95km is tunnel with a design speed of 80km/h and 9.97km is bridge and 6.58km is land connection with a design speed of 100km/h. The project is designed as dual 6 lanes expressway, and rail traffic provision is made below the road bed. Seismic fortification level is 7. Design service life is 100 years. The project consists of land connection of Pudong side, river-crossing tunnel and land connections on Changxing Island. The river-crossing part is twin-tube bored tunnel. The longitudinal profile of bored tunnel is in a shape of "W" with a longitudinal slope of 0.3% and 0.87%. The land connections have a longitudinal profile of 2.9%. The minimum curvature radius of horizontal plane is 4000m and vertical profile 12000m. The ring width is 2000mm and thickness is 650mm. The lining ring consists of 10 segments, i.e. 7 standard segments, 2 adjacent segments and 1 key segment.

II. Terms and terminology

immersed tube tunnel	沉管隧道
trench	沟槽
dredge	(用挖泥船等)疏浚;挖泥船,疏浚机
section	管段,管节
bulkhead	隔板;防水壁
backfill	回填
prefabricated section	预制管段
estuary	河口;江口
rock dike	岩墙
wharf	靠泊码头
shellfish	甲壳类动物;贝类等有壳的水生动物
settlement	沉降
alignment	线形
bending stress	弯应力
crack control	裂缝控制

watertightness	防水
dry dock	干坞
pontoon	趸船；驳船
ballast	压载
prestressing	预应力
synthetic neoprene	合成氯丁橡胶
vinyl type rubber	乙烯基橡胶
epoxy coating	环氧树脂涂层
buoyancy	浮力
main navigation channel	主航道
leveled gravel bed	整平碎石垫层
ship impact	船撞力
environmental impact assessment	环境影响评估
open ramp	敞开段
award of concession contract	授予特许经营权合约
adjoining roads	连接线
steel fibre-reinforced concrete (SFRC)	钢纤维混凝土

Ⅲ. Questions and difficult sentence analysis

1. Questions for brainstorming discussion

(1) What are the advantages and disadvantages of immersed tube tunnel method compared with TBM tunneling method?

(2) What physical conditions such as weather, current and geology should be utilized in immersed tunnel construction?

(3) Briefly state the principal works procedures of IMT method and point out the principal control factors in this given construction technique.

2. Difficult sentences analysis

(1) Permits for construction and jurisdictional conflicts with other governmental agencies over environmental protection, natural resources, and local conditions must be evaluated and resolved. Approval of these agencies should be obtained during the preliminary dredging stage.

译文：施工许可证书以及辖区与其他政府主管机构在环境、自然资源和当地条件的保护问题上的冲突必须加以评估和解决，并在初步疏浚阶段应该取得这些主管机构的批准。

(2) Under normal conditions, immersed tube tunnels are relatively insensitive to soil settlement, because their buoyant weight differs only slightly from that of the original submerged soil or the adjacent backfill. However, when the soil types and the loading pattern vary significantly along the tunnel alignment, differential settlements will take place.

译文：在正常条件下，沉管隧道对于土沉降相对来讲不敏感，因为沉管的浮重与原来的水下土体或相邻填筑体的重量相差不大。但是，当沿隧道轴线的地质和荷载作用模式变化很大时，会发生不均匀沉降。

(3) In European practice, the required factor of safety for buoyancy at the element's permanent state is 1.05, based on minimum weight and maximum water density, excluding the friction forces from backfill and excluding the weight of operational installations, finish work, pavement, safety walks, and backfill.

译文：按照欧洲惯例，沉管永久状态的抗浮安全系数取1.05，该系数的选择是根据最小重量和最大水密度，不包括回填产生的摩擦系数，也不包括作业安装设施、饰面工程、路面、安全墙和回填料的重量。

(4) For the 58 tubes of the BART tunnels in San Francisco, a special screed rig was built consisting of a steel truss of 240ft in length, supported by flotation tanks that could be partly ballasted with water to reduce buoyancy, permitting anchoring the assembly against tide level changes, thus eliminating adjustments during screeding.

译文：旧金山的巴特隧道（BART tunnels）由58根管节组成，搭建了一个专门的刮平工作台，由一个240英尺长的钢桁架组成，支承在一个装有部分压载水的浮船上，以减轻浮力、能抗潮位变化锚固组件，因此不需要在刮平作业中调整。

Ⅳ. Translation case study

Case 1

Chinese	English translation
项目概况 　　拟建的港珠澳大桥跨越珠江口伶仃洋海域，是连接香港特别行政区、广东省珠海市、澳门特别行政区的大型跨海通道，是国家高速公路网规划中珠江三角洲地区环线的组成部分和跨越伶仃洋海域的关键性工程。主体工程采用桥隧组合方案，穿越伶仃西航道和铜鼓航道段约5.99km采用沉管隧道方案（不含岛上隧、桥过渡段），其余路段约22.9km采用桥梁方案。为实现桥隧转换和设置通风井，主体工程隧道两端各设置一个海中人工岛，人工岛各长625m，东人工岛东边缘距粤港分界线约366m，西人工岛东边缘距伶仃西航道约2000m，两人工岛最近边缘间距约5584m。	The project overview 　　The proposed Hong Kong-Zhuhai-Macao Bridge is a large marine link across the Lingdingyang sea areas at the Pearl River estuary and spanning linking Hong Kong Special Administrative Region, Zhuhai city of Guangdong province and Macao Special Administration Region and is a critical engineering works across Lingdingyang Sea as well as a part and is part of the ring road in the Pearl River Delta Zone in the State planned under State express way network program and a key works across seas of Lingdingyang. The principal part of the mega project works adopts a bridge-tunnel combination, An immersed tunnel in total length of 5.99km (excluding the tunnel section under the artificial islands and tunnel-bridge transition) is taken to cross the Lingdingxi navigation channel and Tonggu channel and bridge is taken to cover the rest distance in approximately 22.9km solution of combination of bridge and tunnel and the tunnel covering around 5.99km across Lingdingxi navigation channel and Tonggu navigation channel adopts immersed tunnel solution (excluding the tunnel on artificial island and bridge transition section) and the remaining road section around 22.9km adopts bridge solution. To enable the bridge-tunnel transition and arrangement of ventilation shaft, one offshore artificial island is arranged respectively at the both ends of the immersed tunnel with each island in length of 625m. The east

Chinese	English translation
	edge of the East Island and the demarcation line of Guangdong/Hong Kong are approximately 366m apart while the east edge of the West Island and the Lingdingxi channel are approximately 2000m apart. The minimum edge-edge distance between the two islands is approximately 5584m. realize transition between bridge and tunnel and provision of ventilation shaft one marine artificial island is set respectively at both ends of the tunnel principal works with each artificial island of length of 625m respectively. The boundary line from east edge of east artificial island to the demarcation line between Guangdong and Hong Kong is around 366m and the distance between east edge of west artificial island and the navigation channel of Lingdingxi is around 2000m. The shortest distance between edges of the two artificial islands is around 5584m.

Case 2

Chinese	English translation
隧道横截面 　　隧道设计将在不降低施工与运营期间隧道安全度的前提下，尽量降低工程量和造价。造价与风险方面的优化应考虑安全、可行、风险优化的施工方法、设计寿命期、环保以及节约能源等。设计将考虑结构与基础之间的共同作用，以寻求最优方案。综合通风、消防救援、经济与技术等因素，港珠澳大桥沉管隧道最终确定采用二孔单管廊的横断面，两侧为行车道孔，中间为综合管廊，管廊内分为三层，上层为专用排烟通道；中层为安全横通道，建筑限界高2.2m；下层为电缆沟和海底泵房。隧道中隔墙上每间隔90m设置一处横向安全门，连通两车道孔及横向安全通道。中间管廊细部设计根据排烟道面积、安全通道高度以及给排水管道高度等综合需求确定。	The Tunnel Cross Section 　　Tunnel design shall reduce works amount and build cost to greatest extent without compromising reducing safety level margins during construction and operation periods. The optimization in respects of cost and risk shall consider A safe, feasible, low risk optimized construction method, design life span, environmental protection and energy saving shall be overall considered to reduce the cost and risk, design life span, environmental protection and energy saving etc. An optimum design shall be selected by considering the joint actions of the structure and the foundation. The design will consider the composite actions of structure and foundation to seek most optimized solution. By combination of such factors as ventilation, fire fighting, and rescue and aid, economy and technology it is finally determined that the IMT of Hong Kong-Zhuhai-Macao link project will adopts the cross section of two bilateral motorway tubes and one central gallery in which the bilateral two tubes are motorway and central tube is the integrated pipe gallery in which three levels are divided and the upper lever is the specialized smoke extraction gallery; the middle level is safety cross passway with construction gauge height construction gauge height of 2.2m and bottom level accommodates the is electrical power cable trench and the sea floor pump room. One cross safety door is set at interval of 90m on tunnel partition wall to link the two traffic bores and the cross safety cross passway. The detailed design for the central middle tube gallery shall be determined according to the overall requirements on the smoke gallery areas, height of the safe passway and height of the drainage duct.

Case 3

Chinese	English translation
橡胶止水带接头：在该类接头中，首道接头止水是靠安装在沉管端面的橡胶止水带与相邻管节上的光滑面相压缩实现的。采用不同形状的止水带，其止水原理是相同的。被沉放管节端面内侧装有一条连续的止水带，管节下沉后，将管节朝已经沉放就位管节的光滑表面外侧靠拢，将拉合千斤顶从其中一个管节上伸出，与另一个管节上的匹配部分连接，这些千斤顶拉拢并对接这两个管节，使止水带首次压缩并实现接头充分密封，然后从管内向外抽排端封门之间的水，使管节另一端的静水压力发生作用，进一步压缩止水带，临时密封该接头。安装限位装置将止水带的压缩量控制在设计范围内。排水之后，可以通过端封门一端的门进入该管节内，进行永久性连接。	**Rubber gasket joint**: In this type of joint, the initial seal of the joint is provided by the compression of rubber gaskets attached to the face of one tube and bearing against a smooth face on the adjoining tube. While various shapes of gaskets have been used, the principle is the same. The tube being placed carries a continuous gasket on the periphery of its inboard face. After lowering, the tube is moved close to the outboard smooth-faced end of the tube in place so that hydraulic coupling jacks, extending from one of the tubes, can be engaged into mating parts on the other tube. These jacks pull the tube into contact and give an initial compression to the gasket. This seals the joint sufficiently for it to be drained from the inside, which brings into action the entire hydrostatic pressure on the far end of the tube, compressing the gasket, temporarily sealing the joint. Positive stops are provided to limit the compression of the gasket to its design range. After dewatering, the joint then can be entered through the doors in the end bulkheads, and the permanent connection made.

Ⅴ. Assignment

（1）在规划沉管隧道时，首先要充分调查建设现场的地理、物理及人为等各种条件，并与桥梁及其他水底隧道方案进行比较；在充分调查的基础上，进行选址、交通量和交通组成规划、线形和横断面选择、管节结构等规划。

（2）在管段沉放前，基槽开挖不平整，使槽底表面与沉管底面之间存在很多不规则的空隙，这样会使地基受力不均，引起地基不均匀沉降，并使沉管结构受到较大的局部应力而开裂。因此在沉管隧道施工中必须进行基础处理，使管段底面与地基之间的空隙充填密实，均匀接触。

（3）由于是软土，该隧道基础包括地基加固措施，采用砂桩和水泥深层搅拌桩。

（4）一个管节含八个节段，在管节起浮之前，用数根后张拉预应力索将节段在纵向上拉紧。

（5）所选方案为隧道方案，包括双向双管廊沉管混凝土隧道，长度约700m，隧道两端接暗埋段。

Unit 8　Cut and Cover Method
明　挖　法

I. Text

Text A　Underground Works Construction by Cut and Cover Method
地下工程明挖法

The cut and cover method is the general term of the said construction method by which excavation is executed from ground surface downward to the prescribed position of the structure to be built, and is a tunnel construction method by vertical excavation method (relative to the method of tunnel heading in horizontal direction). In municipal underground works, particularly in shallowly burialed subway works, the cut and cover method has been extensively used. Further, the submerged tunnel ends section at river banks and proximity to tunnel ports are commonly constructed by cut and cover method.

While in flat topography with burial depth less than 30m, application of cut and cover method has demonstratedachieves very good practical value; the cut and cover method is highly adaptable and suitable for any rock (soil). The structures of various shapes can be built by this method. Cut and cover method can create maximum working face for underground works execution and all works procedures can be carried out at full-scale and allowing parallel flow process thus expediting construction speed. The construction technique by cut and cover method is relatively simple and easy for operation and the works quality can be assured. Cut and cover method shall be the priority choice to be applied to the regions where surface traffic and surrounding conditions permit.

In recent years, the technology on foundation pit excavation and support has been greatly developed with the expansion of underground space expansion. In early time the foundation pit excavation was shallow and the foundation pit bracing was dominantly a slope excavation or a cantilever type support. With the incrementalprogressively deepening of foundation pit excavation, the foundation pit bracing by means of slope excavation or cantilever support is not economical and cannot satisfy requirements. Therefore, diaphragm walls as support means are dominant. In later time, the comprehensive technology of soil nail and soil-nail wall plus prestresssing anchor cable emerged. With the increase of deep foundation pit excavation works, the deep foundation pit bracing technology has great development. Reverse construction method is one newly invented foundation pit support technology developed recently.

With the increased burial depth the works cost and construction time by cut and cover method will be increased. In addition, open cut construction exerts is of great environmental impacts around such as the impact on surface traffic, commercial activities and residential life. The amount of demolition and replacement of underground pipeline is greater than that of cover and underground excavation method. While the ground water level is high, dewatering and ground improvement stiffening cost is high. Thus, in application of open cut method, the characteristics of all types of construction methods shall be fully considered and the construction method whose special advantages can be made use of shall be selected.

The major problems by cut and cover constructions are foundation pit stability and its construction procedures, selection of retaining structure and dewatering. In cut and cover design the care shall be given to following issues.

1) tunnel depth determinationsetting

The principal problem of tunnel construction by cut and cover method is the determinationsetting of tunnel burial depth. Generally, tunnel shall be placed in sound strata to most extent and adequate investigationngestion in aspects of technology, economy, operation and strata shall be performed and the burial depth in question to be set shall be studied with caution. In normal condition the burial depth shall be less than 20m to ensure the performance and safety of the completed tunnel.

Usually, according to the geology, the strata displacement can be possible after completion of tunnel completion and the influence of the displacement on the tunnel shall be investigated and corresponding countermeasures shall be designed. Particularly Especially in the case of great variation of soft strata thickness, the differential settlement along longitudinal of strata may occur which may causes structural longitudinal abnormal deformation. In addition, in saturated loose soils an and, earthquake may trigger liquefaction of sand layer, which will place the structure under great stress. Adequate concern must be paid to the above-mentioned problems during tunnel planning.

2) Tunnel structure form

The tunnel structure form by cut and cover method is various and can be roughly classified into straight wall arch, single span, double span or multi-span rectangular enclosed frame and other forms. But box-shape and longitudinally connected structures are commonly adopted. The intermediate elements are mostly column structure or wall structures. In box-shape structure, diaphragm wall is taken as a part of main structure. The sectional shape of box structure differs to meet different intended usages of tunnel. There are various forms as illustrated in figure 8.1.

The longitudinal structure of tunnel is always continuous and is generally placed in sound ground and impact on tunnel longitudinal is immaterial and is not considered. But, under the conditions of apparent variation of loading state and stratum conditions and apparent variation of tunnel section, the influence from above mentioned situations of the tunnel stability shall be thoroughly studied.

3) Waterproofing and anti-earthquake of tunnel structure

The cut and cover tunnel is generally built below groundwater level. Thus, the tunnel structure shall be of sound waterproofing performance for which the structure should be as simple as possible to improve the reliability of waterproofing works.

The cut and cover tunnel differs from any surface structure. The tunnel-surrounding ground interaction is very complex, for which special attention shall be paid to tunnel dynamic state in seismic occurrence. In tunnel design, seismic effect on the tunnel dynamic state shall be studied in addition to the societal and economic impacts after the tunnel suffers from a seismic event.

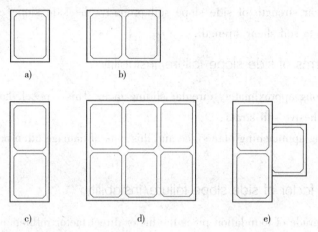

Figure 8.1 Tunnel Structure Form by Cut and Cover Method

1. Foundation pit excavation

Open slope cut method is also called open foundation pit method including two types of complete slope excavation and semi-slope excavation. The complete slope method refers to the foundation pit excavation by complete slope cut without pit wall bracing. Appropriate side slope gradient is used according to geology and excavation by sections shall be carried to require position before structure works commencement and after structure is completed, backfill works shall be followed to reinstate. By semi slope excavation method, a cantilever steel pile of some height is placed at bottom of a foundation pit to enhance the stability of the soil wall and the trench bottom width is determined according to the width of the underground structure and consideration of space needed for execution and operation. In order to retain the side slope stability, dewatering well points are often set along the bilateral sides of the foundation pit.

Application conditions:

While in vacant region without buildings, and excavators and dumpers of high efficiency can be used with convenience' and the foundation pit type by complete slope or semi slope excavation without bracing is often practiced.

The application of above excavation approach is economical of low cost compared with commonly practiced piling works of excavation. Since no road pavement on the covering plate is needed and thus construction cost is reduced and construction time is shortened. But due to large area occupation, large amount of resettlement and cut and fill and traffic interruption in works site, this method is not feasible in region of narrow road and busy traffic. This method is rarely applied in urban central area. The key factors which determine whether this method is to be used or not are the geological conditions, the water infiltration amount and the excavation depth. In the application of opening foundation pit excavation method, adequate concern shall be paid to the impacts from pit side slope protection and excavation on adjacent buildings and embedded parts.

Design and execution:

Two fundamental parameters need to be determined in side slope design: the side slope excavation depth and grade. Since the stability of the side slope of foundation pit is mainly achieved through shear strength of side slope soil property, the side slope excavation depth and grade are all subject to soil shear strength.

1) damage forms of side slope failure/instability

(1) Rotating along approximately circular sliding face. This type of damage often occurs to relatively uniform adhesive soil strata;

(2) Sliding along approaching plane face and this type of damage often occurs to non-adhesive soil strata.

2) influencing factor of side slope failure/instability

The side slope grade of foundation pit is the major direct factor influencing the stability of the foundation pit. While the shear stress in side slope soil of foundation pit exceeds the shear strength of the soil, the side slope will fail and collapse. In addition, improper execution will also cause side slope failure for following reasons:

(1) Side slope is not excavated in conformity with design grade.

(2) Excessive loading on slope crown of the foundation pit.

(3) In sufficient efficient pit dewatering and drainage measures; groundwater is not lowered to till below background while the surface storm drainage and underground supply and drainage pipelines around the foundation pit leak, which and the result in water infiltrating into the soils of side slope of the foundation pit and soil moistening, increase of the soil self weight and thus the increased shear stress in the soil.

(4) The foundation pit is exposed to open air for over long time after its excavation and slope cutting is not performed in time. Further reverse slope excavation is performed, which result in soil instability.

3) The method for determination of the stability of side slope of a foundation pit.

There are three methods as to determine the stability of side slope of foundation pit and they are calculation method, illustration method and table lookup. In the open excavation of municipal underground works, while the geological conditions are sound and soil is homogeneous and the underground water level is low or is kept below groundbase through dewatering, table lookout method is often used to determine the side slope grade of the foundation pit. The table 8.1 and table 8.2 are provided in accordance with groundbase foundation design specification in combination with experiences on municipal underground engineering works and the construction time may be used as reference.

Rock Foundation Pit Side Slope Grade   Table 8.1

Rock category	Weathering degree	Slope gradient(height width ratio)	
		Within 8m	8-10m
Hard rock	Slight Micro weathering	1:(0.1-0.2)	1:(0.2-0.35)
	Moderate weathering	1:(0.2-0.35)	1:(0.35-0.5)
	Highly weathering	1:(0.35-0.5)	1:(0.5-0.75)
Soft rock	Slight Micro weathering	1:(0.35-0.5)	1:(0.5-0.75)
	Moderate weathering	1:(0.5-0.75)	1:(0.75-1.0)
	Highly weathering	1:(0.75-1.0)	1:(1.0-1.25)

Soil Foundation Pit Side Slope Grade   Table 8.2

Soil type	Density or state	Slope grade value(height width ratio)		
		5m	5-10m	10-15m
Gravel soil	Highly dense	1:(0.35-0.5)	1:(0.5-0.75)	1:(0.75-1.0)
	Moderate dense	1:(0.5-0.75)	1:(0.75-1.0)	1:(1.0-1.25)
	Slight dense	1:(0.75-1.0)	1:(1.0-1.25)	1:(1.25-1.5)
Adhesive soil	Hard	1:(0.75-1.0)	1:(1.0-1.25)	1:(1.25-1.5)
	Hard plastic	1:(1.0-1.25)	1:(1.25-1.5)	1:(1.5-1.75)

4) Notes of foundation pit excavation

Out of various reasons, construction situations in reality constantly differ from the original design conditions or the cases beyond considerations of designers. Then the side slope of foundation pit must be reviewed through re-calculationed. If the safety allowance is not adequate, corresponding remedying measures shall be taken up; hence following items shall be noted in works execution.

(1) Determining the grade of the side slope of foundation pit according to soil physical property and folding line shaped slope shall be made in different soil strata or bench shall be reserved.

(2) Dynamic driven pile or static pressure driven pile operations shall not be carried out within the region of impact on excavated foundation pit. While pile driving must be carried out, the side slope must be cut and the load must be reduced. Heavy hammer shall be used and strike from low distance in the pile driving and the piles shall be driven alternatively at intervals.

(3) No excessively heavy loads shall be increased on side slope of foundation pit. While loads shall be increased or vehicle travel on the slope crown, the side slope must be calculated and reviewed to control the loading index.

(4) The construction organization shall be favorable for maintaining the stability of the side

slope of foundation pit. It is ideal that the earth volume be taken out from the excavated part to the unexcavated part in order instead of removing the soil from the top of side slop excavated. Excavations shall be performed from top to bottom in order and the slope toe shall not be cut initially.

(5) Care shall be taken to the reasonable discharge of surface water to prevent surface water from flowing into the foundation pit or infiltrating into the side slope.

(6) Taking drainage measures as well points and lowering groundwater level.

(7) Observing jobsite carefully and upon identifying early sign of the side slope instability (such as cracking) stop execution immediately and meanwhile taking effective measures, improving the stability of undergoing side slope and the execution works may be resumed when the safety requirement is met.

(8) In the process of foundation pit excavation, side slope shall be excavated and cut simultaneously. Reverse slope excavation is not allowed.

(9) For the foundation pit which is exposed for over one1 year, generally slope protection measures may be taken.

5) Foundation pit side slope instability preventions

(1) Slope cutting. Changing the outer appearance of side slope and making the side slope gentle or forming it into bench shape (Figure 8.2). This method aims at reducing the downsliding weight of the side slope and it will be more effective in combination with unloading (including discharging soil) the slope crown.

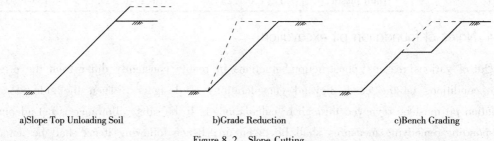

a) Slope Top Unloading Soil　　　　b) Grade Reduction　　　　c) Bench Grading

Figure 8.2　Slope Cutting

(2) Providing side slope surface protection. The provision of concrete protection of the side slope of foundation pit is intended intends to control the surface water infiltration through cracks into the interior of the side slopes so as to reduce the possibility of soil softening and rise of void water pressure due to the infiltration of water (Figure 8.3). In order to enhance the anti-crack strength of the surface of the side slope, some amount of constructional reinforcement in slope interior (as rebar of $\phi 6@300$) are required.

(3) Anti-slide stiffening at slope toe. While the foundation pit excavation depth is great and the side slope cannot be made gentle due to the site constraints of site, the slope can be made gentle by strengthening the soils within the range of side slope slip resistance and such specific methods are: setting anti-slide pile, jet grouting method, grouting in layers and, DCM.

In the application of above-mentioned this methods, care must be taken that the stiffened region shall penetrate through the slide face and some distance shall be kept away from the bilateral sides of the slip face and the range shall be in excess of 5 times the hole diameter for concrete slip-resistant anti-slide piles.

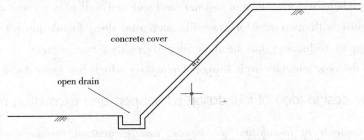

Figure 8.3 Slope Surface Protection

6) Foundation pit excavation works

Since the foundation pit by slope excavation is provided generally for purpose of shallow burial underground works, the earth excavation is in great volume. If the excation is made by hands, the involved labor load will be great stress is great and construction time accounts for up to 25%-30% of total construction time, which is the major influence on construction progress. Thus, large scaled earth excavator and conveyance of high efficiency shall be used to most extent.

For open slope excavation, the current methods currently being adopted are manual excavation, and the excavation by means of small-sized excavator and large-sized excavation machines.

Manual excavation is a performance of of low efficiency and with high labor intensity and thus is generally used in the conditions of small earthwork volume such as slope cutting or in the situations of condition of excavation in short of lack of excavation machines.

The common small-sized machines are simple excavators such as crab bucket and rope-conveyor and the small-sized excavating machines are normally used in limited construction space where large-sized machine can be used.

For large area earthwork excavation, large-sized machines such as single-bucket excavator and scraper are used. Those large-sized machines are of high working efficiency and one large-sized machine can replace labor of hundreds of men and thus can greatly save manpower and expedite works progress.

Digging soil by machine disturbs soil greatly and cannot accurately excavate basement to design level and over-excavation occurs from time to time easily. It is required that soil excavation by machine can only reach to the position at 20-30cm above the groundbase and the rest remaining earthwork in depth of 20-30cm will be removed by hand or other methods.

2. Brief statement of foundation pit support

With the development of underground works, the foundation pit excavation depth is increased constantly and the technical requirement of foundation pit support is continually upgraded higher and higher. Before 1990, foundation pit excavation depth is small and foundation excavation is mainly performed by means of slope excavation or cantilever typed support. After 1990, foundation pit excavation is dominated by means of diaphragm wall pile anchor support or wall-anchor support. Although this type of support technology is safe and reliable, the construction cost is even higher. The comprehensive technology of soil nail and soil nail wall plus prestressing anchor cable is adopted. Recently with increment of gradually increased deep foundation pit works, the deep foundation pit support technology has been developed greatly. For instance reverse construction method is one of the new foundation pit support technology which has been developed recently.

1) The basic design idea of foundation pit support and excavation method

The design contents of foundation pit support and excavation include enclosure structure, supporting system, and earth excavation solution, bracing replacement measure, dewatering scheme and ground improvement. These contents are interrelated and must be comprehensively considered in foundation pit design. The basic design steps are given in table 8.3.

Design Steps   Table 8.3

Design step	Preliminary work	Design and planning	Fence structure calculation	Preparation of construction drawing	Works execution
Content	(1) Understanding works environment; (2) Familiarizing works design intention; understanding construction condition, study engineering geology and engineering	(1) Enclosure structure form and support system plan preparation, (according to needs of work and excavation depth, propose penetration depth in soil, structure form and size); (2) Determining the soil in stratum, soil pressure, surface surcharging, the reaction coefficient k (sandy soil-water and soil respective calculation; adhesive soil water and soil combined calculation); (3) Determining the fence structure's penetration depth in soil stability analysis (overall, upheaval, swelling pipe, bottom bulging, calculating trench wall stability); (4) correct the form of fence structure (including increasing support, penetration depth in soil, ground improvement and dewatering)	(1) Internal force calculation, strength calculation; (2) Displacement calculation $\leqslant$ allowable value	(1) Construction drawing design; (2) Construction notes; (3) Detailed design	Technological delivery to constructor

2) Enclosure structural form and its characteristics

The enclosure structure for foundation is categorized by its prefabrication methods as shown in table 8.4.

Enclosure Structure Categorization Table 8.4

Enclosure Structure				
Prefabrication method			Cast in-situ method	
Simple support	Steel support		Column type	Cast-in-place pile
Timber plate + Longitudinal beam	Steel sheet pile	Prefabricated concrete sheet pile (including prefabricated diaphragm wall)	Wall type	SMW Diaphragm wall (reinforced concrete diaphragm wall and prestressing concrete diaphragm wall) Stabilizing wall Mixing pile wall (concrete)
	Steel pipe pile			

The characteristics of above mentioned types of enclosure structures are given in table 8.5.

Characteristics of All Types of Enclosure Structures Table 8.5

Type	Characteristics
Simple support	Generally applied to local excavation for short time in small range. Method: self stability excavation and wooden retaining plank and longitudinal beam are provided to control stratum collapse concurrently. Features: low rigidity, easy deformation and water infiltration
Sheet pile wall	Spacing of H shaped steel ranges between 1.2-1.5m. Low cost, simple method can change spacing when meeting obstacles. Poor water stop, not applicable in locations of high groundwater level
Steel sheet pile wall	Product fabrication, may be used repeatedly. Simple and easy works execution, but with noise of construction, low rigidity, large deformation, in combination with multiple rounds of bracings, can also be used in soft soil stratum, sound waterproofing when newly built, if any leaking sign occurs, additional waterproofing measures are needed
Steel pipe pile	Sectional rigidity in excess of that of steel sheet pile, large excavation depth in soft soil stratum. Waterproofing measures are needed as aid
Prestressed concrete sheet pile	Simple and easy construction, but generating noise; need to be aided with waterproofing; large self-weight, limited by lifting equipment, not suitable for deep and large foundation pit
Cast-in-place pile	High rigidity can be applied to deep and large foundation pit. Small constructional impact on surrounding stratum; need to be used in combination with water stopping measures, such as mixing pile, jet grouting pile

continue

Type	Characteristics
Diaphragm wall	High rigidity, large excavation depth, applicable to all soil stratums. High strength, small deformation, sound water separation meanwhile can serve as one part of main structure. Can be used in proximity to buildings (structures) with little environmental impact, high cost
SMW method	High strength, sound waterproofing performance, the inserted section steel can be extracted and recycled repeatedly, good economy
Stabilizing liquid curing wall	Extensive application in Japan
CDM-cement deep mixing	With support, sound wall waterproofing, low cost, great wall displacement

3) Supporting system

Supporting system is used to support the enclosure wall body, undertake backside soil pressure and lateral pressure from surface surcharge loading on the enclosure wall. Supporting system is made up of support, enclosing purlins and vertical column and the latter are provided in accordance with the requirement on specific size and deformation of foundation pit. The support material shall be determined in accordance with surrounding environmental requirement and foundation pit deformation requirement, construction technology and construction equipment. Table 8.6 listed the advantages and disadvantages of various support materials.

Advantages and Disadvantages of Various Materials   Table 8.6

Support material	Advantage	Disadvantage
Steel support	Installation, easy remove, and can add prestressing	Small stiffness, large wall displacement, installation deviation may generate bending moment
Reinforced concrete support	High rigidity, small deformation, flexible plane layout	Time is required for reinforced concrete support to gain strength, removal requires blasting, fabrication and removing time takes longer time than that for steel support and axial force cannot be imposed in advance, self weight is large
Steel and reinforced concrete combined support	Use of respective advantages of steel and reinforced concrete	Not suitable for wide and large foundation pit
Pull anchor	Large working space	Soft soil stratum has small bearing capacity, lots of anchors are densely placed and most of the anchors cannot be withdrawn thus causing high cost

3. Sheet-pile retaining for support of foundation pit

Under the constraints of urban narrow streets, the foundation pit width shall be reduced to minimum and the foundation pit type with vertical trench support with combination of steel piles and well point dewatering is commonly adopted. The general practice is to drive I beam pile into soil strata as per design positions to form such supports of continuous sheet piled wall or spacing standing column and bracing. The foundation pit is excavated under the protection of the support. With progress of foundation pit soil excavation, single-level or multi-level supporting structure composed of wooden barrier plates and ceiling support, pull anchor or soil anchor shall be provided between piles to ensure the pile strength and stability under the actions of lateral soil pressure. Provided that soil collapse or ground subsidence still occurs due to use of wooden retaining plank, continuous sheet pile support structure shall be adopted.

1) Applicable conditions

I beam steel piled enclosure structure is applicable to the ground of adhesive soil, sandy soil and sandy cobble with diameter no greater than 10cm. While the groundwater level is high, manual dewatering measures shall be carried out jointly. While piling the constructional noise is generally in excess of 100dB which is greatly in excess of the limit value stipulated in "Law of Environmental Protection". Hence this type of enclosure structure is only suitable for thein foundation pit works in suburb area far away from residential zone.

2) Design and construction

Large I beam of $50^{\#}, 55^{\#}$ and $60^{\#}$ are used as main enclosure structures of foundation pit. Prior to commencement of foundation pit excavation, I beam is driven one by one with impact typed piling machine from surface into soil along the design edge line of foundation pit and the pile spacing is generally set at 1.0-1.2m. Provided that the ground is saturated, muck soft soils, pile can be driven with static pressing piling machine and vibratory piling machine. During foundation pit excavation, 5cm thick horizontal wood back plane is inserted between piles while digging soil to block the soil between piles. After the foundation pit is excavated to some depth, provided that the stiffness and strength of cantilever I beam is not adequate, waist beam and bracing or anchor bolt (cable) are needed. Breast beam is generally made of large channel steel and I beam while bracing can be steel pipe or composite steel beam and support plane.

4. Continuous steel sheet or steel tube piles support

Steel sheet pile is of high strength and the piles are tightly connected which provide sound isolation and can be reused from time to time. Sheet piles are mostly used in the foundation pit where groundwater level is high.

The sectional shapes of sheet piles are often U shaped or Z shaped. In most subway construction in China, U shaped sheet piles are often used whose driving and extracting methods, machines used are all similar to that of I beam piles. But the constructional method can be classified into single level sheet piled enclosure, two-level sheet piled enclosure and screen. Since the foundation pit in subway works is of great depth, to ensure the verticality and ease for execution and enclosure screen construction is mostly adopted.

Both sheet piled enclosure structure and I beam enclosure structure have similar applicable ranges.

5. Digging cast-in-place pile (artificial dig-hole pile)

Digging cast-in-place pile, also called artificial dig-hole pile is extensively applied in foundation pit enclosure structure and building foundations due to its such advantages as flexibility, lack of machine noise and short of mud pollutions and easy adjustment and correction of deviations and accuracy control, low demand on construction site and plant and equipment and low cost. It is defined as hand-dug caisson in BS 8004 1986 and HDC in Hong Kong and called California well and Chicago caisson in USA.

Drilling method and steps are as follows:

Digging piles are normally formed by digging hole by portable tools and extracting the soil by hand-operated or power-driven winch and hanging bucket. After earth excavation for each segment of pile shaft, immediately erect formwork and cast concrete protective lining, which alternates by segments from top to down till reaching design level? With the increased penetration of well shaft, ventilation, illumination and communication equipments shall be installed. While the excavation reaches below groundwater level, general submerged water pump is adopted to draw the water. But to prevent bore bottom collapse, water discharge amount shall not exceed 60L/min. In case of large water amount, dewatering by hand or grouting as reinforcement shall be conducted before hole boring.

The minimum diameter of digging piles is 800mm and for easy operation diameter no less than 1200mm is preferred.

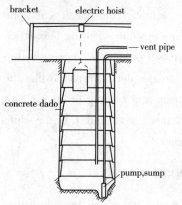

Figure 8.4 Digging Piles

To prevent collapse and assure constructional safety, the digging depth for each segment of pile shaft is controlled in range of 0.9-1.0m and in difficult geological conditions, the digging depth for each pile segment shall be shortened. The concrete lining is in thickness range of 10-15cm and some reinforcement of diameters $\phi 6$ to $\phi 10$ may be placed as required, and C20 concrete is used. For digging piles of super large diameter, its concrete lining dimension and construction shall be specially designed. The concrete lining is all kept inside the bore and became becoming one part of the pile shaft (body) (Figure 8.4).

For the digging piles, pile body concrete mixing, cast method and technical requirement are the same as that of bored pile.

The safety of digging pile construction is priority and in addition to the above mentioned requirement, attention shall be paid to following matters issues:

(1) Sufficient site investigation information and site management with experiences shall be

available and works shall be executed in strict accordance with operation manuals.

(2) Enhance observation of surface and check for any signs of abnormal settlement.

(3) Provide fence and working platform at hole opening.

(4) All the earthwork workers in well must wear safety helmet, safety sling, anti-toxic musk and life-saving ladder shall be provided in the dug hole.

6. Deep mixing method retaining structure

Deep mixing method is one type of method by which mixing machine mixes cement, lime and similar consolidating agents with base soil so as to achieve foundation improvement. General deep mixing method retaining structure is featured with competent impermeability, so in foundation pit excavation, well point dewatering is not used, as avoids harms to surrounding pipelines and buildings. This type of construction method is also free of pollutions thus basically free of vibration and noise, which results in low cost and has become one of the principal forms of enclosure structure of foundation pits recently.

The construction procedures and technology of deep mixing method retaining wall are illustrated in figure 8.5.

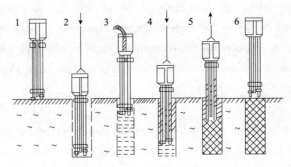

Figure 8.5 Construction Technology

1-Positioning; 2-Pre-mixing while sinking; 3-Jetting mixing while sinking; 4-Repeating mixing while sinking; 5-Repeated mixing while lifting upward; 6-Finish

(1) Positioning. Hoisting mixing machine by crane (or tower crane) to the appointed pile position and center.

(2) Pre-mixing while sinking. After the cooling water cycling of deep mixing machine is normal, activate mixer and slack steel wire rope of crane to enable mixer to cut soil while sinking down along guide bracket.

(3) Prepare cementitious grout. While deep mixing machine sinks to certain depth, namely mixing cementitious grout as per designed mixing ratio, pour the cement grout into aggregate hopper before commencement of grouting.

(4) Lifting, grout while mixing. After the deep mixer sinks to the designed level, activate grout pump pumping grout to foundation and grout while mixing. Meanwhile lift up mixer at designed speed.

(5) Repeat mixing up and down. The rotating edge of mixer can be plunged into soil again to achieve uniform mixing of soil and cementitious grout before the mixer is raised again above ground

surface after the design depth is reached.

(6) Cleaning: inject proper amount of clean water to emptied hopper, activate grouting pump, remove the entire cement residue in whole pipelines and eliminate the soft soil attached on mixing head.

(7) Move to next following pile and repeat above steps (1) to (6) and execute next following pile.

7. SMW method

SMW retaining wall is a method by which soil is cut on spot with mixing equipment and then cementitious mixture is injected and mixed to form a uniform retaining wall in which section steel (such as H steel) is inserted finally by certain form finally, namely forming a type of stiffened composite enclosure structure.

This type of enclosure structure is featured with such advantages as sound water-tightness, simple construction procedure, the shallowsmaller penetration of H steel into the penetration of mixing pile, fast construction, repeated usage of the H section and lower cost.

By SMW method, tri-axle type or multi-axle typed mixers drills on site to reach certain depth meanwhile cement consolidating agent is sprayed out at drill pit to ground soil repeatedly and superimposing overlapping works is conducted among respective construction units. Then before cement mixture hardens, insert section or reinforcement cage as stiffening material until cement soil hardens. This way, as forms a continuous retaining wall of certain strength and stiffness is formed.

8. Soil anchor support

Soil anchor support is a new technology recently developed since past 20 years. The key points are drilling an inclined holes of certain penetration depth (hole diameter approximately 90-130mm) with horizontal driller in the side wall of foundation pit and then placing reinforcement or high strength tendon in the hole center and finalizing with injecting cementitious grout into the hole. To increase grip force, special purpose interior hole expanding drill bit can be used to expand hole diameter 3-5 times larger or blasting can be used for hole expanding and end of hole is expanded.

When the foundation pit is very deep and needs multi-level tie bars, earth anchor support can be used. Earth anchor supports can be arranged in multi-levels and is a very ideal support form in I steel pile and wooden plank support, continuous steel pile support and diaphragm wall and can serve as a permanent structure such as retaining wall structure, anchorage of ship dock bottom plate for resistance against floating or improvement of bridge foundation. But where the soil stratum is soft and loose, anchorbolt installation is complex and difficult. Currently anchorbolts have been used at large and were used in subway tunnel of West Station of Tianjin.

Text B Shoring System
支 挡 系 统

Neat-line excavation in soils requires that temporary walls (commonly referred to as "sheeting" or "shoring walls") be in place before significant cut-and-cover excavation commences. As the excavation progress, the shoring walls must be supported so that they retain the vertical faces of the excavation. The function of the supported shoring walls (shoring system) is usually to prevent detrimental settlement of the ground, utilities, and buildings at the side of the cut as well. The design of the support system will depend on many factors, including the following:

(1) The physical properties of the soil throughout and beneath the cut.

(2) The position of the groundwater table during construction.

(3) The width and depth of the excavation.

(4) The configuration of the subsurface structure to be constructed within the cut.

(5) The size, foundation design, and proximity of adjacent buildings.

(6) The number, size, and type of utilities crossing the proposed excavation. Also, the presence of utilities adjacent to the excavation.

(7) Requirements for street decking across the excavation.

(8) Traffic and construction equipment surcharge adjacent to the excavation.

(9) Noise restrictions in urban areas.

The depth of excavation required for the construction of subsurface structures discussed in this unit is rarely less than 25ft. For the sake of clarity and reference in this unit, it is arbitrarily assumed that "cut-and-cover excavation" exceeds 25ft in depth. Additionally, cases where bedrock lies above the bottom of the bottom of the excavation are not addressed in this unit.

1. Common types of shoring walls

Soldier pile and often classified as "rigid" or "semirigid" walls, depending upon actual stiffness.

1) Soldier Piles and Lagging

A very common type of shoring wall is soldier piles and lagging. The soldier piles are usually steel wide flange (WF) or bearing pile (HP) shapes installed prior to the excavation by driving or drilling. Spacing of soldier piles can range from 3ft or less to 10ft or more; 5-8ft spacing is most common. The soil between the soldier piles is retained with horizontal wood lagging placed between the soldier piles as the excavation progresses. The wood lagging is usually placed behind the inside flanges of the soldier piles but is occasionally placed in front of the soldier piles ("contact lagging") using proprietary hardware or welded, threaded studs with retaining plates to secure the lagging to the soldier piles. During excavation, the depth of exposure below the last-placed lagging may be as little as 1ft, as in the case of say saturated silt (see below), or as much as 4 or 5ft in competent, cohesive or semicohesive soils. The restriction in depth of unsupported cut is the height of the cut that will remain stable until the lagging can be placed, but in soils it should not be more than 5ft.

When soldier piles are placed in drilled holes, the portion of the drilled hole below excavated subgrade is sometimes backfilled with 3000psi (or more) concrete, either to provide for needed bearing capacity when the soldier pile is axially loaded or to improve available passive resistance below subgrade. More commonly, however, this portion of the drilled hole is backfilled with a lean concrete. Above excavated subgrade, good construction practice can range from filling the hole with lean concrete to filling it with a soil-cement mix, depending on the importance of avoiding loss of ground when excavating the soil face to fit the lagging boards in place.

Soldier pile and lagging walls are particularly advantageous when many underground utilities will cross over the excavation. The utilities are exposed prior to installation of the soldier piles can be placed so that they straddle the utilities. After the soldier piles are installed, and during the first step in the cut-and-cover excavation, the utilities are either independently supported across the excavation, or they are suspended from street decking that spans the excavation.

When the cut is in saturated, pervious, or semiprecious soils; or when there are zones of saturated soils within the cut, soldier piles and lagging are rarely feasible unless the groundwater table lies a few feet above the excavated subgrade in semi precious soils, but this practice is not recommended, except in some otherwise very difficult circumstances.

When the groundwater table lies at or has been lowered to a level below excavated subgrade, soldier piles and lagging can be used more or less routinely in a wide variety of soils. Soldier piles and lagging are also used when the cut lies in weak or of being supported with modern shotcrete and rock bolt techniques. Soldier piles and lagging are not ordinarily considered suitable for cuts in very soft clays, saturated silts, loose silty sands, or in any soil that is potentially unstable during excavation.

2) Steel sheet piling

Continuous steel sheet pile walls are composed of rolled Z-shaped or arch-shaped interlocking steel sections. Because of their greater stiffness and resistance to bending, Z-shaped sections are almost exclusively used as steel sheet piling for cut-and-cover construction.

Interlocking steel sheet piling is typically used in saturated pervious or semipervious soils and other loose or weak soils that do not permit the easy placing of lagging. When the groundwater table cannot be lowered, interlocking steel sheet piling is normally adequately effective in cutting off concentrated flow through pervious ground both above and below the excavated subgrade.

Interlocking steel piling is used as well in competent sandy soils when groundwater is not a concern, if there are sufficiently few utility crossing and other subsurface obstacle and it is found economically advantageous to do so. The he sheet piles are driven with either impact-type or vibratory-type hammers, depending in part on the type of soil. In modern pile driving practice, with the assistance of augering techniques, sheet piles can be driven with a vibratory hammer in dense sand to a depth of 65ft or more with relatively good driving production. For the San Francisco Clean Water Program, in soft to medium clays, sheet piles up to 90ft long were driven with a vibratory hammer.

3) Diaphragm walls

In shoring system design and construction, the term diaphragm wall refers to continues shoring walls that are reinforced concrete, a combination of concrete and structural steel, or similar systems. The walls are constructed form the ground surface and are ordinarily designed so that rheumatoid are, for construction purposes, watertight. The more common diaphragm walls, and their applications, are discussed briefly below.

Slurry walls. Although the term slurry wall sometimes has a broader meaning, it usually refers to a reinforced concrete wall placed in a deep trench usually 2-3ft wide. The wall is constructed in increment, or panels. Panel lengths have ranged from 7 to 20ft, but in cut-and-cover construction they are usually 10-15ft long. The panel is excavated with a special clamshell-type bucket. The sides of the panel excavation are stabilized by filling the panel with bentonite slurry and maintaining the level of the slurry at or near the ground surface throughout the excavation. Upon completion of the panel excavation, a preassembled steel reinforcing "cage" is lowered into the slurry-filled panel. Concrete is then placed in the panel by tremie techniques, displacing the slurry.

It is important (almost always) in slurry wall construction that the joints between panels be watertight. The most common type of joint is formed with a circular end pipe. The end pipe is a steel tube inserted at one end of the excavated panel as a stop for tremie concrete. Some time after the start of the tremie concrete pour, the end pipe is rotated to break bond; it is subsequently slowly extracted to produce a formed, semicircular joint, which can be cleaned when the next panel is excavated. There are many variations to the more common procedures described. Polymer drilling fluid has been used in lieu of bentonite slurry on several recently constructed slurry wall projects. More sophisticated types of slurry wall joints have been used to improve watertight at the joints.

Slurry walls can be constructed in soil to depths exceeding 180ft. For cut-and-cover construction, slurry walls deeper than about 100ft are not common, however. Occasionally it is necessary to key he bottom of the slurry wall into rock. Shallow keys in soft to medium-hard rock have been successfully excavated using percussion tools developed for this purpose. Keys into medium-hard to hard rock have been difficult to achieve.

Soldier pile and tremie concrete walls. Soldier pile and tremie concrete (SPTC) walls are composed of soldier piles spaced at relatively close centers with a good-quality very stiff continuous wall. Soldier piles are typically 24-36in. deep, rolled beams or deeper, built-up sections. The principal steps in the construction of an SPTC wall are as follows:

(1) Alternate soldier piles are placed in predrilled holes. Bentonite slurry is used for hole stabilized if required. Each hole is then filled with sand or other weak backfill.

(2) The slot between alternate soldier piles is then excavated with a specially designed clamshell tool. Bentonite slurry is used to stabilize the sideshow of the excavated slot in similar manner to that for slurry walls.

(3) The intermediate soldier pile is lowered into the slot. Unreinforced concrete is then placed in the slurry-filled slot on both sides of the intermediate pile simultaneously, using the tremie method.

Soldier pile spacing for SPTC walls typically ranges from 4 to 6ft, with the upper limit being held to about twice the nominal wall thickness. Apart form the great strength that can be achieved using these walls, there is the added advantage that soldier pile element of the wall can be extended deeper than the tremie concrete element. Thus, the soldier piles can be extended below the tremie concrete into very strong soil or into bedrock when there is a structural reason to do so.

Drilled pile walls. In this chapter, "drilled pile walls" refers to walls formed by abutting cast-in-place concrete or reinforced concrete piles, concrete and soldier beams placed in drilled holes, or combinations of these concepts. Drilled holes range in diameter from about 2 to 4ft. Depending on soil and groundwater conditions, the excavation can be made with rolled without casing, either in dry or slurry-stabilized holes. Cast-in-place concrete or reinforced concrete piles placed in a single line or row, tangent, nearly tangent, or slightly overlapping with each other, have been called "contiguous", "secant", or (sometimes) "tangent" pile walls. With this configuration, considerably more strength can be built into the drilled pile wall. Drilled pile walls are especially suitable when the soil-rock contact lies near or above the cut-and-cover subgrade and a diaphragm wall is either required or most suitable above the rock line. This type of wall (or a wall of similar configuration) can be keyed into rock or constructed as a wall to support weak rock, using commercially available drilling equipment.

Soil-cement mixing walls. Soil-cement mixing walls are composed of soldier piles placed in overlapping columns of in situ soil that has been mixed with a measured amount of cement or cement and bentonite. The soil-cement columns are constructed with special proprietary equipment, which employs a bank (usually three) of hollow-shaft augers. The augers penetrate the soil to the depth of the wall and then are withdrawn, mixing the soil with cement (and bentonite if needed) in the process, thus creating the overlapping circular columns of soil-cement. Before the soil-cement has hardened, soldier piles are pushed into the alternate (usually) soil-cement columns. The augers are normally 24-36in. in diameter. Soldier piles range form W18 to W30 spaced appropriately 3ft on center (with 24in columns) to 4ft on center (with 36in columns). The unconfined compressive strength of the soil-cement ranges form about 75 psi in soft clays and saturated silts to about 200psi in stronger sandy soils. Soil-cement mixing walls may be constructed to any reasonable depth required for cut and cover construction. Wall depths up to 180ft have been reported in other applications.

Applications for diaphragm walls. Diaphragm walls are used generally where it is required that the shoring wall be watertight and where, at the same time, more wall stiffness or resistance to bending is needed than can be provided by heavy steel sheet pile sections. Diaphragm walls have been constructed in virtually all soil types, but usually in very soft to medium clays, saturated silts, or saturated, loose silty or clayey sand. They are usually constructed where surface settlement adjacent to the cut must be minimized. The stiffer of the diaphragm walls have; been special in many urban cut-and-cover projects to obviate the need for underpinning adjacent buildings.

The construction of diaphragm walls causes much less noise and vibration than does the driving of sheet piles and a diaphragm wall may be chosen over a sheet pile wall in some cases on this account alone. Where a diaphragm wall is to be used, the choice of the type will depend primarily on the required stiffness and resistance to bending and shear, actual subsurface conditions, and cost.

Occasionally, slurry walls or SPTC walls are utilized both as shoring walls and as the wall element if the permanent structure to be constructed within the cut. SPTC walls were utilized in this capacity in the design of several BART subway stations.

2. Common types of shoring wall support

1) Internal bracing

Most cut-and-cover excavations are relatively narrow and, as a result, internal bracing composed of multiple tiers of horizontal, structural steel framing is the most common type of shoring wall support used. In a typical excavation, the principal components of each internal bracing tier are longitudinal beams, or "wakes", and transverse compression members, or "struts".

The bracing tiers must be positioned so that they support the shoring wall and permit efficient construction of the permanent structure. The shoring walls are shown as constructed at the structure neat line (except for wall tolerance allowed), as is usually the case. During the excavation stage, vertical spacing of bracing tiers is often specified to be a maximum of 15-16ft, sometimes 12ft when it is crucial to minimize adjacent ground settlement. The maximum depth of cut in any excavation step is usually specified to be 3ft below the centerline of the next bracing tier to be installed. The amount of settlement of the ground adjacent to the cut is generally considered to be largely a function of vertical spacing of bracing tiers and shoring wall stiffness. It is sometimes better to increase wall stiffness to permit larger vertical spacing of bracing tiers, when the larger spacing is needed to avoid interference of the bracing with the reinforced concrete construction. Occasionally, it is not feasible to avoid such interference, and different removal techniques or supplementary bracing methods are required. During the bracing removal stage, the shoring wall does not depend upon the soil below subgrade for support, and larger vertical shoring wall spans can ordinarily be permitted.

Struts in the internal bracing framing need to be spaced far enough apart so that excavating equipment can operate efficiently. Struts spacing is usually in the range of 10-15ft, but larger spacing (up to 25ft) is sometimes used to permit more clearance for construction activities. However, such large spacing is often very costly because of the much heavier wales that result, and it can be undesirable as well because of the inward wall movement that accompanies the increased wale deflection. Where there is no axial load in wales it is usually more economical to make the wales two to three spaces long and discontinuous at the wale ends.

Internal bracing is compatible with any of the shoring wall types already discussed. Horizontal force from the shoring wall is transferred to the wale at each soldier pile web, or in the case of slurry walls, at heavy steel bearing plates embedded in the slurry wall at its inside face. (The bearing plates are fastened to the reinforcing cage when the slurry wall is construed.) The shoring walls cannot be placed with sufficient accuracy to permit the wales to bear directly on the soldier piles, sheet piles, or slurry wall bear plates. The gap between these wall elements and the wale is typically filled with a structural "packing". The wales are supported by structural steel brackets ("lookouts") mounted on the soldier piles, sheet piles, or slurry wall bearing plates.

Many framing concepts different from the typical framing are employed. Irregular framing is usually required for irregularly shaped cut-and-cover excavation. When slurry wall panels can be constructed so that they are installed symmetrically about the longitudinal centerline of the cut-and-cover excavation, slurry wall panels are sometimes braced directly by struts, thus eliminating the need for wales.

2) Tie-backs

A tie-backs is a form of support in which the horizontal earth pressure (E) acting on the shoring wall is resisted by an anchor assembly, which in turn deposits its load into soil or rock far enough behind the wall to have no significant effect on the wall. Tie-backs anchored in soil are commonly referred to as "soil anchors"; tie-backs anchored in rock are "rock anchors." A tie-back consists of three principal elements:

(1) An anchor zone, which acts as a reaction to horizontal earth pressure (E) on the shoring wall.

(2) A tie element, which transfers the load from the wall to the anchor zone.

(3) A wall reaction assembly at the point of wall support.

To locate the anchor zone safely behind the shoring wall, the anchor zone is typically placed behind an "assumed failure plane." Theoretical establishment of this plane so that it is representative of a safe installation requires complex analysis. In most cases, the assumed failure plane is established by an experienced geotechnical consultant, who in turn relies on both experience from past performance of tie-back installations and theoretical considerations.

There are many types of soil and rock anchors. The tie element for all of the more commonly used tie-backs is either a single threadbar 1 to 13/8in. in diameter (usually high strength, as manufactured by Dywidag), or multiple high-strength strands, each (in most cases) 0.6in in diameter. The tie elements are installed in holes drilled from inside the excavation through the shoring wall at an inclination usually in the range of 15°-30° from horizontal for soil anchor, and up to (commonly) 45° for rock anchors. The anchor zone is created by filling the drilled hole throughout the anchor zone with sand-cement grout or neat cement grout, depending upon the type of anchor. The zone between the anchor zone and the shoring wall is commonly referred to as the "unbounded zone" or "unbounded length." Throughout this length the tie element is covered with a plastic tube so that none of the tie-back load is transferred into the ground. (Other techniques are also used to create the unbounded length.)

Drilled holes for the most common tie-backs range from 8 to 18in in diameter; about 12in is typical. Grout is placed in the drilled hole by gravity or at modest pressure (about 50psi) when hollow-stem augers are used to drill the hole. The anchor resistance is developed through grout-to-soil friction. For these "conventional" tie-backs, working capabilities in competent soils ranging from 70 to 140kips are common.

More sophisticated tie-backs of much higher capacity are also utilized on cut-and-cover projects. The type commonly referred to as "regroutable" employs equipment, hardware, other materials and methods that permit the injection of grout within the anchor zone at very high pressure (up to 300psi or more) and in multiple applications. These regroutable tie-backs require a relatively small drilled hole (usually about 5in). In competent soils, tie-back capabilities up to 400kips or more have been installed successfully in medium clays (S_u = 500-1000psf) with a working capacity up to 150kips.

Tie-backs are also compatible with any of the shoring wall types discussed. When the shoring wall is soldier and lagging, sheet piles, or any of the diaphragm walls that use soldier piles, usual practice is to mount the anchor head assembly on double-channel wales, which in turn are mounted on and react against the soldier piles or sheet piles. When the shoring wall is a slurry wall, the anchor head assembly typically reacts directly on the slurry wall concrete.

When tie-backs are utilized as support for shoring walls, excavation proceeds in lifts that correspond to the vertical spacing of the tie-backs. Each succeeding increment of excavation cannot commence until the tie-back at that lift has been successfully post-tensioned to its design working load at the wall reaction assembly. Normally, the tie-backs cannot be posttensioned until 5 days after completion of the grouting of the anchor zone.

Tie-backs can be considered an alternative to internal bracing when the following conditions exist:

(1) There is ample width within the excavation for tie-backs installation.

(2) Permission is granted by the property owner to install tie-backs in the ground adjacent to the cut.

(3) There is no significant piezometric head behind the shoring wall at the level of the tie-back installation. (To date, attempts to install tie-backs when there is piezometric head exceeding a few behind the shoring the wall have had limited success.)

(4) The soil behind the shoring wall is sufficiently competent to permit successful tie-back installation.

(5) There are no subsurface obstacles such as deep basements beneath adjacent buildings.

Although all these conditions are often present, it is uncommon to find that tie-backs are economical alternative when the excavation is less than about 65ft wide.

3) Soil nailing

In some of the shallower cuts, installation of a shoring wall prior to the excavation can be avoided by utilizing the soil nailing method. Soil nailing is an in situ reinforcing technique that consists of installing passive inclusions (nails) into the undisturbed natural soil mass to retain excavation. The inclusions are usually steel reinforcement bars that either are placed in drilled bore holes or grouted along their entire length or (sometimes) are driven into place. To provide local stability between the nails, an outside facing is provided. The facing generally consists of 3-6in of reinforced shotcrete. Nailing differs from tie-back support: the nails are passive elements that are not posttensioned. In addition, the nail density in the retained soil is much larger and the nails are shorter than for tie-back systems.

The soil nailing technique is best suited to dry or moist noncohesive or semicohsive soils that will stand vertically for short durations during construction. In heterogeneous soils with cobbles, boulders, and weathered rock zones, this method offers the advantage of small-diameter, shorter drill holes. In cohesive soils subject to creep, however, soil nailing is usually either not feasible or is uneconomical, even at relatively low stress levels.

In North American, the retained depth of excavation using this system has generally been less than 30ft. However, excavations as deep as 60ft have been supported.

The mobilization of soil reinforcement interaction requires a relative displacement of soil and reinforcement. Therefore, in urban sites, the use of this technique can be limited by requirements for minimal settlement and movement of the ground adjacent to the excavation.

Text C Open Cut Section of Xiamen Urban Rail Transportation Line 1
厦门地铁一号线明挖段

The entrance and exit sector of Xiamen North Station Project -the stage one works of Xiamen Urban Rail Transportation line 1 is located at chainage No. 1 right YCK32 + 845. 184 ~ right YCR2CK1 +300. 000 with the sector total length approximately 1383. 961m, which consists of two cut and cover tunnels and one tunnel by mine tunneling method. The interface section of the open cut section and station enclosure structure are connected and excavated by sloping. The subsequent following section due to the rapid rise of ground level adopts forms of sloping excavation + interior support in enclosure structure and sloping excavation + anchor cable form in the enclosure structure and the total length is 218. 961m. The open cut section two adopts sloping excavation at the location of crossing water pond and close to the tunnel portal and the rest remaining section adopts the form of enclosure structure with interior support and the horseshoe shaped underground sector of the tunnel and is executed by means of method of boring the two portal open sections from counter-directions of entrance and exit from counter-directions.

The works details of given sections are shown in table 8. 7.

Works Details of the Given Sectors   Table 8.7

Section	Method	Section length (dual line running meter m)	Minimum curve radius(m)	Maximum longitudinal slope(‰)	Range of burial depth (m)
Length from North square station in roc to Entrance and exit section	Cut and cover	218.961	500	2	3.56 -9.54
	Mine tunneling method	945	250	26	2.24 -39.27
	Cut and cover	320	250	26	0 -7.91

1. Technical standard for open cutting section

(1)The safety level of the open cut section is I and environmental protection rating of the foundation pit is class I.

(2) The structure design shall meet such requirements of building, operation, construction, fire fighting and prevention, water prevention and prevention of stray electrical currents. Adequate structural durability should be assured. The design service life of the main structural works is 100 years with class I safety level and seismic fortification intensity of 7 in magnitude degrees (0.15g). The underground structure is designed by seismic fortification intensity class III.

(3) For general underground structure, only the cross sectional force to be sustained by taking of the structure is analyzed and calculated. But if one of the following cases is encountered, longitudinal strength and deformation shall be analyzed.

①While cover soil thickness undergoes relatively great changes along tunnel longitudinal.

②While the structure directly sustains great local loads of building and structures.

③While when there is obvious apparent variation of ground or foundations.

④While the foundation undertakes differential settlement along longitudinal.

⑤Under the seismic effect when seismic is acting, the structural longitudinal deflection and tensile and compressive strengths shall be calculated and checked.

When thermal deformation joint distributes is at great spacing, the temperature effect and concrete contraction along the longitudinal of the structure influence of temperature change and concrete contraction on the longitudinal of the structure should be considered. For the section subjected to apparent spatial effect, the space structure shall be analyzed preferably.

(4) The underground structural strength, stiffness and stability shall be calculated separately for construction phase and normal service phase shall be calculated separately. For the reinforced concrete structure the crack width in service phase shall be calculated. When accidental loads are considered in the load combination, crack width of the structure is not calculated.

(5) The structural seismic fortification intensity is 7 degrees and design seismic grouping is group two.

(6) In the seismic design for underground structure, the analyzing approach which well reflects seismic working status shall be selected according to the fortification and precaution requirement, ground conditions, structure types and burial depths and necessary configuration measures shall be taken to improve the seismic capacity of the structure at joint location. Seismic resistances shall be applied to non-load bearing members (decorative members, pipe installations) which do not sustain loads.

(7) In underground structure the bearing member shall be of fire resistance rating I and other structural members shall meet corresponding in-house fire fighting specifications.

(8) This given engineering works falls into category of civil works of rating A and engineering works shall be of resistance against nuclear weapons of rating six and resistance against regular weapon of class six respectively and resistance against chemical weapons shall not be less than rating C. The requirement on the service in protective unit shall conform to the "requirement on general civil works with enclosure or waterproof requirement" and meanwhile conversion of functions for peace time and war time shall be duly performed.

(9) Underground structures shall meet the specification on waterproof ratings and the waterproofing for the section tunnel and linking corridor and likely ancillary tunnel structures shall

be rating II.

(10) When underground structure is located at corrosive areas, additional suitable corrosion protections or anti-corrosion steps shall be taken according to the rating of environment at the tunnel site.

(11) Food control or tunnel interior flooding shall be designed at tunnel entrance between sections.

Comparison and selection of types of the enclosure structures type in open cut sections: The enclosure structure options shall be in compliance with the policy of "safety, economy, easy execution for works performance" and shall take such factors into comprehensive consideration as the engineering geological and hydrological conditions, environmental conditions, excavation depth, construction methodology, works period, works cost and the common enclosure envelope structures in that region. Based on comparison among many alternatives, the most suitable enclosure envelope alternative shall be selected.

In the section from the North Station Square Station in rock to the inward and outward section, the foundation pit excavation depth ranges approximately from 0m to 19.0m. In light of the investigation data on mass deep foundation pit in Xiamen and surrounding areas, the alternative foundation pit enclosure structures are mainly sloping excavation, secant pile wall, bored pile plus waterproof curtain, diaphragm wall and SMW method (steel concrete mixture wall).

1) Slope excavation

The slope excavation without support is a kind of common foundation pit excavation method, by which the foundation jobsite shall be located in space environment and there are no buildings (structure) and underground pipelines in need of support in vicinity. The slope gradient of slope excavation and the slope protections shall be comprehensively determined in accordance with the local experiences, rock property and excavation depth. In the soft soil, in single graded slope excavation, the foundation pit excavation depth shall not exceed 6m and in multiple graded slope excavation, the foundation excavation depth shall not exceed 12m preferably.

2) Diaphragm wall

The application of diaphragm wall method works execution causes little vibration and low noise and can make construction possible in buildings and structure concentrated zone. The hard rock shall be grooved by means of percussion drilling which will affect the surrounding buildings. The diaphragm walls are of great stiffness and can sustain great horizontal lateral load and small and the deformation occurs is little during foundation pit excavation with, little settlement of surrounding ground surface. Hence, the impact on adjacent buildings, structures and underground pipelines can be well controlled and reduced. The enclosure walls of underground stations on second floor and third floor generally all adopt diaphragm wall in thickness from 600 to 1000mm and the foundation pit penetration depth is to be confirmed subject to foundation pit deformation and stability calculation. The diaphragm wall and interior structure jointly sustain load effect during service phase.

3) Drilling (percussion) bored pile

When bored pile serves as an enclosure structure, waterproof curtain is placed between piles (or waterproof between piles) to block groundwater. Hard rock needs to be percussion bored to form into trench and drillhole collapse is vulnerable in sandy soil is vulnerable to drillhole collapse due to long time period of spent in trench formation.

4) Secant pile

Secant piles are dominantly mainly drilling secant pile and rotary excavation secant pile depending on according to the piling machines. Bored secant pile is mainly applicable to soft soil stratum including such adverse geological conditions as silt, drift sand and high groundwater. After the meeting high strength soil stratum or order I pile initial setting is met, the stratum strength improves and the second pile formation will become even harder. Rotary excavation secant pile can smoothly stand uphold on due to application of total rotary boring machine in bore formation and for the soil rock with uniaxial compressive strength less than 10000kPa. The biggest strong point lies in the application of steel sleeve to protect the wall (after penetrating soil filled soil and sandy soil stratum, total sleeve can be omitted) to prevent hole wall collapse in soil filled soil and sandy soil. Piling can be executed closely near buildings and underground pipelines, the environmental impact during trench formaiton is weak, and in trench formation phase impact on surroundings is little. Hence, for some stations on which environmental protection requirement level is rigorous high and strict, bored secant pile can be used as an enclosure structure.

5) SMW method (steel concrete mixture wall)

SMW method is a method by which cement soil mixture pile with H profile steel serves as enclosure wall meanwhile functioning also as soil retaining and permeation resistance. After completion of interior structure works, H profile steel can be withdrawn as appropriate and thus works cost is relatively low. The SMW method is generally used in the foundation pit enclosure structure for the underground station with excavation depth less than 13m. If SMW serves as enclosure wall, generally it is only considered that the cast in situ side wall and interior structure bear loads in service period.

One outstanding characteristics of this project is that the foundation pit excavation is shallow and its present surroundings are farmland and ground conditions are simple without any road and controlling buildings. Most part of the station structure is located in muck, silty clay, medium coarse sand, residual sandy clayey soil and most part of bottom slab is in residual sandy clayey soil.

In the light of different structural forms, ground geological conditions and surrounding environmental protection requirements, in combination with local experiences often deep foundation pit construction and through calculation analysis, the enclosure structure of the open cut tunnel from the north square station in rocks to the inward and outward lines adopts slope excavation + bored piles.

Design for enclosure structure in the open cut section: The tunnel open cut section is in of total length of 538.961m and divided into fore and aft parts. The foundation pit depth ranges between 5.8-19m. Different enclosure forms are set according to the foundation pit depth, surrounding geological conditions required of and needs of the works. The slope excavation is applied within the range from right out of station at chainage number YCK32 +845.184 ~ YCK32 +885.000 and cofferdam range at chainage number YCR2CK0 +980 ~ YCR2CK1 +070.000 and exit portal at chainage number YCR2CK1 +280.000 ~ YCR2CK1 +300.000, slope excavation is applied. In the range of fore open cut section at chainage number YCK32 +885.000 ~ YCR2CK0 +48.500, fender post + one concrete support + one steel support serve as enclosure forms. In order to ensure the construction space for cut and cover tunnel section, in the range of between chainage numbers YCR2CK0 +48.500 ~ YCR2CK0 +124.000, fender post + two anchor cables are applied. At the interface between open cut and underground cut between chainage numbers of YCR2CK0 +124.000 ~ YCR2CK0 +135.000, fender post + one steel inclined support as enclosure is applied. In the aft open cut section between chainage number YCR2CK1 +070.000 ~ YCR2CK1 +280.00, fender post + one concrete support + one round of steel support are applied as enclosure.

2. The principal engineering materials used in the open cut section

Concrete: The reinforced concrete top slab (beam), middle slab (beam), bottom slab (beam) and inner lining wall of interior structure all use concrete C35. The column uses concrete of grade C45; bored pile uses concrete with strength grade of underwater C35; the plain concrete bed below bottom slab is of grade C20 and early hardening concrete is used. Except for middle slab, middle slab beam and ring beam, support and column, concrete permeability rating is not less than P8.

Steel: Q235B.

Steel bar: uses steel with grade HPB300、HRB400.

Profiled steel and steel plate uses steel with grade Q235B.

Weld rod: E43XX、E50XX.

This given section is executed concurrently in two parts fore and aft. The part in range between chainage numbers of YCK32 +845.184 ~ YCR2CK0 +550.000 is fore section while the part in range between chainage numbers YCR2CK0 +550.000 ~ YCR2CK1 +300.000 is aft section. Mobilization for open cut works is scheduled to begin on January 1 2013 and the enclosure works for the two open cut sections are scheduled to begin on February 1 2014. In the enclosure works flow works execution flow of enclosure works, interior structures are executed concurrently. When the open cut section approaches close to underground excavation section, the underground excavation section shall be completed before the commencement of the main structure.

II. Terms and terminology

    cut and cover method   明挖法
    burial depth   埋深

flow process	流水作业
foundation pit	基坑
cantilever	悬臂
slope excavation	放坡开挖法
diaphragm wall	地下连续墙
soil nail	土钉
soil-nail wall	土钉墙
well point dewatering	井点降水
enclosure structure	围护结构
supporting system	支撑系统
bracing replacement	换撑
ground improvement	地基加固
SMW	型钢水泥土搅拌墙(Soil Mixed Wall)
cast-in-place pile	灌注桩
steel sheet pile	钢板桩
steel pipe pile	钢管桩
enclosing purlin	围檩
artificial dig-hole pile	人工挖孔桩
electric hoist	电葫芦
deep mixing method	水泥土深层搅拌法
profile steel	型钢

III. Questions and difficult sentence analysis

1. Questions for brainstorming discussion

(1) Briefly state the applicable conditions and advantages of the cut and cover method.

(2) State respectively the types and features of various fence structures of foundation pits by cut and cover method.

(3) Briefly state the work flow of reinforced concrete diaphragm.

2. Difficult sentences analysis

(1) The cut and cover method is the general term of the said construction method by which excavation is executed from ground surface downward to the prescribed position of the structure to be built, and is a tunnel construction method by vertical excavation method (relative to the method of tunnel heading in horizontal direction).

译文:明挖法是从地表面向下开挖,在预定位置修筑结构物方法的总称。它是一种垂直开挖方式修建隧道的方法(对应于水平方向掘进隧道而言)。

(2) The cut and cover tunnel differs from any surface structure. The tunnel-surrounding ground interaction is very complex, for which special attention shall be paid to tunnel dynamic state in seismic occurrence. In tunnel design, seismic effect on the tunnel dynamic state shall be

studied in addition to the societal and economic impacts after the tunnel suffers from a seismic event.

译文:明挖隧道与地面结构不同,隧道与周围地层的相互作用是非常复杂的,因此,要特别注意地震时隧道的动态。在设计时,要研究地震对隧道动态的影响,同时还要研究隧道受震害后的社会、经济的影响。

(3) The design content of foundation pit support and excavation include enclosure structure, supporting system, and earth excavation solution, bracing replacement measure, dewatering scheme and ground improvement. These contents are interrelated and must be comprehensively considered in foundation pit design.

译文:基坑支护开挖法的设计涉及的内容包括:围护结构、支撑系统、挖土方案、换撑措施、降水方案、地基加固。这几方面内容相互关联,在基坑设计时必须综合考虑。

(4) Deep mixing method is one type of method by which mixing machine mixes cement, lime and similar consolidating agents with base soil so as to achieve foundation improvement. General Deep mixing method retaining structure is featured with competent impermeability, so in foundation pit excavation, well point dewatering is not used, as avoids harms to surrounding pipelines and buildings.

译文:深层搅拌桩是一种用搅拌机械将水泥、石灰之类的固化剂和地基土相互拌和,从而达到加固地基目的的方法。一般的水泥搅拌桩挡土结构具有良好的抗渗特点,在基坑开挖时可以不用井点降水,从而避免了对周围地下管线和建筑物造成危害。

Ⅳ. Translation case study

Case 1

Chinese	English translation
当基坑深度较大,开挖时除采用围护结构外,还常采用支撑加强围护结构以抵抗较大的侧压力。支撑分为水平支撑、斜支撑以及采用锚杆加固围护结构。水平支撑常用的形式有横撑和角撑,基坑拐角或断面变化处用角撑,其他一般用横撑。采用水平支撑的优点是:墙体水平位移小,安全可靠,开挖深度不受限制;但要求围护结构的平面形状比较规则,以矩形为佳。开挖基坑宽度较大时,支撑应加设中间支柱来保持其稳定性。	When foundation trench depth is large, during excavation, in addition to use of envelope enclosure, support is often used to reinforce the envelope enclosure structure in resisting large lateral pressing forces. The supports are divided into horizontal bracing, inclined support and bolted exterior protection structure. The common horizontal bracing forms consist cross bracing and angle brace. Corner brackets are used at corners of foundation trench or section variation points. Cross bracings are used in rest other locations. The use of horizontal bracings has following advantages: small horizontal displacements of wall body, safe and reliable, unrestrained excavation depth. But the plan shape of the exterior protection structure is required to be regular and rectangular shape is the optimum. When the trench excavated is of large width, bracing should be placed between the two sides to retain its stability.

Case 2

Chinese	English translation
明挖法是从地面向下分层、分段依次开挖,直至达到结构要求的尺寸和高程,形成基坑,然后在基坑中进行主体结构施工和防水作业,最后回填恢复地面。明洞以及隧道洞口段不能用暗挖法时,都采用明挖法施工。在城市地下工程特别是浅埋的地下铁道工程中获得了广泛的应用。	Tunnel construction is characterized as "cut and cover" construction when ground is excavated downward in layers and sections till the foundation trench with structural required dimension and level is formed. Then tunnel structure is built with waterproof jobs executed in the foundation trench and finally is subsequently covered with backfill and the ground surface is restored. When cut and cover section and tunnel portal section cannot be executed by subsurface excavation method, cut and cover method is used as the construction method. The cut and cover construction method is extensively used in urban subsurface works, especially in shallow-depth underground railway tunnels.

Case 3

Chinese	English translation
在城市街道狭窄的条件下,基坑宽度应减至最小,这时常采用钢桩与井点降水结合的直槽支护基坑形式。一般用工字钢,按设计位置打入土层中,形成连续板桩墙或间隔立柱,并架设横板等支撑。基坑在支护的保护下进行开挖。随着基坑土的开挖,应在桩间安设木挡板和顶撑、拉锚或土锚等组成的单层或多层支护结构,以保证桩在地层侧压力作用下的强度与稳定性。若使用木挡板仍会导致土体崩塌或地面沉陷时,应采用连续钢板桩支护结构。	Under the constraints of urban narrow streets, the foundation pit width shall be reduced to minimum and the foundation pit type with vertical trench support with combination of steel piles and well point dewatering is commonly adopted. The general practice is to drive I beam pile into soil strata as per design positions to form such supports continuous sheet piled wall or spacing standing column and bracing. The foundation pit is excavated under the protection of the support. With progress of foundation pit soil excavation, single-level or multi-level supporting structure composed of wooden barrier plates and ceiling support, pull anchor or soil anchor shall be provided between piles to ensure the pile strength and stability under the actions of lateral soil pressure. Provided that soil collapse or ground subsidence still occurs due to use wooden retaining plank, continuous sheet pile support structure shall be adopted.

V. Assignment

(1) 主要施工步骤按如下顺序:施作围护结构→第一道混凝土支撑→基坑内降水→基坑开挖→钢管支撑→底板垫层混凝土→铺设防水层→浇筑底板混凝土→施工侧墙及顶板混凝土→拆除支撑→顶板防水层施工→回填基坑。

(2) 根据本工程的功能及使用方便的要求,明挖区间隧道设计为地下一层一孔和二孔现浇钢筋混凝土箱型框架结构。主要施工步骤:采用自上而下开挖基坑,自下而上浇筑结构的明挖顺筑法施工。

(3) 区间明挖段结构形式为矩形框架结构,分单跨、双跨断面。其组合形式是从区间隧道和出入段线共用的双跨断面,过渡为各自的单跨断面,最终出入段线左右线又合并为双跨断面,从线路纵坡看出入段线和区间隧道也由同一标高过渡为不同标高,结构变化较为复杂。

（4）区间明挖段顶板采用钢管扣件式脚手架搭设满堂支架支模灌注混凝土。结构顶板采用组合钢模板,侧墙采用大块模板,结构的腋角采用特制钢模板。

（5）明挖结构外防水主要是在底板、侧墙、顶板外侧全包防水方案,形成一个封闭的防水层,以达到止水的目的。

Unit 9　Tunnel Excavation and Lining
隧道开挖与衬砌

Ⅰ. Text

Text A　Types and Selection of Excavation Methods
隧道开挖方法类型及选择原则

1. Types of excavation methods

For the cross section of tunnels, tunnels can be shaped by full-face excavation and also can be divided into several smaller parts which are formed in parts and excavated in parts into shape. For the longitudinal section of tunnels, regardless of the division into various parts of the cross section, the rock mass within the tunnel range is anyway divided into several sections to be excavated in order. Namely, some volume of rock mass is excavated and removed in each excavation (V = excavation sectional area S × longitudinal penetration length L = section width B × section height H × advancement span L). That is to say, an underground space in some volume shapes after each excavation finally forming an continuous underground gallery.

According to the conditions of tunnel cross sections, the excavation methods can be categorized as following methods. Each method is illustrated and introduced severally.

Excavation methods are as follows:
(1) Full face excavation method.
(2) Bench excavation method:
①Micro bench excavation method;
②Semi section excavation method.
(3) Partial face excavation method:
①Ring cut method;
②Lower drift excavation method;
③Center diagram method (CD method);
④Center cross diagram method (CRD method);
⑤Single side-wall drift pilot excavation method;
⑥Double side-wall drift pilot excavation method;

⑦Column-heading method.

2. Selection of excavation methods

The choice of tunnel excavation methods is subject to determining the size of transverse excavation face for partial excavation (width × depth) and length of longitudinal excavation sections and its dynamic adjusting measures. *The surrounding rocks of different classes are of different stability while different excavation methods cause different disturbances of surrounding rock and the mutual disturbances among working faces also differ.*

Therefore, the principle for choice of tunnel excavation methods shall be selecting an excavation method both favoring stabilization of the surrounding rock and satisfying requirement for operating space by comprehensive analysis which takes into account of the stability of the surrounding rock and the impacts of rock stress redistribution and structural system conversion during course of construction and also size of operation space, supporting conditions and operating capability, support conditions and operating capability, construction time required, working area length and economy.

The construction law of modern surrounding rock bearing theory in tunneling emphasized that regardless of the designed tunnel section size, only if the surrounding rock permits, generally large section excavation shall be applied to most extent and the adaptation to the variation of stability of the surrounding rock is mainly achieved through adjusting heading length adjustment.

As for cross section, the application of large section excavation can reduce of number of excavations by partial face excavation method so as to reduce number of disturbances of the surrounding rock. In addition, large section excavation can provide large working operating space thus facilitating various executions. It can be avoided that there are excessive working faces in one working area, which can reduce the mutual disturbances among working faces in favor of construction management.

In terms of longitudinal section of tunnels, while the surrounding rock stability is poor, the advancing length of excavation should be shortened, as can both provide competent space for arch forming and gain convenient retain the convenience for large-section excavation. Accordingly, due to poor rock stability, in the application of large section excavation and shortened penetration length, disturbance of surrounding rock due to blasting shall be strictly controlled and support shall be erected and reinforced in time.

Namely, if the satiability of the surrounding rock is competent, sound, larger volume of rock can be excavated in each operation, namely larger sectional areas and longitudinal length can be excavated. If the stability of the surrounding rock is poor, smaller volume of rock shall be excavated in each operation, namely the larger excavation cross section area but shorter longitudinal length of excavation.

Taking express transit railway for example, various applicable conditions for various corresponding excavation methods are listed in following table 9.1.

Applicable Conditions for Various Excavation Methods (Express Transit Railway)　　　Table 9.1

Excavation method	Applicable to size of tunnel cross section, the surrounding rock engineering geology	Note
Full face excavation method	1. Single-track tunnel with surrounding rock in class I, II, III; 2. Double-track tunnel with surrounding rock in class I and II; 3. Groundwater state: dry or moist	1. The better the stability of the surrounding rock is, the larger area can be the section of excavation in one operation and the, penetration can also be longer; the poorer is the rock stability is, the smaller is the section of excavation in one operation and the, advancing length is shorter accordingly; 2. For the surrounding rock in class III, IV, the maximum sectional area of one excavation can reach 70-80m^2, with cyclic penetration controlled in range of 4-5m; for rock in class V and VI, the sectional area of one excavation shall be smaller with cyclic penetration controlled within range of 0.5-3m; 3. Large section excavation shall be applied to maximum to reduce number of parts (divisions); 4. The bench length shall facilitate constructional operation and development of machine efficiency meanwhile shall facilitate looping of support; micro bench or multi-bench excavation shall be applied; 5. Sectional areas of tunnels: 50-60m^2 for railway single-track tunnel; 80-90m^2 for double-track; 60-70m^2 for highway single-lane tunnel, 90-100m^2 for double-lane; 70-85m^2 for express single-track railway tunnel; 100-120m^2 for double-track railway tunnel
Bench excavation method	1. Single-track tunnel with rock in class III, IV; 2. Double-track tunnel with rock in class III; 3. Groundwater state dry or moist	
Ring cut method	1. Single-track tunnel with rock class IV, V and VI; 2. Double-track tunnel with rock class III, IV, V, VI; 3. Groundwater state: with water infiltration and jet water	
Lower drift excavation method	1. Single-track tunnel with rock in class III, IV; 2. Double-track tunnel with rock class II and III; 3. Groundwater state: with water infiltration and jet water	
Double side-wall drift pilot excavation method	1. Single-track with rock in class V, VI; 2. Double-track tunnel with rock in class IV, V, VI; 3. Groundwater state: with water infiltration and jet water	
Column-heading method	Multi-arch tunnel	
Center diagram method (CD method)	Single and double-track tunnel with rock in class V, VI; Shallow burial tunnel; three-track tunnel	
Center cross diagram method (CRD method)	Double-track, three-track tunnel, rock class IV, V, VI, shallow burial tunnel	

Full face excavation method

By the full face excavation method, some length of rock in the designed section of adit is excavated and removed in one operating cycle namely an unlined opening with some depth is shaped in one excavation operation before lining and other operations as illustrated in figure 9.1.

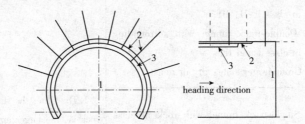

Figure 9.1 Full Face Excavation Method
1-Full face excavation; 2-Anchoring and shotcreting; 3-Secondary lining

1) Applicable conditions for the full face excavation method

The full face excavation primarily applies to the conditions of sound rock stability and small tunnel sections.

2) The advantages and disadvantages of the full face excavation method

(1) Full-section excavation facilitates construction organization and control due to single cycle operation in single same working area. But single cycle operating is of low utilization of the operating capacity of various procedures.

(2) The full face excavation has large sectional driving rate (namely the proportion of sectional areas to penetration length $= S/L$) namely facilitating both mechanical blasting operation or drill and blasting operation as well as can achieve sound result of blasting.

(3) The full face excavation reduces number of excavations in parts thus reducing the number of disturbances of the surrounding rock. But while blasting and breaking the rock, each blasting creates high intensity vibration. Thus blasting design shall be strictly controlled, particularly for the surrounding rock of poor stability.

(4) In full face excavations, the rock stress redistribution occurs least often, as facilitates rock self-stability retention and eases initial lining operation, formation of enclosure bearing ring in sense of mechanics thus achieving essentially stabilized adit.

(5) By full face excavation, larger operating space can be obtained which enables the usage of large construction machines in a complete set and speeds up the construction. But the due to large excavation face, relatively low stability of surrounding rock and relatively large amount of work in cycle, powerful excavation and mucking capacity and corresponding support capacity are required.

3) Technical essentials of full face excavation method

(1) Generally, excavation and primary lining are categorized into one working face and

invert, backfill (or bottom slab) and side wall into one working face; waterproofing layer and inner lining into one working face. Proper spacing is kept among several working faces enabling concurrent operation (parallel operation) and avoiding mutual disturbances so as to speed construction. In the super long tunnel where construction time is tight, cross tunnel, inclined shaft and side tunnel or cross tunnel between twin-tubes of tunnel can be utilized for establishing multi-working planes, thus realizing "shaping long tunnel by short length excavations". Of course, while the increase of increasing auxiliary tunnels, the work time and its cost investment shall be compared.

(2) In the full face excavation, single cycle operation is carried out in same one working area, as enables the major operations as excavation, mucking and initial lining carried out in one operation cycle. If the operation capabilities of various procedures are not in balance, considerable delayed long cycle time will occur and construction will be slow. To improve construction speed, the operation capability should be improved to shorten the operation time and cycling time.

(3) It is required that all procedures in aspects of time, space, personnel, plant and equipment, material supply and logistical support shall be complete, rationally organized and dynamically adjusted to ensure a high construction speed of all working faces (working areas) and further assure the construction time or shorten the construction time.

(4) *By the full face excavation method, the section of one excavation is substantial. If adverse geological conditions are encountered with, (such as faulting fracture zone, groundwater, karst cave, gas stratum and similar ground), emergent engineering safety incidents are vulnerable (such as collapse, water inrush, mud bursting, gas burst) and they can be in large scale.* Hence, advancing geological investigation shall be carried out strictly to forecast the geological conditions ahead of the excavating face and emergency counter measures shall be ready and the excavation method shall be changed to ensure the construction safety.

Bench excavation method

By the bench excavation method, the rock mass in the design section of adit is divided into two parts—upper and lower, which are excavated simultaneously in same one working circle and the upper half section excavation is always kept ahead of the lower half section thus forming one step. The step length by the bench excavation method is generally 3-5m as illustrated in figure 9.2. If the step length is set to be over short, the upper and the lower sections will disturb each other.

1) The application conditions for application of bench excavation method

The bench excavation method is mainly applied to the conditions of the surrounding rock with sound stability and large section; or tunnel with small section and the surrounding rock with poor stability.

2) The advantages and disadvantages of the bench excavation method

(1) The upper and lower sections are combined into one operation face and excavated concurrently. Basically similar to full face excavation method, bench excavation method can provide adequate space and rapid works progress. If the upper and lower semi sections are to be

excavated separately, the two working faces may disturb each other considerably, which is rarely practiced.

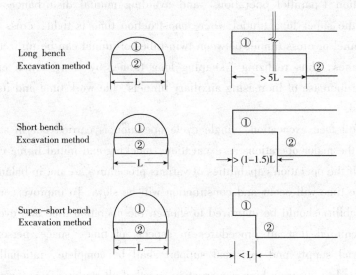

Figure 9.2 Bench Excavation Method

(2) By bench excavation, the lower semi section excavation lags behind and always one micro bench is existed in heading face, which both facilitates the stability of the excavation as well as the stability of surrounding rock and also providing a working platform for upper semi-section which facilitates working on the upper section. Particularly, after the upper bench section is finished with excavation and initial lining, the working on the lower section will be safe. But attention shall be paid to the influence of lower operation on the existed lining of upper section.

(3) By application of bench excavation method, large-scale construction machine can be used as well as the medium-small machines. Particularly, mucking and loading material conveyance are basically similar to that of full face excavation method.

(4) By application of bench excavation method, while unexpected sudden variations of geological conditions of surrounding rock ahead (such as sudden change into weak fragments, water inrush, debris flow and karst caves), better prevention and precaution is expected compared with full face method. Thus major loss and damages can be avoided and change to application of ring cut excavation method or other partial excavation method will be more convenient.

3) The technical essentials of bench excavation method

(1) Proper bench length is required. Namely the stability of surrounding rock shall be considered meanwhile the advancing length shall be considered; the requirements on the supporting capacity of construction machines and size of work space shall be considered.

(2) Proper solution to the problem of mutual disturbance of the operations on upper semi section and lower semi section. Micro bench is basically combined into one work face on which heading is carried out concurrently, as is basically similar to full face excavation method. For short

tunnels, "semi-section excavation method" is applied. Namely the upper semi section is broken through initially then the lower semi section is excavated, which may avoid disturbances of both sections to maximum extent.

(3) While the lower half section is being excavated, care shall be taken to control the disturbance intensity of the surrounding rock and care shall also be taken to prevent damages of upper existed support.

(4) With the construction progress, sudden variation of geological conditions is encountered; and conversion of excavation method shall be in time.

(5) When the self-stability of surrounding rock is not adequate and the design section is large, to shorten the period of rock exposure, core soil can be retained on upper bench temporarily. *Initially shape by excavation the upper arch pilot cavity and after the upper initial lining is placed, remove by excavation the core soil and carry out lower part excavation and its lining. The core soil is retained for the purposes of reducing the voided height of heading face, moderating the slope surface angle of the heading face, reducing down slip of the heading face, shortening the exposure period of rock excavated and assuring the stability of the surrounding rock.* It can be considered that the lower semi section is to be excavated and lined separately as two parts.

(6) In the construction of tunnels with weak fragmentary broken surrounding rock or large section, by application of bench excavation method, the stabilization or the temporary stabilization of the excavation face is the significant issue constraint to works progress. To maintain the stabilization or temporary stabilization of excavation face, which enables other operations possible, the excavation method should be considered and solution shall be the foundation from lining methods. Before the commencement of excavation of lower semi section, temporary closing of upper initial lining should be considered, for which is greatly very necessary for the stabilization of upper initial ling and the surrounding rock.

Partial face excavation method

By partial face excavation method, the rock mass within the design tunnel section of tunnels is divided into several parts, one of which is excavated and removed ed as per some depth in different time, and in different working face before erection of followed with initial lining; Then proceed to excavate and remove rest remaining other parts in sequence and erect lining respectively.

By application of the partial face excavation method, the complete tunnel section shaping is completed by several excavation operations and the excavation of one part excavation shall always be kept ahead of that of other parts. The tunnel shaping initially is called "pilot tunnel". The pilot tunnel is generally advancing deeper forward than that of rest remaining other parts. Thus partial face excavation method is also called "pilot tunnel advance excavation method". The primary role of the pilot tunnel aims at detecting in advance the engineering geology of rock in front.

The common partial face excavation methods are as the following table 9.2.

Partial Face Excavation Method   Table 9.2

Method	Cross-section	Longitudinal
ring cut method	① ② ③ ②	① ②
lower drift excavation method	② ①	② ①
single side-wall drift pilot excavation method	① ② ③	② ③ ①
double side-wall drift pilot excavation method	② ① ③ ①	② ③ ①
center diagram method (CD method)	① ④ / ② ⑤ / ③ ⑥	④ ① / ⑤ ② / ⑥ ③
center cross diagram method (CRD method)	① ③ / ② ④ / ⑤ ⑥	③ ① / ④ ② / ⑥ ⑤
column-heading method	③ ⑥ / ② ④ ① ⑦ ⑤	⑥ ③ / ⑦ ⑤ ④ ② ①

1) Applicable conditions for partial face excavation method

The partial face excavation method applies to the excavation under the conditions of large tunnel section or the surrounding rock with poor stability.

2) The advantages and disadvantages of the partial face excavation method

(1) In the excavation in parts, the tunnel section is divided into several smaller sections to be excavated in order, which makes smaller excavation span of adit of each smaller section and enhances the relative stability of the surrounding rocks of adit. Further, the smaller section of the adit facilitates local support to surrounding rock. Hence, the method of excavation in parts method mainly applies to in the tunnel with large design section or severely fragmented weak surrounding rock with and poor stability.

(2) By method of excavation in parts, due to many working procedures, different procedures disturb each other and the number of disturbance of the surrounding rock is increased. While boring tunneling method is applied, it is more harmful to the stability of surrounding rock and makes construction organization and management even more difficult.

(3) Pilot adit excavation in advance facilitates clear knowledge of the geology in advance and timely treatment of such ground. But if the pilot adit used is of excessively small section, the construction speed will be slow.

3) Technical key points of partial face excavation method

(1) Due to many working faces which disturb each other, attention shall be given to construction organization and coordination by implementing unified command and control.

(2) Care shall be given to enhancement of control enhancement and management of blast and excavation and avoidance of the damages to the completed support by subsequent excavation and the reduction of reducing disturbance of surrounding rock.

(3) The excavation and support of respective parts following different sequences thus imposing different disturbances on the surrounding rock and different impacts on support. Hence, to apply the method of excavation in parts, full consideration shall be given to the mutual influences of excavation and support of various parts and that of adjacent working faces and proper control over the sequences of excavation and support.

(4) *In compliance with the basic principle of "maximizing the excavation section to the greatest extent" of the New Austrian Tunneling Method, efforts shall be made to create conditions, reduce number of excavations in parts and to achieve large-section excavation to provide larger interior operation space for working of large-medium machines realizing speedy construction.*

Text B Heading Mode and Category
掘进方式及类型

Heading mode is the mode of rock excavation (rock breaking and smashing mode) within adit. By modes of rock breaking and smashing, heading modes are classified into four categories as drill and blast heading, full-face boring machine heading, free section excavator heading and manual heading.

1. Heading by drill and blast

Heading by drill and blast is firstly drilling blast holes in all parts of the rock to be blasted, and then distributing explosives in all cut holes and detonating the explosive thus the rocks within adit are blasted. In tunnel works "cut blasting" is usually adopted.

Rock blasting exerts great disturbance to surrounding rocks and causes reducing of stabilizing capacity of the rocks. Sometimes, blasting induced vibration may cause collapse of surrounding rocks. Hence blasting is generally only used in stone-natural rock tunnels around which rocks are of sound stability. But with the development of controlled blasting technology, blasting method is more and more widely used, such as the loosening blasting of weak stone and hard soil. Heading by drill and blast is the most common method applied in general mountainous tunnel works. Hole-drill blasting requires special boring equipment and consumes large amount of explosives and similar blasting materials and heading can only be carried out in sections in cycle.

2. Heading with full-section TBM

In heading with full-section tunnel boring machine, the rock body is smashed by the cutter head set in circular cutter disc at fore end of boring machine and it can accomplish heading by forming full section of tunnel in one operation. Full section excavator avoids the damages to the surrounding rock due to blasting-induced vibration. In TBM while heading exerts the little disturbance and damages to the surrounding rocks while its self rock breaking capacity is high, thus is generally applicable to hard rock ground with sound surrounding rock integrity and stability. The TBM is highly mechanized and integrated resulting in fast construction.

3. Free face excavator heading

By free face excavator heading, rocks are smashed by the cutter head installed on mobile mechanical arm and tunnel sections are developed gradually completely. The free section excavator avoids the damages to the surrounding rocks due to blasting-induced vibration. In heading, the surrounding rocks are slightly disturbed and damaged but its own rock breaking capacity is also small. Thus this heading type is generally used in weak rock tunnel with poor stability of the surround rock and earth tunnel, particularly being applicable to cooperating with the operation of open type shield.

Free section excavator with high adoptability can excavate in tunnels in any shape, any size and also can drill continuously. Free section excavator which is mostly equipped with equipment capable of continuous mucking. The common types of mucking machines comprise crab type, vertical claw type, bucket-type, digger type. The common used conveyors comprise two types as scraper plate type and chain plate type. Free section excavator mostly adopts crawler walking equipment adaptable to tunnel temporary road with poor bearing capacity and even muddy conditions. While the road in tunnel is muddy and track transport is used, the free section excavator with track walking device can be selected.

The common free section excavator is divided into three categories as mining machine, digging bucket excavator and bucket-type mucker. Among the above types, the milling disc cutting type mining machine is the type in which the column shaped or cone shaped cutting head is mounted on hydraulic telescopic rig where the cutting head can rotate both in horizontal and vertical directions. This machine can excavate in all types of soils with low moisture content and rocks below medium hardness but not applicable to muddy soil. Further, when digging bucket excavator or bucket-type mucker is used in tunneling, excavation and mucking can be accomplished by one same machine. These machines with limited rock breaking capacity are only suitable for excavating hard soil to soft plasticity muddy soil with cooperation of periphery trimming by hand.

4. Manual heading

Rock mass is dug out by hand with pickaxe or pneumatic pick by manual heading. Manual digging exerts little disturbance and damages of surrounding rock thus facilitating preserve the original stabilizing capacity of the surrounding rock. But manual digging speed is very slow with high labor intensity, poor safety thus being generally used in earth tunnel with poor stability or soft rock tunnels.

Manual heading is only accidentally used in tunnel works of special geology or super small sections. In case of small works amount and loose works schedule, unavailability of machine or machine being not preferred, manual heading can be adopted. Muck can be loaded for removal manually with shovels and buckets. During manual heading, care must be paid to safety and special person should be designated for observing the safety of working face.

The principle of selecting heading mode are as follows.

The rock body which originally fully occupied position of the tunnel excavated was of various hardness and broken extent. The difficult level of breaking and removing those rocks differs. On the contrast, different tunneling methods cause disturbances of rocks in different degree. So mode of tunneling is another significant element affecting stability of surrounding rock. For different rock mass, different modes of breaking rock are adopted.

Selection of tunneling method is determining the ways of breaking and removing of each portion of rocks and the controlling measures of the disturbance of rock. In practical tunneling, disturbance extent of surrounding rock by the tunneling way to be applied, the surrounding rock' resistance against disturbance (namely its stability), and the secondary considerations are influences of such factors as the excavation method to be adopted, size of working space, machine capacity equipped, construction time required, construction zone length and economy and through overall analysis the tunneling method shall be selected which is both economical, fast and without serious impact on the stability of the surrounding rock.

To sum up, although drill and blast method is economical, it exerts excessive disturbance of surrounding rocks, particularly adverse to stabilization of soft and fragmentary surrounding rock. Although mechanical boring causes little distance of surrounding rock and is of high speed, the machine investment is relatively high. Manual heading exerts small disturbance of surrounding rock but the heading speed is low with excessive labor intensity. At present, drill and blast method is mostly used in mountainous tunnels in stone-natured surrounding rock mainly. It should be noted that while drill and blasting is used in tunneling, blasting should be strictly controlled and managed to reduce the disturbance and damages, due to the vibration of blasting, to the surrounding rock and the existed support.

Text C　Tunnel Lining
隧 道 衬 砌

The lining of a tunnel is never loaded by the stress which initially prevailed in the ground. Luckily, the initial (or primary) stress is reduced by deformation of the ground that occurs during excavation but also after installation of the lining (here "lining" is understood as the shell of shotcrete, which is placed as soon as possible after excavation). Here we shall consider the important phenomenon that deformation of the ground (soil or rock) implies a reduction of the primary stress. This is a manifestation of arching. Since the deformation of the ground is connected with the deformation of the lining, it follows that the load acting upon the lining depends on its own deformation. This is always the case with soil-structure interaction and constitutes an inherent difficulty for design as the load is not an independent variable. Thus, the question is not "which is the pressure acting upon the lining", but rather "which is the relation between pressure and deformation".

The consideration of deformation in tunneling is a merit of NATM. The rock is symbolically represented by a beam. Excavation and installation of the lining is here represented by removal of the central column which is replaced by a lower column. In other words, the central column (which symbolizes the lining) is displaced downwards and, therefore, receives a reduced load. Of course, the principle "pressure is reduced by deformation" is to be applied cautiously. Exaggerated deformation can become counterproductive leading to a strong increase of pressure upon the bearing construction. To point this out was another merit of NATM: softening (and the related loosening) of geomaterials is an important issue. It should be emphasized, however, that this softening does not refer to the gentle stress reduction subsequent to the peak, as it is obtained in laboratory tests on dense soil samples. In contrast, the drastic strength reduction observed in poor rock due to loss of structural cohesion is meant. Civil engineers, by tradition, distinguish between deformation and failure (collapse) structure. It is, however, impossible to find a genuine difference between these two notions. Virtually, failure is nothing but an overly large deformation at any rate, large deformations have to be avoided. How can this be achieved in underpinning/tunnelling? There are two ways: Either early or rigid support (which is not economic) or by keeping the size of the excavated cavities small. The latter option is pursued in tunnelling. There are two ways to do this:

(1) Partial excavation instead of full face excavation;
(2) Small advance steps.

Of course, too small excavation steps would not be economic. So, the art of tunnelling consists in keeping the excavation steps as large as possible and exploiting the strength of the ground.

1. Shotcrete

What distinguishes shotcrete (or "sprayed concrete") from cast concrete is not the strength of the final product but the process of its placement. In tunnelling, shotcrete is applied to seal freshly uncovered surfaces (in thicknesses of 3 to 5cm) and for the support of cavities.

The characteristics of sprayed concrete (shotcrete) are almost the same as those of usual concrete. However, Young's modulus is somewhat lower than with conventional concrete.

Up to the age of 28 days the stiffness and the strength of shotcrete develop approximately as they do with cast concrete. Afterwards, with sufficient humidity, the strength increases considerably due to post-hydration. Up to the age of two years it increases by ca 50%. The strength of fast-setting sprayed concrete increases with time as follows (Table 9.3):

The Strength of Concrete Increases with Time   Table 9.3

Age	Strength(N/mm^2)	Age	Strength(N/mm^2)
6min	0.2-0.5	24h	8-20
1h	0.5-1.0	7d	30-35

There are two methods to spray shotcrete:

Dry mix: dry cement and aggregates are pneumatically conveyed, water is added at the nozzle (Figure 9.3).

Wet mix: ready mixed concrete is pumped to the nozzle, from where it is driven by compressed air. Due to the increased weight of the nozzle, a wet mix is better sprayed with robots.

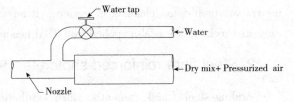

Figure 9.3 Dry Mix Nozzle

Advantages of dry mix:
(1) Machines are smaller and cheaper;
(2) Lower costs for cleaning and maintenance;
(3) Stop and re-start of shotcreting is simpler;
(4) Longer conveying distances (up to 150m);
(5) More precise dosage of additives;
(6) Better concrete (pumping of wet mix requires a higher water content);
(7) Water content can be manually reduced, e.g. when spraying against a wet background.

Advantages of wet mix:
(1) Reduced dust production;
(2) Reduced rebound;
(3) Reduced scatter of concrete properties;
(4) Higher capacity.

Depending on the discharge, shotcrete is sprayed from a distance of 0.5 to 2m, as perpendicular to the wall as possible, in layers of up to 4cm (on vertical walls) and 2 to 3cm (on the roof) thickness. Starting from lower parts, shotcreting moves to the roof. Care should be taken to shotcrete beyond reinforcement, i.e. to avoid "shadows". As the impact velocity is high (20-30m/s), the rebound usually amounts to 15%-30% for vertical walls and 25%-40% for the roof and consists mainly of coarse grains. The aggregates of shotcrete are $\phi = 16mm$, and their diameter should not exceed 1/3 of the layer thickness. The rebound can be reduced by increasing the proportion of fine grains, e.g. by adding cement or silica fume (i.e. SiO_2 powder). The high specific surface of the latter attracts water and thus reduces the consistency of shotcrete. Setting accelerators (such as sodium silicate) may also help, but the resulting concrete has a lower strength. Therefore the chosen accelerator should be tuned with respect to the cement. To achieve sufficient bonding, the target surface (rock or previous shotcrete layer) must be appropriately cleaned and moistened. This is achieved by spraying air and/or water.

Usual additives, aiming to reduce rebound and customize the setting, are alkaline and are therefore hazardous. Recently, non-alkaline additives have been developed. Dust production, rebound and presence of etching materials renders shotcreting an arduous job, which can be mechanized by the use of robots and remote controlled spaying arms. This can considerably speed up the heading. A promising idea to reduce rebound is the rollover shutter belt. Another idea is to replace pressurized air with centrifugal skidding in shotcreting.

The surplus consumption of shotcrete is due to rebound (rebound material should not be reused), overprofile and cleaning of devices. It amounts up to 200%. Shotcrete sealing of the freshly excavated rock surface is also applied with TBM heading. In this case shotcrete is sprayed within a hood.

2. Steel fibre reinforced shotcrete (SFRS)

Figure 9.4 Steel fibres

Adding steel (and, recently, also synthetic) fibres (Figure 9.4) increases the tensile strength and ductility of the shotcrete. Thus, traditional steel reinforcements become dispensable and spraying shadows are avoided. The length of the fibres should not exceed 2/3 of the minimum hose diameter. Usual sizes are 45-50mm length, 0.8-1.0mm diameter. The steel fibre content should be eaqual to 30kg/m^3, while the aggregates should not be coarser than 8mm. The water/cement ratio should not exceed 0.5. If the shotcrete surface is to be covered with an impermeable membrane, then a layer of fibre-free shotcrete should be applied first, otherwise the membrane could be damaged.

3. Quality assessment of shotcrete

The following controls help to assure a sufficient shotcrete quality:

(1) Control of appropriate composition, packing, designation and storage of the ingredients.

(2) Control of the strength of fresh shotcrete. The extraction of core samples is not possible for compressive strengths less than 10N/mm^2 and shotcreting into moulds does not yield representative samples. Therefore, several indirect methods have been proposed. They are based on penetration of pins or on the pull-out of bolts or plates. Ultrasonic and hammer blow tests are inappropriate due to the rough surface of shotcrete.

(3) Stiffness, strength and permeability of hard shotcrete is tested on extracted cores of 10cm diameter. For tunnelling, a shotcrete with an age of 28 days is usually required to have a compressive strength of 23N/mm^2.

(4) The mechanical performance of steel fibre reinforced shotcrete is tested with bending of beams. The content of steel fibres is usually reduced as compared with the initial mixture. It can be measured by smashing a shotcrete sample and extracting the steel fibres with a magnet.

(5) The thickness of shotcrete is measured at random points (roughly one measurement every 100m^2) either with stencils or via coring.

4. Steel meshes

Steel meshes (mesh size =100mm, ϕ <10mm, concrete cover =2cm) are manually mounted and should, therefore, be not too heavy. A usual weight is 5kg/m^2. Mesh installation is labor intensive and relatively hazardous, as the personnel are exposed to small rock falls. For drill and blast heading the mesh adjacent to the face (proximity <1m) can be damaged by the subsequent blast.

5. Rock reinforcement

The mechanical properties of rock (be it hard rock or soft rock and soil) in terms of stiffness and strength can be improved by the installation of various types of reinforcement. Steel bars can be fixed at their ends and pretensioned against the rock. In this way, the surrounding rock is compressed and, as a consequence, its stiffness and its strength increase. Such reinforcing bars are called anchors or bolts. An alternative type of reinforcement consists of bars that are connected with the surrounding rock over their entire length, e.g. by grout. Such bars are not pre-tensioned and are called nails. Rock with nails is a composite material, whose stiffness is increased as compared to the original rock. A third action of reinforcement is given when a steel bar (dowel) inhibits the relative slip of two adjacent rock blocks. In this case the bar is loaded by transverse forces and acts as a plug. The usage of names, stated here (anchor, bolt, dowel) is, however, not unique and they are often interchanged.

6. Connection with the adjacent rock

The connection, i.e. the force transfer between reinforcement and surrounding rock, is either achieved mechanically or by means of grout (cement mortar or synthetic resin). Mechanical connections can be loaded immediately after installation. They comprise following types.

Wedges: Conical wedges are placed at the end of the borehole. They can be moved in longitudinal direction either by hammering ("slot and wedge anchors", figure 9.5) or by rotating a thread ("expanding shell anchors", figure 9.6) in such a way that they force their containment (which is either a slotted bar or a shell) to grip into the rock. The transmission of a concentrated force is only possible in sufficiently hard rock (compression strength >100MPa). Slot and wedge anchors can be loosened by shocks and vibrations (e.g. due to blasting).

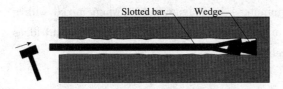
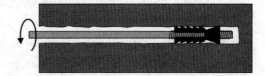

Figure 9.5 Slot and Wedge Anchors   Figure 9.6 Expanding Shell Anchors

Tubular steel rock bolts: A contact over the entire bolt length is achieved by the expansion of a tubular steel (also called hollow anchor) against the borehole wall. The expansion is either elastic (figure 9.7) or is achieved by means of water pressure ("Swellex" rock bolt by Atlas Copco, figure 9.8). The sheer force is transferred to the rock by friction.

Alternatively, the connection with the rock can be achieved by means of cement mortar or resin. The obtained support is not immediate, since setting and hardening needs some time.

Grouted rock bolts: The annular gap between rebar and drillhole wall is filled with cement or resin grout. Before grouting, the drillhole must be thoroughly flushed with water or air to ensure a clean rock surface. It should also be ensured that the rock does not contain wide open joints into which the grout may disappear. This can be avoided by using geotextile containments of the grout.

Cement grout (mortar) consists of well graded sand and cement in ratios between 50/50 and 60/40. To obtain a sufficient strength, the water-to-cement ratio should be equal to 40% by weight. The mortar should set (i.e. obtain the required strength) within 6 hours. To increase plasticity, a bentonite fraction of up to 2% of the cement weight can be added. Note that cement grout can be damaged by vibrations due to blasting. In some cases, grouting is not allowed until the heading has advanced by 40-50m.

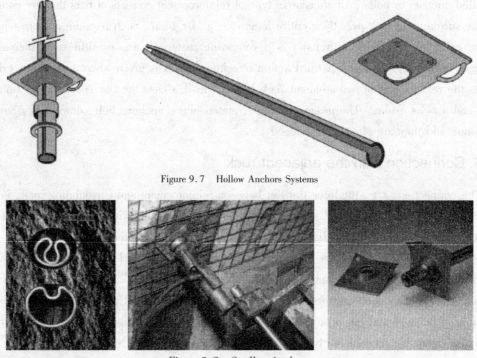

Figure 9.7 Hollow Anchors Systems

Figure 9.8 Swellex-Anchors

Synthetic resins harden very quickly (2-30 minutes) by polymerization when mixed with a catalyst. The two components are either injected or introduced into the drillhole within cartridges which are subsequently burst by introducing the rebar.

Cement mortar can be introduced in several ways:

(1) Grouting into the annular gap between rebar and drillhole wall.

(2) Perforated tubes filled with mortar are placed into the borehole. The subsequent introduction of the anchor (by means of hammer blows) squeezes the mortar into the remaining free space. The perfobolts are now obsolete.

(3) "Self-boring" or "Self-drilling" anchors (SDA)12: the rod is a steel tube of 42-130mm diameter driven into the rock with rotary-percussion drilling equipment, flushing and a sacrificial drill bit. Standard delivery lengths vary between 1 and 6m. Two rods can be connected with couplers. Grouting of mortar occurs through the tube with pressures up to 70bars.

At the head of the anchor the tendon (steel rod) is fixed against a bearing plate or faceplate in such a way that the anchor tension is converted into a compressive force at the rock face. Spherical washers enable to fix the tendon against the faceplate also in cases when the tendon is not perpendicular to the rock surface. The faceplate also helps to fix the wire mesh.

7. Timbering

In the early days of tunneling, timbering was the only means for temporary support. Nowadays it is mainly used for the support of small and/or irregular cavities (e.g. resulting from inrushes). Timbering has been systematically used (according to the old Belgian tunneling method) during the recent construction of the Madrid metro.

Wood is easy to handle and transport and indicates imminent collapse by cracking. On the other hand the discontinuous contact with the rock is problematic.

The spacing of the timber frames is usually 1-1.5m. Care must be taken for a sufficient longitudinal bracing.

8. Support arches

Support arches are composed of segments of rolled steel profiles or lattice girders (Figure 9.9-Figure 9.11). The arch segments are placed and mounted together with fixed or compliant joints (to accommodate for large convergences). The contact with the adjacent rock is achieved with wooden wedges or with bagged packing, i.e. bags filled with (initially) soft mortar. Usually, the arches are subsequently covered with shotcrete. This leads to a garland-shaped shotcrete surface, which protrudes to the cavity at the locations of the arches. To achieve a good contact between the shotcrete surface and a geosynthetic sealing membrane, the sag between two adjacent arches should not exceed 1/20 of their spacing. Together with their contribution to support, arches also help to check the excavated profile. They can also serve to mount forepoling spiles in longitudinal direction. Clearly, ∪ shaped rolled steel profiles have a much higher bearing capacity than lattice girders.

Figure 9.9   Rolled Steel Profiles

Figure 9.10   Grid Steel Frame   Figure 9.11   Profile Steel Arch

9. Forepoling

If the strength of the ground is so low that the excavated space is unstable even for a short time, a pre-driven support is applied in such a way that an excavation increment occurs under the protection of a previously driven canopy.

The traditional method of forepoling was to drive 5 to 7mm thick steel sheets up to 4m beyond the face into the ground or 1.5 to 6m long steel rods (so-called spiles) with a spacing of 30 to 50cm. Nowadays, forepoling is achieved by spiling, pipe roof, grouting and freezing.

Spiling: This method consists of drilling a canopy of spiles, i.e. steel rods or pipes into the face (Figure 9.12). A typical length is 4m. To give an idea, 40-45 tubes, ϕ80-200mm, each 14m long, enable a total advance of 11-12m (the last 2-3m serve as abutment of the canopy). In order for the spiles to act not only as beams (i.e. in longitudinal direction) but also to form a protective arch over the excavated space, the surrounding soil is grouted through the steel pipes or sealed with shotcrete. Thus, a connected canopy is formed that consists of grouted soil reinforced with spiles. Drilling 40 tubes takes 10-12h, grouting other 10-12h. Spile rods can also be placed into drillholes. The remaining annular gap is filled with mortar, whose setting however may prove to be too slow. Alternatively, "self-drilling" rods are used.

Figure 9.12 Forepoling

Pipe roof: This method is similar to spiling with the only difference that large diameter (>200mm) steel or concrete tubes are jacked into the soil above the space to be excavated. The larger diameter provides a larger bearing capacity. Sometimes, the tubes are filled with concrete. The steel tubes only act as beams and do not form an arch. Pipe roofs do not protect the overburden soil from considerable settlements.

Perforex-method: This method is also called "peripheral slot precutting method" or "sciage (sawing)". A peripheral slot is cut using a movable chainsaw (slot cutter) mounted on a rig. The individual slots have a depth up to 5m and a thickness between 19 and 35cm. These are filled with shotcrete, thus forming a vault that protects the space to be subsequently excavated. Immediately after completion the slot is shotcreted while the next one is being cut. The slots are staggered in such a way that consecutive canopies overlap by 0.5 to 2m. This method allows large advance steps. The resulting canopy is relatively rigid and, therefore, does not induce stress relief by yielding. This effect combined with a possible incomplete setting of shotcrete may possibly cause collapse. Peripheral slots are also applied in hard rock in combination with drill and blast. There, the slot protects the surrounding rock from explosion damage.

II. Terms and terminology

lining	衬砌
excavation	开挖
full face excavation method	全断面开挖
bench excavation method	台阶法开挖
partial face excavation method	部分开挖法
micro bench excavation method	微台阶开挖法
semi section excavation method	半断面开挖法
ring cut method	环形导坑留核心土开挖法
lower drift excavation method	下导洞超前开挖法
center diagram method (CD method)	中隔壁开挖法(CD 法)
center cross diagram method (CRD method)	交叉中隔壁开挖法(CRD 法)
single side-wall drift pilot excavation method	单侧壁导坑法
double side-wall drift pilot excavation method	双侧壁导坑法
column-heading method	柱洞法
surrounding rock	围岩
surrounding rock classification	围岩分级
cross section	横截面
longitudinal section	纵截面
single-track tunnel	单线隧道
double-track tunnel	双线隧道
advance length	进尺
working face	开挖面,工作面
anchoring and shotcreting	锚喷
secondary lining	二次衬砌
heading mode	掘进方式
shotcrete	喷射混凝土
fast setting	速凝
nozzle	喷嘴
steel fibre reinforced shotcrete (SFRS)	钢纤维喷射混凝土
steel meshes	钢筋网
grout	注浆
rock bolt	锚杆
expanding shell anchor	胀壳式锚杆
steel profiles	型钢
grid steel frame	格栅钢架
profile steel arch	型钢拱架

III. Questions and difficult sentence analysis

1. Questions for brainstorming discussion

(1) Present the common excavation modes of mountainous tunnels and illustrate them with drawings and figures.

(2) Present the common heading modes of tunnels and point out their respective advantages and disadvantages.

(3) Describe the common types and names of initial linings in tunnels.

2. Difficult sentences analysis

(1) The surrounding rocks of different classes are of different stability while different excavation methods cause different disturbances of surrounding rock and the mutual disturbances among working faces also differ.

译文:不同等级的围岩具有不同的稳定性,而不同的开挖方式对围岩产生扰动程度也不同,从而导致工作面之间的相互扰动不同。

(2) By the full face excavation method, the section of one excavation is substantial. If adverse geological conditions are encountered with (such as faulting fracture zone, groundwater, karst cave, gas stratum and similar ground), emergent engineering safety incidents are vulnerable (such as collapse, water inrush, mud bursting, gas burst) and they can be in large scale.

译文:全断面开挖法一次开挖面较大,如果遇到地质条件的突然变化(如断层破碎带、地下水、溶洞、瓦斯地层等),极易发生突发性工程安全事故(如塌方、突水、突泥、瓦斯涌出等),且其规模也会比较大。

(3) Initially shape by excavation the upper arch pilot cavity and after the upper initial lining is placed, remove by excavation the core soil and carry out lower part excavation and its lining. The core soil is retained for the purposes of reducing the voided height of heading face, moderating the slope surface angle of the heading face, reducing down slip of the heading face, shortening the exposure period of rock excavated and assuring the stability of the surrounding rock.

译文:先行挖出上部弧形导坑,待施作上部初期支护后,再挖除核心土,并进行下部开挖和支护的施作。留核心土的目的是降低开挖面临空高度,减缓开挖面的坡面角度,抵抗开挖面的下滑,缩短开挖后围岩的暴露时间,保证围岩稳定。

(4) In compliance with the basic principle of "maximizing the excavation section to greatest extent" of the New Austrian Tunneling Method, efforts shall be made to create conditions, reduce number of excavations in parts and to achieve large-section excavation to provide larger interior operation space for working of large-medium machines realizing speedy construction.

译文:按照新奥法"应尽可能采用大断面开挖"的基本原则,应尽量创造条件,减少分部开挖次数,尽可能争取用大断面开挖,使具备较大的洞内作业空间,以便于采用大中型机械施工和提高施工速度。

Ⅳ. Translation case study

Case 1

Chinese	English translation
隧道衬砌从不受应力作用,而初始应力对于地面结构普遍存在。幸运的是,在开挖过程中以及安装衬砌之后(此处"衬砌"应理解为开挖后尽快安装的混凝土壳),初始应力(或主应力)随着地层变形而消减。我们应该考虑一个重要现象即地层的变形(土或岩石)意味着主应力的减小。拱的形成证明了这点。由于地层变形与衬砌变形联系在一起,于是,作用在衬砌上的荷载取决于该衬砌结构自身的变形量。	The lining of a tunnel is never loaded by the stress which initially prevailed in the ground. Luckily, the initial (or primary) stress is reduced by deformation of the ground that occurs during excavation but also after installation of the lining (here "lining" is understood as the shell of shotcrete, which is placed as soon as possible after excavation). Here we shall consider the important phenomenon that deformation of the ground (soil or rock) implies a reduction of the primary stress. This is a manifestation of arching. Since the deformation of the ground is connected with the deformation of the lining, it follows that the load acting upon the lining depends on its own deformation.

Case 2

Chinese	English translation
考虑隧道开挖中的变形是新奥法的一大优点。用梁象征性的代表围岩。此处衬砌的开挖与安装表示为拆除中央柱,由一个较短柱取代。换言之,中央柱(象征衬砌)向下位移,承受一个减轻的荷载。当然,主要压力通过变形而减小,然后小心地施加在结构上。开挖变形可能会对生产不利,导致对承重结构的压力增大。	The consideration of deformation in tunneling is a merit of NATM. The rock is symbolically represented by a beam. Excavation and installation of the lining is here represented by removal of the central column which is replaced by a lower column. In other words, the central column (which symbolizes the lining) is displaced downwards and, therefore, receives a reduced load. Of course, the principle "pressure is reduced by deformation" is to be applied cautiously (The principal pressure reduced by deformation is to be applied cautiously). The Exaggerated deformation can become counter-productive leading to a strong increase of pressure upon the bearing construction.

Case 3

Chinese	English translation
增加钢纤维(近来还增加化合物)会加大喷射混凝土的抗拉强度以及延展性。因此,没有必要采用传统的钢筋混凝土,而且还避免了喷射阴影。纤维长度不应超过最小管道直径的2/3。常用混凝土浇筑管子长度为45~50mm,直径为0.8~1.0mm。钢纤维含量应该大于等于30kg/m³而集料直径不得大于8mm,水灰比不得超过0.5。如果采用一层防水薄膜覆盖混凝土表面,首先铺设一层不含纤维的混凝土,否则,该薄膜会被损坏。	Adding steel (and, recently, also synthetic) fibres increases the tensile strength and ductility of the shotcrete. Thus, traditional steel reinforcements become dispensable and spraying shadows are avoided. The length of the fibres should not exceed 2/3 of the minimum hose diameter. Usual sizes are 45~50mm length, 0.8~1.0mm diameter. The steel fibre content should be no less than $30kg/m^3$, while the aggregates should not be coarser than 8 mm. The water/cement ratio should not exceed 0.5. If the shotcrete surface is to be covered with an impermeable membrane, then a layer of fibre-free shotcrete should be applied first, otherwise the membrane could be damaged.

V. Assignment

（1）新奥法的具体做法是，随隧道掘进及时喷射一层混凝土，封闭围岩暴露面，形成初期柔性支护，随后按设计要求系统布置锚杆加固深部围岩。锚杆、喷层和围岩共同组成承载环，支承围岩压力，形成了新奥法初期支护结构，通常把这部分支护结构称为"外拱"。

（2）在混凝土中加入一定量的钢纤维，从而制成钢纤维喷射混凝土。用钢纤维喷射混凝土作初期支护可代替钢筋网喷射混凝土，并可提高喷射材料与岩壁的黏结强度，提高结构的耐久性，改善喷层的受力状态。

（3）整体移动式模板台车采用大块曲模板、机械或液压脱模、背附式振捣设备集装成整体，并在轨道上走行，有的还设有自行设备，从而缩短立模时间，墙拱连续浇筑，加快衬砌施工速度。

（4）混凝土灌注前应按规范规定和设计要求对灌注混凝土地段的地基、基岩、旧混凝土面进行清理和准备工作。必须清除基底虚渣和污物，排除基坑积水。对于先拱后墙法施工的拱圈，灌注前应将拱脚支承面找平。

（5）至于施工中究竟应采用何种台阶法，要根据以下两个条件来决定：初期支护形成闭合断面的时间要求，围岩越差，闭合时间要求越短；上断面施工所用的开挖、支护、出渣等机械设备对施工场地大小的要求。

Unit 10　Tunnel Ventilation
隧道通风

I. Text

Text A　Tunnel Ventilation Mode
隧道通风模式

Highway tunnels, from a ventilation viewpoint, are defined as any enclosure through which highway vehicles travel. This definition includes not only those facilities that are built as tunnels, but those that result from other construction such as development of air rights over highways.

All highway tunnels require ventilation, which can be provided by natural means, traffic-induced piston effects, and mechanical ventilation equipment. *Ventilation is required to limit the concentration of obnoxious or dangerous contaminants to acceptable levels during normal operation and to remove and control smoke and hot gases during fire emergencies. The ventilation system selected must meet the specified criteria for both normal and emergency operations and should be the most economical solution considering both construction and operating costs.* For normal operations, naturally ventilated and traffic-induced ventilation systems are considered adequate for relatively short tunnels with low traffic volume.

Longer and more heavily traveled highway tunnels should be provided with mechanical ventilation system. In addition, many tunnels that do not require mechanical ventilation for normal operation may require a dedicated ventilation system for emergencies.

1. Natural ventilation

Natural ventilated tunnels rely primarily on meteorological conditions and the piston effect of the moving traffic to maintain satisfactory environmental conditions within the tunnel. The chief meteorological condition affecting the tunnel is the pressure differential between the two tunnel portals created by differences in elevation, ambient temperatures or wind. Unfortunately, none of these factors can be relied on for consistent results. A sudden change in wind direction or velocity can rapidly negate all of these natural effects including, to some extent, the piston effect. The total of all pressures must be of sufficient magnitude to overcome the tunnel resistance, which is influenced by tunnel length, coefficient of friction, hydraulic diameter, and air density. None of the natural effects defined above can be considered when addressing emergency ventilation.

Air flow through a naturally ventilated tunnel can be portal to portal or portal to shaft. The portal-to-portal flow-type system functions with unidirectional traffic, which produces a consistent, positive air flow. The air velocity within the roadway is uniform and the contaminant concentration increases to a maximum at the exit portal. If adverse meteorological conditions occur, the velocity is reduced and the carbon monoxide concentration is increased. If bidirectional traffic is introduced into such a tunnel, further reduction in air flow result.

The naturally ventilated tunnel with an intermediate shaft is best suited for bidirectional traffic. However, the air flow through such a shafted tunnel is also at the mercy of the elements. The added benefit of the "stack effect/chimney effect" of the shaft depends on air temperature differentials, rock temperatures, wind direction and velocity and shaft height. The addition of more than one shaft to a naturally ventilated tunnel will most likely be more of a disadvantage than an advantage, since a pocket of contaminated air can be trapped between the shafts, causing high contaminant levels in the zone.

Because of the numerous uncertainties outlined above, historically it is rare that tunnels of greater than 1000ft in length have been ventilated by natural means. There are exceptions to this, such as the Via Mala Tunnel in Switzerland and the Tenda Pass Tunnel between France and Italy. Via Mala, which is 2050ft (625m) long, is located in an area where the traffic flow is extremely low. The 9000ft (2800m) long Tenda Pass Tunnel has a large difference in portal elevations, which creates a large consistent pressure differential and thus adequate air flow. It also is located in an area having favorable wind conditions. Nonetheless, both of these tunnels have been outfitted with booster fans to supplement the natural ventilation if required.

An emergency mechanical ventilation system has been installed in most naturally ventilated urban tunnels more than 600ft (180m) in length. Such a system is required to purge the smoke and hot gases generated during a fire emergency and may be required to remove stagnant polluted gases or haze during severe adverse meteorological conditions.

The reliance on natural ventilation for tunnels more than 600ft (180m) long should be thoroughly evaluated, specifically the effect of adverse meteorological and operating conditions. This is particularly true for a tunnel where a heavy or congested traffic flow may require mechanically generated air flow. If the natural mode of ventilation is not adequate, a mechanical system with fans must be considered. There are several types of mechanical ventilation systems.

2. Longitudinal ventilation

A longitudinal ventilation system is any system where the air is introduced to or removed from the tunnel roadway at a limited number of points, thus creating a longitudinal air flow within the roadway. The injection-type longitudinal system has been used in railroad tunnels. However, it has also found application in highway tunnels. Air is injected into the tunnel roadway at one end of the tunnel, where it mixes with the air brought in by the piston effect of the incoming traffic. This system is most effective in a tunnel with unidirectional traffic. The air velocity within the roadway is uniform throughout the tunnel, and the concentration of contaminants increases from ambient at the entering portal to maximum at the exiting portal. Adverse external atmospheric conditions can reduce the effectiveness of this system. The concentration of contaminants increases as the air flow decreases or the tunnel length increases.

The longitudinal system with a shaft is similar to the naturally ventilated system with a shaft except that it provides a positive stack effect (fan induced). With bidirectional traffic, peak contaminant concentration occurs near the shaft location. This system is generally not used for unidirectional tunnels, because the contaminant levels become unbalanced and excessive amounts of air will therefore be required for ventilation.

An alternative longitudinal system uses two shafts located near the center of the tunnel, one for exhausting and one for supplying. This configuration will provide a reduction of contaminant concentration in the second half, because a portion of the tunnel air flow is exchanged with ambient air at the shaft. Adverse wind conditions can cause a reduction of air flow, a rise in contaminant concentration in the second half of the tunnel, and "short circuiting" of the fan air flows.

3. Jet fans

In a growing number of highway tunnels throughout the world, jet fans mounted at the tunnel ceiling are being employed to generate the longitudinal air flow. This system eliminates the construction required to house ventilation fans in a building, but it may require larger clearances within the tunnel to accommodate the jet fans, and thus, a larger tunnel.

The concept of jet fans mounted at the tunnel ceiling relies on the high-velocity impulse jet of air produced by the jet fans to create an additional induced flow in the tunnel. These fans are usually mounted in groups of two or more and spaced longitudinally in the tunnel at about 300ft intervals.

4. Saccardo Nozzle

The principal feature of Saccardo-nozzle-based longitudinal ventilation system is the use of a high-velocity "nozzle" to inject air into the tunnel, usually in the direction of traffic flow. This concept uses a high-velocity jet flow that will induce additional longitudinal air flow. The Saccardo nozzle functions on the principle that a high-velocity air jet injected into the tunnel roadway at an extremely small angle to the tunnel axis can induce a high-volume longitudinal air flow in the tunnel roadway area. The level of this induced flow depends on the nozzle discharge velocity, the moment exchange coefficient and the nozzle angle.

The induction effect of a Saccardo nozzle is proportional to the square of the discharge velocity. A reasonable value of the discharge velocity is 6000fpm (30m/s), which is about the maximum value that can be used without an adverse impact on the traffic stream.

The basic advantages of the use of Saccard-nozzle-based longitudinal system over a jet-fan-based system are as follows.

(1) Reduced tunnel height;

(2) Reduced number of moving parts to maintain;

(3) Maitenance can be accomplished without impeding traffic flow;

(4) Noise level in tunnel is decreased;
(5) High fan efficiency.

Longitudinal ventilation system, excluding the jet fan system that have either supply or exhaust at a limited number of locations within the tunnel are the most economical systems since they require the least number of fans, place the least operating burden on these fans, and do not require separate air ducts as part of the tunnel structure. However, as the length of the tunnel increases, the disadvantages of these systems become pronounced, such as the excessive air velocities in the roadway and the discharge of pollution at the exiting portal. If the tunnel portal is located in an environmentally sensitive area or near a sensitive environmental receptor, then the latter disadvantage can be severe, and a more complex system may be required. Longitudinal systems are not well adapted to long tunnels with bidirectional traffic, particularly for fire life safety.

5. Semitransverse ventilation

Uniform distribution or collection of air throughout the length of a tunnel is the chief characteristic of a semitransverse system. A supply air semitransverse system produces a uniform concentration of contaminants throughout the tunnel because the air and the vehicle exhaust gases enter the roadway area at the same relative rate. In a tunnel with free-flowing unidirectional traffic, additional longitudinal air flow will be created by the moving traffic within the roadway area. Supply air is transported to the roadway in a duct and uniformly distributed through flues. The most suitable location for the introduction of air to the tunnel roadway is at the level of the vehicles' exhaust pipes to permit immediate dilution of the exhaust gases. To accomplish the air distribution described above, an adequate pressure differential must be generated between the duct and the roadway to counteract the vehicle piston effect and atmospheric winds.

During a fire within the tunnel, the air supplied from a semitransverse system will provide dilution of the smoke. However, to aid in fire-fighting efforts and in emergency egress, the fresh air should enter the tunnel through the portals to create a respirable environment for those activities. For these reasons, the fans in a supply semitransverse system should be reversible.

The exhaust semitransverse system in a unidirectional tunnel will produce a maximum contaminant concentration at the exiting portal. For low traffic speeds with unidirectional traffic or in a bidirectional tunnel, a zone of zero fresh air is located within the tunnel, which, of course, corresponds to the maximum concentration of contaminants.

A combination supply and exhaust system has been used. Such a system is applicable only in unidirectional tunnel where the air entering the traffic stream is exhausted in the first half, and air that is supplied in the second half is exhausted through the exit portal. This system, in effect, creates longitudinal air flow in the roadway area.

The supply system is the only semitransverse system not affected by adverse meteorological conditions or opposing traffic. Semitransverse systems are used in tunnels up to approximately 9000ft (2750m) in length (not altitude), at which point the tunnel air velocities near the portals become excessive.

6. Full transverse ventilation

For longer tunnels, a full transverse system is typically used. A full exhaust duct is added to a supply-type semitransverse system, which achieves a uniform distribution of supply air and a uniform collection of vitiated air. This system was developed for the Holland Tunnel in 1924. with this system, a uniform pressure will occur except that generated by the traffic piston effect, which will tend to reduce contaminant levels. A pressure differential between the ducts and the roadway is required to assure proper distribution of air under ventilation operating conditions.

The desirable location of the supply air inlets from the standpoint of immediate dilution of exhaust gases is at the level of the vehicle emissions near the road surface, with the exhaust outlets located in the ceiling, thus creating transverse air flow. This arrangement originally demonstrated by the full-scale tests conducted by the U.S. Bureau of Mines. The air distribution can be one-sided or two-sided depending on tunnel width and the number of traffic lanes.

7. Single-point extraction

Ever since the ceiling fell down during the Holland Tunnel Fire in 1949, ventilation engineers have been working for ways to apply the concept of enlarged ceiling openings to process a larger rate of smoke extraction. What occurred at the Holland Tunnel fire after the demise of the ceiling was a sudden improvement in the extraction of the smoke from the roadway area. One could arrange for the tunnel ceiling to collapse, but a more meaningful approach is to provide a specialized enlargement of an existing exhaust port or a new large extraction opening. Both approaches have been tried, the enhanced exhaust port in a recent Holland Tunnel retrofit and in the Sydney Harbour Tunnel in Australia and several Swiss tunnels.

An expandable exhaust port is a typical exhaust port, probably 6in × 36in. (152mm × 914mm), which is opened to some large size in the event of a fire incident. This can be accomplished by using a meltable panel-used in Holland Tunnel or an active damper, which can be opened from a central control system. The damper approach is unreasonable due to the high cost of both maintaining and operating the dampers. The meltable panel is a more cost-effective solution. However, finding a material having the proper melting temperature, non toxicity, and structural strength has been extremely difficult.

An oversized extraction port is usually applied in a new tunnel when a large opening (approximately 8ft × 8ft) (2.4m × 2.4m) can be installed in the tunnel ceiling or wall to communicate with the fan system through the exhaust or extraction duct. An early application of the concept, although in a rail tunnel, was in the San Francisco Trans-Bay Tube. This concept has been exposed to a fire and subsequent tests in the 1970s. The purpose of an oversized extraction port is to provide a larger opening close to the fire to provide a large extraction rate to remove the smoke gases. This concept was tested in the Memorial Tunnel Fire Ventilation Test Program in 1994.

Railroad tunnels are tunnels through which rail vehicles travel propelled by diesel engine locomotive power. Tunnels in which electrically propelled trains operation are covered in rapid transit tunnels.

The most important environmental factors in diesel-powered rail tunnels are heat and the products of combustion. Excessive heat will raise the tunnel ambient air temperature to a point at which the locomotive engine can no longer function. The presence of excessive products of combustion will create a hazard to health and a haze within the tunnel. Any criteria established must therefore consider the health of the train occupants, both crew and passengers, and the ability of the locomotive units to function properly within the tunnel.

In a diesel locomotive, the diesel engine drives an electric generator supplying power to the electric traction motors. The throttle, which usually has eight positions, controls engine speed. The diesel engines, in 70% of the locomotives in the United States, are of the two-stroke cycle type. The capacity of these engines ranges from 700 to 4000hp.

8. Diesel exhaust gases in rail tunnels

The composition of railway locomotive diesel exhaust is similar to that of vehicular diesel engines. However, in the railroad tunnel, the significant contaminant becomes the oxides of nitrogen instead of carbon monoxide. Thus the oxides of nitrogen must be studied in depth. It can be shown that, based on the composition of diesel exhaust gas, if the oxides of nitrogen are maintained within specified acceptable limits, all other exhaust gas contaminants will also be maintained within acceptable limits.

The establishment of criteria for oxides of nitrogen must consider the length of time personnel are exposed to the environment, since the nature of the effect on the human body is time-dependent. The American Conference Governmental Industrial Hygienists, in the 1992 edition of Industrial Ventilation (ACGIH, 1992) presents a threshold limit value of 3ppm for nitrogen dioxide and 25ppm for nitric oxide. These threshold limit values are for exposures of 8h per day over a working lifetime. Therefore, since the travel time through a railroad tunnel is on the order of 1h, level of 5ppm for nitrogen dioxide and 37.5ppm for nitric oxide can be tolerated for these short periods of exposure without adverse effects.

The exhaust gases are emitted from the top of most diesel electric locomotives. This creates phenomenon that aids the ventilation of any railroad tunnel. The stratification effect created in the crown of the tunnel and in the annular space around the locomotive by the temperature gradients remain stable, and thus a percentage of the exhaust gas contaminants will remain in the crown of the tunnel and not interact with the train. Tests have shown that about only 45% of the emitted exhaust gases descend from the tunnel crown to interact with the air in the spaces at sides of the locomotive.

The effect of air flow in the annular space has been determined from tests conducted at Cascade Tunnel (1966). These tests show that approximately 50% of the total air flow rate within the annular space surrounding the train is effective for cooling and combustion. A method for determining the oxides of nitrogen emitted from a diesel engine locomotive is described by Berger and McGuire (1946).

9. Heat

Heat from the engine combustion process is released by the locomotive as it travels through the tunnel. The total heat is composed of heat from the exhaust gas, jacket water, lubricating oil, braking resistors, and radiation. The heat from exhaust gases, jacket water, lub oil, and braking resistors is emitted from the top of the locomotive, whereas the radiated heat is emitted from all surfaces of the locomotive.

The final dissipation of this heat is important to the proper operation of the locomotive unit, since air is required for the engine cooling. If the inlet air temperature is raised by this heat to a point above the maximum operating temperature of the engine, the engine will shut down on a high-water-temperature condition. This usually occurs where a large number of locomotive units are operating in a single consist. As in the case of the air, only a porting of this heat affects the locomotive inlet air conditions due to the stratified air flow in the crown of the tunnel.

The total amount of the radiated heat, along with the heat from the exhaust gas, jacket water, lube oil, and braking resistors, interacts with the inlet air.

10. Ventilation

Ventilation is required in all railroad tunnels to remove the heat generated by the locomotive units and to change the air within the tunnel, thus flushing the tunnel of air contaminants. Ventilation can take the form of natural ventilation, piston effect, or mechanical ventilation. While the train is in the tunnel, the heat is removed by an adequate flow of air with respect to the train, whereas the air contaminants are best removed when there is a positive air flow out of the tunnel. The three major forms of railroad tunnel ventilation are outlined below:

(1) Piston effect with an open-ended tunnel. In this type of tunnel, the only means of ventilation is the piston effect of the train on the air. The air in the annular space flows in the same direction as the train, and there is a net flow of air through the tunnel in the direction of the train. This method is satisfactory for short tunnels since the flushing effect is good, and because the oxides of nitrogen levels and the heat have not had an opportunity to build up.

(2) Piston effect with a portal gate. The addition of an operable portal gate at the end of a tunnel will greatly enhance the ability of the ventilation system to remove the heat generated by the locomotive units. However, since there is no net flow from the tunnel, the tunnel under these conditions is not flushed of the air contaminants. This fact precludes the use of a portal gate on a railroad tunnel without mechanical ventilation.

(3) Mechanical ventilation with a portal gate. The addition of a mechanical ventilation system provides the ultimate in the ventilation of a railroad tunnel. The heat along with the contaminants, will be removed, since there will be adequate air flow with respect to the train and an adequate net flow through the tunnel.

11. Pressure

To properly design a railroad tunnel ventilation system, it is necessary to be able to predict the pressures generated in the tunnel for various train speeds as well as the air flow surrounding the train. These air flows must satisfy the cooling requirements of all locomotive units in the consist. The ventilation system components must be designed to withstand the maximum pressures generated by the train and air fans.

12. Flushing

There is a requirement in all diesel-powered railroad tunnels for a flushing cycle after the train has passed through the tunnel. The ventilation of the tunnel during the train passage is never 100% effective. Air contaminants will always remain in the tunnel. The natural ventilation effect created by the pressure differential due to difference in elevation may be sufficient for a short tunnel to provide the necessary flushing. A fan system will be required to provide this flushing effect for longer tunnels or in cases where the train headway requires a more rapid flush cycle.

Text B Environment within Subway System
地铁运营环境

1. Rapid transit systems

The portions of rail rapid transit systems located below the surface in subway structures require control of the environment.

In rapid transit systems, there are two types of tunnels: the standard subway tunnel usually located between stations and normally constructed beneath surface developments with numerous ventilation shafts and exits communicating with the surface; and the long tunnel usually crossing under a body of water, such as the Trans-Bay Tube in San Francisco, also in California. The ventilation concepts for these two types will be different, since in the long tunnel there is usually limited ability to locate a shaft at any intermediate point, as can be done in the standard subway tunnel. The subway tunnel is considered in this section, while the long transit tune is considered in the section "Rail Tunnels".

The evaluation of the environment within the subway system has taken great strides in recent years. Since the BART system was the first new system to be designed in approximately 30 years, the available technology was limited. Efforts have progressed from the analytical tools that were developed for BART to the sophisticated analytical tools developed as a part of the Subway environmental Research Project. The published handbook resulting from this project contains the most up-to-date technical data available for evaluation of the subway environment.

2. Subway environment

During normal train operation, the "piston effect" of the moving train provides air motion within the trainway and station. In most of the systems built in early years, this air movement has been sufficient to maintain adequate environmental conditions within the subway facilities. However, new higher-performance transit vehicles, which are capable of attaining speeds of

80mph (129kph), often generated an amount of heat exceeding the ability of the piston effect ventilation to remove it from the subway. Coupled with this is the increasing use of air-conditioned transit trains and stations. Many of the newer systems being designed and constructed in the world today consider cooling of the station facilities. This occurs on systems in Caracas, Washington, Baltimore, Atlanta, Hong Kong, and Singapore.

The other aspect of subway ventilation is emergency operation. The major purpose of an emergency system is to remove heat and smoke generated during a fire to permit the safe egress of passengers and the entrance of fire-fighting personnel. When an emergency situation occurs, the trains are halted or slowed, and the "piston effect" ventilation ceases. This requires the incorporation of a mechanically driven ventilation system into the subway.

The objectives to be sought in controlling the environment within a subway system are, first, to provide a suitable environment for patrons as well as for operating and maintenance personnel; and second, to minimize the exposure of the equipment to high temperatures, thus prolonging its life. This must be considered for all public and nonpublic spaces within the stations and the normally occupied space in the trainways. Also to be considered is the control of haze, odor, and vapor, and the purging of smoke during a fire.

The Urban Mass Transit Administration (now the Federal Transit Administration) of the U.S. Department of Transportation funded a research project dealing with the subway environment. The rapid transit properties in the United States and Canada sponsored and partially funded this project through the Institute for Rapid Transit (now the American Public Transit Association) and the Transit development corporation. The subway environmental research project had as its objective preparation of a handbook, along with the required methodologies to permit proper evaluation of the subway environment.

The subject of tunnel ventilation in a rapid transit system has taken on a broader meaning over the last 20 years. It now incorporates the tunnel and station environment including both normal and emergency operations. The station environment is severely affected by events in the connecting tunnels. The following text addresses the factors to be considered in the evaluation and design of subway environment control. The subway environmental design handbook provides a detailed description of the evaluation and design process.

Consideration of the environment within the subway system involves three major components: criteria, analysis, and control.

3. Normal criteria

Criteria for the subway environment must be based on the reaction of the human patron to the surrounding environment. The factors to be considered are temperature, humidity, air movement, noise, and vibration. The capacity of human beings to endure the environment is a function of age, occupation, health, acclimatization, and the natural ventilation in human beings. The most critical item is the thermal factor.

Criteria should also be established for maximum air velocity, rapid pressure change, and air quality, including gas particle and odor contaminants. A thorough definition of these criteria and their method of determination is covered in the subway environmental design handbook.

The primary normal criteria to be applied in the subway station are related to platform comfort and tunnel temperature. The criteria for the station are usually based on the specific climatic conditions, the local comfort requirements (demands), and funding limitations set by the operating agency.

Thermal comfort: Thermal comfort is the primary factor in setting the environmental criteria. This factor has the greatest influence on the comfort of the traveling patron. One of the basic underlying philosophies in setting criteria is that the patron in entering a station should not be exposed to a degradation in thermal environment upon entering the subway facilities from the street environment.

The establishment of a specific single value criterion is nearly impossible in this environment. The application of standard office environment criteria would be too costly. Therefore, a method that uses several thermal indices was developed. The indices used are the relative warmth index (RWI) and the heat deficit rate (HDR), which were both developed for a transient or subway environment based on the relative strain index derived by Lee and Henshel and comfort tests conducted by ASHRAE. The RWI was developed to be applied in warm environments, whereas the HDR was developed for cooler environment.

Air quality: The quality of air within a subway system can have an impact on the comfort and health of the traveling patron. The degradation of the air quality can be annoying (such as odor and haze), health related with an impact on the respiratory system, or disastrous as with methane. Most of these contaminants can be contained and the potential hazard mitigated by judicious use of ventilation.

Air velocity: The movement of the train in the tunnel generates a piston effect within the tunnels and stations. Under many circumstances this air flow is useful to maintain a reasonable environment within the tunnels. However, there are circumstances when this air velocity can be objectionable, particularly to patron on the station platform at the tunnel/station junction. The maximum air velocity for a station platform should not be greater than 1000fpm (5m/s). This is intermittent flow.

The other location where air velocity can be a problem is on sidewalk gratings when the vertical velocity should not exceed 500fpm (2.5m/s). However, gratings located in nonpedestrian areas could have velocity up to 1000fpm (5m/s).

Pressure changes: The train movement that creates air flow in the subway also creates transient pressure changes within the subway. These pressure changes have varying physiological effects on subway occupants.

These pressure changes are usually only felt in the patron areas. Some of the reactions of the ear to various levels of pressure changes are reported. Criteria must be set for this phenomenon.

Emergency criteria: An emergency in a subway system, in general, is defined as any unusual situation or occurrence that halts train movement and makes it mandatory that passengers leave the train and enter the tunnel environment, or that requires the evacuation of a subway station.

The only emergency criteria that have an impact on ventilation are those related to air temperature, air velocity and air quality.

Air temperature: Exposure by subway patrons and employees to extraordinarily high temperatures during an emergency can be harmful to the individual. NFPA states in its standard 130 for fixed guideway system that the "ventilation system" shall be so designed that in an emergency situation the air temperature in existing pathways shall be controlled to a design goal of no more than 140 °F (60 °C). This temperature criterion should be at shoulder or head level of the patron, not at ceiling level.

Air velocity: Significant air flow rates may be required to control or evacuate smoke in tunnels and stations during a fire emergency situation. In some circumstances, the evacuating patron may be exposed to this high velocity. This air flow in the faces of evacuating patron is helpful to patrons, giving them a sense of direction (minimum air velocity of 500fpm) and providing more respirable air. A maximum air velocity of 2500fpm in an emergency situation is acceptable.

The magnitude of the air velocity in the tunnel will depend on the size of the fire and thence on the velocity required to control the backlayering of smoke. If the backlayering is controlled, there is a clear evacuation path for patrons.

Air quality: The quality of air within a subway tunnel and/or station during a fire emergency deteriorates rapidly. The combustion can produce gases and aerosols, some of which may be toxic and all of which are, at the least, imitating to the patron.

While oxygen criteria are established by the American Congress of Governmental Institute Hygienists for the most of the gases in the smoke, the type and volume of these substances will depend on the material being consumed by the fire. The best solution is to provide the maximum flow rate required to control the smoke and directing fresh air into the faces of the evacuating patrons.

Analysis: After defining the criteria for a subway system, an analysis of where the heat is in the system and how the air flow created by piston effect of trains and/or fans serve to dissipate this heat is required. A series of sophisticated design tools that permit this form of evaluation have been developed as part of the subway environment research program.

If the heat generated by the equipment and the people in a subway is greater than the capacity of the ground or of ventilation to dissipate it, the temperature within the system will rise. All forms of electrical energy input to the subway eventually are dissipated as heat. The trains account for approximately 85%-90% of all the heat generated within the system. Heat generated within the line sections by trains from their traction, braking, and air conditioning systems will be at substantially higher rate in subway systems now under construction, or being planned for the future, than that speed and acceleration requirements for vehicles, which necessitate significantly higher power input and resultant power losses. Of these inputs, the major portion is derived from breaking and accelerating. There have been and continue to be many efforts to seek ways of reducing this heat source, such as by the use of speed restrictors, wayside dynamic braking resistors, regenerative braking, motor controllers, signaling, vehicle weight, rock profiles, fly wheels, etc.

Approximately 50%-60% of the total heat input attributable to train operation can be assigned to braking or approximately 45%-50% of the total heat input of the subway system. Since braking occurs in the vicinity of the station platform, it is the basic cause of much of the environmental problem.

The heat released into the tunnel or station is partly transmitted into the surrounding soil and partly carried forward by piston action, or mechanical ventilation (if such is used), and eventually exhausted to the atmosphere through the shafts and access openings in the stations. The soil acts as a heat sink when the air in the trainway is at a higher temperature than the soil's temperature, and as a heat source when the reverse takes place.

The heat sink, where it is effective, is a "natural" cooling mechanism, as is the piston effect of moving trains. Cooling is accomplished by the exchange of hot inside air with cooler outside air.

A reliable estimate of the piston effect ventilation, along with the heat sink, and the impact of both on the thermal conditions within the subway, is required prior to determining what measures must be taken to meet established environmental criteria. One of the analytical tools developed as a part of the SERP is a public domain computer model called the subway environment simulation.

Environmental control: Control relates to the methods used to maintain the desired environment within the subway facility. Many types of control systems can be employed in this regard.

Control of the temperature rise in the subway system involves balancing the heat from the system against losses of heat to the surrounding heat sink and to the air flowing losses in the system. When the heat gain from the system is greater than the losses to the sink and to the air, the temperature in the system will rise. Such a rise in temperature will increase the rate of heat flow to the sink. Additional air flow may be required to control the temperature rise. This increase in air flow would reduce the temperature rise, but it would also reduce the cooling effect of the heat sink. Thus, under extreme conditions of maximum heat gain and maximum outside air temperature, an imbalance of heat again and heat losses may result in an overall temperature rise in the system. Under conditions of reduced heat gain and reduced outside air temperature, normal air flow rates resulting from train piston effects may provide the designed control over temperature rises. Frequently, the air flow rate required to provide this control will also be sufficient to replenish the system air with outside air at a desirable rate. If the rise in temperature is not desirable, a system of mechanical ventilation or cooling by refrigeration must be considered.

Knowledge of the available environmental control equipment and its application is required to affect a complete solution for the subway system. The environmental engineer must consider the variety of system concepts appropriate to subway environmental control and the applicability of these systems in the optimization of subway construction and operation. These systems include, in addition to station platform air conditioning, supply and exhaust ventilation systems, trainway or under-platform exhaust systems to remove heat, tunnel line section ventilation systems, and various other possibilities and combinations.

The major contributor to the heat problem in the subway system is the transit vehicle and its propulsion system. Much greater attention must be addressed to this equipment, since optimization of the cost of the vehicle alone may not optimize the cost of building, owning, and operating the entire rapid transit facility. Consideration should be given in the future to propulsion system that provide for rejection of the waste heat out of the enclosed portions of the system and possible reuse of this energy.

Text C Longquanshan Tunnel Ventilation Scheme
龙泉山隧道通风方案

Longquanshan Tunnel(龙泉山隧道) located in the section between Chengdu East to Jianyang South is under the tender section GYSG-1 of the new special railway line for passenger transportation between Chengdu and Chongqing and the tunnel entrance is located in Longquanyi district, Chengdu while the exit in Jianyang city. The total length of Longquanshan Tunnel is 7328m and is a two track single bore railway tunnel with entrance at chainage of DK22 +485, exit at chainage of DK29 +813. The completeentire tunnel is on straight line. One parallel adit and three inclined shafts are arranged and four construction sections are divided: entrance construction section, $1^{\#}$ and $2^{\#}$ inclined shafts construction section, $3^{\#}$ inclined shaft construction section and exit construction section.

1. Selection of ventilation mode

(1) In the entrance section, advanced parallel adit heading method is applied where rail transportation mode is used. In early stage, only pressed ventilation in heading face is suitable and in middle and later stages, jet flow gallery ventilation mode can be used by use of the parallel adit.

(2) In works section of $1^{\#}$ and $2^{\#}$ inclined well, both advanced parallel adit heading and main and auxiliary inclined shafts heading are going on concurrently and rail transportation is applied. In early stage only pressed ventilation in heading face is suitable and in middle and later stages parallel adit and inclined shafts can be used and jet flow gallery ventilation mode can be used.

(3) In $3^{\#}$ inclined shaft construction section, excavations of single inclined shaft and single main tunnel are underway where trackless transportation mode is applied. Only pressed ventilation in heading face is suitable and with extension of tunnel length excavated, volume of air supply is increased.

(4) In exit construction section single main tunnel excavation is underway where trackless transportation mode is applied. Only pressed ventilation in heading face is suitable and with extension of tunnel length excavated, volume of air supply is increased.

Calculation results showed that when rail transportation is applied in the main tunnel, the control wind amount needed at excavation face is $2040m^3/min$ (counted by maximum calculated value of wind speed). Where no trackless transportation is applied in the main tunnel, the control wind amount needed at the excavation face is $4036m^3/min$ (counted by maximum calculated value of total power of internal combustion machines), and the control wind amount needed at parallel adit heading face is $880m^3/min$ (counted by maximum calculated amount of gas emission and rail transportation is applied all in parallel adits).

Taking entrance construction section forexample, the ventilation arrangement in the entrance construction section is divided into six stages.

Stage one is preliminary stage of construction and there are only two excavation faces in main tunnel and parallel adit for both of which pressed ventilation in heading face is applied. One ventilator of type SDF(C)-№13 and PVC air pipe with diameter φ1.6m for air supply are used in main tunnel and one ventilator of type SDF(C)-№11.5 and air pipe with diameter φ1.2mPVC for air supply are used in pilot tunnel. The entrances of main tunnel and pilot tunnel are excavated till reaching 1# cross passageway and the longest distances for air supply are less than 500m for both tunnels and the fans can operate with low capacity.

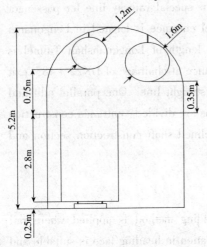

Figure 10.1 Profile of Air Pipe Layout of Parallel Adit

In second stage, the parallel adit heading reached 1# cross passageway and one additional excavation face is created for 1# cross passageway to enter into the main tunnel. All the three excavation faces still use pressed ventilation in heading face technology and the two excavation faces of the main tunnel adopt one ventilator of type SDF(C)-№13 and air pipe with diameter φ1.6mPVC for air supply respectively and the parallel adit still uses one ventilator of type SDF(C)-№11.5 and air pipe with diameter φ1.2mPVC for air supply. Two air pipes need to be suspended in the parallel adit (The air pipe layout is shown in figure 10.1). The main tunnel is excavated in two faces to form the section from the tunnel entrance to the entrance of 1# crossway and the section from 1# cross passageway to 2# cross passageway (the longest distance for air supply for above sections is all less than 500m). The section between the cross passages of nos. 1# and 2# cross passageway in parallel adit is excavated concurrently and (the longest distance for air supply is less than 1000m) is extended to gas emission section. The ventilator runs with full capacity.

In stage three the cross passageways 1# and 2# between the main tunnel and the parallel adit are interconnected and thus ventilation circuit is formed and two excavation faces appear again where jet flow gallery ventilation mode is started. The 1# cross passageway is blocked with air stopping from the side facing main tunnel and the ventilator of type SDF(C)-№13 is provided in 1# cross passageway to supply air to the heading face of main tunnel. Air pipe with diameter φ1.6m PVC penetrates the air stopping to supply air to the main tunnel and the ventilator of type SDF(C)-№11.5 to supply air via φ1.2m PVC air pipe to parallel adit is arranged in 2# cross passageway on the end close to the portal. One jet flow fan of type SSF-№16 is arranged in the pilot tunnel at the position near 1# cross passageway. The general direction of air flow is fresh air in from the parallel adit and polluted air out through main tunnel. The polluted air from the excavation face of the pilot tunnel flows into the main tunnel via 2# cross passageway and is discharged out of the main tunnel together with the polluted air generated from the excavation face of the main tunnel. Over the section between the cross passageways of 2# and 3# in both main tunnel and pilot tunnel, the longest distance for air supply is less than 1000m.

In stage four, the parallel adit excavation proceeds into 3# cross passageway and one excavation face is added for access from $3^{\#}$ cross passageway to the main tunnel and three excavation faces are formed again where simultaneous ventilations are needed. While maintaining the ventilation layout in stage three, one ventilator of type SDF (C)-№13 is added beside the ventilator of type SDF (C)-№11.5 in the parallel adit to supply air via air pipe with diameter ϕ1.6m PVC to the heading face of the main tunnel in $3^{\#}$ cross passageway. Two air pipes need to be suspended in the parallel adit. The main tunnel is excavated in two faces, forming the section between cross passage nos. $2^{\#}$-$3^{\#}$ and nos. $3^{\#}$-$4^{\#}$.

The pilot tunnel is also excavated to form the section between cross passages nos. $3^{\#}$-$4^{\#}$ and the distance for air supply in both tunnels is shorter than 1000m.

2. Requirement of ventilation requirement on construction

(1) It is suggested that professional team manage and execute ventilation works on site. Air pipe must be installed in level and straight manner. Rigid elbow is set at bend of air pipeline and the bending degree should be gentle and flat and bending in sharp angle should be avoided to reduce resistance against pipe along line and local resistance. Daily routine maintenance and care shall be enhanced.

(2) Professional technician should be assigned to check the ventilation effect on site and shall optimize the ventilation scheme in time according to the check results.

(3) If necessary, local adjustment to the ventilation system can be performed according to the check results. It must be ensured that the temperature in tunnel be not higher than 28℃, concentration of CO and No_2 are reduced below 30mg/m^3 and 5mg/m^3 respectively after ventilation lasting for 30min to meet needs for works execution.

(4) All the ventilators must be operated by the professional fan operator and running record shall be duly kept. Before sign-on the operators shall go through professional training and only the qualified through training can take up the job.

(5) Electricians must check and repair ventilators regularly, find and shoot troubles in time and ensure normal running of the ventilators.

(6) The cross passage not in service shall be closed in time and for the cross passage mounted with air door the air door management should be intensified to reduce the impact of polluted air cycle on ventilation efficiency.

In stage five, the main tunnel is interconnected with the section between cross passages nos. $2^{\#}$-$3^{\#}$ and two excavation faces are formed again. The $2^{\#}$ cross passage is closed with air stopping. Shift the fan in $1^{\#}$ cross passage to $2^{\#}$ cross passage to supply air to main tunnel. Shift the fan of type SDF (C)-№11.5 in pilot tunnel to $3^{\#}$ cross passage to be mounted on end close to portal to supply air to the pilot tunnel. Remove the fan in pilot tunnel added in stage four and add one jet flow fan of type SSF-№16 close to $2^{\#}$ cross passage in the pilot tunnel. When $4^{\#}$ cross passage is connected, decision whether axial fan is shifted forward can be made subject to the ventilation efficiency and if shifting forward is confirmed, $3^{\#}$ cross passage must be sealed without need of adding jet flow fan. Main tunnel is excavated in the section between cross passages nos. $3^{\#}$-$4^{\#}$ and the lateral pilot is excavated in the section between cross passages nos. $4^{\#}$-$5^{\#}$. The distances for air supply in both tunnels are shorter than 1000m.

In stage six, the main tunnel is interconnected with the section between cross passages nos. $3^\#$-$5^\#$ and the pilot tunnel excavation works has been completed. Thus there is only one excavation face of main tunnel. Seal the $3^\#$ cross passage with air stopping. Shift the fan in $2^\#$ cross passage to $3^\#$ cross passage to supply air to the main tunnel. Remove the axial fan and air pipe in the pilot tunnel and keep the jet flow fan in original position. The main tunnel is excavated in the section between cross passages nos. $4^\#$-$5^\#$, where the distance for air supply is shorter than 1000m.

II. Terms and terminology

exhaust port	排气口,排气孔
air right	空间所有权;上空使用权
ventilation	通风设备;通风
piston effect	活塞效应
natural ventilation	自然通风
portal	隧道口;隧道洞口;隧道入口;洞门
meteorological condition	气象条件
unidirectional traffic	单向交通
bidirectional traffic	双向交通
stack effect/chimney effect	烟囱效应
contaminated air	污染空气
longitudinal ventilation	纵向式通风
jet fan	射流风机
full transverse ventilation	全横向式通风
oxides of nitrogen	氮氧化物
exhaust gas	尾气
threshold limit value	阈限值;(有害物)容许最高浓度

III. Questions and difficult sentence analysis

1. Questions for brainstorming discussion

(1) Why is ventilation required in long highway tunnels?
(2) What are the principal tunnel ventilation modes?
(3) Discuss the energy saving measures or energy saving ideas which may be applied in common tunnel longitudinal ventilation in group.

2. Difficult sentences analysis

(1) Ventilation is required to limit the concentration of obnoxious or dangerous contaminants to acceptable levels during normal operation and to remove and control smoke and hot gases during

fire emergencies. The ventilation system selected must meet the specified criteria for both normal and emergency operations and should be the most economical solution considering both construction and operating costs.

译文:在正常营运阶段,要求通风系统将隧道内的有害或危险污染物浓度降至合格水平,并在发生火灾时,排除和控制烟雾和热气。所选的通风系统必须满足正常和应急作业时的规定标准并在施工和营运成本方面是最经济的方案。

(2) Because of the numerous uncertainties outlined above, historically it is rare that tunnels of greater than 1000ft in length have been ventilated by natural means. There are exceptions to this, such as the Via Mala Tunnel in Switzerland and the Tenda Pass Tunnel between France and Italy.

译文:由于存在上述诸多不确定性,在历史上,很少有长度超过 1000 英尺的隧道采用自然通风。但也存在例外,比如瑞士的维亚玛拉隧道和连接法国和意大利的腾达山口隧道。

(3) An alternative longitudinal system uses two shafts located near the center of the tunnel, one for exhausting and one for supplying. This configuration will provide a reduction of contaminant concentration in the second half, because a portion of the tunnel air flow is exchanged with ambient air at the shaft.

译文:一个供选择的纵向通风系统是在隧道中心建两个竖井,一个用于排气,另一个供气。由于一部分隧道内气流与该竖井的大气相交换,降低了另一半气流中的污染物浓度。

(4) Uniform distribution or collection of air throughout the length of a tunnel is the chief characteristic of a semi-transverse system. A supply air semi-transverse system produces a uniform concentration of contaminants throughout the tunnel because the air and the vehicle exhaust gases enter the roadway area at the same relative rate.

译文:在隧道全长度范围内,气流的均匀分布或聚集是半横向通风系统的特征。供气半横向系统使整个隧道内的污染物浓度分布均匀,因为新鲜空气和车辆尾气以相同的相对速度进入车道区内。

Ⅳ. Translation case study

Case 1

Chinese	English translation
通风机是把机械能转变为空气压能的一种装置,它是实现隧道机械通风的关键设备。目前,国产通风机有两种类型,即离心式通风机和轴流式通风机。通风机的选择包括选择通风机的类型、通风机的型号、通风机的联合运转方式以及通风机的机号、转速和叶片安装角等。合理的通风机是在满足通风要求(足够的风量)时,工作效率比较高的通风机。通风机选择的依据是隧道的通风阻力和要求的通风量以及其他的一些隧道条件。	Ventilator is a kind of device which transforms mechanical energy into air compression energy and is the critical equipment in achieving tunnel mechanical ventilation. At present, there are two types of domestic ventilator products, namely the centrifugal ventilator and axial flow ventilator. The ventilator selection contents include the selections of ventilator types, specification model, ventilator's union running mode, ventilator's machine number, rotating speed and blade mounting angle etc. A rationally selected ventilator is of higher working efficiency while meeting ventilation requirement (adequate air amount needed in the tunnel) simultaneously. Ventilator selection is based on tunnel ventilating resistance, air volume and other tunnel conditions.

Case 2

Chinese	English translation
确定隧道通风所需风量的计算应遵循以下原则： （1）通风设计中,车辆有害气体的排放量以及与之对应的交通量,都应有明确的远景设计年限,两者应相匹配。计算近期的需风量及交通通风力时应采用相应年份的交通量。 （2）确定需风量时,应对计算行车速度以下各工况车速按 20km/h 为一档分别进行计算,并考虑交通阻滞状态,取其较大者作为设计需风量。 （3）在双向交通隧道中,上坡较长方向的交通量按设计交通量的 60% 进行计算。 （4）应根据隧道建设标准、通风方式等计算隧道在各种工况下的需风量,并取其最大者作为该隧道的设计风量。	The determination of wind amount needed in tunnels shall be made subject to following principles： (1) In ventilation design, there should be a definite perspective design age for the emission of hazardous gas from vehicle and its corresponding traffic volume, both of which should match. In designing the required air flow quantity and piston effect in recent term, the traffic volume of corresponding years should be used. (2) In determination of wind amount needed, vehicular speed under all cases below traffic speed should be calculated by taking 20km/h as one level with consideration of traffic jam situations. The larger is taken as wind amount required. (3) In bidirectional transit tunnel, the traffic volume in longer direction on upward slope shall be calculated by 60% of design traffic amount. (4) The air amount needed in tunnel under all cases shall be calculated in accordance with tunnel construction standard, modes of ventilations and larger value is taken as the design air amount of this tunnel.

Case 3

Chinese	English translation
造成地铁加热问题的主要因素是通过的车辆及其推进装置。由于单独降低车辆的成本不能减少修建、拥有并且营运整个高速交通设施的成本,因此必须对该设备增加关注度。未来应该考虑推进系统,因为该系统能将废热排出该系统的封闭部分并可能再利用该热能。	The major contributor to the heat problem in the subway system is the transit vehicle and its propulsion system. Much greater attention must be addressed to this equipment, since optimization of the cost of the vehicle alone may not optimize the cost of building, owning, and operating the entire rapid transit facility. Consideration should be given in the future to propulsion system that provide for rejection of the waste heat out of the enclosed portions of the system and possible reuse of this energy.

V. Assignment

（1）通风设计中,车辆有害气体的排放量以及与之对应的交通量,都应有明确的远景设计年限,两者应相匹配。计算近期的需风量及交通通风力时应采用相应年份的交通量。

（2）应根据隧道建设标准、通风方式等计算隧道在各种工况下的需风量,并取其最大者作为该隧道的设计风量。

（3）横向通风方式和纵向通风相比较,供风较为均匀、污染空气在隧道内滞留时间短、隧道内可见度高、有利于火灾管理。但横向通风需要在隧道内设车道板和吊顶,还要设风井,从而使隧道建筑工程量大,费用增高；另外,由于受隧道施工断面限制,设在车道板下和吊顶上的送风道和排风道断面小,隧道通风阻力大,通风能耗大,运营管理费用高。

(4)合理的通风方式是安全可靠性高、建设安装方便、投资小、隧道内环境好、对灾害的适应能力强、运营管理方便、运营费用低的通风方式。但是,各种通风方式都既有优点又有缺点,一种通风方式不可能完全满足这些要求。

(5)射流风机是一种特殊设计的轴流风机,风机出口的气流平均速度30m/s左右。由于其具有较大的出口动量,因此被广泛应用于各种中短距离的隧道通风,以降低隧道内废气浓度,提高可见度,维护人员的健康和车辆通行安全。

Unit 11　Tunnel Lighting
隧　道　照　明

Ⅰ. Text

Text A　Lighting of Highway Tunnels
公路隧道照明

The maintenance of traffic volume at design roadway speeds through a tunnel on a bright sunlit day depends on the ability of the motorist to see the interior of the tunnel and objects on the roadway for a safe stopping distance. The geographic location, orientation, and portal surroundings influence the ability of the human eye to adapt from the bright ambient roadway to the "black hole" of the tunnel interior. The lighting of the tunnel interior to eliminate and or diminish the effect of the black hole is achieved through varied lighting concepts. <u>The most prominent lighting concepts employed are the symmetrical and the asymmetrical, of which there are two types: the counter beam and line of sight. Linear or point source luminaires or combinations of types of sources are employed to provide for specific illumination requirements for unidirectional or bidirectional traffic tunnels as appropriate to the system.</u>

1. Definition of terms

Adaptation: The process by which the sensitivity of the retina of the eye adjusts to increases or decreases light from a level it was adjusted to. The resulting sensitivity of the retina is termed the state of adaptation. The luminaires causing this state of adaptation is termed the state of adaptation level.

Adaptation Point: The point on the road where the adaptation of the eye of a motorist approaching a tunnel begins to be influenced by the presence of the dark tunnel entrance.

Brightness: The luminous flux per unit of project area and unit solid angle, either leaving a surface at a given point in a given direction or arriving at a given point from a given direction; the luminous intensity of a surface in a given direction per unit of projected area of the surface as viewed from that direction.

Candela: The international System of Unit (SI) unit of luminous intensity. One candela (cd) is one lumen per square meter.

Candela per Square Meter: The SI unit of photometric brightness. A perfectly diffused surface emitting or reflecting light at the rate of one lumen per square meter.

Count Beam: A technique whereby a directional light control is used opposite to the direction of traffic to provide negative contrast (object luminance is less than background luminance).

Flicker: The result of periodic luminance changes in the field of vision, due to the spacing of the lighting fixtures.

Foot-Candle: The incident illumination a surface $1ft^2$ in area on which is distributed a uniform light output of 1 lumen; $1 lumen/ft^2$.

Lux: The incident illumination a surface $1m^2$ in area on which is distributed a uniform light output of 1 lumen; $1 lumen/m^2$.

Foot Lambert: The unit of photometric brightness (luminance). A perfectly diffused surface emitting or reflecting light at the rate of $1 lumen/ft^2$ would have an equivalent brightness of 1 foot Lambert (fL).

Glare: The sensation produced by brightness within the visual field that is sufficiently more intense than the luminance to which the eyes are adapted to cause discomfort or loss in visual performance and visibility.

Lamp Lumen Depreciation Factor: One of the many factors used in the evaluation of a maintenance factor causing a reduction of lumen output of a lamp during its life cycle.

Louver: A series of baffles used to shield a source from view at certain angles or to absorb unwanted light.

Lumen: The unit of measure of the quantity of light. The amount of light that falls on an area of $1ft^2$, every point of which is 1ft from a source of 1 candela (candle).

Luminaire: A complete lighting device consisting of a light source of together with its direct appurtenances.

Luminaire ambient temperature: The lumen output of fluorescent lamps is affected by operate; the luminaire ambient temperature must be considered when obtaining the maintenance factor.

Luminaire Dirt Depreciation Factor: Another maintenance factor, causing loss of light on the work plane due to the accumulation of dirt on the luminaire.

Luminaire Surface Depreciation: This depreciation of initial luminaire lumen output results from the adverse changes in mental, paint, and plastic components, glass, porcelain, and processed aluminum depreciation negligibly and are easily restored to their original reflectance. Baked enamels and other painted surfaces have a permanent depreciation because all paints are porous to some degree. For plastics, acrylic is least susceptible to change, but in certain atmospheres, transmittance may reduced by usage over a period of 15 to 20 years. For the usage, polystyrene will have lower transmittance than acrylic and will exhibit a faster depreciation. Because of the complex relationship between the light-controlling elements of luminaires using more than one type of material (such as a lensed troffer), it is difficult to predict losses due to deterioration of materials. In addition, some materials are more or less adversely affected depending on the atmosphere in which they are installed.

Luminaire Voltage: High or low voltage at the luminaire will affected the output of most lamps. For incandescent units, deviations from rated lamp voltage cause approximately 3% change in lumen output for each 1% change in primary voltage deviation from rated ballast voltage. When regulated output ballasts are used, the lamps lumen output is relatively independent of the primary voltage with the design range. Fluorescent luminaire output changes approximately 1% for each 1/2%-2% change in primary voltage.

Maintenance Factor: The ratio of the in-service lumens of a lighting system to the initial lumens, which can be determined with reasonable accuracy by the evaluation of various light loss factors that eventually contribute, in varying amounts, to the in-service illumination levels. Some of these light loss factors are luminaire ambient temperature, voltage to luminaire, ballast factor, luminaire refractor depreciation, room surface dirt depreciation, burnouts, lamp lumens depreciation, and luminaire dirt depreciation.

Mate Surface: A surface from which the reflection is predominantly diffused.

Negative Contrast: A dark vertical face of an object toward the viewer relative to a light background.

Optical Guidance: The means by which visible aids indicate the cause of road direction. In tunnel applications, this aid is derived from the light sources as well as curd delineation and lame markers lines.

Positive Contrast: A light vertical face of an object toward the viewer relative to a light background.

Reflectance: The ratio of the flux reflected by a surface or medium to the incident flux. This general definition may be further modified by the use of one or more of these terms: specular, spectral, and diffuse.

Room Surface Dirt Depreciation: The accumulation of dirt on room surface reduces the amount of lumens reflected and interrelated to the work plane; it is one of factors to be considered in the evaluation of the design maintenance factor.

Utilization Factor: Also known as the coefficient of utilization. The ratio of the lumens that reach the work plane to the total lumen output of the bare lamps. It accounts for luminaire photometric characteristics, mounting heights, room dimensions, and surface reflectance.

2. Tunnel ligthing nomenclature

Access Zone: That portion of the open approach of the high way immediately preceding the tunnel façade or portal. It is also referred to as the approach zone. It is a function of the safe stopping distance for the design speed.

Threshold Zone: The fist section at the entrance end of a tunnel, where the first decrease in daylighting takes place. This decrease can be accomplished by a reduction in daylighting with the use of screening or by the use of artificial lighting, or by a combination of these.

Transition Zone: The section at the entrance end that immediately follows the threshold zone and contains diminishing light levels until the interior zone levels are reached. It is sufficiently long to provide for adequate eye adaptation time form open load brightness to interior tunnel brightness.

Interior Zone (sometimes known as the normal day zone): The length of tunnel between a point just beyond the entrance transition zone, where eye adaptation is no longer a consideration for visual perception, and the exit portal.

Exit Zone: That portion at the end of the tunnel that during daytime appears brilliant when a motorist has driven for several minutes in the tunnel interior.

3. Tunnel classification

1) Underpasses

Form the point of view of adequate supplementary lighting, there is no definite line of demarcation between an underpass and a short tunnel. The American Association of State Highway and Transportation Officials (AASHTO) defines an underpass as a point of roadway extending through and beneath some natural or manmade structure, which because of its limited length-to-height ratio requires no supple-mentary daytime lighting. Length to height ratios of approximately 10∶1 or lower will not, under normal conditions, require daytime underpass lighting. Other authorities, such as the Illumination Engineering Society (CIE), generally recognize all covered highways as tunnels and do not recognize an underpass as a separate and distinct structure. There authorities indicate that that for lighting purposes every artificial or natural covering of a road, irrespective of the length and nature of the covering, is considered to be a tunnel.

2) Short Tunnels

IES and ICE define a short tunnel as one where, in the absence of traffic, the exit and the area behind the exit can be clearly visible form a point ahead of the entrance portal. For lighting purposes, the length of a short tunnel is usually limited to approximately 150ft. Some tunnels up to 400ft long may be classified as short if they are straight, level, and have a high width and/or height to length ratio.

3) Long Tunnel

For lighting purposes, IES defines a long tunnel as one with an overall length greater than the safe stopping sight distance. ICE terminology defines every cover a road as included in the concept "tunnel" irrespective of the length and nature of the covering.

4. Entrance lighting

The most critical section of tunnel lighting is the entrance section, which comprises the threshold and transition zones. Recommended illumination and luminance levels at the threshold and transition zones vary somewhat in different countries. To produce luminance levels solely by artificial means using fluorescent lamps requires many luminaires on the walls and ceiling. Use of low-pressure sodium and high-intensity point sources permits reduction in the number of units. *Attention to luminaire type selection, location, and spacing for reduction of glare and flicker is a primary design requisite in the entrance zone and throughout the tunnel.*

To reduce the number of luminaire, some tunnel lighting designers have incorporated a grid at the tunnel entrance to screen out natural daylight in the proper amounts to assist in the eye adaptation process. The subject of sun screens will be treated later in this chapter, but as presently designed, they have not proven to be the ultimate answer to the first step in reduction of natural daylight.

Other factors to be considered in the evaluation of the lighting levels, as well as transition time calculated from the 20° field to the portal, are tunnel orientation, latitude, geographical location, approach grades, terrain, and conditions where the tunnel lighting problem can be readily solved using conventional equipment-for example, is a tunnel located in higher latitudes where the sun or high sky brightness never come into the field of view; The orientation is east-west; the location is through a mountain; and the approach is on an upgrade, which allows the tunnel ceiling (as well as the walls) to act as an appropriate backdrop. An example of unfavorable conditions is a location of a subaqueous tunnel in the lower latitudes having a southeast or southwest orientation, where the sun or its reflection over open water would be directly in the field of view during morning or afternoon rush hours, on a downgrade approach to the entrance portal, where the roadway surface (an eventually soiled and usually poorly reflecting surface) becomes the principal backdrop for silhouette discernment of objects or stalled cars. A good example is the Hampton Roads Tunnel and Bridge Crossing between Hampton and Norfolk, Virginia, where additional rows of luminaire on the tunnel walls provide increased illumination levels.

5. Luminance level in the tunnel interior

Recommendations for tunnel interior lighting levels, as well as methods of measurement, presently vary among authoritative sources. The CIE recommends average luminaire of the road surface to vary with safe sight stopping distance (SSSD) and traffic flow between 1 and 15 cd/m^2 in heavy traffic conditions. The American National Standard Institute practices for tunnel lighting, ANSI/IES RP-22 (1987), suggest at least $5cd/m^2$ maintained luminance on the roadway. AASHTO also recommends an average maintained luminance on roadway $5cd/m^2$. These values are based on a wall reflectance factor of at least 50%. When the reflectance factor is less than 50%, lighting should be increased to compensate. This suggests that the wall luminance is the parameter that should be kept constant. These values are minimum maintained values measured on the road surface. The walls should have at least the same level of luminance up to 2m (6.2ft) above the roadway.

<u>While there is disparity in these recommendations, there are conditions under which the extremes can be shown to be adequate for complete adaptation, such as in long tunnels the interior lighting can approach the criteria for nighttime street lighting.</u> On the other hand, if only partial adaptation can be effected, then the higher values appear to be the better choice during daytime hours. In many cases, economic factors, as well as the availability of the proper lighting equipment, will play an important role in the final interior lighting level.

6. Exit lighting

During the daytime, the exit of the tunnel appears as a bright hole to the motorist. Usually, all obstacles will be discernible by silhouette against the bright exit and thus will be clearly visible. This visibility by silhouette can be further improved by lining the walls with tile or panels having a high reflectance and thus permitting a greater daylight penetration into the tunnel.

When the exit is not entirely clear but partially screened by a large object such as a truck, then a different visibility requirement is present. In this instance, if a smaller object is following the large object, the smaller object may not be readily visible. Whereas the large object screening the exit would be clearly visible, the following small object would have equipment brightness to the large one and, therefore, would not be readily discerned by silhouette.

Under certain conditions and during certain periods of the day, sunlight may penetrate directly into the tunnel exit, creating an extremely difficult visual condition. Coupled with the use of glazed walls and glossy paints, the resulting specular reflection may create considerable interreflections, thus preventing the motorist from identifying the tunnel outlines clearly, as well as creating a situation where discomfort and disability glare would be experienced. Under these conditions, discernment of object by silhouette may be difficult, and a hazardous traffic situation may result. Even sun screens will not offer much help, and so the situation should be avoided. Reorientation of the tunnel exit or the use of materials with diffuse ancestress (matte or flat) should prove helpful.

7. Lighting of short tunnels

In most cases, a lighting system is not required inside short tunnels for adequate driver visibility. Daylight penetration from each end, plus the silhouette effect of the opposite end brightness, generally will assure satisfactory visibility. On the other hand, tunnels between 75 and 150ft in length may require supplementary daytime lighting if the daylight is restricted due to roadway depression, tunnel curvature, or the proximity of tall building in urban areas. Short tunnels appear to the approaching driver as a black frame, as opposed to the black hole usually experienced in long tunnels. After entering the tunnel, the central part of the field of view is taken up by the brightness of the exit, so that the brightness of the walls and ceiling has insignificant adaptation stimulus.

Obstructions in the short tunnel can be seen if they are high enough to silhouette against the bright environment of the exit. If the vertically projected dimension of the dark frame across the roadway is less than the height of the smallest object than must be seen, then the object will be silhouetted against the exit brightness and will be visible.

Due to daylight penetration from both portals, a short tunnel on a straight and level roadway can be as much as 75ft(23m) long and not require daytime lighting for an obstacle having a height of 6in(152mm) silhouetting can be enhance by lining the structure wall with a light-colored colored material to reduce the darkness within the tunnel.

Where local conditions warrant the installation of an artificial lighting system for daytime operation, the level of luminance within the entire length of the tunnel should be at least 0.1 of the expected maximum open approach luminance. This requirement may mean that a luminance level of 300-350flL is needed for satisfactory visibility. Where it is not practical to achieve these levels, visibility can be improved by providing an opening in the ceiling about midway though the structure to permit daylight penetration. In effect, the opening creates two structures and may satisfy the requirement for lighting during the day. Walls and ceilings lined with a light-colored, matte-finished material will enhance visibility. A design with a funneled-up ceiling at the portals will permit additional daylight penetration.

8. Lighting of long tunnel

The Lighting system should be flexible enough to permit its operation at night at a reduced level. The long tunnel requires two daytime lighting levels, one for the intensive zone (the entrance zone comprising the threshold and transitions) and another for the normal day zone (interior zone).

1) The Entrance Zone

The entrance zone is the most critical area, because without sufficient portal brightness, the entrance will appear to the approaching driver as a black hole. The most sever visual task is not when the driver is passing through the plane of the portal shadow. The point in front of the Portal at which must be discerned objects within the tunnel is dictated by the safe stopping sight distance at the posted speed. At 60mph (87kph), this would be 650ft (198m) in front of the portal and, in most cases, will be at a point ahead of the adaptation point. This means that the motorist eye is at that time adapted to the ambient luminance level of the open road. According to the recommendations of IES, CIE, and Schreuder, the portal luminance level should be 1/10, and preferably 1/8, of the maximum expected open approach luminance. This portal luminance should be displayed on the walls, ceiling, and roadway so that these surfaces can serve as effective background for discernment of objects by contrast and silhouette. The effects of the so-called black hole would then be drastically reduced or even eliminated, the first reduction in luminance should occur in the threshold zone depends on the driving speed and the position of the adaption point, which, in turn, depends on the geometry and dimensions of the access zone.

The symmetrical lighting system utilizes illuminates having photometric characteristics that direct light transverse to the longitudinal axis of the tunnel roadway of sufficient magnitude to enable objects to be observed by positive or negative contrast.

The asymmetrical lighting system utilizes illuminates mounted above the road with photometric distribution to direct light toward the driver for the counter beam system and away from the driver for the counter beam system and away from the driver for the pro-beam system. The counter beam system produces a negative contrast between an object and the motorist, which enhances visibility. A common concern of the counter beam system is that there is an increase in glare. Designs currently employ beam angles of 40 from the vertical to minimize the glare. The pro-beam system produces a positive contrast to enhance object visibility; however, there are concerns that reflected glare from vehicle windows ahead will produce diminished visibility. Experiments at Genevieve Tunnel in Belgium were carried out to compare these three systems. Selection by the designer of a tunnel lighting system will require evaluation of proposed ceiling and wall finishes, roadway deflection, roadway treatment, and proposed maintenance and cleaning measures.

2) Stopping Sight Distance

The distance at which a critical object can be seen in the threshold must correlate with the driving speed and the safe stopping sight distance on a wet road, the corresponding vehicle speed would be about 42mph. In a similar manner, the safe stopping sight distance should be used as the distance to the critical object for other speeds in determining the length of the threshold zone.

3) Adaptation Point

The vertical angle shown is a value taken as an average for the shielding angle of vehicle windshields. The two profiles demonstrate that, as the portal height increases, the raising of the facade, consequently, is a very effective expedient to start the length of the threshold zone. Further aids are dark finish of the facade and other neighboring surfaces.

When the motorist has passed the adaptation point his eyes begin to adapt to the dark area of the tunnel entrance. If the luminance within the transition zone of the tunnel decreases, inconvenience caused by afterimages is prevented. This dominance exists at points equal in distance to the safe stopping sight distance in front of the observer.

4) Night Lighting

The requirements for lighting at night in short and long tunnels are identical. The lighting must be designed to avoid flicker and glare, and the illumination level should be the same throughout the entire length. The ratio of the roadway lighting inside the tunnel to that of the roadway outside the tunnel should not be greater than 3:1 and preferably should not exceed 2:1.

At night, the most severe visual task occurs at the exit of the tunnel when the roadway outside the tunnel has no lighting or has a lower level of illumination than inside the tunnel, and the exit appears as a dark hole to the motorist. The common cause for this situation is excessive lighting inside the tunnel. Many tunnels have the same level of illumination for night lighting as for daytime lighting in the interior zone. Inasmuch as the normal daylighting system usually must provide substantially more brightness than is required for night lighting, a single lighting system, without provisions for varying the amount of illumination, will not satisfy both operating requirements. Lighting in excess of the optimum amount is detrimental and may create a hazardous condition at the exit.

In instance when it is not desirable to reduce the night lighting level to a ratio of, at most, 3:1 with the approach roadway lighting, consideration should be given to providing transition lighting. The zone for the transition on the approach roadway should be about 500 to 600ft long (150 to 180m).

Approach roadway to many tunnels are of the depressed type, and these sections of the highway should be provided with roadway lighting. For the comfort of the motorist, the nighttime lighting level in this type of depressed highway should be 50% greater than that required on the open road. If none is provided on the open road, then the lighting level in this section should be 50% of the level within the tunnel.

When sun screens are applied at the entrance and/or exit of the tunnel, the nighttime lighting system must also be extended under and to the end of the sun screens. These sections of the lighting installation must also operate at dusk and at low levels of outside illumination during the daytime.

Very short tunnels that are straight and on a flat grade, and that are not provided with lighting for daytime operation, can usually be provided with satisfactory nighttime visibility by the proper positioning and mounting height of pole-mounted street lighting luminaires at each end of the tunnel. When higher-than-usual mounting heights are used for the luminaires adjacent to the tunnel portals, care must be exercised not to exceed the uniformity ratio; otherwise, some tunnel lighting may be necessary.

5) Use of Daylight in Tunnels

Natural daylight can be employed in lighting the interior of tunnels in three ways:

The use of subdued daylight at the entrance portal of a long tunnel by the use of daylight screening.

(1) The application of light slits in the roof of a short tunnel.

(2) The use of the light that provides a positive target contrast at a tunnel exit.

6) Sun Screens

Daylight screening is used as a means of reducing roadway luminance in way European tunnels, and to a limited extent, in this country (Chesapeake Bay Bridge-Tunnel and Harbor Tunnel, Baltimore). All of these designed with an upper cut-off angle sufficient to prevent direct sunlight penetrating to the roadway, they do not perform with a constant transmission factor when the ambient access illumination level varies from sunrise to sunset and from summer to winter as the sun's altitude gets progressively lower in the sky. As a result, when artificial lighting will be required under the louvers to supplement daylight so that the portal shadow, in effect, will not be transferred to the beginning of the louver.

The important characteristic for a louver to operate successfully is that the transmission factor must remain constant under all outdoor illumination condition. It appears, however, that additional research is required in this field before a satisfactory solution is reached. For these reasons, sun screens are not recommended as a solution to the tunnel entrance visibility problem.

9. Tunnel lining

The interior walls and ceiling of the tunnel are important adjuncts of the lighting system, and their brightnesses and uniformity depend on the reflectance quality of the surface. While the ceiling may not play an important part as a background against which objects may be silhouetted, except in tunnels with an upgrade approach, its light color and high reflectance its desirable because of the higher wall and roadway brightnesses that will result. The surfaces soil and can be easily cleaned. A light-colored matte (nonspecular) finish surface with a reflectance factor of 70% or greater is recommended.

The ceiling should also consist of a durable and reflective surface. Epoxy paint coatings have been applied with mixed success.

The tunnel roadway surface should have as high a reflectance factor as possible. To enhance reflective qualities, natural baked flint is used in England in conjunction with black asphalt. Some European tunnels have used equivalent artificial materials. Concrete, with the same additives, would perhaps produce almost ideal tunnel pavement material.

10. Tunnel lighting luminarires

Development of higher efficacy lamps with significantly greater life has eliminated the use of the incandescent lamp for tunnel lighting. Fluorescent, low-pressure sodium, high-presser sodium, and metal halide offer the tunnel lighting designer options for color and the application of symmetrical and asymmetrical systems.

1) Multilamp Enclosed Fluorescent Lamp Luminaire

This luminaire with internal reflector is placed either on the walls or in the angle between the ceiling and the walls and is one way of adding new lighting to an old tunnel. This type of luminaire has been installed in some recently completed tunnels. It offers considerable flexibility and must be watertight, bug-tight, and dust-tight for efficient lighting and maintenance. The particular advantage of this fixture is the control of the photometric distribution by the design of the reflector in conjunction with the enclosing diffuser and the higher lumen output per unit length. Multilamp luminaries have been used in the Humpton Roads Tunnels and Elizabeth River Tunnels in Virginia.

2) Low-Pressure Sodium Luminaire

The low-pressure sodium lamp has the highest efficacy of lamps applicable for tunnel lighting. The lamp's output is monochromatic yellow, which can be objectionable for color recognition of vehicles in a tunnel. A mix of fluorescent luminaries with low-pressure sodium luminaries has been utilized in the For McHenry Tunnel in Baltimore, Maryland and also the Elizabeth River Tunnels in Norfolk, Virginia. This combination enables the viewing of a broader spectrum of color. Low-pressure sodium lamps have been installed in tandem in 8ft long luminaries, which match the configuration of mutilamp fluorescent luminaires.

3) High-Intensity Discharge Luminaires

High-pressure sodium and mental halide lamps have been utilized for symmetrical and asymmetrical tunnel lighting systems. These lamps are very versatile and enable precise luminaire photometric control for both wall and ceiling mounting applications. These lamps are preferred for counter beam and pro-beam systems. Wall-mounted and ceiling mounted luminaires must be watertight and dust-tight to operate in a tunnel environment for many years.

4) High-Intensity Discharge lamp and Pipe System

The light pipe system uses high-pressure sodium or metal halide lamps in a luminaire coupled to a light guide consisting of an acrylic tube having an internal optical film and reflector. The lighted pipe system is used for symmetrical lighting systems. The system uses a 6in diameter tube in lengths up to 44ft. Luminance of the tube can be varied by varying the length of the tubes and lamp size. Emitting sectors or aperture from 90° to 180° is used to suit the photometric requirements of the tunnel.

Text B Lighting of Railway Tunnels
铁路隧道照明

1. Maintenance

Reliability of the tunnel lighting system is crucial, and its continuous operation without interruption must be assured. The lighting system depends on many factors that should be considered at the design stage. Maintenance of lighting is a most important factor, and the proposed maintenance program must be reflected in the initial design.

The amount of maintenance required depends on the location, type, and volume of the traffic; the type and capacity of the ventilation system; the tunnel cross section and shape; the ceiling and wall finish; operating speeds in the tunnel; the type and location of luminaires; grades and alignment within the tunnel; and the electrical system and supply.

A tunnel must have sufficiently high initial illumination to compensate for the many factors that will reduce it while it is in service. These factors fall into two categories: light loss factors not to be recovered and light loss factors recovered. In the first category are luminaire ambient temperature, voltage to luminaire, ballast factor, and luminaire surface depreciation. In the latter category are room lumen depreciation and luminaire dirt depreciation.

The most important factor, with the exception of the luminaires, is the surface treatment of the walls and ceiling. Reducing the reflection factor of these surfaces may be more detrimental to lighting effectiveness than any other single factor. Vehicular tunnel must be finished with an interior surface that will not deteriorate as time progresses and as chemicals attack it, that will not readily soil, and that can be easily cleaned. These attribute are characteristic of a light-colored matte-finished tile or porcelain-enameled panel with an initial reflectance of 70% or higher.

Luminaires should be sealed to prevent the entry of dust and water when the tunnel is being cleaned by high-pressure water spray. They should be designed to permit quick and easy internal cleaning. The materials used should be resistant to alkaline deposits, to concentrated exhaust fumes, and especially to cleaning solutions that must be used to thoroughly clean the tunnel walls and ceiling.

Lamps should be replaced on a group replacement program, which not only will help to maintain the light output at the desired design level, but will also provide for a balanced maintenance work load. The magnitude of the relamping task will generally dictate that group relamping must be done by sections. To replace lamps on a burnout basis may be acceptable in certain cases, but this usually false economy from the standpoint of the standpoint of lighting output and equipment maintenance cost.

The inside off the luminaire will require cleaning more often than the lamps are replaced, but the maintenance schedules should still prescribe cleaning each time a lamp is replaced. Some tunnels require a program of cleaning on a weekly basis, whereas others may not require cleaning for several weeks. Locations in the more northern latitudes, where freezing conditions may prevail for long periods, make cleaning operations difficult and frequently impractical. All of these factors must be recognized in the initial design of the lighting system.

2. Emergency lighting

Complete interruption of the tunnel lighting, even for an instant, cannot be tolerated, which requires a reliable power supply. For dual-utility power sources, one-half of the tunnel lighting is connected to each supply, so that in case of failure at least one-half the system remains energized until transfer of the entire load to the remaining source. For single-utility service and standby diesel generator, one-sixth of the tunnel lighting is connected to an emergency circuit, which in case of power failure is immediately transferred to a central emergency battery system until the diesel generator picks up to carry one-half of the tunnel lighting. An alternative to a central battery system is to utilize individual battery packs within one-sixth of the fixtures to maintain illumination from portal to portal.

3. Lighting of transit tunnels

The lighting of transit tunnels (rapid transit or subway tunnels) shares similar design features with the lighting of vehicular tunnels. The portal, in bright daylight conditions, presents a "black hole" and diminished visibility or the motorman or train operator. The tunnel interior also requires illumination for both normal and emergency operations, which applies to nighttime conditions from portal to portal. Emergency operations include lighting for passenger egress to exits.

Train operations differ from vehicle operations in a high-way tunnel trough strict regulatory requirement for approach and through speed, signal systems, occupancy control, and public access.

Individual transit operating agencies have criteria defining levels of illumination for both portal and interior zones for the design engineer. For applications where no criteria exist, criteria for vehicular tunnels may be used, with consideration for operational constraints on approach, safe stopping sight distance, and trough speed. Recommendations of ANSI/IES RP-22 (1987) suggest pavement luminance values based on traffic volume and speed, and characteristics of the tunnel. These values require adjustment for the actual use since the traffic volumes and pavement luminance are not applicable. Therefore calculation procedures using an illuminance method should be applied.

4. Lighting of railway tunnels

The design of lighting for railway tunnels is different from the design of highway tunnels and transit tunnels. Highway and transit tunnels typically have intensive lighting for 200-400m from the portal to the interior, for eye adaptation from a high external to low interior illumination level. The railway tunnel lighting design can have an intensive lighting zone greater than 1km, owing to the great mass of the train and stopping distance.

Close coordination with railroad operation agencies to establish intensive zone criteria will be required. Issues such as mandatory train entry speed, grade, alignment, and train mass will provide a basis for engineering judgments. Economic considerations must include capital costs, and energy and maintenance costs.

Portal-to-portal illumination will require assessment of tunnel lining reflectance. Low reflectance resulting from the characteristics of the material and minimal maintenance will require greater lamp lumens than highway tunnels with highly reflective surfaces. This suggests that an asymmetrical lighting concept be employed for positive and negative visibility. Location of luminaries to coincide with refuge niches, to indicate their location as well as providing visibility, is recommended.

5. Design computations

Improvement in tunnel lighting has generated the need for taking a closer look at the accuracy of predicting illuminance and luminance levels. For nearly 70 years, lumen or flux methods for calculation of the illumination level using coefficients of utilization factors have been employed. These original methods used coefficients of utilization that were determined by empirical methods for lighting equipment available at the time. Later developments used mathematical analysis as a method for computing coefficients of utilization data. All of these methods were based on the theory that average illumination is equal to lumens divided by the work area over which they are distributed. Later mathematical methods of analysis took into account the concept of inter-reflection of light, and they have led to progressively more accurate coefficients of utilization data. The Zonal Cavity Method improved older systems by providing increased flexibility in lighting calculations as well as greater accuracy.

For the detailed procedures to be followed in the use of the Zonal Cavity Method, refer to ANSI/IES RP-22, American National Standard Practice for Tunnel Lighting, latest edition. The designer may utilize a computer to aid in calculating illuminance and luminance. Computer software is readily available for this application.

To complement the accuracy in predicting the initial average illuminance and luminance levels in tunnels, the designer should also use the new procedure for evaluating the maintenance factor for the determination of an equally important accurate prediction of the overall average in-service illumination level. A comprehensive procedure for developing a meaningful maintenance factor will be found in the IES Handbook (1990).

Text C Illuminator Installation Construction Lighting of Highway Tunnels
公路隧道照明设备施工

Highway tunnels as special road section of high class motorway can generate a series of vision problems in the course of traffic movement into, through and out of tunnels. Additional electrical illumination need to be arranged to adapt to vision changes. Hence tunnel illumination design and construction is important to highway engineering project.

1. Generalrequirement

(1) Highway tunnel interior must be provided with high luminance and ideal uniformity of illumination to highlight the high standard of highway construction and be supplementary and complementary to the highway outside tunnel to form an organic integrity of mechanical and electrical engineering of transit tunnel.

(2) Tunnel illumination is divided into jump-like control and control mode is required to be flexible with full consideration of such factors as avoiding power consumption peak time and little traffic in some time period and can be controlled separately by time intervals as ordinary, holiday, early night, late night and midnight.

(3) Generally high pressure sodium lamp (HPSL) as light source shall be selected as illuminators which are matured both in luminance and technology and the fixed support shall be top quality cold-roll steel plate. Illuminators shall have high waterproof and dustproof rating (IP65). Light source shall be selected by principle of high efficiency and long life and the selected lamp types for the whole tunnel shall be easily maintained and managed.

(4) Tunnel illumination is usually divided into entrance illumination section, interior illumination section and exit illumination section. Of above entrance illumination is additionally strictly required demanding that the luminance similar to exterior is gradually reduced from the portals towards the interior of the tunnel. Specifically in daytime the luminance of entrance shall be decided according to the luminance outside tunnel, vehicle movement speed and the field of view at entrance and the tunnel length.

According to the International Commission on Illumination tunnel entrance illumination is divided into (starting from portal) threshold value section and transition section. According to the Japanese tunnel illumination standard, the tunnel entrance illumination is further divided into approach section, adaptation section and transition section. The threshold value section is intended to eliminate sign of "black hole" and enable drivers to recognize obstruct from portal. The tunnel transition section of illumination is illumination section intended to avoid sharp contrast between threshold illumination and interior fundamental illumination and to further lower down the illumination level. Thus the light source of tunnel lamps must meet the special requirement on tunnel lighting in addition to the principal requirement for general street illumination and must ensure fine visibility in tunnel even under impact of vehicular emission.

High pressure sodium lamp is the light source of strongest penetration worldwide up to date and is suitable for locations in heavy air dust and smoke dust. The light source of light pressure sodium lamp is used as illumination in developed tunnel to ensure visibility that motorman is able to identify obstructs.

Since man's eye needs time to adapt to luminance variation. During daytime when motorman drives into tunnel from exterior outside tunnel, the apparent difference of luminance between interior and exterior creates black hole effect and at the exit white hole effect will blind vision of the motorman which will seriously endanger driving safety. In order to overcome this phenomenon of vision slag, illumination control measures shall be taken up to enable the luminance at portals and in tunnel interior to be compatible with that of tunnel exterior.

In order to ensure adequate luminance on road pavement, high pressure sodium lamp of power 100W, 150W, 250W or 400W are used generally which are fixed on the support on walls of tunnel in installation upward angle degrees of 30 to facilitate prevention of glare.

Tunnel illumination engineering includes many aspects such as power supply cable, power supply pipeline, and emergency illumination, guiding illumination, cross passage illumination, street lamp illumination, illumination classification control, light intensity detection and luminance requirement. It is a complex and system engineering.

2. Construction requirement and General construction scheme

Tunnel illumination facility works must be executed in strict accordance with relevant design specifications on highway tunnel illumination system installation. The lamp installation angle degree, cable connection and distribution way must strictly conform to specification and design requirement.

After commencement of illumination works, the illumination facility installation team shall make footing for lamp post and grounding system. The circuit installation for illumination control shall be made in cooperation with the equipment installation team. After the capacity of lighting footing reaches 80% of design capacity, light post is installed with crane. Then lifting platform is used in installation of lighting lamps inside and outside tunnel. Finally test the luminance and luminance as specified below:

Before illuminator installation, perform activation performance test and tightness performance test. If there is illuminator detecting element, test the sensitivity of the detecting element. In addition, check for any existence of scratch, rust, coat spalling on the exterior appearance and any existence of crack on front face glass, completion and soundness of electrical ballast and compensation capacitor, firmness of wiring. The level of protection shall be spot checked in compliance with design requirement IP65.

(1) Illuminator installation sequence will follow steps as setting out, hole-drilling, illumination installation, wiring, angle adjustment and testing.

(2) Phasing and grouping of illuminators.

(3) The horizontal tolerance of setting out shall be controlled within range of +1cm every 100m and the tolerance of interval between illuminators is controlled within range of ±2cm. Illuminator installation angle tolerance is no greater than 0.5°.

(4) The wire diameter must conform to design requirement and the wire from junction box to the wire of illuminator must be protected in soft metal flexible pipe and rubber dust proof and waterproof outlet must be arranged at location of illuminators.

(5) The performance of activation of illuminators, glowing and control test of same circuit must meet design requirement.

(6) The installation of illumination control cabin: The illumination control box in tunnel must be strictly humidity-proof and there is no direct contact between the box surface and walls which can be achieved by inserting shim in fixation bolt. Rubber seals are added on both sides at connection between bolt and box body. Opening of distribution box shall be well sealed and no permeation or drop from ceiling wall shall occur. Remote control shall be installed on illumination box for circuit control in compliance with design requirement to ensure site control in priority.

(7) Tunnel illuminators shall be installed in conformity with drawings and are generally installed on ceiling of tunnel walls and installations shall not invade into tunnel construction gauge. Since wire and cables are installed in embedded pipes, during the illumination installation process, care shall be taken to avoid the reserved and embedded facilities in walls of tunnel.

(8) Street light installation shall conform to drawings and relevant technical requirements of specifications.

3. Illuminator installation construction

1) Survey positioning

In light of technical requirement in design document and construction specification, acceptance standard and requirement, all types of lamps, switches, sockets, box locations in tunnel shall be survey positioned and those lamps, boxes, switches and sockets to be mounted in the area in need for second decoration shall be have position fixed in cooperation with the second decoration undertaking unit. The types and numbers and capacity of all the lamps, switches, boxes and sockets shall be checked. In course of survey positioning, supervisor shall be sent on site and check and confirm that all the installations conform to specific requirement.

2) Lamp support processing

In light of various lamp types and installation modes, some lamps require support installation such as hanging lamps. The fixed support shall be processed by design and according to the lamp weight and bearing capacity and reliable fixation must be ensured.

3) Illumination installation

(1) In light of the design requirement, all types of lamps, boxes, switches and sockets shall be precisely properly installed. Before installation commencement, conducting and insulation

performances shall be tested with universal meter and upon being acceptable shall be properly installed with embedded bolt or fastener.

(2) For the area in need of second decoration, before the installation commencement, perform a cooperation and communication with the installation undertaker and perform preservation works for all types of lamps, switches and sockets and embedment works for lamp fastener, box and junction box. After completion of the second installation, install the lamps, switches and sockets.

(3) During the works execution, perform proactive cooperation with the construction undertaker in early stage and install the lamps under the condition of not impacting preliminary works.

(4) When the lamps are received, pre-match all types of lamps safety and precisely in accordance with design document. Before installation commencement, test the conducting and insulation with universal meter and then deliver the lamps on jobsite after being acceptable through testing.

(5) After illuminators are delivered on jobsite, light columns can be moved by site by hands and abut connected with embedded flange. The large and heavy columns shall be uplifted with crane and then connected with flange manually. During the assembling, installation quality shall be strictly controlled. After the columns are connected and assembled, check its verticality and levelness with angle ruler and shim can be used to adjust the column to be vertical or horizontal.

(6) In light of the design requirement, illuminators shall be placed on footing safety and accurately by hands or machine and lamp fasteners and junction box shall be properly installed.

(7) After the lamp installation is completed, electrical wire, maintenance box and grounding poles shall be properly connected via galvanized bolt and well grounded. Every lamp post should be grounded and separate short circuit protection shall be arranged for each lamp post.

(8) The team in charge of illumination equipment installation shall undertake installation of lamp post, lamp support, illuminator, illumination power distribution box and give assistance to energize testing.

(9) After completion of illuminator installation, test and check (including reliability testing) in accordance with relevant specifications.

(10) Technological department and illumination equipment installation team shall conduct appearance check and installation inspection and testing engineering is in charge of electrical equipment check and testing.

II. Terms and terminology

"black hole" 黑洞现象
adaptation （视）适应

illuminance	照度
luminance, brightness	亮度
glare	炫光
luminaries	光源,发光体,照明设备
maintenance factor	维护系数
access zone	接近段
threshold zone	入口段
transition zone	过渡段
interior zone	中间段,基本段
exit zone	出口段
fluorescent lamp	荧光灯,日光灯
low-pressure sodium luminaries	低压钠灯
metal halide lamp	金属卤化灯
emergency lighting	紧急照明
average illumination	平均照度
lighting fixture	照明器材
incandescent unit	白炽灯
photometric characteristics	配光性能

Ⅲ. Questions and difficult sentence analysis

1. Questions for brainstorming discussion

(1) In the process of motorcar's entering and passing through tunnels, what effects on driver's visual sense may occur?

(2) What are the tunnel illumination sections divided?

(3) Discuss how the luminance of various illumination sections in highway tunnels is specified in Chinese specifications on highway tunnels.

2. Difficult sentences analysis

(1) The most prominent lighting concepts employed are the symmetrical and the asymmetrical, of which there are two types: the counter beam and line-of-sight. Linear or point source luminaries or combinations of types of sources are employed to provide for specific illumination requirements for unidirectional or bidirectional traffic tunnels as appropriate to the system.

译文:采用的最优越的照明概念是对称以及不对称照明,其中有两种:反光和视线。采用线性或点发光体光源或者几种光源的组合,对双向或单向隧道提出了具体的适合该系统的照明要求。

(2) Attention to luminaire type selection, location, and spacing for reduction of glare and flicker is a primary design requisite in the entrance zone and throughout the tunnel.

译文:在隧道进口段和全隧道的照明设计中,必须主要注意灯具的选型、位置和间距以便减少眩光和闪烁。

(3) While there is disparity in these recommendations, there are conditions under which the extremes can be shown to be adequate for complete adaptation, such as in long tunnels the interior lighting can approach the criteria for nighttime street lighting.

译文：一方面这些建议意见存在分歧，给出充分的极端条件供完全采纳，比如在长隧道中，内部照明能接近夜间路灯照明的标准。

(4) The symmetrical lighting system utilizes illuminates having photometric characteristics that direct light transverse to the longitudinal axis of the tunnel roadway of sufficient magnitude to enable objects to be observed by positive or negative contrast.

译文：对称照明体系利用照明具有配光性能，能够使光线与隧道道路中线垂直，其程度足以能通过明暗对照度来观察物体。

Ⅳ. Translation case study

Case 1

Chinese	English translation
在白天驾驶员进入隧道直至离开隧道。会遇到以下一些特殊的视觉问题：	During daytime during the time period from a driver entering into a tunnel till his leaving the tunnel, he may encounter following special vision problems:
1. 进入隧道前的视觉问题。由于白天隧道外的亮度相对于隧道内的高很多，如果隧道足够长，驾驶员看到的是黑乎乎的一个洞，这就是"黑洞"现象；如果隧道很短的话，就出现一个"黑框"。	1. The vision problem before one enters into a tunnel: Due to the fact that the sun-lit day brightness outside the tunnel is much higher than the interior tunnel brightness. If the tunnel is long enough, the driver can only see a black hole, which is called "black hole" phenomenon. If the tunnel is very short, a "black frame" appears in front of the driver.
2. 进入隧道即刻会发生的视觉现象。由明亮的外部进入一个较暗的隧道，由于驾驶员的视觉有一定的适应时间，因此他无法迅速地看清隧道内部的情况，这种现象称为"适应的滞后现象"。	2. The vision problem occurring immediately at moment of one's entering into a tunnel: While entering from brightness outside into darker tunnel interior, the driver's vision needs some time to adapt his eyes to the darker interior surrounding of the tunnel and so, he is unable to detect and discern clearly the tunnel interior environment. This phenomenon is called sign of "delay in adaptation".
3. 隧道出口处的视觉问题。处于一个很暗的环境。突然前方出现一个很亮的出处，会产生强烈的眩光，使驾驶员看不清路况，极易发生车祸。	3. The vision problem at tunnel exit portal: Situating in a very dark environment a very bright exit suddenly appears in front a driver. Strong glaring can appear and may blind the driver who is unable to see clearly the road situation and traffic accident is extremely vulnerable in that case.

Case 2

Chinese	English translation
不允许发生隧道照明完全中断，哪怕一瞬间的中断，隧道需要可靠的电源。	Complete interruption of a tunnel lighting, even for an instant, cannot be tolerated, which requires a reliable power supply. For dual-

· 238 ·

continue

Chinese	English translation
如果采用双电源供电设施,一半的隧道照明与每个电源连接,因此,如果发生停电,至少一半的供电系统保持供电,直到将全部荷载转移到剩下的电源。如果采用单个服务设施和备用发电机,六分之一的隧道照明与应急线路连接,如果发生停电,能够立即转换到中央电池系统,直到柴油发电机接着继续承担一半的隧道照明。另一个代替中央电池系统的方案是利用固定装置的六分之一的单个电池组来维持整个隧道的照明。	utility power sources, one-half of the tunnel lighting is connected to each supply, so that in case of power failure, at least one-half the system remains energized until transfer of the entire load to the remaining source. For single-utility service and standby diesel generator, one-sixth of the tunnel lighting is connected to an emergency circuit, which in case of power failure is immediately transferred to a central emergency battery system until the diesel generator picks up to carry one-half of the tunnel lighting. An alternative to a central battery system is the utilization of to utilize individual battery packs within one-sixth of the fixtures to maintain the illumination from portal to portal.

Case 3

Chinese	English translation
为了解决以上各种问题,即使在白天也必须在隧道设置合适的照明设施把必要的视觉信息传递给司机,防止因视觉信息不足而出现交通事故,从而提高驾驶上的安全性和增加舒适感。我国《公路隧道照明设计》规定300m以下的行人稀少且交通量不大的隧道可不设照明,但二级以上公路隧道长度超过100m时必须有可靠的照明设施。	In order to solve the above problems, suitable illumination facilities must be set in tunnels during daytime to transmit necessary visual information to the drivers to prevent occurrence of traffic incidents due to inadequate visual information so as to improve driving safety and increase sense of comfortableness. According to the provisions in the national specification "Specifications for Design of Ventilation and Lighting of Highway Tunnel": for the tunnel in length shorter than 300m with small number of pedestrians and traffic volume, amount no illumination is necessary. But for the highway tunnel of rating II with length in excess of exceeding 100m, reliable illumination facilities must be installed in the tunnel.

V. Assignment

(1)照明器的布置方法很多,可安装在拱顶、墙壁或吊装顶棚上,沿隧道纵向有单排布置的,也有双排布置的。在双排布置的情况下,既有成对布置的,也有交错布置的。总之,灯具的合理布置就是在最经济的条件下达到最好的照明效果。

(2)总而言之,LED 照明是一种节能、环保、具有广阔应用前景的现代照明技术。但是就技术体系而言,需要高效的 LED 电源、合理的电路设计、正确的安装工艺才能充分发挥和利用 LED 光源的巨大优势。同时,需要配套技术标准的制定和相关政策的支持以促进 LED 照明行业的规范化、健康快速发展。

(3)国内已有不少公路隧道采用计算机自动调节控制照明方案,从一定意义上讲基本上解决了安全与节能之间的矛盾,使工作人员从烦劳紧张的手工操作情况下解放出来。

(4)道路照明的眩光可以分为两类:一种叫作失能眩光,另一种叫作不舒适眩光。所谓失能眩光是指由光在眼睛里发生散射过程造成识别能力的下降。来自眩光光源的光在视网膜方向上的散射会引起光幕(等效光幕)作用,在视网膜方向上的散射程度越大,光幕作用也越大。而不舒适眩光是指由于眩光造成驾乘人员的不舒适感。不舒适眩光是心理上的过程,尚无专门的测量仪器,目前主要是用眩光控制等级(G)表示所感到的不舒适程度的主观评价。

(5)在通常情况下,当汽车驶近隧道,但距洞口尚有一定距离时,司机的注意力会自然地集中在观察洞口附近情况上,开始注视之点称为注视点。继续接近洞口时,在司机的视野里,亮度较高的外界景物(其亮度为洞外亮度)逐渐减少,相应地洞内低亮度景物逐渐增加。当汽车到达洞外某一点(约距洞口10m)时,司机视野中的外界景物全部消失,开始适应洞内亮度的变化,不再为"感应现象"所困扰,该点称为适应点。

Unit 12　Water Supply and Drain
隧道给排水

Ⅰ. Text

Text A　Tunnel Water Supply and Drain System
隧道给排水系统

Most tunnels will require systems to provide water to the tunnel and remove wastewater from the tunnel. A water supply system is required primarily for fire protection and possibly for wall-washing operations. A drainage system is necessary to collect, treat, and discharge the waste-water resulting from fire-fighting operations, washing operations, and leakage.

1. Water supply system

Highway, subway, and rapid transit tunnels are usually provided with water mains, hose valves, and fire extinguishers, and in some instances, with water deluge systems on the exhaust fans. Railroad tunnels, because of their extreme length, are usually not provided with water mains.

The most significant aspect of the water supply requirement is the tunnel fire protection system. The water for fire protection is transported through a water main located within the tunnel. The minimum flow and pressure criteria must be established prior to implementation of design.

2. Water supply design criteria

1) Flow Rate

The minimum available water flow rate that should be provided for highway tunnels is stated by the National Fire Protection Association (NFPA) as 1000gpm (3800L/min) at adequate pressure (NFPA, 1991). This will provide sufficient flow for four 250gpm (950L/min) hose streams using the standard 2.5in (63.5mm) fire hose connection. Such a water flow quantity will most likely be sufficient for any auxiliary use of the system, such as wall washing.

2) Pressure

Sufficient pressure must be available at each hose station to create an adequate hose stream. To discharge 250gpm (950L/min) from a 2.5in (63.5mm) hose outlet equipped with 100ft(31m) of hose and a standard tapered hose nozzle, the residual pressure at the hose value must be 60psi(420kPa).

In a subaqueous tunnel, the fire hose valve located at the low point of the tunnel may, because of the difference in elevations, have a greater available pressure than a fire hose valve located near the portal. For the some reason, in a mountain tunnel of the fixed grade, the available pressure at opposing ends of the tunnel may vary greatly due to the large difference in elevation. In either case, the fire hose valve located at the higher elevation may often be the most critical from the standpoint of maintaining a minimum pressure requirement at all valve locations. This fact must be considered when hydraulic calculations for a tunnel water supply system are being performed.

Should the supply pressure be insufficient to provide the required pressure at the hose valve outlet, fire pumps must be considered at the point of water supply, as outlined later in this chapter.

3. Water source

The selection of a source of water for a tunnel must be made early in the design process. In the case of a tunnel located in an urban area, the choice is relatively simple, since large quantities of water are normally readily available from a municipal water supply system. Elsewhere, a dedicated water supply may be necessary, using well or surface water.

1) Municipal Water Supply

A municipal water supply system should be the prime choice as a water source for any tunnel when it is available. This is a valid approach provided that the municipal water lines are relatively close and have a flow rate and pressure adequate to meet the flow and pressure criteria required at the tunnel. If, however, the municipal water lines are not within a reasonable distance from the tunnel, it may be less costly to provide another means of water supply. This could be a dedicated system using an underground water supply, a river, or a lake, together with a storage tank and fire pumps.

As indicated above, a municipal water system may supply the runnel fire protection system if it is capable of providing at least 60psi (420kpa) at any hose outlet while supplying full fire protection demand. The full fire protection demand is a sum of 1000gpm (3800L/min) for hose outlets, cooling water for fans, and sprinkler demand (if any sprinklers are installed).

According to NFPA 502 (NFPA, 1991) a city main may be used for direct connection to the tunnel's fire protection system only if the pressure in the main would not drop below 20psi (140kPa) at the 1000gpm(3800L/min) load applied in addition to its normal nonfire flow.

Therefore, when considering a municipal water system as a source of water supply for a tunnel, the pressure and capacity of the city main at the point of proposed connection must be taken into account. If both are satisfactory, the funnel system should be connected directly to the municipal water system.

If the municipal main satisfies the NFPA's minimum flow requirement of 1000gpm/20psi

(3800L/min /140kPa) but does not have adequate pressure to provide 60psi(420kPa) at any hose outlet in the tunnel at full fire demand, booster fire pumps should be used. The pumps should be installed at the point of water supply to boost the pressure to the required level.

If the municipal main does not satisfy the NFPA's minimum requirement, the city water must be accumulated in a special storage tank and then supplied to the tunnel system by fire pumps having the required capacity and pressure. This arrangement must be used regardless of the pressure that the city mains can provide at any other fire flow rates.

The storage tank reserve capacity must be equal to at least 60min(NFPA,1991) of the full fire protection demand. This 60min reserve is considered a bare minimum, a greater capacity is recommended. Where the municipal water supply is reliable, that is, the storage tank is connected to a city loop; makeup water accumulated in the tank during the fire pump operation may justify selection of a tank with minimum capacity.

2) Dedicated Water Supply

If a municipal water supply system cannot be used, a dedicated system using wells or surface waters must be considered. If wells are used, a storage tank should be used to accumulate the required water reserve and allow reducing the capacity of the well supply system, thus reducing its cost. The tank capacity should be selected to accommodate the full fire protection demand of the tunnel for a minimum of one hour(NFPA,1991). using the recommended flow rate of 1000gpm(3800L/min), a tank of 60000gal(228000L) minimum capacity would be required. A thorough analysis should be made prior to selecting the water supply system for each tunnel to determine which supply system is the most reliable and economical given the specific tunnel configuration.

Where possible, it is advisable to have a dual source of water supply for the tunnel fir protection system; that is, one line from each end of the tunnel. This is usually only practical in a subaqueous or urban tunnel, where the municipal water supplies are close at hand.

4. Water mains

The supply of water for tunnel fire protection is transported through a water main installed in a location that offers protection from both physical and high-temperature damage. Consideration must be given to whether the water main should be wet or dry. The dry main is filled only when water is required.

1) Wet main

The wet main is ordinarily more advantageous for fire protection, since the water is available immediately when required during a fire.

The water in a wet main, however, cannot be allowed to freeze, and in some locations freeze protection will have to be provided. This can be accomplished in several ways. The most effective method involves recirculating heated water in the main to keep its temperature above freezing. Another method is to embed the main in concrete within the tunnel structure, with sufficient cover to prevent freezing. A third method is to keep a continuous movement of water in the pipe, thus reducing the possibility of freezing. This can be accomplished by a simple bleed system, controlled by a thermostatically controlled valve. This system uses the available municipal water pressure to keep the water flowing. This approach will, however, result in a waste of potable water if a municipal water supply system is used.

2) Dry main

The time it takes to fill a dry main before the water becomes available for fire fighting becomes a serious disadvantage in longer tunnels. For example, using normal municipal water pressure and a flow rate of 1000gpm (3800L/min), an 8in (203.2mm) main in a 19000ft (5791m) tunnel would require more than 30min to fill. This is not acceptable since it exceeds the 10min limit set by NFPA 502 (NFPA, 1991) and would create a severe handicap during an emergency. Another disadvantage of a dry main is that it must be drained after each use.

3) Supply arrangement

The water main in a tunnel, where practical, should be provided with two sources of supply, preferably one at each end of the tunnel. The main should be suitably valved and automatically controlled to provide water form either supply when required and to prevent flow from one water source to another.

The water main within the tunnel should also be valved to separate sections to permit repair of a damaged section while minimizing any reduction in fire protection. This can be accomplished by installing sectionalizing valves, provided two sources of water supply are available.

4) Open Approach

The open approach to the tunnel, where the roadway extends beyond the portal, should be considered an extension of the tunnel and, therefore, protected. This will provide available fire protection for a portion of the roadway with limited access. In areas without freezing conditions and in all cases of a tunnel equipped with a dry pipe fire main, the outlets within the open approach should be connected to the tunnel water main.

In areas subject to freezing temperatures and where the tunnel is equipped with a wet pipe main, the approach should be protected by a dry pipe main. A fire protection Siamese connection should be pumped by the fire department from the nearest street hydrant into the dry pipe system of the open approach.

An alternative method would be to protect the open approach from fire hydrants located above, at the surface of the road behind the approach retaining walls. The road must be accessible to fire-fighting equipment at all times.

5) Water Supply to Buildings

Water supply for the building associated with the tunnel should be provided for standpipes and/or sprinklers as required by local codes. NFPA Standards, and the local authorities having jurisdiction, in accordance with the construction group, area and height of the building, and occupancy classification.

6) Size of Main

The water main should be sized to minimize the pressure drop through the system and to provide sufficient pressure at the hose valves as required by code. The hydraulic design considerations should be balanced against the space available within the tunnel cross section. This should be verified by hydraulic calculation whether the system is supplied by a fire pump or directly by a municipal water supply.

7) Material

The piping material used for the fire main can be cast iron, ductile iron, or sufficient strength to withstand the maximum pressure of the system. Sufficient means of compensation for temperature expansion and contraction and projected structural movements must be provided.

5. Drainnage system

A drainage system is required in all tunnels to remove water that could accumulate from rainfall, tunnel washing operations, tunnel seepage, vehicle drippings, fire-fighting operations, or any combination of these sources. Drainage of a tunnel can be accompanied either by a gravity flow system or a pumped system. A gravity flow system will suffice for tunnels with continuous grades, provided that the collected water can be properly disposed of at the lower end of the tunnel. It may be necessary to have a pumped system to dispose of collected water when a low point occurs within the tunnel.

6. Drainage design criteria

The drainage system design must be predicated on a proper determination of the anticipated flow rate, that is, the peak discharge rate of the water to be drained.

1) Drainage of rainfall

To design an adequate drainage system, criteria regarding the amount of expected rainfall in the area to be drained must be available. Three key factors in determining the amount of water to be drained from rainfall are intensity, frequency, and time of concentration.

Intensity. This is the amount of rainfall within a specific period of time, usually given in inch/hour. Intensity-duration curves for many areas of the United States are published by the U. S. Weather Bureau (U. S. Dept. Commerce, 1961).

Frequency. The frequency of a storm is the average number of years between occurrences of a storm of a given or greater intensity. *For normal drainage design a 10-year storm frequency is used; however, for a tunnel where flooding is a serious concern, such as a subaqueous tunnel, a 100-year storm frequency should be considered.*

Time of Concentration. The time of concentration is defined as the time required for run-off from the most remote point of the drainage area to arrive at the point where the entire area exposed to the rain contributes to the flow rate in the drainage system.

Run-off. The amount of water left from a rainfall after the losses from evaporation, transpiration, and infiltration is the run-off.

2) Tunnel Washing Operations

In most highway tunnels, the walls and ceilings are washed periodically, usually in a two-stage procedure. First, a detergent is applied using a wash truck with rotating brushes; second, the detergent and the dirt are rinsed off with water by a separate flush/rinse truck. In a typical tunnel of 7500ft(2286m) in length, the wash process includes a quantity of water and detergent roughly equal to 1500gal (56780L) and a rinse quantity of 15000gal (56780L); the process takes approximately one hour. Thus, an average washwater flow rate for this typical tunnel would be approximately 275gpm (17.4L/s).

3) Drainage from Fire-Fighting Operations

Fire-fighting operations can also contribute a sizable quantity of water to the drainage system. This quantity can be determined by estimating the maximum flow rate of water that could be pumped into the tunnel during a fire emergency within the capacity of the existing fire protection system.

4) Drainage of Vehicle Drippings

Vehicle drippings have been shown to be of minimal consequence and, if the system is designed to handle all the above quantities, the water from vehicle drippings will be adequately handled.

5) Drainage of Seepage

Most tunnels through hills and mountains have water seepage problems. Surface water penetrates through fissures and percolates through permeable soils. Concrete liners are not completely watertight, and water may find its way through cracks in the lining.

Attempts to seal off the rock by grouting with either cement or chemicals usually are not successful. Concrete linings are not completely watertight. Water will find its way through shrinkage cracks in the linings into the interior tunnels. There, it can freeze and cause an unsightly appearance in highway tunnels.

If water appears in considerable quantity during tunneling operations, longitudinal drainpipes should be installed behind the sidewalls, with laterals at regular intervals to the main tunnel drain lines.

Cut-and-cover tunnels can be waterproofed, and with good control, the number of leaks in such a tunnel can be minimized. Seepage in underwater tunnels, either the shield driven or the immersed tube type, is usually limited and can be controlled by caulking joints where leaks do appear in segmented liners.

7. Open approach drainage

The portions of the tunnel roadway that extend beyond the portals are classed as the tunnel approaches. In cases where the approach road slopes into the tunnel and cannot be drained by gravity external to the tunnel, the approach drainage system must be included in the tunnel drainage system. This is especially true in a subaqueous tunnel where the open approaches are below the surrounding grade. The open approach drainage system should be designed to minimize the influx of water from the open approach roadway into the tunnel.

The quantity of drainage water on the open approach can be computed from rainfall alone, since this value, in most instances, will be the greatest.

1) Straight Open Approaches

On straight open approaches without superelevation, transverse interceptors placed approximately 300ft (91m) on centers, with the first one located immediately outside the tunnel portal, are most effective in preventing the run-off from entering the tunnel. The actual interceptor spacing will depend on grade, inlet capacity, and pavement type. The interceptors are approximately 18in (457.2mm) in width, extend from curb to curb, and are covered with heavy cast iron gratings.

2) Superelevated Open Approaches

When the approach is provided with a superelevation, the approach drainage inlets must be placed at regular intervals along the low curb. The drainage water flows by gravity from the approach inlets into portal pump stations or into the tunnel drainage system to discharge into a pump station located at a low point in the tunnel. The gravity line should be a minimum of 8in (203.2mm) in diameter, with cleanouts located at required intervals.

8. Roadway drainage

The roadway drainage system for a tunnel can be either open or closed.

Open drainage system. The open type of roadway drainage consists of a continue system gutter recessed into the curb and has been used in many tunnels. This system, however, may permit propagation of a fire of burning fuel, in the event of a serious accident, due to a continuous source of a serious of air to support combustion.

Closed drainage system. The closed system, on the other hand, will minimize such fire propagation, since the drainage liquid enters the inlets located gravity flow system to a pump station. For this reason, the closed system should be spaced 50-75ft (15-23m) apart on both sides of a level roadway and on the low side of a superelevated roadway.

Drainage inlet. The drainage inlet design is important, since it must remain clear of debris that would prevent influencing of water. The drainage inlet must be a key maintenance item to prevent clogging.

Gravity drain line. The gravity drain line carrying that drainage water from the inlet to the pump station should be a minimum of 8 in (203.2mm) in diamond. Line cleanouts should be located every 100ft (31m), with suitable access.

9. Drainage pump stations

Any tunnel from which the drainage water cannot be properly removed by gravity must be provided with one or more pump stations having the necessary capacity to remove the maximum drainage demand. There are two basic locations for tunnel pump stations: at the low point of a tunnel, in particular a subaqueous type, and at the portals of any tunnel.

1) Low-point pump station

The purpose of the low-point pump station is to collect all the drainage water within the tunnel and pump it out to the portal pump station or to a designed system. The pump type most appropriate for the low-point pump station is a vertical dry pit or horizontal centrifugal type because of the usual limited available headroom at such locations.

2) Portal pump station

The portal pump station in a subaqueous tunnel collects water from the open approach and water pumped from the tunnel low point and the ventilation structures. A portal pump station would be required for a mountain tunnel if the water cannot property drained by gravity. The portal pump station may be construed be either of two methods. The first is in-place construction, where the structure at the portal is formed and construed to create the necessary setting and holding chambers and pump room.

3) Chambers

All pump stations require one or several chambers designed to hold and treat the drainage water. A full evaluation of the drainage water treatment is presented in the next section of this chapter.

The setting well, or sump, is the first line of water treatment. It should be sized to provide adequate time for solids to settling well could be equipped with a skimming weir, or a bar screen across the width of the well, to prevent floating materials from clogging the pumping system or being discharged out of the system.

The holding or storage sump, which receives the water from the settling well, should be sized to allow a minimum of 4 min of running time for each pump. If submersible pumps are used, the need for a separate pump room is eliminated.

Provision must be made in all installation for periodic inspection and removal of sludge from the sumps. Access manholes and proper drainage facilities are necessary. Portable housekeeping pumps can be used to empty the chambers for maintenance purpose.

10. Drainage pumps

There broad categories of pumps are available: reciprocating, rotary, and centrifugal. However, since only the centrifugal pump is used in tunnel drainage applications, only this type of pump will be discussed in this section.

The centrifugal pump can be operated against a completely blocked discharge without overloading the drive, and it is the most suitable pump for tunnel drainage service. Centrifugal pumps can be obtained in several arrangements: horizontal, vertical dry pit, submersible, and vertical wet sump. Each of these is suitable for a particular situation or situations.

The horizontal pump is suitable where the headroom is limited and plan space is available, or when high flow capacity and pressures are required. The horizontal split casing pump is easy to maintain because half of the casing can be removed for inspection and maintenance without removing the piping or bearings.

The vertical dry pit pump can be used where the vertical space is limited but plan space is available adjacent to the sumps. This pump requires less floor space than does the horizontal type. The entire pump is accessible for ease of maintenance. The vertical dry pit pump is a type most often used in a package pump station.

The vertical sump pump is appropriate where floor space is limited, but vertical space is available above the sumps. The impeller and the bearings of this type of pump are located below the water, thus creating some maintenance problems. When the pump must be removed, considerable space is required to lift the pump.

The submersible pump is installed completely below the surface of the water in the sump. The only connection from the pump to the space above the sump is the discharge pipe, the power cable, and the removal cable. These pumps can be mounted on vertical rails for lifting the pumps to the surface for maintenance. It is not recommended where traffic in the tunnel must be interrupted to service the pump. This pump requires a minimum of floor area and vertical space.

The centrifugal pumps outlined above should, if possible, be installed in tunnel drainage systems with a flooded suction. If a suction lift is unavoidable, a reliable priming system must be installed.

1) Pump drives

Most tunnel drainage pumps are driven by electric motors. However, there are instances where an internal combustion engine drive would be appropriate. This could be during a power failure when emergency pumping isabsolutely necessary.

2) Pump arrangement

In most tunnel drainage systems, more than one pump should be installed to provide an adequate factor of safety to what is a critical system, particularly in a subaqueous tunnel. Other benefits of multiple pump installation include smaller individual installations and servicing loads, reduced electrical starting loads and cable sizes, smoother pumping, and overall installation economies. The use oftwo pumps in each pumping station, each having 100% capacity, implies full spare capacity, and would give too large a pumping increment. Normal inflow is much less than peak capacity, making it undesirable to run one high-capacity pump. *If three pumps are used, each having 50% capacity, then as in flow increase the second and third pumps would start sequentially; such a system will have a margin of safety and a smaller pumping increment.*

11. Flood protetion

The only tunnels subjected to serious flooding are subaqueous, either in tidal areas or in flood plains of rivers. Where possible, flooding should be prevented by raising the elevation of the approaches above maximum flood levels. Where this is too expensive or impractical, flood gates must be installed.

It may be possible to raise the approach walls above the flood level and install flood barriers at the upper end of the open approaches. This would be less expensive than raising the approach elevation and would prevent flooding of the tunnel and the open approaches.

Flood gates installed at the tunnel portals will provide a closure to restrain rising flood waters from entering the tunnel and permit collection of flood water at the portals. These gates are constructed of steel and designed to withstand the hydraulic forces present during maximum flood conditions. The gate travels in vertical frames and seals against a seat built into the roadway to minimize the leakage into the tunnel. An enclosure may be provided above the gate while it is in its raised or stored position.

Leakage criteria should be established for each portal flood gate installation and should be considered in the selection of pumps for the tunnel pumping stations.

Valves are required on the flood gate to permit rapid drainage of the water collected in front of the gates prior to raising the gates. This water can be drained and permitted to enter the tunnel drainage system prior to raising the gates. Gate valves of a minimum 2.5in (63.5mm) size with threaded connection for 2.5in(63.5mm) hose are most appropriate for this application.

In subaqueous tunnels where there are no portal pump stations, the open approach drain lines are connected to the tunnel drainage system. A means must be provided to isolate these two systems during flooding to prevent the ingress of flood waters through the open drainpipes, which could cause flooding of the tunnel. A method of providing such isolation is to place a shut-off valve in a valve box on the tunnel side of each portal flood gate. This will permit inspection of the valve to confirm that the drainpipe leading from the open approach is clear of debris and can be sealed tightly against the flood waters.

Testing. The floodgate should be tested against a head of water equal to the maximum flood level anticipated. This test is required to assure that the leakage criteria are not exceeded. Construction of a watertight bulkhead on the open approach side of the flood gate will permit development of such a head and testing of the flood gate.

Operation. When flood conditions are imminent, the flood gates should be lowered to seal the tunnel portals. The drainage system isolation valves, along with the dewatering valves on the flood gates, must be in the closed position at this time.

12. Drainage of rail tunnels

Rail tunnels include both those carrying railroad trains and those carrying rapid transit trains, with both ballast and concrete roadbeds. A railroad tunnel with ballast is usually drained by installing a perforated pipe below the track ballast. Where there is no ballast used, such as in a rapid transit tunnel, an open channel or drainage trough is often used. The drainage water is carried through this channel to inlets located at specified intervals. These inlets permit the water to enter the gravity flow line, thus transporting the water either to a low-point sump, in the case of a subaqueous tunnel, or to the low portal in the case of a mountain tunnel.

The water quantity anticipated in the rail tunnel drainage system will consist of water from fire-fighting operations, vehicle drippings, seepage, or rainfall on the approach tracks and onopenings to the surface.

1) Subway

Drainage in the subway portion of a rail rapid transit system is accomplished by use of a center channel tocollect and transport water, which is then piped to pump station located at each low point.

2) System descriptions

Drainage system with two low points. The Trans-Bay Tube is a 4.5mile (7.25km) subaqueous rapid transit crossing of the San Francisco Bay in California. It is a part of the Bay Area Rapid Transit system. This tunnel has two low points. The Drainage system consists of two low-point pump stations, four intermediate-gallery pump stations located at changes in grades, and two ventilation-structure pump stations. The four intermediate-gallery pump stations are arranged so that two comprise the intermediate pump stations at grade changes and two are included in the low-point pump stations.

The drainage water is collected and transported in the open channel located between the rails in the concrete roadbed and then collected either at the intermediate points or at the low points. At the intermediate point, the water is collected in a trackway sump and then flows by gravity into the intermediate sumps, from which it is pumped through the main discharge line to the pump station located in the ventilation structure at the rear end of the tunnel, either in Oakland or in San Francisco. At the tunnel low point, the water is collected in a trackway sump, drained by gravity to the gallery sump, and then pumped into the main sump of the low-point pump station. From the low-point sump station, the water is pumped through the main discharge line to the vent structure pump station and then discharged to the surface.

This system is equipped with an emergency bypass arrangement, whereby either low-point pump station can pump its effluent to either ventilation structure; this provides a method of removing water should there be a break in either end of the discharge line. A recirculating arrangement has also been build into this system to provide the means to exercise the pumps with a minimum of water in the sumps.

Drainage system with one low point. The Potomac River Crossing, on the Huntington Route of the Washington Metro, is a 6000ft (1830m) subaqueous rail tunnel. It is a double-track, two-bore tunnel. The water is drained from the trackway by an imbedded drainage pipe. The water will flow in an open channel to drain inlet sumps, which are spaced approximately 300ft (90m) on centers. Through these inlets, the water enters the imbedded gravity drain line and then flows to the low-point pump station, which is of a package construction with two pumps. The water is then pumped to the surface through a pressure discharge line.

Text B To Drain or to Seal
排 或 堵

1. Inflow in the construction phase

Heading inflows occur when a water-bearing zone is penetrated during tunneling. Appropriate resources (pumps etc.) must be available on site, because inflows are very difficult to predict. Water inrush can be critical, especially if the tunnel is headed downhill or starting from a shaft. The flow rate can be very high (cases with more than 1000L/s are reported), but usually slows down quickly as the water stored in the rock is depleted. If not, one possible countermeasure is to grout the water carrying joints using cement mortars with up to 10% sodium silicate or polyure than foams. A successful grouting may require the reduction of the water inrush by pressure relief (achieved with draining boreholes or with diaphragm walls).

During heading of the Tecolate pressure tunnel in California water inrushes at the face of up to 580L/s were encountered. The water had a temperature of 40℃. A source with a supply of 180L/s could not be plugged in with grouting and the heading had to be stopped for 16 months. Also the construction of the road tunnel at Füssen was considerably delayed in 1996/97 by water inrush (Figure 12.1). During construction of the 8.6km long twin tube Hallandsas tunnel of the Swedish rail, water inrushes up to $15m^3$/min were encountered. Grouting with cement did not help; therefore a chemical product based on acrylamide was grouted. Usually, this toxic substance is bonded and therefore harmless. In this case, however, the ground water velocity was too high and the bonding was incomplete. As a result, the environment was contaminated. Within an area of $10km^2$ all agricultural products were spoilt and 24 wells of drinking water had to be abandoned.

a)Füssen tunnel   b)Simplon tunnel

Figure 12.1 Water Inrush

Clearly, groundwater and other waters must be withdrawn from the tunnel. In case of water-sensitive rock (e.g. rock containing dispersive clay minerals), the contact with water should be minimized.

The water ingress into tunnels can be measured by dams in the tunnel floor and an overflow V-notch. The acceptable limits of water ingress depend on the excavation method (e.g. $2.0 \sim 2.5$ m^3/m for TBM $= 0.5 m^3/m$ for drill and blast).

2. To drain or to seal

Tunnels below the groundwater table can be either sealed or drained. Sealed tunnels do not influence the groundwater but their lining has to support the full water pressure. This is technically possible down to depths of 60m below the groundwater table. The hydrostatic pressure can be relieved if the tunnel is drained. Note, however, that also a drained tunnel can be sealed (waterproofed) in the sense that the water is guided to the longitudinal drainage pipes but is not allowed to enter the tunnel interior.

Drainage can influence the surrounding groundwater considerably. An intermediate solution is the so-called partial pressure relief: The pressure is limited by special valves. This solution reduces the disturbance of the groundwater. The condition "sealed" can be easily changed to "drained" by the appearance of cracks in the lining or by opening a valve in the circumferential drainage. Note, however, that a redistribution of pore pressure and the corresponding discharge of pore water will need some time, which can be considerable in case of soil/rock with low permeability.

3. Drainage

Drainage affects the distribution of hydraulic head by attracting groundwater and relieving the lining from hydrostatic pressure. The groundwater is then collected and appropriately discharged. These needs to be achieved in a permanent way and maintenance must always be possible. It should be added that there are tunnels, exclusively devoted to drainage, e.g. to stabilize a slope. The drainage path of the groundwater is as follows:

(1) The groundwater penetrates the shotcrete shell through fissures and bored holes (to enhance the mobility of groundwater towards the drainage system, radial boreholes may be drilled into the ground).

(2) The interface drainage systems consist either of fleece (for low discharge) or of composite geosynthetics or air-gap membranes (for high discharge) and are placed in the interspace between shotcrete and concrete lining. There are many types of geosynthetics (so-called geospacers), designed to provide a stable interspace for water discharge. Higher water discharges emanating from local sources are caught with separate pipes and guided to the drainage pipes (Figure 12.2).

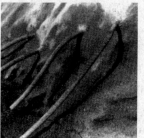

Figure 12.2 Draining Pipes in Shotcrete, Connection to Main Drainage

This area drainage receives the groundwater flowing to the crown and the sides of the tunnel and guides it to the longitudinal drainage pipes, which are installed at the merges of the sides with the invert (Figure 12.3). The interface drainage and the drainage pipes are embedded within granular filters ("dry pack"), the pipes are perforated in their upper parts (Figure 12.4).

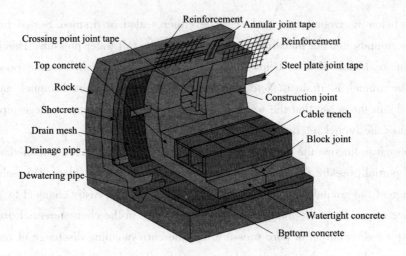

Figure 12.3 Drainage of a Rail Tunnel

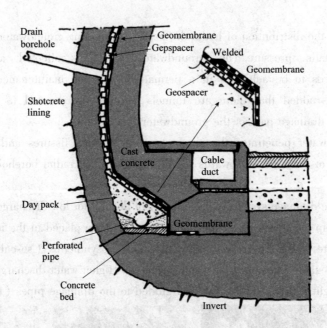

Figure 12.4 Example for Drainage into the Side Pipe

(3) Transversal slots guide the groundwater from the side pipes to the main collector which is placed underneath the carriageway.

(4) The groundwater flowing into the tunnel invert is collected in a similar way, i. e. with a granular filter and a perforated pipe in longitudinal direction, placed in the deepest part of the invert.

· 254 ·

Polluted water and other liquids are drained from the carriageway into longitudinal pipes. The access to these pipes is given either via gullies or slots. An aim of this drainage system is to collect leaking inflammable fluids in case of accidents. The polluted water is temporarily piped into reservoirs outside the tunnel to be treated elsewhere later.

The longitudinal pipes underneath the carriageway are accessible via shafts (manholes) for inspection and cleaning. The longitudinal pipes along the tunnel sides are accessible via niches. The cleaning is performed with pressurized water (up to 150 bars at the nozzle) at a discharge of up to 500L/min. The details of cleaning should be contained in a manual of maintenance.

The following items are of interest with respect to drainage:

Clogging: Drainage can be clogged by sintering (i. e. precipitation of carbonates) and/or fouling. Calcium (lime), dissolved in groundwater, can precipitate due to changes of pressure, temperature, pH, entrance of oxygen and interaction with cement. Countermeasures are (apart from regular cleaning) siphoning the drainage lines (to prevent contact with air) and use of hardness stabilizers. Asparagine acid impedes the precipitation of carbonates. It can be added as a fluid to drainage pipes (if the water discharge is more than 1-2L/s) or it can be placed into the drainage system as solid cubes. This additive reduces the amount of sinter and renders it softer. Maintenance (cleaning) of the drainage pipes is very costly and inhibits the operation of tunnels. The same holds for the related inspections which are preferably done by video scanning. The cleaning of clogged pipes is done with water jets, as explained before. Alternatively, chain and rope flails or impact drilling cutters can be used. The German Rail (DB) had to pay up to 60 € per m tunnel drainage annually for cleaning the drainage. Therefore, German Rail tunnels are now generally sealed.

Temporary drainage: Localized outflow of water impedes the application of shotcrete or waterproofing geomembranes. Therefore, a temporary drainage must be provided for to catch and divert the water. This can be achieved, e. g., with semi-cylindrical flexible pipes or with strips.

Porous concrete: It has a void ratio = 15%, and consequently, a high permeability and a reduced strength. To obtain such a high porosity, gap graded aggregates, recommendably siliceous ones, should be used. The cement content should be no less than $350kg/m^3$ and its chemical composition should not enhance clogging.

Text C Tunnel Waterproofing
隧 道 防 水

Waterproofing: Above the groundwater table, a tunnel has to be protected against downwards percolating water. This is achieved with a so-called umbrella waterproofing. Below the groundwater table, groundwater is pressurized so that an all-embracing waterproofing must be applied. Up to water pressure of 3 bars, water-tight concrete can be used, above 3 bars, and up to approximately 15 bars, watertight membranes should be used in addition. The sealing membrane is fixed between the outer and inner linings. For pressures higher than 15 bars in permeable rock, a sealing ring around the tunnel has to be obtained with advance grouting. When advance grouting proves to be insufficient, post-grouting can be applied. At any rate, advance grouting should be tried first, as it is much more efficient and economic than post-grouting.

A properly fabricated cast concrete is watertight if some conditions, regarding the grain size distribution of the aggregates and the water content, are adhered to. In this case, its pores are not interconnected and the concrete can be considered as impermeable (for thicknesses = 30cm). Its impermeability can only be reduced by fissures, which may appear due to too large tensile stresses, temperature gradient, creep and shrinkage. With respect to watertight concrete attention should be paid to:

Hydration heat: This is produced during the setting process. The subsequent cooling may lead to incompatible stressing and, thus, to fissures. Remedies are late dismantling of formwork, heat isolating formwork, cooling of the aggregates and of the mixing water and long (10-14 days) moistening of the concrete.

Shrinkage: Only a part of the mixing water is chemically bonded (corresponding to ca 25% of the cement mass). The remaining water occupies the pores. Thus, low water content helps to keep the porosity small. Shrinkage is due to the evaporation of the free water. Thin parts are more prone to shrinkage, their length reduction corresponds to the one caused by a temperature reduction of 15-20℃.

Cement: Portland cement is preferably used for watertight concrete, while blast furnace slag cement produces less heat but needs longer time for setting.

Longitudinal reinforcement reduces the spacing and the width of the fissures but does not avoid them. The only remedy is to keep short sections of concreting. On the other hand, too many joints should be avoided. As a compromise, sections of ca 12-20m length are usually applied. To avoid fissures due to inhibited contraction, the shotcrete should be separated from the cast concrete lining with a foil.

An advantage of watertight concrete (as compared with synthetic membrane) is that leakages can be easily localized, whereas in case of membranes the leaking water is spread.

It should be noted that the watertightness of tunnels is often over-emphasized and the related measures are overdone. Some droplets of water are in most cases tolerable. What should be avoided (especially in road tunnels) are water puddles, reduction of visibility due to inrushing water, black ice and icicles. It should also be taken into account that, in the end, every waterproof lining will have some leakages so that what counts more is the reduction of the related damage (e. g. with drainages of the leaking water and vents for grouting) and provisions for an easy repair.

Geosynthetics intunneling: Geosynthetics are applied for drainage (geospacers, geocomposite drains) and for waterproofing (geomembranes). Polyester should not be used, as it can be destroyed by hydrolysis in alkaline environment, such as concrete. PVC (polyvinyl chloride) produces hydrochloric acid in case of fire. It may, however, be used if it is covered by concrete lining. Geomembranes are not mounted directly on the rough shotcrete lining. To protect them against puncturing or tearing, a geotextile or geocomposite protective barrier of 600 to 1200 g/m^2 is interposed. Geomembrane strips are mounted with synthetic disks and welded with each other. This is done with hot air of 200-300℃, which, however, must not deteriorate the underlying protective barrier.

II. Terms and terminology

wall-washing	侧墙清洗
leakage	渗漏
water mains	总水管;给水总管
hose valve	水带阀门;消火栓阀
fire extinguisher	灭火器
water deluge system	大水量喷洒系统
exhaust fan	抽风机;排风机
hose	软管
hose station	墙式消火栓
hose stream	消防射流
roadheader	巷道掘进机
municipal water line	市政供水管
gpm	每分钟加仑数(gallons per minute)
discharge rate	排水速率
run-off	径流
detergent	清洁剂;去垢剂
superelevation	超高
transverse interceptor	横向截水沟
clogging	堵塞
pump station	水泵房,泵站
sump	水坑,污水坑
centrifugal pump	离心泵
flood gate	防洪闸,潮门;坞门;水闸
invert	仰拱
porous concrete	多孔混凝土
geosynthetic	土工合成材料
geomembrane	土工膜;隔泥网膜
PVC (polyvinyl chloride)	聚氯乙烯

III. Questions and difficult sentence analysis

1. Questions for brainstorming discussion

(1) Why is water supply needed in operation phase of rail tunnels or highway tunnels?
(2) Please list the types of principal water supplies to tunnel.
(3) Discuss the types of water to be discharged through drainage system in tunnels.

2. Difficult sentences analysis

(1) Highway, subway, and rapid transit tunnels are usually provided with water mains, hose valves, and fire extinguishers and, in some instances, with water deluge systems on the exhaust fans. Railroad tunnels, because of their extreme length, are usually not provided with water mains.

译文：公路隧道、铁路隧道和高速交通隧道通常都安装输水总管、软管阀门及灭火器，有些隧道中还在排气扇上安装雨水排除系统。由于铁路隧道很长，通常不安装水总管。

(2) The water main within the tunnel should also be valved to separate sections to permit repair of a damaged section while minimizing any reduction in fire protection. This can be accomplished by installing sectionalizing valves, provided two sources of water supply are available.

译文：隧道内的水总管应该安装阀门，将管道分成几段，便于修理损坏部分，同时尽量减少消防用水的损失。如果可提供两个水源，可以安装分段阀门。

(3) For normal drainage design a 10-year storm frequency is used; however, for a tunnel where flooding is a serious concern, such as a subaqueous tunnel, a 100-year storm frequency should be considered.

译文：常规设计采用10年重现期，但是，对于洪水是一个隧道严重关注的问题时，如水下隧道，应该考虑100年一遇的暴雨。

(4) If three pumps are used, each having 50% capacity, then as in flow increase the second and third pumps would start sequentially; such a system will have a margin of safety and a smaller pumping increment.

译文：如果使用3台水泵，每台水泵的容量为50%，如果水流增大，可依次采用第2台和第3台水泵。这种系统即具有安全裕度同时泵增加量较小。

IV. Translation case study

Case 1

Chinese	English translation
模筑混凝土本身就具有一定的抗渗阻水性能，但普通混凝土的抗渗性较差，尤其是在施工质量不高的情况下，如振捣不密实，施工缝，沉降缝，伸缩缝处理不好，配比不当等，则更易形成水的渗漏、漫流。当地下水有侵蚀性时，对混凝土的腐蚀就更为严重。如果能保证混凝土衬砌的抗渗防水性能，则不需要另外增加其他防水堵水措施。因此，充分利用混凝土衬砌的防水性能，是经济合算的和最基本的防水措施。	Form concreting itself has certain permeability resistance and water resistance performance, but common concrete is of poor permeability resistance, especially in the case of poor construction quality. For example, in cases of uncompacted vibratory mixing, poor handling of construction joint, settlement joint and movement joint and improper mixing ratio, leakage and cross flow will occur. When there exists groundwater erosion, concrete corrosion becomes even more severe. If the permeation resistance and waterproofing performance of concrete lining can be ensured, no additional waterproofing and water resistancewaterblocking measures are necessary. Hence, full utilization of the waterproofing performance of concrete lining is the economically worthwhile and most essential waterproofing measure.

Case 2

Chinese	English translation
在运营期间,地下水常从混凝土衬砌的施工缝、变形缝(伸缩缝和沉降缝)、裂缝甚至混凝土孔隙等通道,渗漏进隧道中。造成洞内通信、供电、照明等设备处于潮湿环境而发生锈蚀;使路面积水或结冰,造成打滑,危及行车安全;由于结冰膨胀和侵蚀性地下水的作用,不仅使衬砌受到破坏,而且使得以上危害更加严重。总之隧道工程中,地下水的存在是必然的,但它对工程的危害却是可以避免和减少的。	In operation stage, groundwater often ingresses into tunnel through such passages as the construction joints, deformation joints (movement joint and settlement joint), cracks in concrete lining even voids in concrete, which causes the tunnel communication, power supply and illumination facilities situated in moist environment, induces rust and corrosion; brings about water catchments on road surface creating slippery road surface and endangering traffic safety. Due to actions of icing-induced expansion and erosive groundwater, not only the linings are subjected to damages but also above mentioned hazards are getting worse and worse. In general, in tunneling, groundwater is inevitable but its harm and damages to the tunnel works can be avoided and reduced.

Case 3

Chinese	English translation
如果有城市供水系统,它应该是所有隧道用水的首选。如果城市供水线路距离隧道较近,其流速和水压足以满足隧道供水对水流和水压的要求,这是一个有效的供水途径。但是,如果城市输水管线距离隧道较远,采用另外水源会更经济,该水源应为隧道专用水源,利用地下水、河流或湖泊并配合采用蓄水池及消防水泵。	A municipal water supply system should be the prime choice as a water source for any tunnel when it is available. This is a valid approach provided that the municipal water lines are relatively close and have a flow rate and pressure adequate to meet the flow and pressure criteria required of the tunnel. If, however, the municipal water lines are not within a reasonable distance from the tunnel, it may be less costly to provide another means of water supply. This could be a dedicated system by using an underground water supply, a river, or a lake, together with a storage tank and fire pumps.

V. Assignment

(1)在隧道施工期间,地下水的作用不仅降低围岩的稳定性(尤其是对软弱破碎围岩影响更为严重),增加开挖难度,且增加了支护的难度和费用,甚至需采取超前支护或预注浆堵水和加固围岩。

(2)在运营期间,地下水常从混凝土衬砌的施工缝、变形缝(伸缩缝和沉降缝)、裂缝甚至混凝土孔隙等通道,渗漏进隧道中,造成洞内通信、供电、照明等设备处于潮湿环境而发生锈蚀;使路面积水或结冰,造成打滑,危及行车安全。

(3)隧道常用的堵水措施有:喷射混凝土堵水,塑料板堵水,衬砌堵水。当水量水压都较大时,则可采取注浆堵水;注浆既可以堵水也可以起到加固围岩的作用。

(4)隧道内的排水一般均采用排水沟方式,类型主要有中心排水沟和路侧排水沟,在严寒地区应设置防冻排水沟。

(5)为避免和减少水的危害,中国隧道工作者总结出"防、排、截、堵相结合"的综合治水原则,并以模筑混凝土衬砌作为防水(堵水)的基本措施。

Unit 13   Tunnel Safety Provisions
隧道安全规定

I. Text

Text A   Tunnel Safety Introduction
隧道安全概述

At one time, tunnel accidents claimed one life for every half mile of tunnel conducted. Increased concern over construction safety has led to improvements in the miner's working conditions, with a subsequent reduction in the frequency of deaths and disabling accidents. However, based on 1986 OSHA statistics, lost-time accidents still occur at more than twice the frequency for underground workers compared with other construction workers, and three times the rate for manufacturing workers. Approximately the same adverse ratio applies to fatalities. Obviously, there is a need for more improvements in safety for underground workers.

In discussing safety provisions, we must keep two facts in mind. First—and contrary to some beliefs—accidents are not inevitable. Second, accidents are extremely costly, and so accident prevention makes sound economic sense.

The major causes of accidents are:

(1) Uncontrolled contact between personnel and materials or equipment.
(2) Failure of temporary structures.
(3) Inherent constructional hazards such as the sue of explosives.
(4) Unsafe practices or carelessness by individual workers.

The employer must recognize these causes and establish programs, rules, regulations, guidelines, and whatever else might be necessary to reduce accidents. Reducing the number and severity of accidents reduces many costs in addition to insurance and other items obviously affected by accidents. Injured employee, but also lost time of coworkers due to general work stoppage; lost time of supervisors attending to the injured person, investigating and preparing accident report; costs associated with damaged equipment or property; as well as many other partially hidden costs. Adherence to safety regulations in the sensitive tunnel construction industry is the prudent economic course to follow.

1. Safety engineer and safety program

On virtually every underground project, the contractor is required to employ at least one full-time, properly qualified safety engineer. On the same project, owners and engineers often have their own safety engineers who visit the project occasionally. In the early stages of construction planning, the contractor's safety engineer should design a safety program tailored to the project. All personnel should be obliged to comply with the provisions of the program. It is often desirable to offer incentives or rewards in the safety program to encourage active, enthusiastic participation.

All personnel should be instructed on the recognition of hazards, observance of precaution, and use of protective and emergency equipment in enclosed underground spaces. When personnel are underground, an accurate record of their location must be kept on the surface.

On tunnel operation with 25 or more workers underground, at least two rescue crews should be trained in rescue procedures and the use of oxygen breathing apparatus and fire-fighting equipment. At least one crew should be trained in routine safety operations. A safety inspection of the job site, including all materials and equipment, should be made at least once per shift.

2. Emergency measures

Tunnel excavation plans and procedures should be developed and make known. These plans should incorporate a separate communications system independent of the tunnel power supply as well as provisions for emergency hoisting or other egress in shafts.

3. Protective Clothing

Tunnel personnel should wear protective head gear (helmet), footwear (safety shores or safety boots), and any other special garments that applicable codes require. Safety glasses, rubber gloves, goggles, or face shields should be worn when handling corrosive, toxic or injurious substances and should be made available for use when required. Working molten metal (e.g. welding) requires fire-resistant clothing and face shields. Moving machinery necessitates the wearing of snug-fitting clothes, and handling of sharp, rough, and splintery material requires protective gloves. In New York, the state's Industrial Code Rule governing tunneling operations (called the New York State Regulations) also requires waterproof clothing in wet areas and safety belts for shaft workers where the drop is 10ft or more. Other jurisdictions may have other specific protective clothing requirements.

4. General precautions

Specific working areas in underground construction can have their own unique hazards that personnel should be made aware of. These hazards should be addressed in the safety program.

Safe means of access and egress should be available in all working areas, and all ladders and stairways should comply with applicable code requirements. Subsidence areas presenting safety hazards should be fenced and posted. In New Jersey, the Construction Safety Code requires the surface working site to be walled or fenced to a height of 8ft again; other jurisdictions may have other requirements for overall construction sites and/or specific areas.

The crown, face, and walls of rock excavation areas should be tested frequently, and loose rock scaled down or supported. Rock bolts should be tested frequently for proper torque with a calibrated torque wrench. All steel or timber ground support sets should be properly installed and blocked to prevent movement of rock, and lateral bracing can be provided between sets to further stabilize the support. Damaged or dislodged tunnel supports must be required or replaced immediately. Properly designed shields, forepoling, or other devices should be provided as required for soft ground tunneling. Suitable provisions for breasting the face should also be incorporated.

Walls, ladders, timbers, blocking wedges, and supports should be inspected for loosening following blasting operations. Corrections to unsafe areas must be made immediately.

Safety belts should be worn by crews on skips and platforms in shafts when the clear distance between the skip or cage and the sides of the shaft is greater than 1ft, unless guard rails are provided. The New York State Regulations provide much more extensive and detailed precautions to be observed in the shafts and hoisting operations.

In caisson work in compressed air, a protective bulkhead should be erected in the working chamber when the chamber is less than 11ft in height and the caissons are at any time suspended or hung so that the bottom of the excavation is more the 19ft below the deck of the working chamber while work is in progress. Shafts must be made tight and hydrostatic, or air pressure tested. The test pressure must be stamped on the outside shell about 12in from each flange. Accurate and accessible gauges should be located in the lock and on either side of each bulkhead. Caissons greater than 10ft in diameter or width should be provided with a manlock and shaft exclusively for personnel.

5. Localized operational hazards

All equipment to be used during a shift should be inspected before use by either the prospective user or a supervisor. Unsafe equipment should be repaired immediately or removed from any location where it might accidentally be used.

Safety in drilling: Before drilling, the roof must be scaled down by an experienced miner, and the area inspected and made safe from all potential hazards. All personnel should be warned of the possibility of residual explosives from previous blasting. Lifter holes should not be drilled through previously blasted rock. No one should be allowed on a drill boom while the drill is in operation, and no one except the driver should be allowed on a moving jumbo. Jumbos should have storage receptacles for drill steel, a mechanical heavy materials lifter, stair access to decks for at least two people, and removable guard rails on all sides and at the back of platforms if the deck is more than 10ft high. When a jumbo is being moved, equipment should be secured and booms should be in a safe position. Drills on columns should be anchored firmly before drilling, and retightened frequently. Scaling bars should always be sharp and in good condition. Water, air, or other utility lines in the area of the drilling should be clearly identified.

Safety in blasting: The blaster should be fully qualified to handle and use explosives safely as required. All jurisdictions require the blaster to be licensed.

Only the explosives or blasting agents required for one blast should be taken underground. Explosives and blasting agents should be hoisted, lowered, or conveyed in a special powder car. The hoist operator should be notified before explosives are transported in a shaft, and personnel, material, supplies, detonators, or equipment should not be transported in the same conveyor with the explosives. Explosives should not be transported in unmarked conveyances or in a locomotive during man-haul trips. *A physical separation of 24in, should divide the compartments of detonators and explosives in a vehicle, and no one except the operator, his helper, and the powderman should be permitted to ride in a vehicle or train transporting explosives and blasting agents.*

Trucks used for the transportation of explosives underground should have the electrical system checked for electrical hazards, and a written record of such inspections should be kept on fire.

Explosives must be stored in the types of facilities required by relevant regulations and specifications. Permanent storage of explosives or blasting agents should not be permitted underground unless at least two modes of exit for personnel have been provided. However, most jurisdictions prohibit any storage of explosives underground where men are employed.

Smoking and open flames should not be permitted within 50ft of explosives and detonator storage magazines. Blasting caps, detonating primers and primed cartridges should not be stored in the same magazine with other explosives or blasting agents. Nor should detonator magazines be located closer than 50ft to a magazine containing explosives.

6. Hauling

Powdered mobile equipment should be provided with adequate brakes, audible warning devices, and lights at each end. Visible or audible warning should be given before equipment is started and moved. Cabs should have clean windows constructed of safety glass.

Adequate backstops or brakes should be installed on inclined conveyor drive units. No one should ride on power driven chains, belts, or bucket conveyors, in dippers, shovel buckets, forks or clamshells, in the beds of dump trucks, or on haulage equipment.

Electrically powdered mobile equipment should not be left unattended unless the master switch is in the off position, all operating controls are in the neutral position, and the brakes are set. Parked railcars should be blocked securely. Means should be provided to prevent overtravel and overturning at dumping locations and at all track deadends. Rocker-bottom or bottom-dump cars should have positive-locking devices. Supplies, materials, and tools (other than hand tools) should not accompany personnel on man-trip cars. Equipment that is being hauled should be protected against sliding or spillage.

The most recent OSHA regulations as well as the regulations of other agencies address haulage specifics concerning braking requirements, whether personnel-carrying work trains can be pushed or must be pulled, the prevention of injuries when derailments occur, and many other items. These regulations must be consulted when formulating haulage plans.

7. Hoisting

Hoisting machines should be worm-geared or powered both ways, and if the power is stopped, the load should not move. Power hoist controls should have a nonlocking switch or control, and a device to deactivate the power should be installed ahead of the operating control. Hoist machines with cast metal parts should not be used. All anchorages of hoists should be inspected at the beginning of each shift, and every hoist should be annually tested to at least twice the maximum load.

Recently OSHA, other agencies and even crane manufacturers have promulgated more stringent regulations regarding the hoisting of personnel. All of these sources must be consulted when equipment for hoisting personnel is being considered.

An enclosed covered metal cage designed with a safety factor of 4 should be used to raise and lower personnel in the shaft. The cage must be load tested prior to use, and the exterior should be free of projections or sharp corners. Only closed shackles should be used in the cage rigging, and a positive locking device should be installed on the cage to prevent the door from opening accidentally while in operation. Maximum rates of speed for transporting persons should be established and adhered to in accordance with the applicable regulations, whether federal or local, and signal codes should be employed in the operation of the hoist.

8. First aid station

Weatherproof first aid kits should be provided at appropriate locations. These kits should contain materials recommended by the consulting physician and should conform to Red Cross standards with individual sealed packages for each item. The contents of the first aid kit should be checked by the safety engineer before being released for use and at least weakly to ensure that expended items are replaced. Equipment for prompt transportation of an injured person to service should be provided. The New York State Regulations and most other jurisdictions also require that blankets and at least one stretcher per 100 workers underground be made available.

Sufficient competent personnel (with at least one person currently certified in first aid training) should be available either on or near the work site to perform first aid or any rescue work that may be required in the tunnel. Many agencies and/or project specifications may require more on-site first aid/or other medical personnel. This usually depends on the size and complexity of the underground work.

Provisions should be made to ensure the availability of medical personnel for continual consultation and of prompt medical attention in case of serious injury. The telephone numbers of the doctors, hospitals, and ambulances should be posted in conspicuous locations.

9. Fire hazards

Matches, lighters or other flame-producing smoking materials must be prohibited in all underground operations where fire or explosion hazards exist. It is preferable that this restriction apply in all underground work, whether known fire hazards exist or not. Gasoline or liquefied petroleum gases should not be taken underground. Paper, combustible rubbish, and scrap wood should not be allowed to accumulate. Only the current day's supply of diesel fuel should be stored underground, the oil, grease, and fuel should be stored underground, and they should be well sealed and kept a safe distance from sensitive areas. Only approved fire-resistant hydraulic fluids should be used in hydraulically operated equipment. Air that has passed through underground oil or fuel storage areas must not be used to ventilate working areas. When compressed-gas cylinders are being moved to a new location underground, the safety caps for protecting the cylinder valves should be secured in place.

Noncombustible barriers should be installed below welding or burning operations in or over a shaft or raise. During and for 30min after welding or flame cutting underground, a person with a fire extinguisher should stand by.

Fire extinguishers should be provided at the head and tail pulleys of underground belt conveyors, at 300ft intervals along the belt line, and wherever combustible materials are stored. These extinguishers must be suitable for extinguishing fires of wood, oil, grease, and electrical equipment. Other fire-fighting equipment or fire barriers may be required on certain projects.

Bureau of mines—approved self-rescuers (in good condition) should be available near the advancing heading, on the haulage equipment, and in any area where personnel could be trapped by smoke or gas.

All electrical cables taken or used underground should be completely encased in an armored, noncombustible casing or jacket. Power lines should be well separated or insulated from water lines, telephone lines, and air lines. Oil-filled transformers should not be used underground unless they are in a fire-resistant enclosure.

Caution must be exercised when relying on local codes governing electrical equipment. For example, the New York State Regulations are far more comprehensive with regard to electrical equipment safety in tunnels than many other codes.

10. Ventilation during construction

Major tunnel explosion disasters thatoccurred in 1970s and 1980s provided much of the impetus for updating of underground safety regulations which define gassy, potentially gassy, and nongassy areas, and stipulate strict adherence to specify safety guidelines for each type of area. Regulations are designed and promulgated to promote better understanding of the hazardous conditions of gassy atmospheres and the safety precautions that must be taken to prevent accidents. Top management as well as safety engineers must be aware of the possible gassy conditions on a project and must comply with whatever regulations govern in providing proper safety for the site and the personnel.

Testing for the presence of gasses at principal work locations should be conducted continuously. Other locations should be spot-checked frequently. The allowable quantities given in following table were taken from the "Threshold limit Values". Many similar tables are available. Some include quantities, and others include times of exposure and other more detailed information.

The presence of flammable or toxic gases, mists, and fumes should be determined and if 1.5% or higher concentrations are detected, personnel should be evacuated and power cut off to the affected area until concentrations are reduced to 1% or less. A record of all tests should be kept on file.

Gas detection equipment has been vastly improved and simplified in recent years. Easy-to-operate gas detectors that can be equipped to monitor virtually any gas that might be encountered in an underground project are on the market. All detectors have both visual and audio alarms, and most have digital readouts. Some detectors even record and retain the information from an entire shift of gas monitoring: this data can be plugged into a computer to generate readout of the gases detected, concentrations, times, etc. Choosing the appropriate gas detection equipment for an individual project is an important task for the safety engineer and project manager. The allowable quantities of various gases is shown in table 13.1.

Allowable Quantities of Various Gases Table 13.1

Gas	Maximum allowable quantity
Carbon monoxide	50ppm
Carbon dioxide	5000ppm
Methane	1%
Nitrogen dioxide	5ppm
Nitric oxide	25ppm
Hydrogen sulfide	10ppm

a. from "threshold Limit values" safety regulation No. 3 New Jersey Department of Labor and Industry

11. Air quality maintenance

Tunnels should be provided with mechanically induced reversible-flow primary ventilation for all work areas. Ventilation doors should be self-closing and remain closed regardless of direction of flow. When primary ventilation has been discontinued for any reason, employees should be evacuated and qualified personnel should examine the tunnel for gas and other hazards before activating power or readmitting employees to the work areas.

The supply of fresh air should not be less than $200 ft^3/min$ per employee, and the velocity should be at least 30ft/min where conditions can produce harmful dusts or gases. Respirators should not be used in place of environmental ventilation controls except in welding, blasting, and lead-burning operations. Internal combustion engines other than mobile diesel must not be used underground. After blasting, smoke and fumes should be exhausted through the vent line to the outside air.

Access to unattended underground work areas should be restricted by gates. Unused chutes, manways, or other openings should be tightly covered, bulkheaded, or fenced off and posted.

Should tunneling operations be interrupted, the heading should be securely supported. Hydraulic pressure or collapsible rams or struts should not be used for securing the faces of inactive headings. If a shield invert is below the water table, watchmen should be on duty at the heading at all times when excavation is suspended. However, used in some cases to monitor the heading.

If a tunnel is inactive for a relatively long period of time, it is recommended that a bulkhead with a valve be installed in the face. The valve should be opened frequently to check for water pressure or noxious fumes and before the bulkhead is removed.

12. Compressed-air work

A licensed physician, qualified and experienced in treating decompression illness and willing to enter a pressurized chamber, should be consulted prior to beginning work and be available whenever work is in progress. In addition, a fully equipped first aid station and a vehicle equipped with one litter should also be available.

Prospective compressed-air workers should be examined by the physician to determine if they are physically qualified for the work. If a worker is ill or injured, or has been absent for 10 days, he should be reexamined before returning to work under compressed air. In addition, compressed-air workers should be reexamined at least annually. The examination results should be kept on record along with the record of any decompression illnesses reported by the physician. The records should be available for inspection, and a copy should be sent to the Bureau of Labor Standards following a death, accident, injury, or decompression illness.

Under relevant regulations, a medical lock must be maintained whenever air pressure in the working chamber is increased above the atmospheric pressure. The lock must conform to the specifications in the regulations.

Identification badges must be furnished to the compressed-air workers indicating the worker's name, the nature of his job, the address of the medical lock, the phone number of the physician on the project, and instructions that in case unknown or doubtful cause of illness the wearer should be taken to the medical lock. The badge should be worn on and of the job at all times.

Records and communications: There should be one person who represents the employer and who is knowledgeable about and responsible for complying with compressed-air regulations. Every employee should be instructed in the rules concerning safety when working under compressed air. The time of decompression as shown in the applicable decompression table should be posted on each lock. Also, appropriate signal codes should be posted at workplace entrances. Communications should be maintained at all times among the following locations: working face, work chamber side of the man-lock door, the manlock, lock attendant's station, compressor plant, first aid station, emergency lock, and special decompression chamber.

For each shift, a record of each employee's time under air pressure and his decompression time must be kept by an employee remaining outside the lock near the entrance, and a copy of the record should be submitted to the physician after each shift.

Compression and decompression: All personnel going under air pressure for the first time should be instructed on how to avoid excessive discomfort.

Compression procedures: First minute, Up to 3psig maximum, hold to determine if any discomfort is experienced. Second minute, Raise uniformly at a maximum rate of 10psi/min.

When personnel signal discomfort, hold the existing pressure for 5min. If the discomfort does not cease after 5min. reduce pressure gradually until the discomfort eases. If it persists, release the affected parties from the lock. No one should be subjected to a pressure greater than 50psi. Decompression to normal atmospheric conditions must be in accordance with decompression tables.

Decompression proceeds by two or more stages, with a maximum of four for a working chamber pressure of 40psi or over. Stage 1 consists of a reduction in ambient pressure ranging from 10 to a maximum of 16psi, but in no instance will the pressure be reduced below 4psi at the end of stage 1. This reduction in pressure in stage 1 will always take place at a rate not greater than 5psi per minute. Further reduction in pressure will take placed during stage 2 and subsequent stages as required at a slower rate, but in no event at a rate greater than 1psi per minute.

If repetitive exposure to compressed air is required (more than once in 24 hours), the physician should establish and be responsible for compression and decompression procedures. The physician is also responsible for decanting methods, if these methods are required. In decanting, no more than 5min. should elapse in atmospheric pressure before recompression.

Manlocks and muck locks: Controlled decompression of employees from a compressed-air atmosphere must always take place, except in emergency. Except when the air pressure is below 12 psig and there is no danger of rapid flooding, each bulkhead in tunnels of 14ft or more in diameter, or an equivalent area, should have at least two locks—a manlock, the other a materials lock. If only a combination man and materials lock is required, the lock should be able to hold an entire heading shift. A lock attendant, responsible to the physician, should be at the controls of the manlock whenever men are in the working chamber or in the lock. If the air pressure is 12psi or above, decompression must be regulated by automatic controls supplemented by manual controls to allow the lock attendant to override the automatic controls if required. Manual controls for an emergency must also be provided inside the manlock. The manlock must contain the following equipment: a clock and a continuous recording pressure gauge outside the lock; a pressure gauge, a clock, and a thermometer inside the lock. In addition, 4in minimum diameter observation ports should be installed so the lock occupants can be observed from the chamber and free air side. Ventilation should be provided, and the temperature should be at least 70°F in the lock. The lock must contain 30ft^3 of air space per occupant and have 5ft clear headroom minimum at the center. Also, each bulkhead should have a pressure/gauge on both faces.

When locks are not in use and employees are in the working chamber, lock doors should be kept open to the working chamber. In an emergency, if the working force were to become disabled, provisions should provide for rescue parties to enter the tunnel quickly. A special decompression chamber to accommodate the entire force of employees being decompressed at the end of a shift should be provided whenever the required time of decompression exceeds 75min. This chamber is commonly known as the "Luxury Lock".

Special decompression chamber: The headroom in the special decompression chamber should be at least 7ft. For each person there should be 50ft^3 of air space, 4ft^2 of walking area, and 3ft^2 of seating space exclusive of lavatory space. The rated capacity of the chamber will be based on the stated minimum space per employee and should be posted. The capacity should not be exceeded except in case of emergency. Each special decompression chamber should be equipped with the following: clocks, pressure gauge, valve to control the supply and discharge of air, an oral communication system among the occupants, attendant and compression or plant, and an observation port at the entrance.

Seating space, at least 18 by 24in wide, should be provided per occupant, and normal sitting posture permitted. Proper and adequate toilet and washing facilities in a screened or enclosed recess should also be provided. Fresh pure drinking water should be available. Community drinking vessels should be prohibited.

Unless the special decompression chamber is serving as the manlock to atmospheric pressure, the chamber should be adjacent to the manlock on the atmospheric pressure side of the bulkhead.

Compressor plant: At all times a thoroughly experienced, competent, and reliable person should be on duty at the air control valves as a gauge tender, regulating the pressure in the working area. During tunneling operations, one gauge tender only should regulate the pressure in two headings, provided the gauge and controls are all in one direction.

The low air-compressor plant capacity should permit the work to be done safely and provide a margin to meet emergencies and repairs. Low air-compressor units should have at least two independent source of power supply. The compressors should be of sufficient capacity to maintain the necessary pressure in the working chamber even during periods of breakdown, repair, or emergency.

Switching from one independent source of power supply to the other should be done periodically to ensure the workability of the apparatus in an emergency. Duplicate low-pressure air feedlines and regulating valves should be provided between the source of air supply and a point beyond the locks, with one of the lines extending to within 100ft of the working face. All high-and low-pressure air supply lines should be equipped with check valves. Low-pressure air will be regulated automatically, but manual valves should be provided for emergency. The air intakes should be located at a place where fumes, exhaust gases, and other air contaminants will be at minimum. Gauges indicating the pressure in the working chamber should be installed in the compressor building, the lock attendant's station, and the employer's field office.

Bulkheads and safety screens: Intermediate bulkheads with locks, or intermediate safety screens, or both, are required where there is a danger of rapid flooding. The New York Regulations limit the length between work face and bulkhead to 1000ft if the possibility of rapid flooding exists.

In tunnels of 16ft or more in diameter, where there is a danger of rapid flooding, hanging walkways should be provided from the face to the manlocks, as high in the tunnel as practicable, with at least 6ft of headroom. Walkways should be constructed of noncombustible materials. Standard railing should be securely installed throughout the length of all walkways on open sides. Where walkways are ramped under safety screens, the walkway surface should be skid-proofed by cleats or by equivalent means. Bulkheads used to restrain compressed air should be tested to prove their ability to resist the highest air pressure expected to be used.

Ventilation and air quality: The working chamber should be well ventilated. The air in the work area should be analyzed at least once per shift and a record of analyses kept. Test results must fall within the threshold limit values set forth by the applicable regulations; otherwise, immediate corrective action must be taken. During the entire decompression period, forced ventilation of fresh air must be provided.

Whenever heat-producing equipment is used, a positive means of removing the heat buildup at the heading should be provided. The temperature of all working chambers should be maintained at temperatures not in excess of 850°F.

Sanitation: Clean, heated, lighted, and well-ventilated dressing rooms and drying rooms should be provided for all employees engaged in compressed-air work. Such rooms should contain suitable benches and lockers. Bathing accommodations (showers at the ration of 1 to 10 employees per shift), equipped with running hot and cold water and with suitable toilet accommodations (1 toilet for each 15 employees per shift) should be provided. All parts of caissons and other working compartments should be kept in a sanitary condition.

Fire prevention and protection: Proper fire-fighting equipment must be available for use at all times. While welding or flame cutting is being done, a firewatcher with extinguisher should stand by. Shafts and caissons containing flammable material of any kind should be provided with a fire hose arranged so that all points of the shaft or caisson are within reach of the hose stream.

Tunnels should be provided with a 2in minimum diameter water line extending into the working chamber and to within 100ft of the working place. The line should have hose outlets with 100ft of fire hose attached and maintained as follows: one at the working face, and one immediately inside of the bulkhead. In addition, hose outlets should be provided at 200ft intervals throughout the length of the tunnel, and 100ft of fire hose should be attached to the outlet nearest to the location of flammable material or any area where flame is being used.

Fire hose should be at least 1.5in in nominal diameter, and water pressure and supply should at all times be adequate for efficient operation of the type of nozzle used. The powerhouse, compressor house, and all buildings housing ventilating equipment should have at least one hose connection in the water line. A fire hose should be maintained within reach of any wood structure over or near shafts. The compressor building should be constructed of noncombustible material.

In addition to the fire hose protection required on every floor of every building used in connection with compressed air work, there should be at least one approved fire extinguisher of the proper type for the hazard involved. At least two approved fire extinguishers should be provided in the working chamber as follows: one at the working face, and one immediately inside the bulkhead (pressure side). Extinguishers in the working chamber must use water as the primary extinguishing agent and may not use any extinguishing agent that could be harmful to the employees in the working chamber. Highly combustible materials should not be used or stored in the working chamber.

Manlocks should be equipped with a manual fire extinguishing system that can be activated inside the manlock and also by the outside lock attendant. In addition, a fire hose and portable fire extinguisher should be provided inside and outside the manlock. The portable fire extinguisher should be constructed of noncombustible materials. Bedding and like materials must be chemically treated to be fire resistant. Headframes should be constructed of structural steel or open framework fireproofed timber. Temporary surface structures within 100ft of any shaft caisson, or tunnel opening should be built of fire-resistant materials.

Oil, gasoline, or other combustible material should not be stored within 100ft of any shaft, caisson, or tunnel opening.

However, oil may be stored in suitable tanks in fireproof buildings if the buildings are at least 500ft from any tunnel-connected building or opening. Positive means should be taken to prevent leaking flammable liquids from flowing into the tunnel-connected openings or buildings. The handling, storage, and use of explosives must comply with all applicable regulations in connection with compressed-air work.

Electricity: All lighting in compressed-air chambers should be by electric method exclusively. Two independent electric lighting systems, with independent sources of supply, should be used. The minimum intensity of light on any walkway, ladder, stairway, or working level should not be less than 10-foot-candles, and in all work areas the lighting should at all times enable personnel to see clearly.

All electrical equipment and wiring for light and power circuits must comply with the requirements relevant electrical code for use in damp, hazardous, high-temperature, and compressed-air environments. External parts of lighting fixtures and all other electrical equipment, when within 8ft of the floor should be constructed of non-combustible, nonabsorptive, insulating materials, except that metal may be used if it is effectively grounded. Portable lamps should be equipped with noncombustible, insulating sockets, approved handles, basket guards, and approved cords. The use of worn or defective portable and pendant conductors should be prohibited.

Text B Fire Safety in Tunnel
隧道消防安全

The Permanent International Association of Road Congress (PIARC, 1987) data show that a fire occurs about once per six million vehicle miles. Most of these fires start without an external cause; thus, accident frequency is a minor influence on fire risk. With the high standards of equipment and control in road tunnels, death and/or injuries due to fire are extremely rare.

Nonetheless, while highway tunnel fires have been rare, they can be very serious due to the difficulties of fighting fires in an enclosed space, the possible concentration of poisonous gases, temperature that can be in excess of 1800°F, and the possibility of panic among the tunnel users. Serious fires resulting in loss of life have occurred in the past in the Holland and Caldecott Tunnel in the United States, the Velsen Tunnel in Holland and the Nihonzaka Tunnel on the Tokyo-Nagoya-Kobe motorway in Japan.

The experience of most operating tunnels indicates that the most common fires are small in size and attributable to electrical and mechanical faults in vehicles (brake, tires, fuel systems, short circuits, etc.). The size of a fire is nearly always limited and can be easily extinguished, although rapid intervention is critical. Fire extinguishers are the most appropriate means for bringing this type of fire under control when it first begins. Hence, regularly spaced placement of easily accessible portable fire extinguishers is now common practice in most vehicular tunnels. It is also a fact that fires due to accidents (frontal or front-rear collisions, hitting of obstacles) are much less frequent inside than outside of tunnel. Drivers are most careful in a tunnel. They drive at lower speeds and are not exposed to risks due to weather and the condition of the roads that apply outside the tunnel.

The characteristics of heat and smoke propagation in the event of a vehicular fire in a tunnel are similar to those which occur in a fire of equal intensity on an open highway, in that buoyancy created by the heat at the roadway level causes smoke and heat to rise. On an open highway, the smoke and heat can dissipate and disperse vertically into the atmosphere. In a tunnel, however, the ceiling or roof precludes such dispersal, thereby creating a serious hazard to move longitudinally at the ceiling or roof of a tunnel.

Experience has proven that toxic gases and particles in undiluted smoke are more life threatening than heat. Thus, people have a greater chance of escaping harm when the ventilation succeeds in keeping the lower portions of the traffic space free of smoke, and provides enough air and visibility to enable people to evacuate the tunnel. The ventilation system should be capable of removing smoke from the traffic space as soon as possible and preferably at a higher rate than it is being generated.

Basic factors that influence the determination of the safety equipment and system to be installed in a tunnel include the tunnel's length and the amount of traffic. Other factors include the location of the tunnel (within or outside an urban area, under water), the number of traffic lanes, the amount of heavy-goods traffic and the regulations in force for the transit of dangerous materials through the tunnel.

The size of a fire is also a function of the type of vehicle involved, and if it is a truck, the nature of its cargo. In the event that vehicles are involved in a collision, there also may be a rupture of fuel tanks and consequently spillage of fuel, which may spread according to the grade of the roadway. If ignited, a spill can result in a rapid propagation and spread of the fire. The magnitude of a fire corresponding to various sources can be approximated by the values.

It is difficult to accurately predict the magnitude of a fire scenario. Even where hazardous cargoes are precluded from using tunnels, they cannot be detected. In fact, the Holland Tunnel fire of 1949 was a consequence of a prohibited hazardous cargo in the tunnel.

Documented reports of research on tunnel fires show the behavior of the fire and associated tunnel fire flows to differ significantly from more familiar fire situations outside the confines of a tunnel. The most noteworthy distinction is the buoyant effect that tends to create a layer of hot smoke and gases flowing away from the fire near the crown of the tunnel, while air supporting combustion moves toward the fire beneath the smoke layer. For example, in a level, unventilated tunnel with the fire near the longitudinal midpoint, the buoyant effect will establish a symmetrical circulation pattern with the hot, smoky air leaving both ends of the tunnel and air outside the tunnel drawn in beneath it.

A longitudinal ventilation system forcing air to flow through the tunnel will shift the balance of heated air in the direction of the forced flow. If the ventilation is of sufficient capacity, it will cause all of the heated air to flow toward the downstream direction. If the ventilation capacity is more limited, the upper layer of heated air may flow in a direction contrary to the forced ventilation (a phenomenon called backlayering). Whether backlayering occurs depends upon several factors, including the intensity of the fire, the grade and geometry of the tunnel, and the velocity of the ventilating airstreams.

Allowing for the uncertainties of the rate of fire growth and propagation in a tunnel, the objectives of a viable emergency ventilation system are to keep the smoke and heat of a fire away from people who may be in a tunnel.

In all of the following mentioned major tunnel fires, the common parameter that significantly influenced the magnitude of the fire and the resultant impact on life safety was time. The significance of time can best be identified by the key sequence of events in a fire situation as follows:

(1) Time to detect a fire;
(2) Time to send an alarm;
(3) Time to verify the source of life;
(4) Time to implement emergency response procedures.

In recent years, technological advances have combined to minimize the time factors identified above. The subsystem appropriate to minimize total time, and therefore improve life safety capabilities in highway tunnels are widely death with.

1. Detection of fires

Thermal and/or smoke detectors come to mind when one thinks of fire detection. While some are in use in tunnels, they are limited in their capabilities. Smoke detectors of virtually any type are unsuitable for tunnel applications due to the products of combustion in the vehicle exhaust emissions. Most thermal detectors are also unsuitable.

First, detectors must be rugged and reliable in the harsh corrosive ambient atmospheric environment of a tunnel and be able to withstand the high-pressure water nozzles used on tunnel washing machines. Second, there is a possibility of frequent false alarms, particularly during congested operations, due to vertical exhaust stacks on large trucks or buses. Current state-of-the-art heat detectors suitable for tunnels include dual rate of rise detectors (spaced approximately 75ft on centers for a two-lane tunnel), or linear thermal detectors (usually arranged in a serpentine pattern at the ceiling of the tunnel).

Given that most vehicular fires initiate under the hood or floors of the passenger compartment (or in the passenger compartment), there may be a substantial time delay before the heat is detected by thermal detectors at the ceiling. In fact, if and when such a situation occurs, it would be reasonable to conclude that the fire has had time to increase to some significant size. For the above reasons, thermal detectors are not often installed in tunnels, other than as a secondary detection system, if deemed necessary.

Subsystems facilities frequently will include traffic loop detectors embedded in the roadway pavement for monitoring traffic flow rates and speeds. They can detect stopped traffic and thereby usually will become the first means of detecting an incident and altering the Operation Control Center staff of a problem.

Many modern highway tunnels including an Operations Control Center (OCC), which is continuously named by trained operators. Operators in the OCC, using closed-circuit television

(CCTV) cameras positioned to view the length of the tunnel roadway, can then assess the cause of the traffic being stopped and effect an appropriate response. In a fire situation, this means of early detection can be most effective toward initiating an appropriate and timely response.

2. Alarm

The detection of stopped traffic by a roadway loop detection system will be alarmed to the OCC. If a fire situation is verified, the OCC can transmit alarms as appropriate to the various emergency response agencies, so that suitable personnel and equipment may be dispatched to the scene. Thermal (heat) detectors at the ceiling will transmit alarms to the OCC and, if desired, directly to the emergency response authorities, including fire, police, and other emergency service units.

Manual fire alarm pull station and/or emergency telephone installations in wall niches along the length of the tunnel roadway are also employed as supplementary alarm devices.

3. Incident location

Knowledge of the location of a fire incident in a tunnel is critical to implementing an appropriate plan of emergency response. Loop detectors and heat detectors can be arranged in zones, or, if a thermal linear detector is used, the location along the length of the detector (currently available up to 1000ft per power and control unit) can denote the specific location of the fire incident on a graphic display panel or CRT monitor. The OCC will also use the CCTV monitors, if possible, or dispatch personnel to the scene to effectively verify and establish an incident location.

4. Communication

Relatively recent advances in the state of the art in electronic communications have substantially improved incident management—including fires—in tunnels. Some of those which seem to be most effective include:

(1) AM-FM rebroadcast antennas, which permit the OCC to convey message, instructions, etc, to motorists via their car radios. Public address systems in tunnels are not suitable because of the high ambient noise level.

(2) Variable-message signs can provide information to notify and assist motorists in a fire situation, including guidance in evacuation to safety areas or exits by foot or vehicle.

(3) Traffic control signals can be set and warning notices can be flashed on an electronic sign at the tunnel entrance portals, activated simultaneously with a fire alarm, to preclude further entry to the tunnel by motorists. The OCC can also position lane traffic signal controls most appropriate to expeditious vehicular evacuation or to facilitate access by emergency response vehicles.

(4) Emergency telephones are available in tunnel wall niches at frequent intervals for motorists to contact the OCC as required. Other dedicated telephone and two-way radio support system compatible with emergency response services communication requirements should also be provided in the tunnel installation.

(5) Locations of exit doors to safety areas are generally unknown to the average motorist in a tunnel. Illuminated fixed directional signs, flashing strobe lights at the exit doors, and emergency lighting systems are used to guide people in the event they are devised to abandon their vehicles and evacuate the tunnel on foot.

5. Planned responses

Emergency response plans should be developed in conjunction with the fire department and other emergency response services as appropriate. The OCC should be equipped with computer hardware and software systems from which preprogrammed or manual emergency response plans application may require a combination of automatic, semi-automatic, or manual actions as most appropriate to the situation. The emergency response plans should be capable of addressing all types of incident management situations.

In the case of a fire situation, the emergency response plan should include the collection and verification of input data such as alarms and incident location, notification to police, fire department and other response units as appropriate, dispatch of emergency tunnel personnel and vehicles, setting of traffic control signs, activation of smoke control ventilation and fire suppression systems, procedures and means for effective communications with motorists, and advice and guidance for their evacuation when necessary. The major elements and subsystems of the fire life safety program should function as follows:

(1) The OCC should be manned 24 hours a day by trained operators. Operator proficiently in dealing with minor and major incidents and plant failure should be maintained by regular refresher training using incident simulation programs.

(2) CCTV cameras should be located throughout the project roadways. Pictures from the cameras would be relayed to the OCC for display on monitors located in the OCC and available for selection by the operator.

(3) Roadways should be provided with a system of loop detectors embedded in the pavement. The OCC computer should continuously monitor traffic passage time over successive loops within the tunnels to determine when a breakdown in traffic flow occurs, and alert the operator to a possible incident. An alarm would be displayed in the OCC. The appropriate CCTV output would be automatically directed to a dedicated monitor at the master control console. The operator should assess the situation and provide the appropriate response.

(4) Traffic control systems should include lane-use signals mounted over each lane to control traffic flow in each lane and advisory message signs located on the tunnel approaches and throughout the tunnels to advise motorists.

(5) The radio rebroadcast system, with override capability, should provide a means for the OCC to communicate directly with motorists via FM frequencies (variable message signs should advise motorists to switch on radios).

(6) Motorists "lift to call" telephones located throughout the tunnels should provide communications between motorists and the OCC.

(7) Zoned thermal detectors should provide additional data to the OCC to indicate and locate

fire incidents, with simultaneous automatic notification of the fire departments.

(8) Preprogrammed options for the operation of themechanical ventilation system should be available for selection and implementation by the operator. Manual operation should also be available if required.

(9) Cross-passageways between the roadways or emergency exits to the surface should provide easily accessible escape routes should evacuation be required.

(10) Emergency response vehicles, manned by personnel trained to provide assistance ranging from fighting minor fires to clearing accident sites, should be provided. The personnel should respond to instructions issued by the OCC and should be able to locally assess the situation and render appropriate assistance. The vehicles should be equipped with two-way radios, public address facilities, emergency lights, fire-fighting equipment including foam extinguisher, metal-cutting equipment, and medical supplies.

(11) the fire detection, alarm, and protection systems should include thermal detectors, thermal and smoke detectors, and sprinklers as appropriate in ancillary buildings, chemical suppression systems in OCCs, thermal and smoke detectors in switchrooms, fire indicator panels located in ancillary buildings, a main fire indicator panel located in the OCCs, a continuous standpipe system with 2.5in fire department hose valves (or otherwise as appropriate) at approximately 150ft centers, portable extinguishers, and a communication system using the radio rebroadcast system.

(12) Emergency response plans should be developed in conjunction with fire departments and other local agencies as applicable. These plans should include the assembly of equipment operating modes, which may be selected during a fire incident and should be part of an integrated package. The implementation of any emergency response plan option for fire fighting should be OCC operator-initiated at the direction of the senior fire department officer upon arrival on the scene. Manual operation of all systems should be available in case of control system failure, or to accommodate a particular situation.

In addition to the emergency response plan being documented and distributed to all necessary individuals of the tunnel operating authority, copies should also be provided to all emergency response units. Regular programs of training should be mandatory for all individuals who are likely to have to participate in a fire emergency situation. This training should be repeated at suitable regularly scheduled intervals if effective responses are to be expected. Coordinated simulation exercises involving all emergency response units and individuals must also be accomplished on a regular basis. Since the frequency of occurrence of a major emergency incident (especially one involving a major fire situation) is rare, only through all involved personnel participation in repetitive regularly scheduled training courses and field exercises will the emergency response team be effective when needed. Modern electronics and computers can minimize the critical response time, but the response personnel have to be ready to act.

6. Personnel evacuation

The need to evacuate personnel (i.e. motorists and passengers abandoning their vehicles in the tunnel) will be determined at the OCC. Evacuation pathways and procedures are presented as preprogrammed scenarios graphically displayed by the computer on monitors in the OCC. The display will reflect the incident input data and al the interdependent relevant information to support an evacuation including smoke control, fire suppression, and traffic control status. Evacuation is to be implemented when the OCC operator or fire commander at the scene verifies the applicability of all the indicated subsystems are activated at the OCC (by a single master control button or switch), the variable-message signs, appropriate exitways, and safety lighting will be energized to guide the personnel evacuation.

7. Smoke control

The common parameter critical to all fires is time. In effect, therefore, it can be said that the objective of a good tunnel emergency ventilation system is to buy time. That is, time to allow people to escape from a tunnel involved with a fire incident. The longer the ventilation system can keep the concentrations of smoke and heat away from escaping motorists, the greater their chance of reaching a safety exit from the tunnel.

Today's technology is such that systems of detection, alarm, verification, and communication can effectively assist in guiding passengers to points of safety if they must evacuate a tunnel and abandon their cars. However, one must also design and operate an emergency ventilation system in a manner that will maintain a safe pathway of escape for the maximum amount of time.

While it is unlikely that an emergency ventilation system could be engineered to meet all possible conditions of fire and smoke propagation, it is possible to mathematize the effectiveness of certain emergency ventilation system for a variety of fire scenarios.

Over the years, full transverse ventilation systems (a type usually associated with urban tunnels than 1/2 mile in length) have generally been regarded as the type of ventilation system that would provide the maximum safety in a fire situation. The popular theory associated with full transverse systems has been that the air flow in a tunnel is always transverse from the supply ports to the exhaust grills and therefore no longitudinal flow will take place. Therefore, the theory contends that the smoke and heat can be contained local to the fire. Unfortunately, observation of actual tunnel fire scenarios demonstrates that this is not the case when the fire is large.

In the event of a fire involving a vehicle or vehicles disabled in a tunnel, the ventilation system should be able to control the direction of smoke movement to provide both a clear and safe path for evacuating people and to facilitate fire-fighting operations. The ability to prevent backlayering should therefore be a major objective in the design of the ventilation system and its operation during an emergency.

Given the advance in state-of-the-art analytical techniques, coupled with knowledge derived from the afore-described experience and research, a design tool to analyze the performance of certain concepts of mechanical ventilation systems in a fire situation was developed in recent years.

This fire model simulation computer software program evolved from an original Subway environment simulation (SES) computer program capable of evaluating the environmental conditions under normal operations in tunnels and underground stations of a rapid transit system. That program, developed between 1970 and 1975, is a numerical simulation model that incorporates the results of theoretical research, scale model and field testing data, and has been verified through full-scale subsystem tests and by comparisons with measurements taken in operating transit systems.

The SES Program comprises from interdependent computation sequences developed for underground rapid transit systems simulation: a train performance subprogram, an aerodynamic subprogram, a temperature/humidity subprogram, and a heat sink/environmental control subprogram.

Sometime after 1975, the aerodynamic subroutine of the SES, which determines the piston action air flows (longitudinal air flow in a tunnel caused by vehicle travel), was extended to vehicular tunnel applications. While the piston effect is a function of traffic speed, density, and a number of other variables, in all cases, and for any type of ventilation system, it causes longitudinal air flow in the roadway in the direction of traffic movement.

8. Fire suppressions systems

Systems of fire suppression in highway and rapid transit tunnels are usually provided with wet or dry pipe water fire mains feeding a standpipe system throughout the tunnel. They are sprinkler systems, halon systems and fire extinguishers.

In a limited number of tunnels, foam-or deluge-type sprinkler systems have been applied. While the fire safety effectiveness of automated sprinkler systems for most types of buildings is unquestioned, consideration of their possible use in tunnels requires evaluation of several factors that are significantly different from a building.

Much evidence suggests that sprinklers are not only ineffective in controlling a fuel fire, but can actually contribute to the spread and severity of the fire. Vehicular tunnel conditions cannot exploit sprinkler system strengths and turn most of them into disadvantages.

Tests with sprinklers have been undertaken in Switzerland, Austria, and Japan. They all indicated that the water shower induces a strong vertical mixing that the cooled smoke cannot resist, thus eliminating all chances for the stratification: thus, smoke gets immediately spread over the entire cross section of a tunnel. There also is a risk of explosion of vapors generated by the sprinkler after the fire extinction. Depending on the fire intensity, the air vapor mixture may attain 212 °F and more.

If consideration is given to the use of sprinklers in tunnels, the only type that has chance at al of controlling large fires would be an AFFF (foam) discharge system. Experience dictates that it must be a deluge system and be manually activated. The complexity of a sprinkler installation with its attendant requirements for zoning valves, preaction valves, foam storage and dispensing facilities, control system, etc., in the corrosive atmospheric environment of highway and rapid transit tunnels would mandate a maintenance program of enormous proportions. Also, to ascertain a minimal level of service for such a system, periodic testing of the foam sprinklers would have to be performed, at great financial and operational expense (traffic limitations, etc.). Consequently, without regard to the massive capital cost incurred for a foam sprinkler system, its overall reliability would be very uncertain unless the required maintenance could be assured. With the anticipated years of service to be expected from highway and rapid transit tunnels and the probably infrequent use of a sprinkler installation, its potential deterioration with time would further reduce its reliability.

Where some sprinkler systems have been installed in tunnels, their use-in some cases-is no longer advocated by the local fire-fighting authorities, due mainly to inherent maintenance problems and resultant lack of reliability. Their preference is to rely on a fire standpipe and tunnel ventilation system in case of fire.

Consequently, it is generally the practice in almost all U.S tunnels, and in most other countries, not to recommend the use of sprinklers in vehicular or rapid transit tunnels. The sprinkler systems are generally not recommended for tunnels for the following reason:

(1) Many of the perceived benefits of a sprinkler system that apply to building use do not apply to vehicular or rapid transit tunnels. Differences in combustible content and the physical relationships of the discharge from a sprinkler system in a tunnel upon a vehicle with an on-board fire, where the vehicle has been designed for exposure to water, limit a sprinkler's effectiveness.

(2) One of the key disadvantages (potential hazard) of a sprinkler system in a tunnel, which could adversely impact life safety, is the delamination of thestratified smoke layer, inducing turbulence and mixing of the air and smoke.

(3) Sprinkler systems for tunnels are not recommended by most tunnel operators and tunnel/ fire protection related organizations.

(4) The cost of a proper foam sprinkler installation, with all its attendant special features and requirements necessary for a tunnel installation, would be extraordinarily high compared with that for a building of equivalent floor area.

Current state-of-the art system of detection, alarm, operation and surveillance, response, access and egress, and alternative suppression methods can be applied to constitute an effective integrated fire safety program for highway and rapid transit tunnels. A sprinkler system (if required) would have to be a preaction, manually remote-controlled zoned AFFF (foam) type. The complexity and maintenance needs of such a system would substantially reduce its reliability.

9. Halon system

These systems are commonly applied to control and/or communication centers or critical electrical or electronic equipment areas. Subsequently the halon distribution systems are integrated within cabinet housings of the equipment it is designed to protect. It is also frequently applied to the operating OCCs for most tunnel-type applications.

In all cases, due to the toxicity problems associated with the fumes from the discharge of halon gas, such systems must be installed with the appropriate safeguards.

10. Fire extinguisher

Fire extinguishers are the most appropriate means for bringing many small types of fire under control at initiation. Hence, interval placement of easily accessible portable fire extinguishers is now common practice in most vehicular tunnels. The extinguisher should be of the multipurpose, dry chemical type with an ABC rating. The minimum capacity should be one with a 4-A, 40-B: C rating. The maximum size considered convenient for this use is a 20lb unit.

The extinguishers should be spaced so that the distance between units is not greater than 150ft on each wall of the tunnel. It is preferable, where possible, to have fire extinguishers on both sides of a vehicular tunnel nowadays. A staggered spacing arrangement would place the extinguishers at a maximum distance of 75ft from any possible fire.

The extinguisher should be mounted in a well-marked flush wall enclosure, preferably with a door. Often the fire extinguisher is located in the same enclosure with the fire hose valve.

The cabinet should be arranged so that when the door is opened or the extinguisher removed, an audible alarm is sounded in the OCC to alert the operator of the use of this equipment. This arrangement will discourage and signal unauthorized use or theft of fire-fighting equipment.

The appropriate subsystems and their details for achieving an effective integrated fire safety program for a tunnel can vary considerably with the physical characteristics, location, and planned use of the tunnel. In turn, careful attention to the design of each of the applicable subsystems will determine the overall level of fire safety.

Text C Tunnel Fire Disaster Cases
两个隧道火灾案例

Knowledge acquired in recent years through experiences with fires in tunnels, as well as from various research and development activities, including analytical studies and field measurement test programs, has contributed significantly to more effective design and performance of tunnel life safety programs.

Over the past 40 years, the most significant tunnel fires include the Holland Tunnel fire in 1949 (New York-New Jersey), the BART (Bay Area Rapid Transit) Trans-Bay Tube fire on January17,1979 (California); the Nihonzaka Tunnel fire in 1979 (Japan); the Caldecott Tunnel fire on April7,1982(California) and the Kings Cross Station fire in the London Underground in November 1987. From these experience, it has been found that overall, tunnels do survive fires; however, people may not.

Several significant factors were learned from the world's major tunnel fires. For example, during the Holland Tunnel fire in 1949, enormous quantities of heat and smoke traveled along the ceiling of the tunnel for distances of more than 300ft (100m), subsequent causing secondary fires in vehicles trapped behind and uphill from the primary fire source. The Holland Tunnel has a full transverse system of ventilation. When the ceiling above the primary fire source collapsed, large quantities of air flowed longitudinally in the roadway toward this large opening in the ceiling exhaust duct. In effect, the ventilation system changed at that moment from a full transverse system to one of single-point exhaust. This served to reduce the spread of heat and smoke along the ceiling and eliminated further occurrences of secondary fire.

The BART Trans-Bay Tube fire occurred in the inbound trainway January 17, 1979. The 3.6 m-long subaqueous tunnel runs between ventilation structures at both sides of San Francisco Bay. There are no exitways, vent shafts, or other external openings throughout the tube length. One vent structure is on land on the Oakland side of the bay. The vent structure on the San Francisco side is located 400ft off-shore in the bay.

The two trainways are separated by a service passageway (galley) between and parallel to the trainways. Cross-passageways at approximately every 320ft (100m) interconnect the two trainways via the gallery. Fire-rated doors insolate the trainways at each cross-passage.

An emergency ventilation duct in the upper part of the gallery, connected to fans in ventilation structures at both ends of the subaqueous crossing, provides smoke removal from selected locations via remote-controlled selective damper openings to each trainway, spaced at approximately 320ft (100m) intervals for the length of the tube. Beneath the ventilation duct, the maintenance passageway (gallery) provides access for fire-fighting personnel.

The fire began when a metal cover plate on a control box mounted on the undercarriage of a car on the train came loose, struck the third rail, and created a short circuit with the power rail. The fire began at about 6 P.M. on a normal workday, and few passengers were on board the eight-car inbound train. Outbound traffic was heavy at this peak rush hour period. The train crew evacuated the passengers from the fire train to the tunnel walkway and through a cross-passage to the adjacent trainway, where they were picked up by a train traveling in the opposite direction. All passengers and crew escaped before the fire engulfed and consumed the train. The fire was hot enough to melt and eventually ignite the aluminum bodies of the transit vehicles.

The fire was declared out about 6 hours later. There was one fatality, a fire department lieutenant, who was overcome by smoke in the gallery due apparently to a fire door having been blocked open. The involved train was destroyed by the fire.

A report on the subsequent investigations of the fire noted that there was inappropriate response by the various transit operating personnel and/or by the emergency response services agencies involved. The operating personnel had difficulty determining the location of the fire, and hence in deciding which dampers to operate. Rehabilitation included the installation of frequent location markers in the trainways.

Concrete spalling occurred in the arch of the structural lining for a length of about generally only to reinforcing steel depth, which a few isolated small spots extending 2-3in (5-7.6cm) deeper.

1. Caldecott Tunnel

A third two-lane bore of the Caldecott Tunnel went into service in October 1964. it was in this bore that the accident occurred. The tunnel length is 3370ft (1027m). The tunnels were interconnected by periodic maintenance-only passageways (not accessible to passengers) protected by simple steel plate doors at each tunnel.

Traffic in the third tube was being operated unidirectional from east to west. The tunnel is graded uphill from west to east, so that the traffic was going downhill. Prevailing winds are west to east, the direction of fire travel.

The ventilation system consists of an overhead full transverse system using a ceiling duct divided into two parts, with supply from ceiling outlets on one side of the tunnel and extraction through the adjacent ceiling duct.

The ventilation capacity for supply and exhaust was approximately 500000ft^3/min (9236m^3/s) for each system. The tunnel traffic is monitored by the tunnel authority. In the control room, operators can observe the fire alarm anunciators, carbon monoxide recorders, television monitors, and fan operation. The operators were equipped with an emergency telephone connection to phones in the tunnels.

The fire began shortly after midnight in very light traffic conditions, following a collision involving an abandoned automobile, a transit bus, and a tank-truck trailer full of gasoline. The initial fire stated in the tractor engine, and within several minutes the trailer tank exploded. The tanker explosion produced a fireball that filled the tunnel for several hundred feet uphill from the back of the tanker. The tanker was fully fire-involved with heavy black smoke moving uphill toward the eastern portal: no smoke traveled westward downhill.

From studies by the National Transportation Safety Board (NTSB), it was estimated that the maximum flame temperature during the fire did not exceed 1950°F (1066°C). Fire-fighting personnel were able to approach the burning tanker (which was overturned) to within about 150ft.

After 40min from initiation of the fire, the firefighters were able to go in right up to the tanker itself, which at that time melted. The burning tank trailer was located at the approximate midpoint of the tunnel.

Near the rear of the tanker, the flames reached the ceiling and smoke extended from head height to the tunnel ceiling. Visibility was estimated by firefighters at about 30ft (10m) in all directions. As the firefighters moved east, visibility decreased. At a distance of approximately 550ft (168m) east of tanker, visibility was reduced to about 3-6ft (1-2m) and smoke was within 1.5ft (0.5m) of the roadway.

Based on subsequent analysis by the NTSB, physical evidence indicated that temperatures had reached a maximum of 1900°F (1038°C) for at least 20min in the areas of the involved level from 1600ft (488m) to about 900ft (275m) from the east end. In this same location, temperatures near the roadway exceeded 1100°F (593°C). Between 25ft (8m) and 550ft (168m) from the east end, temperatures near the roadway ranged typically between 350 and 1075°F (177 and 580°C) except in the areas of the burning vehicles, where temperatures reached 1900°F (1038°C).

Two elderly people trapped in their car only 115ft (35m) from the eastern end of the tunnel did not escape the smoke and fire, and died. The truck and bus drivers escaped through the west portal. Several people got out of their cars and tried to run back to the entering portal, but most were engulfed in the fire stream or overcome by smoke. Skeletons were found in some cars; others were on the roadway.

None of the motorists who tried to flee on foot used cross-passages. The cross-passage doors were not equipped with handles, signs, or lights.

The members of NTSB were of opinion that had the Caldecott Tunnel been equipped with video monitors or loop detectors, the number of fatalities would probably have been less than the seven that in fact occurred. The NTSB (National Transportation Safety Board) also concluded that due to the intensity of the gasoline fire, fire response or changes to ventilation probably would have had little effect in this accident.

There was no ceiling collapse. Finish ceiling tiles had been removed at an earlier date. Concrete spalling was limited to the ceiling over the trailer and to the nearest sidewall. The depth of spalling was generally limited to mid-depth of the reinforcing steel with only a few longitudinal rears exposed.

Tiles on both walls were burned off and spread across the roadway for a considerable distance behind the tanker. Roadway debris was about 3in (7.5m) deep over this area.

The two fire hydrants' brass or bronze fittings nearest the trailer were badly damaged by the heat. A sizable jet of water was still spouting from one of them 36 hours after the fire.

2. Kings Cross Station

In November 1987, a fire in the Kings Cross Station of the London Underground resulted in 34 fatalities. Kings Cross is a multilevel underground station that includes three levels of trainways interconnected via stairs and escalators, and a ticketing hall (fare collection) concourse below the street level. The fire apparently began in an escalator between the uppermost trainway station platform level and the ticketing hall. It was concluded that the cause of the fire was probably a cigarette that had fallen through the risers of the escalator into the substructure below. The escalator was an old unit that included wooden treads. In addition, debris mixed with oil and/or grease from lubricants for the escalator mechanism in the escalator truss provided the initial source of fuel for the fire. Subsequent to the start of the fire in the truss structure of the escalator, the fire erupted through the moving stairs as a fireball and rapidly ascended to the ticket hall, which provided additional combustibles to feed the fire (ceiling construction, etc.). Most of the fatalities occurred in the ticketing hall or on the affected escalators.

The fire progressed upward from the original source. Thus, individuals who remained in the lower levels of the station were safe from the effects of the fire.

Smoking is now prohibited in the London Underground. Automatic sprinkler systems have been or are being installed in all London Underground escalator machine rooms and escalator trusses, and maintenance to preclude accumulations of combustible debris has been intensified. All of the older escalators in the London Underground that contain combustible components and are not sealed as effectively as the currently available escalator systems are being replaced with newer models.

Summary: The time of the fire occurrence in above fires described above likely was a major factor in limiting the number of fatalities. In addition, several design elements for new tunnels or the retrofit of existing ones to improve fire life safety were learned. These include:

(1) Improvements in signing on the walls of tunnels to guide people to an exit from the tunnel or to a place of refuge.

(2) Low-height placement of illuminated exit signs.

(3) Recessed fire protected enclosures for fire hydrants and related emergency equipment.

(4) Duct banks or other fire rated enclosures for critical emergency equipment.

(5) Duct banks or other fire rated enclosures for critical emergency power and communication circuits.

(6) Illuminated electronic signs for communicating instructions to people in highway tunnels and at the portals during an emergency.

(7) Radio rebroadcast systems to communicate with people via their car radios.

(8) Escape from an emergency-involved tunnel via pedestrian cross-passages to a parallel bore.

3. Mont Blanc Tunnel

The Mont Blanc Tunnel is a highway tunnel in Europe, under the Mont Blanc mountain in the Alps. It links Chamonix, Haute-Savoie, France with Courmayeur, Aosta Valley, Italy, via European route E25. The passageway is one of the major trans-Alpine transport routes, particularly for Italy, which relies on the tunnel for transporting as much as one-third of its freight to northern Europe. It reduces the route from France to Turin by 50km (30miles) and to Milan by 100km (60mile). Northeast of Mont Blanc's summit, the tunnel is about 15km (10mile) southwest of the tripoint with Switzerland, near Mont Dolent.

Begun in 1957 and completed in 1965, the tunnel is 11.611km (7.215mile) in length, 8.6m (28ft) in width, and 4.35m (14.3ft) in height. The passageway is not horizontal, but in a slightly inverted "V", which assists ventilation. The entrance elevation on the French side with a maximum of 1395m (4577ft) near the center, a maximum difference of 121m (397ft). The tunnel consists of a single gallery with a two-lane dual direction road. At the time of its construction, it was more than triple the length of any existing highway tunnel. Plans to widen the tunnel were never implemented because of lack of financing and fierce opposition of local residents who objected to the harmful effects of increased heavy traffic.

The Mont Blanc Tunnel was originally managed by two public companies, each managing half of the tunnel:

French side: ATMB (Autoroutes et tunnels du Mont-Blanc) founded 30 April 1958.

Italian side: SITMB (Società italiana per azioni per il Traforo del Monte Bianco), founded 1 September 1957.

After the 1999 fire, which showed how lack of coordination could hamper the safety of the tunnel, all the operations are managed by a single entity: MBT-EEIG, controlled by both ATMB and SITMB together, through a 50-50 shares distribution. A commemorative plaque is on the French side of the tunnel, remembering those who were killed in the fire.

On the morning of 24 March 1999, 39 people died when a Belgian transport truck carrying flour and margarine caught fire in the tunnel. After several kilometers, the driver realized something was wrong as cars coming in the opposite direction flashed their headlights at him; a glance in his mirrors showed white smoke coming out from under his cab. This was not yet a fire emergency; there had been 16 other truck fires in the tunnel over the previous 35 years, always extinguished on the spot by the drivers.

At 10:53 CET, the driver of the vehicle, Gilbert Degrave, stopped in the middle of the tunnel to attempt to fight the fire but he was suddenly forced back by flames from his cab.

At 10:55, the tunnel employees triggered the fire alarm and stopped any further traffic from entering. At this point there were at least 10 cars/vans and 18 trucks in the tunnel that had entered from the French side. A few vehicles from the Italian side passed the Volvo truck without stopping. Some of the cars from the French side managed to turn around in the narrow two-lane tunnel to retreat back to France, but negotiating the road in the dense smoke that had rapidly filled the tunnel quickly made this impossible. The larger trucks did not have the space to turn around, and reversing out was not an option.

Most drivers rolled up their windows and waited for rescue. The ventilation system in the tunnel drove toxic smoke back down the tunnel faster than anyone could run to safety. These fumes quickly filled the tunnel and caused vehicle engines to stall because of lack of oxygen. This included fire engines which, once affected, had to be abandoned by the firefighters. Many drivers near the blaze who attempted to leave their cars and seek refuge points were quickly overcome.

Within minutes, two fire trucks from Chamonix responded to the unfolding disaster. The fire had melted the wiring and plunged the tunnel into darkness; in the smoke and with abandoned and wrecked vehicles blocking their path, the fire engines were unable to proceed. The fire crews instead abandoned their vehicles and took refuge in two of the emergency fire cubicles (fire-door sealed small rooms set into the walls every 600 meters). As they huddled behind the fire doors, they could hear burning fuel roll down the road surface, causing tires to pop and fuel tanks to explode. They were rescued five hours later by a third fire crew that responded and reached them via a ventilation duct; of the 15 firefighters that had been trapped, 14 were in serious condition and one (their commanding officer) died in the hospital.

Some victims escaped to the fire cubicles. The original fire doors on the cubicles were rated to survive for two hours. Some had been upgraded in the 34 years since the tunnel was built to survive for four hours. The fire burned for 53 hours and reached temperatures of 1000℃ (1830℉), mainly because of the margarine load in the trailer, equivalent to a 23000-litre (5100 imp gal; 6100 US gal) oil tanker, which spread to other cargo vehicles nearby that also carried combustible loads. The fire trapped around 40 vehicles in dense and poisonous smoke (containing carbon monoxide and cyanide). Due to weather conditions at the time, airflow through the tunnel was from the Italian side to the French side. Authorities compounded the effect by pumping in further fresh air from the Italian side, forcing poisonous black smoke through the length of the tunnel. Only vehicles below the fire on the French side of the tunnel were trapped, while cars on the Italian side of the fire were mostly unaffected. There were 27 deaths in vehicles, and 10 more died trying to escape on foot. Of the initial 50 people trapped by the fire, 12 survived. It was over five days before the tunnel cooled sufficiently to start repairs.

Ⅱ. Terms and terminology

OSHA (Occupational Safety And Health Administration)	职业安全与健康管理局
safety provisions	安全措施；安全设施
Safety engineer	安全工程师
rapid transit artery	高速交通干道
safety program	安全计划
precaution	预防措施
emergency equipment	应急设备
safety inspection	安全检验
per shift	每班
helmet	钢盔,头盔
safety boot	安全靴
special garment	特种服装
Safety glasses/goggle	护目镜
face shield	面罩
welding	焊接,电焊
safety belt	安全带
jurisdiction	行政辖区
ladder	梯子
caisson work	箱涵作业
flange	法兰,轮缘；边缘
deadly smoke	致命烟雾
emergency ventilation	应急通风
detonator	雷管
hauling	搬运
bottom-dump car	底卸式车
first-aid station	急救站；救护站
first aid kits	急救药箱
fire extinguisher	灭火器
pulley	滑轮
Methane	甲烷
Hydrogen sulfide	硫化氢
Bureau of Labor Standards	美国劳工部标准
Identification Badges	身份徽章

Ⅲ. Questions and difficult sentence analysis

1. Questions for brainstorming discussion

(1) What are the principal safety assurance measures of the operators working in tunnel?

(2) What the items of attention are compulsory to assure the safety in operations by drill-blast method?

(3) Collect the fire incidents which have occurred in highway tunnels of China in recent ten years and discuss and propose the preventions and countermeasures for such similar accidents from technical or management point of view.

2. Difficult sentences analysis

(1) At one time, tunnel accidents claimed one life for every half mile of tunnel conducted. Increased concern over construction safety has led to improvements in the miner's working conditions, with a subsequent reduction in the frequency of deaths and disabling accidents. However, based on 1986 OSHA statistics, lost-time accidents still occur at more than twice the frequency for underground workers compared with other construction workers, and three times the rate for manufacturing workers.

译文：曾经，隧道事故中，每修建半里隧道就夺取一条人命。对隧道施工的日益关注导致了矿工的工作环境的改善，从而降低了人员伤亡和残疾的频率。但是，根据OSHA的统计数据，地下工程施工人员发生事故而导致工程延误的频率为其他工程类型的施工人员事故率的两倍，是制造业工人的三倍。

(2) Safe means of access and egress should be available in all working areas, and all ladders and stairways should comply with applicable code requirements. Subsidence areas presenting safety hazards should be fenced and posted. In New Jersey, the Construction Safety Code requires the surface working site to be walled or fenced to a height of 8ft again; other jurisdictions may have other requirements for overall construction sites and/or specific areas.

译文：在所有工区中，进出段应该具备安全措施，应该安装符合适用规则要求的爬梯和台阶。在出现安全隐患的沉降区，还应该安放围栏结构并张贴标识。在新泽西，施工安全条例要求地面工程施工区应该安装高度8英尺的围栏结构，其他不同辖区对于整个施工现场及/或特定区域提出其他的要求。

(3) A physical separation of 24in. should divide the compartments of detonators and explosives in a vehicle, and no one except the operator, his helper, and the powderman should be permitted to ride in a vehicle or train transporting explosives and blasting agents.

译文：车上的炸药和雷管应设置间距为24英寸的间隔间单独装载，除了驾驶员、助理和炸药装卸人员以外，任何其他人员不允许搭乘运送炸药和爆炸剂的机动车或火车。

(4) Prospective compressed-air workers should be examined by the physician to determine if they are physically qualified for the work. If a worker is ill or injured, or has been absent for 10 days, he should be reexamined before returning to work under compressed air. In addition,

compressed-air workers should be reexamined at least annually. The examination results should be kept on record along with the record of any decompression illnesses reported by the physician.

译文:拟参加压缩空气下作业的人员应该接受医生的体检,以确定是否身体条件合格参与这项作业。如果某个作业人员生病或受伤,或持续旷工10天,该人员应该重新接受体检,合格后方能重返压缩空气下的作业岗位。此外,从事压缩空气下作业的人员应接受至少每年一次体检。该体检结果应该连同医生关于解压疾病的报告一起保存。

Ⅳ. Translation case study

Case 1

Chinese	English translation
在养护工作上,养护公司努力做到"养护精细化、管理规范化、服务标准化",不断探索养护管理新思路,积极推行科学化养护,努力提高养护管理水平,确保秦岭终南山公路隧道美观舒适通畅。首先从细节着手,加强路容路貌的全面治理,坚持每季对全线路容路貌进行排查,对细节问题进行集中整治,疏通清理了排水沟,增设隧道南口路沿轮廓标,对隧道南口铁路挡墙上防抛网全部进行除锈刷漆,清理了隧道洞口路基边沟垃圾。	In curing, curing company tries his best to achieve "fine and detailed curing, normalized management and standardized service", continuously explore and investigate new thoughts of curing management, vigorously promote scientific curing, makes effort to improve curing management level so as to ensure Qinling Zhongnanshan Highway Tunnel to be beautiful, comfortable and free and smooth passage. Start with details in first place, enhance overall handling of road appearance and outlook, insist on quarterly inspection on road appearance and outlook throughout whole route; detailed problems are dealt with collectively; drainage ditches are cleared up; Curb profile labeling is increased on south portal ; the anti-throwing steel wire mesh on the retaining wall for railway at south portal is repainted for derusting and garbages at side trenches of subgrade at tunnel portals are removed and cleaned up.

Case 2

Chinese	English translation
首先,必须包裹探测器使之在隧道大气环境的严重腐蚀条件下保持性能可靠,能够承受冲洗隧道机器的高压水冲刷的压力。第二,探测器可能发出假报警信号,在当交通拥堵的情况下,由于安装大型卡车上或大巴车上的排气管排出尾气的时候。最新技术的热量探测器适用于隧道的类型包括双功率升降探测器(间距大约为75英尺,安装在双线隧道中央),或线性温度探测器(通常悬挂在隧道顶部)。	First, detectors must be rugged and reliable in the harsh corrosive ambient atmospheric environment of a tunnel and be able to withstand the high-pressure water nozzles used on tunnel washing machines. Second, there is a possibility of frequent false alarms, particularly during congested operations, due to vertical exhaust stacks on large trucks or buses. Current state-of-the-art heat detectors suitable for tunnels include dual rate of rise detectors (spaced approximately 75ft on centers for a two-lane tunnel), or linear thermal detectors (usually arranged in a serpentine pattern at the ceiling of the tunnel).

Case 3

Chinese	English translation
公路隧道和高速交通隧道安装的灭火器通常装有湿的或干的消防总管,与一根立管连接,并贯穿整条隧道。隧道中还安装有水喷淋和灭火器。 在数量有限的一些隧道中,还使用了泡沫或暴雨式水喷淋系统。对于大多数建筑种类,该自动水喷淋系统的安全有效性是无可非议的,如果考虑用于各种隧道中,需要对不同于建筑房屋的几个重要参数进行评估。 大量证据表明,水喷淋系统不仅能有效控制燃料起火,还能有助于控制火蔓延和火势。机动车隧道条件不能充分利用水喷淋系统的优点,反而会将这些优点变为不利。	Systems of fire suppression in highway and rapid transit tunnels are usually provided with wet or dry pipe water fire mains feeding a standpipe system throughout the tunnel. They are sprinkler systems, halon systems and fire extinguishers. In a limited number of tunnels, foam-or deluge-type sprinkler systems have been applied. While the fire safety effectiveness of automated sprinkler systems for most types of buildings is unquestioned, consideration of their possible use in tunnels requires evaluation of several factors that are significantly different from a building. Much evidence suggests that sprinklers are not only ineffective in controlling a fuel fire, but can actually contribute to the spread and severity of the fire. Vehicular tunnel conditions cannot exploit sprinkler system strengths and turn most of them into disadvantages.

V. Assignment

(1)民用爆炸物品的储存,必须设置专门的库房储室,其选址及库房建筑结构图,必须报所在地公安主管部门批准。库房必须远离城区、风景名胜区及职工(村民)住宿,与水利设施、交通要道、桥梁、隧道、高压输电线路、通信线路、输油输气管道等重要设施的距离,必须符合安全规定。

(2)地质灾害发生后,立即启动项目安全应急预案,判定地质灾害级别及诱发因素、规模等,并立即将灾情向当地市人民政府和国土资源局报告,在处置过程中,应及时报告处置工作进展情况,直至处置工作结束。

(3)隧道工程项目部要广泛利用音像、标语、画廊等各种形式开展教育培训,广泛宣传应急法律和预防、避险、自救、互救、减灾常识,增强全体员工的安全意识,社会责任意识和自救、互救能力,要有计划地对应急救援的管理人员进行培训,提高其专业技能。

(4)施工用电和照明用电要符合规定要求,严禁乱拉乱接和使用电炉等器具,施工用电必须三相五线制,配电箱内应设触电保护装置,配电箱加锁。

(5)专职安全员应参加作业伤亡事故的调查、分析与处理,按照"四不放过"的原则,认真处理好事故隐患,及时整改;并向上级如实统计报告,并做好事故建档工作。

Unit 14　Tunnel Contract Management
隧道合同管理

I. Text

Text A　Tunnel Construction Contracting
隧道施工合同

A whole separate book (or several) could be written about tunnel construction contracting. The purpose of this brief chapter is to explain why tunnel construction, and why and how the philosophic basis for modern tunnel construction contracting has evolved.

In English law, from which American practice is derived, a contract is an agreement between two parties in which one party undertakes to perform for the other a definite, mutually understood task for a defined compensation. Construction contract law is generally based on this underlying premise. The American system of competitive bid contracting is based on the assumption that the work to be performed, and the conditions under which it is to be performed, are perfectly and unambiguously defined in the contract documents, so that a simple comparison of bid prices is made to the lowest responsive bidder.

This ideal is rarely reached in any construction contract, but it is especially illusory for tunnel (or any underground) construction, owing to several peculiarities inherent in underground work:

(1) Tunnels are invariably lengthy structures, and over extended lengths the characteristic of the ground (and groundwater) may vary widely and unpredictably. Despite the most astute interpretations (neither of which are universally attained), the exact nature of the ground is never completely disclosed until it is exposed by excavation at the tunnel heading (and, indeed, this nature may change subsequently owing to time-dependent effects). As a result, the work that is actually performed may differ in small or large measure from that expected by either or both parties at time of contract award.

(2) The methods, equipment, and skills required for safe and economical tunnel construction depend on the nature of the ground, and may be disproportionately sensitive to small changes in ground characteristics. In particular, small changes in groundwater content or permeability, which are especially difficult to predict accurately, may have large effects on how the work must be performed.

(3) Preconstruction investigations can determine the characteristics of (more or less

representative samples of) the existing ground. The processes of construction may change these characteristics (e. g. distressing rock joints by excavation may cause them to open, and convert a dry tunnel into a waterfall). The contractor's choice of equipment and construction methods, and the skill of his workers, may increase or decrease deleterious changes in ground characteristics during construction.

(4) In urban tunnel work, the existence and location of unknown buried obstructions and hazardous conditions (such as gasoline derived from abandoned leaking underground storage tanks) is difficult to determine beforehand and can have major effects on the work.

(5) In urban work, it is not uncommon that cost of dealing with third parties (government regulations, adjacent structure protection, support and relocation of utilities, hauling and disposal of excavated materials, traffic maintenance, site clearance and preparation, and restoration of the surface after completion of construction) may equal or exceed the cost of constructing the desired facility. The best of agreements between two parties regarding how third parties will act or behave is considerably less than infallible.

In traditional construction contracting practice, the owner allocated all risks to the contractor, saying in effect, "you deal with all construction problems and all third parties, and don't bother me." The contractor's bid price was supposed to cover the costs of mitigating all problems related to unknown site or geotechnical conditions, as well as all delays or difficulties introduced by the actions or omissions of third parties. These were essentially gambles, which the owner asked the contractor to make.

But at the same time, the owner told all bidders that the contract would be awarded to the lowest responsive bid. A bid that included reservations or exclusions regarding any risk was deemed "nonresponsive."

This practice produced two results:

(1) Experienced and prudent contractors, who included in their bids substantial contingencies to cover perceived risks, found that their bids were rarely low. In the minority of contracts that they did win (generally the more difficult ones that scared inexperienced contractors away), they found that if they did materialize they went broke. In this boom-and-bust climate, if the boom came first, he went out of business. Tunnel construction contracting was a short-lived occupation.

(2) Less experienced, or more adventurous, contractors took an optimistic view of risks of underground construction, and included little or no contingencies in their bids. They won more contracts, and when the risks materialized they mounted a vigorous campaign of claims and litigation, generally on the assertion that the contract was defective, in that the owner knew, or should have known, or failed to take adequate measures to discover, conditions of which the contractor should have been advised in the solicitation of bids.

This was the situation in the 1950s, when a great surge in urban underground construction occurred across the United States. Construction litigation became an increasingly popular and lucrative (for the lawyers) occupation, and tunnel construction developed a bad name among owners and the general public, as prone to large, unexpected overruns of projected costs and schedules.

Differing site conditions clause

The greatest source of conflict was the allegation of "changed conditions," or more specially, "differing site conditions." The first attempt to mitigate this problem was the development by the Corps of Engineers of a standard contract clause, which has evolved into the following, which is now almost universally included in tunnel contracts:

(1) The Contractor shall promptly, and before such conditions are disturbed, notify the Owner in writing of subsurface or latent physical conditions at the contract, or unknown physical conditions at the site, of an unusual nature, differing materially from those ordinarily encountered and generally recognized as inherent in work of the character provided for in this contract. The Owner shall promptly investigate the conditions, and if he finds that such conditions do materially so differ and cause an increase or decrease in the Contractor's cost of, or time required for, performance of any part of the work under this contract.

The Owner shall promptly investigate the conditions, and if he finds that such conditions do materially so differ and cause an increase or decrease in the Contractor's cost of, or time required for, performance of any part of the work under this contract, whether or not changed as a result of such conditions, an equitable adjustment shall be made and the contract modified in writing accordingly.

(2) No claim of the Contractor under this clause shall be allowed unless the Contractor has given the notice required in (1) above; provided, however, the time prescribed therefore may be extended by the Owner.

(3) No claim by the Contractor for an equitable adjustment hereunder shall be allowed if asserted after final payment under this contract.

One valuable attribute of this particular clause is that it has been through the courts for a long enough time that there is general agreement among judges and lawyers as to what the words mean, and on that account it is desirable to follow this wording scrupulously.

The Differing Site Conditions clause enabled the owner's contracting officer to make equitable contract adjustments for the more egregious cases, where he could in good conscience find that site conditions did indeed differ so clearly that he could not, by accepting the contractor's claim, be held to breach his duty to the owner, to protect his interests. General acceptance of this clause by the courts eased the strain of loosening the rigid contract bonds, and the climate for tunnel construction improved. Prudent contractors found that they were protected from the more outrageous risks, their contingencies came down, and they started to gain more contractors improved, and their litigation became less raucous.

Nonetheless, many cases remained in which the owner and the contractor did not agree on whether the conditions differed, and these cases still ended up, after the contract appeals process was exhausted, in court.

It became apparent that tunnel construction is an arcane art to the legal profession, and much of the time and cost of litigation was being expended on educating the lawyers and judges (to say nothing of juries) on the technical terms and practicalities of tunnel construction. Since this education was perforce rudimentary, and the field remained obscure and mysterious to the lawyers and case on the basis of fine points of law and alleged legal precedents (which they understood). July cases tended to be decide by the relative persuasiveness of the opposing lawyers rather then by any consideration of the relative equity of the parties.

This situation satisfied neither the owners nor the contractors. A particular burden was the length of time the litigation process consumed, which meant that final settlement was frequently delayed until years (sometimes many years) after construction was completed.

One of the most prominent tunnel contract disputes of this time concerned the first bore of the Eisenhower (Straight Creek) Tunnel in Colorado. The final settlement doubled the original contract price, long after the tunnel was completed. The Colorado Highway Department determined that on the second bore there should be a better way to resolve contract disputes. Mr. A. A. Mathews, a construction engineering consultant, recommended a Mediation Board to resolve any disagreements between the owner and the contractor that could not be settled through the claims process of the contract. This was so successful that it became a model for what has evolved into the Disputes Review Board process, which is a standard feature of modern tunnel construction contracts.

A Disputes Review Board is composed of three members, all of whom are experts in tunnel construction or tunnel engineering. One member is selected by the owner, one by the contractor, and the third by the first two. They provide informal mediation of technical and contractual issues on which the owner and contractor are unable to reach agreement under the provisions of the contract. The Board provides a written report and recommendation regarding each dispute, which is not binding but carries great weight because the members are chosen, and recognized, for their professional experience and perspective. If either party rejects the Board's recommendation, it is with the knowledge that in subsequent litigation the courts will value the Board's recommendation highly.

The Disputes Review Board (DRB) procedure has been found to have a number of advantages for both the owner and the contractor:

(1) The DRB procedure is much less costly and time consuming than formal litigation.

(2) Recommendation of professional experts is more likely to be based on practical consideration than on abstruse points of law.

(3) The saving in senior management time devoted to contract dispute resolution is significant.

(4) Disputes are settled promptly while the construction continues to go forward, and consequential delays and costs are reduced.

(5) The process is much less adversarial than litigation, and the climate of contract administration is improved.

The DRB process has also been found to have some unexpected benefits:

(1) By its very existence, the Board reduces the incidence of claims and fosters settlement between the two parties, because both parties know that the Board cannot be bluffed and that insecure claims (or arbitrary disallowances) are likely to be rejected by the Board.

(2) Since the contracting officer is relieved of the onus of being both the owner's representative and the judge of the contractor's claim, he is enabled to be more flexible in dealing with unanticipated developments during construction. Since he can pass ambiguous issues to the

Board for equitable resolution, he does not have to find black and white solutions to gray problems.

With respect to the largest classification of tunnel construction contract dispute, Differing Site Conditions, an important companion to the DRB procedure is the Geotechnical Design Summary Report (GDSR), which is a part of the contract documents, is a record of the engineer's preconstruction site investigation and laboratory tests, as well as a discussion of the engineer's interpretation of how this information has affected the design and may affect construction. In particular, the GDSR is intended to illuminate any restrictions on construction methods, equipment, or sequences that may be included in the specifications.

In broad terms, the GDSR is intended to define a basis for the solicitation of bids. It provides the assumptions with respect to site geotechnical conditions that are to be used by both the contractor and the owner in performance of their respective duties under the contract. The GDSR defines a box-if the actual conditions disclosed during construction fall within this box, they are covered by the contract; If they fall outside the box, they require modification to the contract.

In cases of disagreement about whether a condition falls inside or outside, the matter may be settled directly by negotiation between the owner and contractor, through the stipulated claims process, and if this fails, the DRB mediates the dispute and recommends a settlement.

More than 25 years of experience with the DRB process has now been accumulated. The reduction in the cost and time required for dispute resolution has been so substantial that the process has spread from tunnel and underground construction to general heavy construction and even to complex commercial building projects. The scope of DRB activities has similarly been extended from its original focus on differing site conditions to include all forms of technical and contractual disputes between the owner and contractor.

A comprehensive discussion of the history, operation, and effects of the DRB process is given in the Construction Disputes Review Board Manual, by Mathews, Matyas, Smith, and Sperry, 1995 (McGraw-Hill).

A few words are in order on the use and misuse of the Geotechnical Design Summary Report. It is intended to clarify, insofar as the imperfect state of engineering art permits, incidence of surprises during construction. It is not a promise or warranty, to either the owner or the contractor, that condition different from those described will not be encountered. It is, rather, a definition of what is to be covered by the contract (and the bid price), and a notice that excursions beyond what is described in the GDSR will be legitimate grounds for a contract modification. (Note however, that disputes about what is an inclusion and what is an excursion are contemplated, and these are to be settled through the DRB process.)

The preparation of a GDSR is perhaps the greatest moral challenge faced by a tunnel engineer. It is possible to draw up a GDSR that predicts such great hazards that all contractors will raise their prices and the likelihood of differing site conditions claims and disputes is minimized. This is not likely to serve the owner's best interests.

It is also possible to draw up a GDSR that predicts such benign conditions that all bids will be low, but the risk of disputes, changes, and cost overruns is sharply increased. This is also not in the owner's (or engineer's) interest.

If the owner dose not choose to found an adequate geotechnical exploration and testing program (as discussed in Chapter 4), the engineer's basis for predicting construction conditions is reduced. But even the most comprehensive preconstruction investigation is never perfect. No engineer, owner, or contractor has yet been found who can outsmart nature all the time.

The engineer must therefore draw his "box" with what information he was at hand, and use his experience and intuition to illuminate the dark crevices where nature has squirreled away her surprises for contractors, engineers, and owners. In the end, he must choose to draw his box where, in his professional judgment, it will yield the best balance of risk and price for his client, the owner.

Tunnel engineering and construction remain a field in which honest professionals can and will disagree, as well as one in which an experienced of other parties. *Over the past 25 years the concepts of the Disputes Review Board and the Geotechnical Design Summary Report have evolved to provide the means for resolving honest disagreements and for protecting the innocent, and to cast a spell of civilization over the jungle that has been the venue of tunnel construction contracting for so long.*

Text B Part of FIDIC Clause
部分 FIDIC 合同条款

14 Contractor price and Payment

14.1 The contractor Price

Unless otherwise stated in the Particular Conditions:

(a) the Contract Price shall be agreed or determined under Sub-Clause 12.3 [Evaluation] and be subject to adjustments in accordance with the Contract;

(b) the Contractor shall pay all taxes, duties and fees required to be paid by him under the Contract, and the Contract Price shall not be adjusted for any of these costs except as stated in Sub-Clause 13.7 [Adjustments for Changes in Legislation];

(c) any quantities which may be set out in the Bill of Quantities or other Schedule are estimated quantities and are not to be taken as the actual and correct quantities:

(i) of the Works which the Contractor is required to execute, or

(ii) for the purposes of Clause 12 [Measurement and Evaluation]; and

(d) the Contractor shall submit to the Engineer, within 28 days after the Commencement Date, a proposed breakdown of each lump sum price in the Schedules. The Engineer may take account of the breakdown when preparing Payment Certificates, but shall not be bound by ft.

14.2 Advance Payment

The Employer shall make an advance payment, as an interest-free loan for mobilization, when the Contractor submits a guarantee in accordance with this Sub-Clause. The total advance payment, the number and timing of installments (if more than one), and the applicable currencies and proportions, shall be as stated in the Appendix to Tender.

Unless and until the Employer receives this guarantee, or if the total advance payment is not stated in the Appendix to Tender, this Sub-Clause shall not apply.

The Engineer shall issue an Interim Payment Certificate for the first installment after receiving a Statement (under Sub-Clause 14.3 [Application for Interim Payment Certificates]) and after the Employer receives (i) the Performance Security in accordance with Sub-Clause 4.2 [Performance Security] and (ii) a guarantee in amounts and currencies equal to the advance payment. This guarantee shall be issued by an entity and from within a country (or other jurisdiction) approved by the Employer, and shall be in the form annexed to the Particular Conditions or in another form approved by the Employer.

The Contractor shall ensure that the guarantee is valid and enforceable until the advance payment has been repaid, but its amount may be progressively reduced by the amount repaid by the Contractor as indicated in the Payment Certificates. If the terms of the guarantee specify its expiry date, and the advance payment has not been repaid by the date 28 days prior to the expiry date, the Contractor shall extend the validity of the guarantee until the advance payment has been repaid.

The advance payment shall be repaid through percentage deductions in Payment Certificates. Unless other percentages are stated in the Appendix to Tender:

(a) Deductions shall commence in the Payment Certificate in which the total of all certified interim payments (excluding the advance payment and deductions and repayments of retention) exceeds ten per cent (10%) of the Accepted; Contract Amount less Provisional Sums; and

(b) Deductions shall be made at the amortization rate of one quarter (25%) of the amount of each Payment Certificate (excluding the advance payment and deductions and repayments of retention) in the currencies and proportions of the advance payment, until such time as the advance payment has been repaid.

If the advance payment has not been repaid prior to the issue of the Taking-Over Certificate for the Works or prior to termination under Clause 15 [Termination by Employer], Clause 16 [Suspension and Termination by Contractor] or Clause 19 [Force Majeure] (as the case may be), the whole of the balance then outstanding shall immediately become due and payable by the Contractor to the Employer.

14.3 Application for Interim Payment Certificates

The Contractor shall submit a Statement in six copies to the Engineer after the end of each month, in a form approved by the Engineer, showing in detail the amounts to which the Contractor considers himself to be entitled, together with supporting documents which shall include the report on the progress during this month in accordance with Sub-Clause 4.21 [Progress Reports].

The Statement shall include the following items, as applicable, which shall be expressed in the various currencies in which the Contract Price is payable, in the sequence listed:

(a) the estimated contract value of the Works executed and the Contractor's documents produced up to the end of the month (including Variations but excluding items described in sub-paragraphs (b) to (g) below);

(b) any amounts to be added and deducted for changes in legislation and changes in cost, in accordance with Sub-Clause 13.7 [Adjustments for Changes in Legislation] and Sub-Clause 13.8 [Adjustments for Changes in Cost];

(c) any amount to be deducted for retention, calculated by applying the percentage of retention stated in the Appendix to Tender to the total of the above amounts, until the amount so retained by the Employer reaches the limit of Retention Money (if any) stated in the Appendix to Tender;

(d) any amounts to be added and deducted for the advance payment and repayments in accordance with Sub-Clause 14.2 [Advance Payment];

(e) any amounts to be added and deducted for Plant and Materials in accordance with Sub-Clause 14.5 [Plant and Materials intended for the Works];

(f) any other additions or deductions which may have become due under the Contract or otherwise, including those under Clause 20 [Claims, Disputes and Arbitration];

(g) the deduction of amounts certified in all previous Payment Certificates.

Schedule of Payments

If the Contract includes a schedule of payments specifying the installments in which the Contract Price will be paid, then unless otherwise stated in this schedule:

(a) the installments quoted in this schedule of payments shall be the estimated contract values for the purposes of sub-paragraph (a) of Sub-Clause 14.3 [Application for Interim Payment Certificates];

(b) Sub-Clause 14.5 [Plant and Materials intended for the Works] shall not apply;

(c) if these installments are not defined by reference to the actual progress achieved in executing the Works, and if actual progress is found to be less than that on which this schedule of payments was based, then the Engineer may proceed in accordance with Sub-Clause 3.5 [Determinations] to agree or determine revised installments, which shall take account of the extent to which progress is less than that on which the installments were previously based.

If the Contract does not include a schedule of payments, the Contractor shall submit non-binding estimates of the payments which he expects to become due during each quarterly period. The first estimate shall be submitted within 42 days after the Commencement Date. Revised estimates shall be submitted at quarterly intervals, until the Taking-Over Certificate has been issued for the Works.

14.4 Plant and Materials

If this Sub-Clause applies, Interim Payment Certificates shall include, under subintended for the Works paragraph (e) of Sub-Clause 14.3, (i) an amount for Plant and Materials which have been sent to the Site for incorporation in the Permanent Works, and (ii) a reduction when the contract value of such Plant and Materials is included as part of the Permanent Works under sub-paragraph (a) of Sub-Clause 14.3 [Application for Interim Payment Certificates].

If the lists referred to in sub-paragraphs (b)(i) or (c)(i) below are not included in the Appendix to Tender, this Sub-Clause shall not apply.

The Engineer shall determine and certify each addition if the following conditions are satisfied:

(a) The Contractor has:

(i) Kept satisfactory records (including the orders, receipts, Costs and use of Plant and

Materials) which are available for inspection, and

(ii) Submitted a statement of the Cost of acquiring and delivering the Plant and Materials to the Site, supported by satisfactory evidence.

or

(b) The relevant Plant and Materials:

(i) are those listed in the Appendix to Tender for payment when shipped;

(ii) have been shipped to the Country, en route to the Site, in accordance with the Contract; and

(iii) are described in a clean shipped bill of lading or other evidence of shipment, which has been submitted to the Engineer together with evidence of payment of freight and insurance, any other documents reasonably required, and a bank guarantee in a form and issued by an entity approved by the Employer in amounts and currencies equal to the amount due under this Sub-Clause: this guarantee may be in a similar form to the form referred to in Sub-Clause 14.2 [Advance Payment] and shall be valid until the Plant and Materials are properly stored on Site and protected against loss, damage or deterioration.

or

(c) The relevant Plant and Materials:

(i) are those-listed in the Appendix to Tender for payment when delivered to the Site, and

(ii) have been delivered to and are properly stored on the Site, are protected against loss, damage or deterioration, and appear to be in accordance with the Contract.

The additional amount to be certified shall be the equivalent of eighty percent of the Engineer's determination of the cost of the Plant and Materials (including delivery to Site), taking account of the documents mentioned in this Sub-Clause and of the contract value of the Plant and Materials.

The currencies for this additional amount shall be the same as those in which payment will become due when the contract value is included under sub-paragraph (a) of Sub-Clause 14.3 [Application for Interim Payment Certificates]. At that time, the Payment Certificate shall include the applicable reduction which shall be equivalent to, and in the same currencies and proportions as, this additional amount for the relevant Plant and Materials.

No amount will be certified or paid until the Employer has received and approved the Performance Security. Thereafter, the Engineer shall, within 28 days after receiving a Statement and supporting documents, issue to the Employer an Interim Payment Certificate which shall state the amount which the Engineer fairly determines to be due, with supporting particulars.

However, prior to issuing the Taking-Over Certificate for the Works, the Engineer shall not be bound to issue an Interim Payment Certificate in an amount which would (after retention and other deductions) be less than the minimum amount of Interim Payment Certificates (if any) stated in the Appendix to Tender. In this event, the Engineer shall give notice to the Contractor accordingly.

An Interim Payment Certificate shall not be withheld for any other reason, although:

(a) if any thing supplied or work done by the Contractor is not in accordance with the Contract, the cost of rectification or replacement may be withheld until rectification or replacement has been completed; and/or

(b) if the Contractor was or is failing to perform any work or obligation it accordance with the Contract, and had been so notified by the Engineer, the value of this work or obligation may be withheld until the work or obligation has been performed.

The Engineer may in any Payment Certificate make any correction or modification that should properly be made to any previous Payment Certificate. A Payment Certificate shall not be deemed to indicate the Engineer's acceptance, approval, consent or satisfaction.

14.5 Payment

The Employer shall pay to the Contractor:

(a) the first installment of the advance payment within 42 days after issuing the Letter of Acceptance or within 21 days after receiving the documents in accordance with Sub-Clause 4.2 [Performance Security] and Sub-Clause 14.2 [Advance Payment], whichever is later;

(b) the amount certified in each Interim Payment Certificate within 56 days after the Engineer receives the Statement and supporting documents; and

(c) the amount certified in the Final Payment Certificate within 56 days after the Employer receives this Payment Certificate.

Payment of the amount due in each currency shall be made into the bank account, nominated by the Contractor, in the payment country (for this currency) specified in the Contract.

14.6 Delayed Payment

If the Contractor does not receive payment in accordance with Sub-Clause 14.7 [Payment], the Contractor shall be entitled to receive financing charges compounded monthly on the amount unpaid during the period of delay. This period shall be deemed to commence on the date for payment specified in Sub-Clause 14.7 [Payment], irrespective [in the case of its sub-paragraph (b)] of the date on which any Interim Payment Certificate is issued.

Unless otherwise stated in the Particular Conditions, these financing charges shall be calculated at the annual rate of three percentage points above the discount rate of the central bank in the country of the currency of payment, and shall be paid in such currency.

The Contractor shall be entitled to this payment without formal notice or certification, and without prejudice to any other right or remedy.

14.7 Payment of Retention money

When the Taking-Over Certificate has been issued for the Works, the first half of the Retention Money shall be certified by the Engineer for payment to the Contractor. If a Taking-Over Certificate is issued for a Section or part of the Works, a proportion of the Retention Money shall be certified and paid. This proportion shag be two-fifths (40%) of the proportion calculated by dividing the estimated contract value of the Section or part, by the estimated final Contract Price.

Promptly after the latest of the expiry dates of the Defects Notification Periods, the outstanding balance of the Retention Money shall be certified by the Engineer for payment to the Contractor. If a Taking-Over Certificate was issued for a Section, a proportion of the second half of the Retention Money shall be certified and paid promptly after the expiry date of the Defects Notification Period for the Section. This proportion shall be two-fifths (40%) of the proportion calculated by dividing the estimated contract value of the Section by the estimated final Contract Price.

However, if any work remains to be executed under Clause 11 [Defects Liability], the Engineer shall be entitled to withhold certification of the estimated cost of this work until it has been executed.

When calculating these proportions, no account shall be taken of any adjustments under Sub-Clause 13.7 [Adjustments for Changes in Legislation] and Sub-Clause 13.8 [Adjustments for changes in-cost].

14.8　Statement of Completion

Within 84 days after receiving the Taking-Over Certificate for the Works, the Contractor shall submit to the Engineer six copies of a Statement at completion with supporting documents, in accordance with Sub-Clause 14.3 [Application for Interim Payment Certificates], showing:

(a) the value of all work done in accordance with the Contract up to the date stated in the Taking-Over Certificate for the Works;

(b) any further sums which the Contractor considers to be due; and

(c) an estimate of any other amounts which the Contractor considers will become due to him under the Contract. Estimated amounts shall be shown separately in this Statement at completion.

The Engineer shall then certify in accordance with Sub-Clause 14.6 [Issue of Interim Payment Certificates].

14.9　Application for Final Payment Certificate

Within 56 days after receiving the Performance Certificate, the Contractor shall submit, to the Engineer, six copies of a draft final statement with supporting documents showing in detail in a form—approved by the Engineer:

(a) the value of all work done in accordance with the Contract, and

(b) any further sums which the Contractor considers to be due to him under the Contract or otherwise.

If the Engineer disagrees with or cannot verify any part of the draft final statement, the Contractor shall submit such further information as the Engineer may reasonably require and shall make such changes in the draft as may be agreed between them. The Contractor shall then prepare and submit to the Engineer the final statement as agreed. This agreed statement is referred to in these Conditions as the "Final Statement".

14.10　Discharge

When submitting the Final Statement, the Contractor shall submit a written discharge which confirms that the total of the Final Statement represents full and final settlement of all moneys due to the Contractor under or in connection with the Contract. This discharge may state that it becomes effective when the Contractor has received the Performance Security and the outstanding balance of this total, in which event the discharge shall be effective on such date.

14.11　Issue of Final Payment Certificate

Within 28 days after receiving the Final Statement and written discharge in accordance with Sub-Clause 14.11 [Application for Final Payment Certificate] and Sub-Clause 14.12 [Discharge], the Engineer shall issue, to the Employer, the Final Payment Certificate which shall state:

(a) the amount which is finally due; and

(b) after giving credit to the Employer for all amounts previously paid by the Employer and for all sums to which the Employer is entitled, the balance (if any) due from the Employer to the contractor.

If the Contractor has not applied for a Final Payment Certificate in accordance with Sub-Clause 14.11 [Application for Final Payment Certificate] and Sub-Clause 14.12 [Discharge], the Engineer shall request the Contractor to do so. If the Contractor fails to submit an application within a period of 28 days, the Engineer shall issue the Final Payment Certificate for such amount as he fairly determines to be due.

14.12 Cessation of Employer's Liability

The Employer shall not be liable to the Contractor for any matter or thing under or in connection with the Contract or execution of the Works, except to the extent that the Contractor shall have included an amount expressly for it:

(a) in the Final Statement and also

(b) (except for matters or things arising after the issue of the Taking-Over Certificate for the Works) in the Statement at completion described in Sub-Clause 14.10 [Statement at Completion].

However, this Sub-Clause shall not limit the Employer's liability under his indemnification obligations, or the Employer's liability in any case of fraud, deliberate default or reckless misconduct by the Employer.

Currencies of Payment

The Contract Price shall be paid in the currency or currencies named in the Appendix to Tender. Unless otherwise stated in the Particular Conditions, if more than one currency is so named, payments shall be made as follows:

(a) If the Accepted Contract Amount was expressed in Local Currency only:

(i) the proportions or amounts of the Local and Foreign Currencies, and the fixed rates of exchange to be used for calculating the payments, shall be as stated in the Appendix to Tender, except as otherwise agreed by both Parties;

(ii) Payments and deductions under Sub-Clause 13.5 [Provisional Sums] and Sub-Clause 13.7 [Adjustments for Changes in Legislation] shall be made in the applicable currencies and proportions; and

(iii) Other payments and deductions under sub-paragraphs (a) to (d) of Sub-Clause 14.3 [Application for Interim Payment Certificates] shall be made in the currencies and proportions specified in sub-paragraph (a)(i) above.

(b) Payment of the damages specified in the Appendix to Tender shall be made in the currencies and proportions specified in the Appendix to Tender.

(c) Other payments to the Employer by the Contractor shall be made in the currency in which the sum was expended by the Employer, or in such currency as may be agreed by both Parties.

(d) If any amount payable by the Contractor to the Employer in a particular currency exceeds the sum payable by the Employer to the Contractor in that currency, the Employer may recover the balance of this amount from the sums otherwise payable to the Contractor in other currencies; and

(e) If no rates of exchange are stated in the Appendix to Tender, they shall be those prevailing on the Base Date and determined by the central bank of the Country.

Text C   A Contract Agreement
合同协议书

Through open tendering, it is confirmed that _____ is the prime contractor of contract section 01 of Beijing Rail Transportation Fangshan Line North Extension Line Engineering Design. Hereby Beijing Municipal Rail Communication Construction Management CO., Ltd. (the Employer) and _____ (the prime contractor) through bilateral negotiation agreed to enter into the design contractor of section 01 for the engineering design of Beijing Rail Transport Fangshan Line North Extension Line Project.

In accordance with the provisions of the design contract, the prime contractor shall perform design service under contract section 01 of Beijing Rail Transport Fangshan Line North Extension Line, accept the designer management performed by the employer and network-based designer and provide design results in conformity with national specification and the contract requirement.

An agreement on following items is reached and the given contract is concluded.

Under contract section 01 for the engineering design of Beijing Rail Transportation Fangshan Line North Extension Line Project the mileage ranges _____, in length of _____; the specific design scope and associated requirements are specified in the contract.

The following documents shall be deemed as constituents of the contract for reading and interpretation. The constituent contract documents of the given contract shall be mutually explanatory explain each other and supplementary to each other. Provided any conflicts disputes or inconsistancy mutual contradiction arise among the contract documents or obvious mistakes identified in the contractual documents, explanation shall be made in following order of priority.

(1) Contract agreement;
(2) Letter of acceptance;
(3) Letter of Tender and Appendix to the Letter of Tender;
(4) Contract terms;
(5) Appendix to the contract;
(6) Other tender documents and Clarification supplementary document;
(7) Principal work content;
(8) Principal technical requirement.

Further provisions as follows:

(1) For the same type of contract documents, the latest version or latest issuance governs.

(2) In the contract conclusion and performance, all the agreements signed, issued and received by bilateral parties and associated with conclusion or performance of given contract, correspondence, minutes and memorandum are constituents of given contract. The order of priority for interpretation shall be determined subject to the correlation between their contents and other contract documents.

(3) The appendix to the contract and the contract are indivisible and shall take effect upon the confirmation by signature of the client and designer including but not limited to the following contents.

①Appendix 1 Requirement on design staff management
②Appendix 2 Requirement on design progress control
③Appendix 3 Design management methods (separate volume)
④Appendix 4 Design quality management
⑤Appendix 5 List of design results
⑥Appendix 6 Design interfaces
⑦Appendix 7 Design schedule
⑧Appendix 8 Design organization and personnel

(4) Considering the payment of contractor in the contract document, the contractor hereby makes a commitment of performance of the service prescribed in this contract to the client.

(5) The total contract price to be paid to the designer for his completion of design assignment and design service in associated assistance prescribed in the contract is: RBM(in number) _____ Yuan, (in word) _____ Yuan only.

(6) The project responsible person in charge of the design under given contract section is _____.

(7) The Client and the employer hereby agree to pay the amount stipulated in the contract to the Contractor as per the payment schedule and mode noted in the contract as the payment for the design service provided by the Designer.

(8) This contract is done in fifteen copies of which two are in original and thirteen in replication copies. The Employer and Designer hold one original copy respectively. The Employer holds 10 replication copies and the Designer three copies.

Both parties in the contract agreed that this given contract only takes effect upon the contractor's payment of effective performance security in adequate amount and the signatures of the bilateral parties in the contract.

Employer: Beijing Municipal Rail Transport Construction Management CO., Ltd.
Legal Person:
or
Authorized agent:
Date: Y   M   D
Address:
Telephone No. :

Prime Contractor:
Legal Person:
or
Authorized agent:
Date: Y   M   D
Address:
Telephone No. :

II. Terms and terminology

competitive bid contract	投标合同
contractor	承包人
owner	业主
Appendix to Tender	投标函附录
FIDIC	国际咨询工程师联合会
DAB	争端裁决委员会
retention Money	保留金
temporary Works	临时工程
force Majeure	不可抗力
site	现场
variation	变更
contract agreement	合同协议书
letter of acceptance	中标函
letter of tender	投标函
particular conditions	专用条件
general conditions	通用条件
specification	规范
drawings	图纸
confidential details	保密事项

III. Questions and difficult sentence analysis

1. Questions for brainstorming discussion

(1) What are DAB and its performance?
(2) What is force majeure referred to?
(3) Briefly state the project tender procedures.
(4) Briefly state the general obligations and duties of works Owner, Employer and Contractor. Contractor.
(5) What is the purpose of retention money in a works contract?

2. Difficult sentences analysis

(1) In English law, from which American practice is derived, a contract is an agreement between two parties in which one party undertakes to perform for the other a definite, mutually understood task for a defined compensation. Construction contract law is generally based on this underlying premise.

译文：英国法律是美国实践的依据，根据英国法律，合同是双方达成的协议，其中一方接受为另一方实施明确的，达成共识的任务并为此获得补偿。建设合同法律通常基于该基本前提。

(2) This ideal is rarely reached in any construction contract, but it is especially illusory for tunnel (or any underground) construction, owing to several peculiarities inherent in underground work.

译文：任何建设合同都很难实现该理想，由于地下工程固有的特点，在隧道（或任何地下工程）建设中，尤其成为幻想。

(3) A Disputes Review Board is composed of three members, all of whom are experts in tunnel construction or tunnel engineering. One member is selected by the owner, one by the contractor, and the third by the first two. They provide informal mediation of technical and contractual issues on which the owner and contractor are unable to reach agreement under the provisions of the contract. The Board provides a written report and recommendation regarding each dispute, which is not binding but carries great weight because the members are chosen, and recognized, for their professional experience and perspective.

译文：争端审查委员会由三名成员组成，他们都是隧道建设或隧道工程领域的专家。业主挑选一名，承包人选一名，这两名成员共同挑选第三名成员。该委员会就业主和承包人未能在合同条件下达成共识的技术和合同事项，提供非正式的调解，并出具一份解决每个争端问题的书面报告和建议，该书面报告和建议不具约束力但很有分量，因为这三名专家之所以被挑选和认可作为委员会成员，正是由于他们丰富的专业经验和独特的观点和视角。

(4) Over the past 25 years the concepts of the Disputes Review Board and the Geotechnical Design Summary Report have evolved to provide the means for resolving honest disagreements and for protecting the innocent, and to cast a spell of civilization over the jungle that has been the venue of tunnel construction contracting for so long.

译文：在过去的 25 年中，已经形成了争端审查委员会和岩土设计总结报告的概念，作为解决诚实的分歧和保护无辜的措施和手段，一直以来成了裁决隧道建设合同纷争的文明之举。

Ⅳ. Translation case study

Case 1

Chinese	English translation
1 合同各方权利与义务	1 The obligations and rights of all concerned parties under the contract
1.1 业主的权利和义务	1.1 Owner's obligations and rights
1.1.1 业主为北京轨道交通房山线北延工程投资人，委托发包人对北京轨道交通房山线北延工程设计进行全面管理工作。	1.1.1 The project owner is the investor of Fangshan Line North Extension Line of Beijing Municipal Rail Communication and entrusts the contractor to carry out overall management on engineering design for Fangshan Line North Extension Line of Beijing Municipal Rail Communication.
1.1.2 业主对本项目的实施、终止具有抉择权，对本项目有关设计功能和重大投资等重大管理问题具有抉择权。	1.1.2 The Owner is entitled to the right of decision on the project execution and termination and has the right of decision on such major management issues concerning design performance and major investment.

continue

Chinese	English translation
1.1.3 业主有权参与设计全过程,对工程设计过程的抉择,控制,实施等环节实行监督管理。 1.1.4 业主有权对项目提出商业需求及其他用户需求,提出设计方案改进意见,参与商业规划编制及方案设计的全过程,并对方案进行审定。 1.1.5 业主负责筹措项目资金,通过发包人向各参建单位支付工程价款和费用。	1.1.3 The Owner has the right to participate in the whole design process, execute supervision and control over the decision-making, the control and execution in the project design process. 1.1.4 The Owner is entitled to raise commercial needs and other user's demands and has the right to propose comments on design improvement participate in the whole process of commercial plan compilation and design solution and make review and confirmation of design solutions. 1.1.5 The Owner is responsible for fund raise for the project and pay works price and expenditure through the Contractor.

Case 2

Chinese	English translation
1.2 发包人的权利和义务 1.2.1 发包人受业主的委托,对工程设计过程的抉择,控制,实施等环节实行全面管理,协调和监督设计工程开展。 1.2.2 发包人负责检查总包人职责的执行情况,确保设计工作有序进行,对不能胜任合同职责的,发包人有权给予处罚,直至解除合同。 1.2.3 发包人有权对建设项目提出用户需求,提出设计改进意见,检查,督促建设项目的进展情况。 1.2.4 发包人负责落实审定主要技术标准,技术参数,设备类型等。 1.2.5 发包人负责组织审查和确认设计各阶段的设计成果及重大技术方案,做好对方案设计的组织评审工作,要求总包人依据审查意见对其成果性文件予以完善。 1.2.6 发包人负责施工设计变更终审,设计变更审批,设计节约投资评价等工作。 1.2.7 发包人有权审核与调整总包人和设计人编制的设计概算。	1.2 the Employer's obligations and rights 1.2.1 The Employer, under the entrustment of the Owner, carries out overall management of the decision-making, the control and the execution during whole process of the project design and coordinates and supervises the design. 1.2.2 The Employer is responsible for checking the Primer Contractor's obligation fulfillment and ensuring the design progress in order. The Employer is entitled to impose punishment till contract termination for incompetence. 1.2.3 The employer has the right to raise user's demands on the construction project, to provide comments for the improvement of design, to check and supervise the works progress. 1.2.4 The Employer is responsible for execution of review on major technical specifications, technical parameters and equipment types and so on so forth. 1.2.5 The Employer is responsible for initiating calling on expert's review and determination of design results and major technical solutions of all phases, duly organize the review on design solutions and request the Prime Contractor to complete and make perfect his design solutions in compliance with review comments. 1.2.6 The Employer is responsible for construction and design variations and review and approval of such design variations and evaluation on design economical investment. 1.2.7 The Employer is entitled to review, make adjustment of design budget made by the Prime Contractor and Designer.

Case 3

Chinese	English translation
1.4 总包人的权利和义务	1.4 Primer Contractor's obligations and rights
1.4.1 总包人接受发包人的委托,负责北京轨道交通房山线北延的工程设计,以及全线工程的设计质量,设计安全,设计进度及设计投资控制全面负责,并对本线路其他设计人的工作进行监督指导,标准统一,设计审查和技术把关。	1.4.1 The Prime Contractor, under the entrustment of the Employer, is responsible for the engineering design of Fangshan Line North Extension Line of Beijing Municipal Communications and undertakes overall responsibility for the whole line engineering works design quality, design safety, design progress and design investment and supervise and guide the design of other designers for this line, unify design standard, review design solutions and perform technical control.
1.4.2 总包人接受发包人的委托,根据工程设计依据文件及有关的技术说明,国家有关的设计标准,技术规范,规程完成全线工程设计工作(含导向标识设计,不含车站公共区装修设计,车站地面附属建筑物设计),包括并不限于方案设计,初步设计,招标图设计,施工图设计及后续设计施工配合等。	1.4.2 The Prime Contractor, under the entrustment of the Employer, completes the engineering design of the whole line (including the guide sign design, excluding the station public zone decoration design and station surface ancillary building design) and the design includes but is not limited to the concept design solution design, preliminary design, pre-bidding drawing design, detailed design for execution and subsequent design and rendering cooperation during works execution in accordance with the project design document and associated technical specification, associated national design standard, technical specification and code.
1.4.3 总包人负责审查设计人提交的成果性文件,对设计文件的正确性,完备性,可靠性,可操作性,经济性付总体审查责任。总包人应对设计人的设计质量负有连带保证责任,发包人或政府部门组织的审查并不减免其上述责任。	1.4.3 The Prime Contractor is responsible for the check on the result-natured document submitted by designers and undertakes the responsibility of overall review for the correctness, completeness, reliability, operatability and economy of the design document. The Prime Contractor shall undertake joint and several liabilities for the assurance of design quality of the designers. The inspection and review organized by Employer or governmental authority shall not relieve the Prime Contract of above-mentioned responsibilities.
1.4.4 总包人须接受发包人和规划部门对其成果性文件的修改意见,并对其成果性文件进行完善,或者根据服务内容提出优化方案。	1.4.4 The Prime Contractor shall accept the comments and opinions of Employer and the planning department on modification of the result-natured documents and shall complete and make perfect his result-natured document or provide optimization on his services.
1.4.5 总包人应该按照发包人在委托合同中约定的服务内容,标准和要求,在不同施工阶段,重要施工部位,关键施工工序等环节提供现场技术服务,并对参加驻场服务情况记录保存,工程施工前,应向施工,监理单位说明设计情况,解释设计文件,指导施工单位按照设计要求和相关技术标准进行施工,对施工不符合设计标准的可要求施工单位予以纠正。	1.4.5 The Prime Contractor shall render technical service on site in different works stages, at important works parts and at key procedures and steps in accordance with the services, specification and requirements agreed in the contract with the Employer and shall keep record of field service rendered, and shall make clear explanation of design solutions, interpretation of design documents to the supervisor and constructor prior to commencement of execution and guide constructor to perform works by design standard and relevant technical specifications. The Prime Contractor can request the constructor to correct those executions unacceptable by the design standard.

V. Assignment

(1)在合同双方之间,雇主应对规范、图纸和其他由雇主(或雇主授权的人员)编制的设计文件保留版权和其他知识产权。承包人可为合同的目的,自费复印、使用及传输上述文件。除非因履行合同而必需,否则不经雇主同意,承包人不得为第三方复印、使用或传输上述文件。

(2)然而,如果雇主的过失(并且在一定程度上)是由于承包人的某些错误或延误造成的,包括承包人的文件中的错误或提交的延误,则承包人无权要求获得此类延长的工期、费用或利润。

(3)雇主应任命工程师,该工程师应履行合同中赋予他的职责。工程师的人员包括有恰当资格的工程师以及其他有能力履行上述职责的专业人员。

(4)承包人应执行每项变更并受每项变更的约束,除非承包人马上通知工程师(并附具体的证明资料)并说明承包人无法得到变更所需的货物。在接到此通知后,工程师应取消、确认或修改指示。

(5)承包人应在现场或工程师可接受的另一地点保持用以证明任何索赔可能需要的同期记录。工程师在收到根据本款发出的上述通知后,在不必事先承认雇主责任的情况下,监督此类记录的进行,并(或)可指示承包人保持进一步的同期记录。承包人应允许工程师审查所有此类记录,并应向工程师提供复印件(如果工程师指示的话)。

Glossary
专业词汇表

access Zone	接近段
adaptation	（视）适应
adjoining roads	授予特许经营权合约
advance length	进尺
air supply and exhaust	输气和排气
air right	空间所有权；上空使用权
alignment	沉降
anchoring and shotcreting	锚喷
ancillary buildings	附属建筑
apex	顶点
articulation shield	铰接式盾构
artificial dig-hole pile	人工挖孔桩
axial fan	轴流风机
average illumination	平均照度
award of concession contract	敞开段
backfill	回填
back filling	背回注浆
back-fill grouting	壁后注浆
ballast	压载
bench excavation method	台阶法开挖
bending stress	弯应力
bidirectional traffic	双向交通
"black hole"	黑洞现象
blade	切削刀
blast hole	炮眼
blasting cap	起爆雷管（火帽）
bored tunnel	钻掘隧道
bottom-dump car	底卸式车
bottom cut	底眼
bracing replacement	换撑
ancillary building	附属建筑
bulkhead	隔板；防水壁
buoyancy	浮力
Bureau of Labor Standards	美国劳工部标准
burial depth	埋深
burn cut	直眼掏槽
cable trench and other trenches for pipelines	电缆槽与其他设施预留槽
caisson work	箱涵作业
cast-in-place pile	灌注桩

continue

centrifugal pump	离心泵
center diagram method(CD method)	中隔壁开挖法(CD 法)
charging	装炸药
climbing lane	爬坡车道
clogging	堵塞
collecting sample(sample-collecting)	采样
column-heading method	柱洞法
competitive bid contract	投标合同
cone penetration testing (CPT)	静力触探试验
contour blasthole	周边钻孔
consolidation	固结
contract agreement	合同协议书
contractor	承包人
contaminated air	污染空气
cross section	横断面
crack control	裂缝控制
curve in small radius	小半径曲线
cut and cover tunnel	明挖隧道
cut and cover method	明挖法
cutter head	切削刀头
cylinder cut	桶形掏槽
DAB	争端裁决委员会
deadly smoke	致命烟雾
deep mixing method	水泥土深层搅拌法
degree of lighting	照明度
depth of bury	埋深
detergent	清洁剂;去垢剂
detonation speed	炮轰速度
detonating cords	引爆线,导爆索
detonation velocity	爆轰速度
detonation	引爆,爆轰
diaphragm wall	地下连续墙
discharge rate	排水速率
double side-wall drift pilot excavation	双侧壁导坑法
downbound	下行
double-track tunnel	双线隧道
drainage pipe	排水管
drainage	排水设施
drainage ditch, interception	排(截)水沟
drawings	图纸
dredge	疏浚;挖泥船,疏浚机

continue

drill and blasting	钻爆法施工
drill and split	钻裂
drill jumbo platform	钻孔车台车
drill hole	钻孔
dry dock	干坞
dynamite, explosive	炸药
Earth pressure balance (EPB) shield	土压平衡盾构
electric detonator	电雷管
electric glow wire	导电线
emergency equipment	应急设备
emergency lane and lay-by	紧急停车带
emergency lighting	紧急照明
emergency telephone	应急电话
emergency ventilation	应急通风
enclosing purlin	围檩
enclosure structure	围护结构
end wall typed portal	端墙式洞门
engineering geology	工程地质学
enter cross diagram method (CRD)	交叉中隔壁开挖法(CRD 法)
epoxy coating	乙烯基橡胶
erector	管片拼装器
escape corridor	逃生管廊
escape route	逃生线路
excavation	开挖
exhaust fan	抽风机;排风机
exhaust gas	尾气
exhaust port	排气口,排气孔
exit zone	出口段
explosive emulsions	乳化炸药
exploratory boring	勘探钻孔
extraction by ventilation	通风排气
face shield	面罩
fast setting	速凝
fire ax	消防斧头、太平斧
fire extinguisher	灭火器
free surface	自由面
firefighting equipment	消防设备
fire hydrant	消防栓
fire hydrant	消防软管
fire life safety	消防及人身安全
first-aid station	急救站;救护站

continue

first aid kits	急救药箱
flange	法兰,轮缘;边缘
flood gate	防洪闸,潮门;坞门;水闸
flow process	流水作业
Fluorescent Lamp	荧光灯,日光灯
foam extinguisher	泡沫灭火器
force Majeure	不可抗力
foundation pit	基坑
frame	反力架
full face excavation method	全断面开挖
full transverse ventilation	全横向式通风
gelatin dynamites	胶质炸药
general conditions	通用条件
geologic exploration	地质勘探
geomembrance	土工膜;隔泥网膜
geosynthetic	土工合成材料
geotechnics	地质学
glare	炫光
gpm	每分钟加仑数(gallons per minute)
grab	抓斗
grid steel frame	格栅钢架
ground improvement	地基加固
grout	注浆
ground condition	地基条件
ground support	地基支护
ground treatment	围岩处理
grouting	注浆、灌浆
hauling	搬运
heading mode	掘进方式
height control	机动车高度控制
helmet	钢盔,头盔
heterogeneity	不均匀性、多相性
highway tunnel	公路隧道
hobbing cutter	滚刀
horizontal and vertical alignments	水平和竖向线型
hose valve	水带阀门;消火栓阀
hose	软管
hose station	墙式消火栓
hose stream	消防射流
threshold limit value	阈限值;(有害物)容许最高浓度
hydrogen sulfide	硫化氢

hydroelectric tunnel	水电站隧道
hydrological survey	水文调查
hypabyssal rock	半深成岩
Identification Badges	身份徽章
ignition	点炮
illuminance	照度
immersed tube tunnel	沉管隧道
impermeable layer	不渗水层
impermeable settlement	不均匀沉陷、不均衡下沉
incandescent unit	白炽灯
inclinometer	倾斜计、倾斜仪
initial spalling	初期剥落
inlet duct	送风道
Interior Zone	中间段，基本段
invert	仰拱
jackhammer	手提钻
jack	（盾构）千斤顶
jacking pit	顶管井
jet fan	射流风机
jointing	节理
Jointed rock mass	节理岩体
jumbo	钻孔台车
jurisdiction	行政辖区
KANZASHI-beam method, support beam protection	托梁法
karst	岩溶
key	刺尖
kible cage	出渣用吊桶
kick up	预留余空、向上弯曲
knife sheet	梅塞尔钢插板
Koepe winding/Koepe hoisting	提升、卷扬机
ladder	梯子
leakage	渗漏
letter of acceptance	中标函
letter of tender	投标函
leveled gravel bed	整平碎石垫层
lighting fixture	照明器材
lighting system	照明系统
lighting for operation	营运照明设施
lining	衬砌
longitudinal section	纵截面
longitudinal ventilation	纵向式通风

continue

lower drift excavation method	下导洞超前开挖法
low-pressure sodium luminaries	低压钠灯
luminance, Brightness	亮度
luminaries	光源,发光体
main navigation channel	主航道
maintenance factor	维护系数
metal halide lamp	金属卤化灯
meteorological condition	气象条件
method	方法
methane	甲烷
micro bench excavation method	微台阶开挖法
muck	石渣
mucking	出渣
municipal water line	市政供水管
natural ventilation	自然通风
New Austrian Tunneling Method (NATM)	新奥法
nitroglycerine	硝化甘油
nitropenta	四硝酸酯
nonel	诺雷尔管,由瑞典科学家诺雷尔发明
nozzle	喷嘴
observational method	观察法
open ramp	环境影响评估
OSHA	职业安全与健康管理局(Occupational Safety and Health Administration)
over excavation (overbreak)	超挖(超爆)
ovality	椭圆度
oversized vehicles	超高车辆
owner	业主
oxidation	氧化反应
oxides of nitrogen	氮氧化物
parallel cut	直眼掏槽,平行掏槽
particular conditions	专用条件
partial face excavation method	部分开挖法
per shift	每班
pedestrian passageway/ walkway	人行通道
perimeter cut	周边眼
photometric characteristics	配光性能
piezometers	压力计,压强计
piston effect	活塞效应
planning the route (route-planning)	线路规划
pneumatic leg	气腿

· 314 ·

continue

pontoon	干坞
portal	隧道口；隧道洞
porous concrete	多孔混凝土
position and stance	姿态
precaution	预防措施
prefabricated section	预制管段
prefabricated section	回填
presplit	预裂
prestressing	压载
primary charge	主装药
profile steel	型钢
profile steel arch	型钢拱架
propagate	传递,传爆
protective shield	保护屏
pulley	滑轮
pump station	水泵房,泵站
PVC (polyvinyl chloride)	聚氯乙烯
quartz	石英
quartz porphyry	花岗斑岩
quartz diorite	石英闪长岩
quartz porphyry	石英斑岩
quaternary (system)	第四纪
quick sand	流砂现象
quick setting grouting	即时注浆
quotation, estimation	估价单、报价单
radio communication	无线电通信
rapid transit artery	高速交通干道
raging fire	烈火
rail tunnel	铁路隧道
rapid transit artery	高速交通干道
retention Money	保留金
refugee access	行人,行车横洞和预留洞室
relief cut	缓冲眼
retarding agent	延迟剂,延期药
rear void	盾尾空隙
ring cut method	环形导坑留核心土开挖法
rock dike	河口；江口
rock bolt	锚杆
roadheader	巷道掘进机
road signs	道路标识
roof cut	顶眼

· 315 ·

continue

run-off	径流
safety provisions	安全措施；安全设施
safety engineer	安全工程师
safety program	安全计划
safety inspection	安全检验
safety boot	安全靴
safety glasses/ goggle	护目镜
safety belt	安全带
sampling intervals	取样间距
scraper cutter	刮刀
segment	管片
sealing gasket	防水密封条
section	机
settlement	靠泊码头
semi section excavation method	半断面开挖发
secondary lining	二次衬砌
settlement	沉降，沉降量
seepage	渗流
service telephones	公共电话
semi-transverse ventilation	半横向通风
secondary charge	副装药
shield	盾构
shield work shaft	盾构工作井
shield launching	盾构始发
shield arrival shaft	盾构接收井
shield cradle	盾构基座
ship impact	整平碎石垫层
shellfish	甲壳类动物；贝类等有壳的水生动物
shotcrete	喷射混凝土
single side-wall drift pilot excavation method	单侧壁导坑法
single-track tunnel	单线隧道
site	现场
site exploration	现场勘探
slope excavation	放坡开挖法
slurry shield	泥水平衡盾构
smooth blasting	光面爆破
SMW	型钢水泥土搅拌墙(Soil Mixed Wall)
soil nail	土钉
soil-nail wall	土钉墙
special garment	特种服装
specification	规范

speed limit sign	限速标识
steel sheet pile	钢板桩
steel fibre reinforced shotcrete (SFRS)	钢纤维喷射混凝土
steel meshes	钢筋网
steel profiles	型钢
stack effect/chimney effect	烟囱效应
standard penetration testing (SPT)	标准贯入试验
steel fibre-reinforced concrete (SFRC)	连接线
steel pipe pile	钢管桩
stemming	炮泥
stand-up time	自持时间
supporting system	支撑系统
surrounding rock	围岩
surrounding rock classification	围岩分级
superelevation	超高
sump	水坑,污水坑
subaqueous tunnel	水下隧道,水底隧道
sunlight shed, sunlight grid, dimmer section	遮阳棚,遮光格栅,减光段
surrounding rock conditions	围岩状况(条件)
support	支护
synthetic neoprene	预应力
tamping	封堵炮孔,炮孔堵塞
tail avoid	盾尾间隙
temporary Works	临时工程
temporary segment	负环管片
Threshold Zone	入口段
trench	沟槽
Transition Zone	过渡段
transverse interceptor	横向截水沟
train's piston effect	列车的活塞效应
traffic surveillance	交通监控
traffic lights	交通灯
traffic census	交通控制
Triaxial test	三轴试验
Tunnel boring machines (TBM)	隧道掘进机
tunnel clearance	隧道净空
tunnel parlance	隧道用语
tunnel portals	隧道洞口
unbound	上行
unidirectional traffic	单向交通
U-turn turn around	调头

continue

variation	变更
ventilation	通风设备;通风
ventilation facilities	通风设施
ventilation shaft for operation	运营通风竖井
ventilator	通风机
video-monitoring	摄像机监控
vinyl type rubber	合成氯丁橡胶
wall-washing	清洗
wastewater treatment plant	废水处理厂
water deluge system	大水量喷洒系统
water mains	总水管;给水总管
watertightness	裂缝控制
welding	焊接,电焊
well point dewatering	井点降水
wedge cut	楔形掏槽
wharf	岩墙
working face	开挖面,工作面
X-ray analysis of fabric	结构的 X 射线分析

References
参 考 文 献

[1] 中华人民共和国行业规范.JTG D70—2004 公路隧道设计规范[S].北京:人民交通出版社,2004.

[2] 中华人民共和国行业规范.JTG/T D70/2-01—2004 公路隧道照明设计细则[S].北京:人民交通出版社,2000.

[3] 中华人民共和国行业规范.TB 10204—2002 铁路隧道施工规范[S].北京:中国铁道出版社,2002.

[4] BICKEL J O,KUESEL,T R,KING E H. Tunnel engineering handbook [M]. 2nd. New York: Chapman & Hall,1996.

[5] 赵萱,郑仰成.科技英语翻译[M].北京:外语教学与研究出版社,2006.

[6] 彭立敏,刘小兵.隧道工程[M].长沙:中南大学出版社,2009.

[7] 覃仁辉,王成.隧道工程[M].重庆:重庆大学出版社,2013.

[8] 陈秋楠.隧道工程[M].北京:机械工业出版社,2007.

[9] 朱永全.隧道工程[M].北京:中国铁道出版社,2007.

[10] Dimitrios Kolymbas. Tunneling and Tunnel Mechanics [M], Springer-Verlag Berlin Heidelberg,2008.

[11] 丁文其,杨林德.隧道工程[M].北京:人民交通出版社,2012.

[12] 王长柏,旺鹏程.隧道工程[M].武汉:武汉大学出版社,2014.

[13] 张俊儒.隧道工程[M].成都:西南交通大学出版社,2013.

[14] 李德武.隧道[M].北京:中国铁道出版社,2004.

[15] 陈建勋.隧道[M].北京:人民交通出版社,2012.

[16] 崔玖江.隧道与地下工程修建技术[M].北京:科学出版社,2005.

[17] 霍润科.隧道与地下工程[M].北京:中国建筑工业出版社,2011.

[18] 刘石年.勘察技术[M].长沙:中南工业大学,1999.

[19] 陈成宗,何发亮.隧道工程地质与声波探测技术[M].成都:西南交通你大学出版社,2005.

[20] 何发亮.隧道工程地质学[M].成都:西南交通大学出版社,2014.

[21] 王石春,何发亮.隧道工程岩体分级[M].成都:西南交通大学出版社,2007.

[22] 孙家齐,陈新民.工程地质[M].武汉:武汉工业大学出版社,2007.

[23] BICKEL J O,KUESEL,T R,KING E H. Tunnel engineering handbook [M]. 2nd. New York: Chapman & Hall,1996.

[24] 齐景狱.隧道爆破现代技术[M].北京:中国铁道出版社,1995.

[25] 李术才.钻爆法施工的海底隧道最小岩石覆盖厚度确定方法[M].北京:科学出版社,2013.

[26] 徐颖.爆破工程[M].武汉:武汉大学出版社,2014.

[27] 高文蛟,陈学习.爆破工程及其安全技术[M].北京:煤炭工业出版社,2011.

[28] 赵德刚.津秦客专隧道钻爆法施工技术[J].铁道建筑技术,2010(5):118-119.

[29] 王燕,黄宏伟. 钻爆法施工隧道塌方风险分析[J]. 沈阳建筑大学学报,2009(1): 23-27.

[30] 白云. 隧道掘进机施工技术[M]. 北京:中国建筑工业出版社,2013.

[31] 宋清秀,刘杰. 隧道施工[M]. 北京:人民交通出版社,2009.

[32] 王道远. 隧道施工技术[M]. 北京:中国水利水电出版社,2007.

[33] 鲍绥意. 盾构技术理论与实践[M]. 北京:中国建筑工业出版社,2012.

[34] 周文波. 盾构法隧道施工技术及应用[M]. 北京:中国建筑工业出版社,2004.

[35] 朱文会,陈静. 重庆轨道交通6号线敞开式TBM过站技术研究[J]. 隧道建设,2012(10):741-748.

[36] 陈馈,冯欢欢. TBM施工风险与应对措施[J]. 隧道建设 2013,920:91-97.

[37] 周志强,钟显奇,宋金良,等. 广州地区盾构施工风险及控制技术要点[J]. 隧道建设,2010,30(5):608-611.

[38] 杨其新,王明年. 地下工程施工与管理[M]. 成都:西南交通大学出版社,2009.

[39] 陈韶章. 沉管隧道设计与施工[M]. 北京:科学出版社,2002.

[40] 沈永芳,黄醒春. 沉管隧道注浆效果检查与评价的实验研究[J]. 地下空间与工程学报,2013(4):758-763.

[41] 陈清军,朱合华. 沉管隧道结构的空间受力性态分析[J]. 力学,2000(6):237-242.

[42] 刘卫丰. 隧道工程[M]. 北京:北京交通大学出版社,2012.

[43] 王智远,张宏. 隧道工程[M]. 北京:人民交通出版社,2014.

[44] 杨晓杰,刘冬明. 地铁隧道明挖法施工基坑支护稳定性研究[J]. 地下空间与工程学报,2010(6):516-520.

[45] 胡纯,李大庆. 明挖法地铁车站地基反力分析[J]. 武汉大学学报,2013(3):208-211.

[46] 古兰玉. 双线铁路隧道明挖法边坡与衬砌技术[J]. 国防交通工程与技术,2008(2):67-72.

[47] 奥洛克. 隧道衬砌设计指南[M]. 北京:中国铁道出版社,1999.

[48] 邓德祥. 隧道开挖[M]. 北京:中国铁道出版社,1981.

[49] 傅鹤林,韩汝才. 隧道衬砌荷载计算理论及岩溶处治技术[M]. 长沙:中南大学,2005.

[50] 李世辉. 隧道支护设计新论:典型类比法与分析法应用和理论[M]. 北京:科学出版社,1999.

[51] 晏启祥,程曦. 水压条件下盾构隧道双层衬砌力学特性分析[J]. 铁道工程学报,2010(9):56-59.

[52] 张云军,宰金珉. 隧道开挖对临近桩基的二维数值分析[J]. 地下空间与工程学报,2005(12):832-836.

[53] 李文秀,翟淑花. 隧道开挖引起地表下沉及其影响分析[J]. 岩石力学与工程学报,2004(7):4752-4756.

[54] 王汉青. 通风工程[M]. 北京:机械工程出版社,2007.

[55] 王新泉. 通风工程学[M]. 北京:机械工程出版社,2008.

[56] 金易学,陈文英. 隧道通风机隧道空气动力学[M]. 北京:中国铁道出版社,1983.

[57] 王毅才. 隧道工程·上册[M]. 北京:人民交通出版社,2006.

[58] 王成. 隧道工程[M]. 北京:人民交通出版社,2009.

[59] 曾艳华,李永林. 隧道通风网络及调节[M]. 西南交通大学学报,2003(4):183-187.
[60] 李永林,毛遵训. 二郎山隧道运营通风设计方案浅析[J]. 公路,2000,(12):28-32.
[61] 冯炼,刘应清. 地铁通风网络的数值分析[J]. 中国铁道科学,2002,23(1):131-135.
[62] 赖涤泉. 隧道施工通风与防尘[M]. 北京:中国铁道出版社,1994.
[63] 陈秋南. 隧道工程[M]. 北京:机械工业出版社,2007.
[64] 岳强. 隧道工程[M]. 北京:机械工程,2012.
[65] 刘卫丰. 隧道工程[M]. 北京:北京交通大学出版社,2012.
[66] ADRIAN W K. A Method for the Design of Tunnel Entrance Lighting[J]. Journal of Engineering Society,2000,3(9).
[67] ADRIAN W K. Adaptation Luminance When Approaching a Tunnel in Daytime[J]. Lighting Research and Technology,1987,19(3):73-79.
[68] American Association of State Highway and Transportation Officials (AASHTO) (1984) Guide for Roadway Lighting,Washington,D. C.
[69] 涂耘,王少飞. 西汉高速公路隧道照明系统评估研究[J]. 照明工程学报,2010(9):15-21.
[70] 王毅才. 隧道工程[M]. 北京:人民交通出版社,2000.
[71] 傅鹤林,赵朝阳. 隧道安全施工技术手册[M]. 北京:人民交通出版社,2010.
[72] 李术才,张庆松. 隧道及地下工程突涌水机理与治理[M]. 北京:人民交通出版社,2014.
[73] 冯卫星. 隧道塌方案例[M]. 成都:西南交通大学,2002.
[74] 刘学增,俞文生. 隧道稳定性评价与塌方预警[M]. 上海:同济大学,2010.
[75] 曹文宏,申伟强. 长大隧道安全保护条例[J]. 地下工程与隧道,2012(1):1-4.
[76] 杜益文,韩直. 公路隧道安全模糊评价方法[M]. 公路交通技术,2006(6):120-123.
[77] 谢明. 地下空间开发对下方铁路隧道安全影响分析[J]. 地下空间与工程学报,2013(9):1449-1456.
[78] 张雷,袁戟. 城市地下工程对周围建筑风险评价的价值模型[J]. 地下空间与工程学报,2010,6(5):1098-1103.
[79] 王雪青,杨秋波. 工程项目管理[M]. 北京:高等教育出版社,2011.
[80] 宣卫红,张本业. 工程项目管理[M]. 北京:中国水利水电出版社,2006.
[81] 栋梁工作室. 隧道工程预算定额与工程清单计价应用手册[M]. 北京:中国建筑工业出版社,2004.
[82] 吴焕道,催永军. 隧道施工及组织管理指南[M]. 北京:人民交通出版社,2004.
[83] 刘志杰,高仁良. 合同管理[M]. 北京:人民交通出版社,2003.
[84] 刘志杰,李静. 合同管理[M]. 北京:人民交通出版社,2013.
[85] 邹应. 合同管理[M]. 北京:人民交通出版社,2007.
[86] 李锦辉,陈悦. 土木工程专业英语[M]. 上海:同济大学出版社,2012.
[87] 邬万江,马丽丽. 交通工程英语[M]. 北京:机械工业出版社,2012.
[88] 陈瑛,邵永波. 土木工程专业英语[M]. 北京:机械工业出版社,2010.
[89] 钱永梅,庞平. 新编土木工程专业英语[M]. 北京:化学工业出版社,2012.
[90] 马彩玲,张梅英. 土木工程英语[M]. 北京:清华大学出版社,2011.

[91] 秦卫红. 土木工程专业英语[M]. 武汉:华中科技大学出版社,2012.
[92] 教育部《土建英语》教材编写组. 土建英语[M]. 北京:高等教育出版社,2000.
[93] 张倩. 土木工程英语[M]. 北京:科学出版社,2009.
[94] 周开鑫. 土木工程英语教程[M]. 北京:人民交通出版社,2000.
[95] 赵永平. 路桥工程专业英语[M]. 北京:人民交通出版社,2007.
[96] 傅勇林,唐跃勤. 科技翻译[M]. 北京:外语教学与研究出版社,2012.